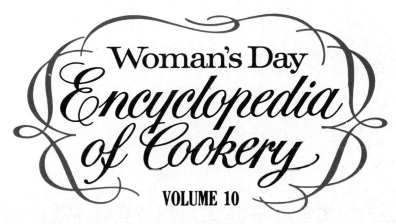

# Woman's Day
# *Encyclopedia of Cookery*

## VOLUME 10

*in 12 volumes—over 2,000 pages—*
*with more than 1,500 illustrations in color,*
*1,000 entries and 8,500 recipes*
*1,200 menus, 50 specialty cook books*
*and a host of delightful features by distinguished food writers.*

*Prepared and edited by the Editors of Woman's Day*
*Editor:* EILEEN TIGHE
*Managing Editor:* EVELYN GRANT      *Food Editor:* GLENNA MCGINNIS
*Art Consultant:* HAROLD SITTERLE      *Photographic Editor:* BEN CALVO
*Associates:* OLIVIA RISBERG, CHARLOTTE SCRIPTURE,
CAROLYN STORM, JOHANNA BAFARO

SPECIAL PROJECT STAFF
*Editor:* NIKA STANDEN HAZELTON      *Art Director:* LEONARD A. ROMAGNA
*Associates:* L. GERALDINE MARSTELLER, HELEN FEINGOLD,
SUSAN J. KNOX, INEZ M. KRECH

FAWCETT PUBLICATIONS, INC.      NEW YORK

Printed in U.S.A. by
**FAWCETT-HAYNES PRINTING CORPORATION**
Rockville, Maryland

# Table of Contents

## VOLUME 10

### QUAIL TO SORREL

Definitions and 825 Recipes
How to buy, store, prepare, cook, and serve ·
Nutritive Food Values · Caloric Values

To help you plan more varied meals
with the recipes in this volume

# *Foreword*

To the best of our knowledge, no work of this magnitude ever has been undertaken by any author, editor, or publisher in America. The editors of Woman's Day, with a special staff of experts, present to you this Encyclopedia of Cookery, a comprehensive and colorful library on all culinary matters. The twelve-volume encyclopedia contains in its 2,000 pages over 8,500 recipes from all over the world, 1,500 food illustrations in color, 1,200 menus, 50 special cook books and over 1,000 food definitions. In addition, there are full details about all foods, their nutritive and caloric values, how to buy, serve, prepare, and cook them. There is a history of food and cooking, articles on nutrition, diet, entertaining, menu planning, herbs and spices. Every topic of culinary interest is covered. Five years of intensive work have gone into its preparation, backed by twenty-five years of food and cookery experience in the publication of Woman's Day.

We think you will find this Encyclopedia of Cookery the most complete and authoritative work ever published on the subject. It is a library for everyone who cares about good food and the fine art of preparing it.

*The Editors*

**QUAIL**—A small gallinaceous game bird which resembles a tiny plump chicken. Quail have a strong short round beak and their plumage is a modest soft brown or a brown mottled with white, black, or chestnut. This is true self-protective coloring, for quail hover in the grass, since they prefer walking (or running) to flying. They make their nests on the ground. They are sociable birds, living in small flocks called coveys. Quail are found in most parts of the United States.

There are several varieties. The best-known American species is often called a bobwhite. Many people use the words quail and partridge interchangeably.

American quail are white-meated and the flesh has a delicate flavor. Quail are cooked like all game birds. When young, they can be panfried, panbroiled, broiled, or roasted. Older birds should be potroasted with a marinade or with sour cream.

*Availability*—Frozen eviscerated quail are available in pairs, as are canned whole quail stuffed with *pâté de foie gras* in sherry sauce, smoked quail meat, and quail eggs.

**Storage**

☐ Frozen, refrigerator frozen-food compartment: 4 to 5 weeks

☐ Frozen, freezer: 6 months
☐ Canned, kitchen shelf: 1 year
☐ Canned, refrigerator shelf, opened: 4 to 5 days

**Caloric Value**

☐ 3½ ounces, raw = 168 calories

*Basic Preparation*—Wild quail should be bled and eviscerated immediately. Remove crop. Rub dry inside and out with a clean dry cloth or dry grass. When removing entrails handle gall bladder carefully to avoid breakage. Plucking can be done best dry, by pulling out feathers, starting at the base of the neck, and singeing them down with a small flame; or else birds can be plucked by dipping into water heated to 165°F. to 175°F. until feathers loosen. However, of all methods used, dry plucking is far superior and results in a bird of excellent eating quality. After plucking, remove head and feet. Hang carcasses singly and protect against dirt and insects until cool. Quail are used from the fresh state but may be hung for a day or two, if desired. However, they should not be hung for more than 3 days. If not to be used at once, they should be frozen.

□ **To Freeze**—If hunting period lasts several days, birds can be frozen in a frozen-food locker, if a convenient one can be found. To freeze in freezer, wash birds thoroughly and wipe dry. Chill overnight. Wrap for freezing in moisture-vapor-proof paper or polyethylene bags and freeze at 0°F. or lower.

### BROILED QUAIL ON TOAST

Clean quails, split down the back, and brush with olive oil. Sprinkle with salt and pepper. Put on well greased broiler rack and broil for about 8 minutes, or until done. Serve on hot buttered toast. Garnish with parsley and lemon slices.

### PANBROILED QUAIL

Clean quails and split down the back. Sprinkle with salt. Put quails split-side down in a hot buttered skillet. Cover and cook for 3 minutes. Turn and put 1 teaspoon butter on each bird. Cook, turning occasionally, until browned and tender. This will take about 20 minutes for tender birds. When done, remove birds to a hot platter and add a little hot water to drippings in skillet. Pour over birds.

### ROAST QUAIL

Allow 1 quail per serving. Wrap thoroughly cleaned birds in grape leaves if available. Cover with slices of fat salt pork and tie in place with string. Put, breast-side up, in heated shallow open roasting pan. Spread with a little butter. Roast, uncovered, basting often, for 15 to 20 minutes, depending on degree of rareness desired. When done, remove from pan. Remove leaves and put birds under broiler for a few minutes to brown. If desired, add some water to drippings in pan and thicken with a little flour-and-water paste to make gravy. Serve birds on toast, topped with gravy.

### QUAILS YUGOSLAV STYLE

Clean 4 quails and brown on all sides in hot butter in a large skillet. Put 8 rounds of buttered white bread in a buttered shallow baking dish. Cut quails into halves and put each half on a slice of bread. Put in preheated hot oven (400° F.) until butter melts and bread begins to brown. Beat 1 egg yolk with ½ cup white wine and ¼ cup melted butter. Pour over birds and bake for 10 to 15 minutes longer. Garnish with watercress and lemon slices. Makes 4 servings.

**QUANTITY COOKING**—The process of producing food, ready-to-serve, in amounts larger than those customarily needed for a family meal. It may be done for home entertaining or for such group entertaining as a church supper, a lodge dinner, a P.T.A. tea, or a food sale designed to raise money for a charity. It may, of course, also be the quantity cooking involved in the preparation of food in restaurants, summer camps, schools, or the armed forces, but this type of day-in, day-out quantity cooking is not covered in the material which follows because it requires institutional equipment, highly professional techniques, and specialized recipes.

### The Selection of Menus and Recipes

Generally speaking, simple menus and recipes are the best to use for quantity meals. Choose foods everyone knows and likes, ones that are pleasing to children as well as to men and women. They are frequently the easiest to prepare, to transport, to store, and to serve. The nature of the group and seasonal specialties may also affect the choices.

Do not try to multiply low-quantity home recipes: cakes, cookies, pies, pastry, bread (baked goods), soufflés, or candies. These depend on chemical reactions under given conditions, and changing the amounts of ingredients affects time, temperature, and often the behavior of the mixture itself. These recipes, when used to prepare a large amount of food, must be made over and over in their original quantities. (Five cakes, each of which serves ten people, must be made to serve fifty people.) But soups and mixtures such as a macaroni salad can be made in any amount which is convenient as far as ordering, precooking, and mixing are concerned. The amounts to be made are determined by the size of the kettles and mixing bowls available and the physical strength of whoever is doing the cooking. (If the home recipe serves five, multiply everything by ten to serve fifty.) If some of the foods are to be brought from homes already prepared or partially prepared, it is a good policy for all the cooks to use the same recipe. Have the necessary number of copies typed, checked for accuracy and clarity, and distributed to the volunteer cooks ahead of time.

### Buying in Quantity

■ Make shopping lists and order well ahead of time to allow stores to meet your requirements.

■ Be sure to include in the shopping list such items as cleaning supplies, paper napkins and plates, if they are being used, or other non-food items which must be shopped for.

■ Shop around for source which can give the best buy.

■ Order in quantity units where possible. Gallon sizes of pickles, mayonnaise, #10 cans (about 3 quarts) of fruits, juices, tomatoes, etc., may be available, especially if ordered well ahead of time. They can save both money and handling.

■ Read labels on cans for information which can be of help such as the number of pear halves in a can, slices of pineapple, etc.

■ Shop for the best buy in money and labor. Don't choose the more expensive whole tomatoes if they are to be cooked in a sauce, or sliced pineapple if it is to be cut up into small pieces.

■ Make use of labor-saving items such as chopped frozen onions or green peppers if they are to go into cooked foods. They are frequently no more expensive, and save time when time is precious.

■ Some meat markets, or sometimes a restaurant, will agree to cook and/or slice large roasts or turkeys, a real contribution to saving labor and time. In addition it may result in servings which are more attractive and professional-looking. In some areas freshly made-up hamburgers can be obtained from the meat market.

■ Plan far enough ahead to take advantage of items which might be donated if enough advance notice is given, for example: home-grown products, specially baked cakes, etc.

■ Decide on the most convenient place and time to have grocery orders or prepared foods delivered or picked up.

The amounts of certain staples considered standard for serving twenty-five people are given below:

American cheese: 1½ pounds for 25 sandwiches

Beef, ground for patties: 8 to 9 pounds

Butter for rolls: 1 pound, cut 32 pats to the pound

Butter for 50 slices of bread: ¾ pound, softened and creamed

Butter or margarine for vegetables: ½ pound, allowing about ½ tablespoon per serving

Carrots, raw sticks: 1 to 1½ pounds

Celery for relish curls: 4 to 5 bunches

Coffee (regular): 1 pound

Coffee (instant): one 2-ounce jar makes about 40 cups

Crackers: 3 pounds

Cranberry sauce: 4 cups (two 1-pound cans)

Cream for coffee: 1½ pints

Cream for whipped toppings: 1 pint

Frankfurters: 6 to 7 pounds, allowing 2 per serving

French dressing, 1½ to 2 tablespoons per serving: ½ to ¾ quart

Ham, boned, rolled, ready to eat: 5 to 6 pounds

Ice cream, brick: 4 quarts, cut 7 slices per quart

Juices: 3 cans (46 ounces each), allowing 5 ounces per serving

Ketchup: 3 bottles (14 ounces each)

Lemon, for tea: 4, cut 8 slices per lemon

Lettuce, 2 to 3 leaves per serving: 3 heads

Lettuce for hearts, 1/5 head per serving: 6 medium heads

Mayonnaise, 1 tablespoon per serving: 1 pint

Milk for tea: 1 quart

Mints, after dinner: 1¼ pounds

Nuts, salted: 2 pounds

Olives, 2 per serving: 1 quart

Peanut butter: 3 cups to spread 25 sandwiches

Peas: 7 cans (1 pound each) or 4 packages (1 pound each) frozen

Pickles, 2 small per serving: 1 quart

Potatoes, boiled, 1 medium per serving: 9 to 10 pounds

Potatoes, mashed, ½ cup per serving: 9 to 10 pounds

Potato chips: 2 pounds

Radishes: 4 to 5 bunches

Rolls: 3 to 4 dozen

Sherbet: 1 gallon, 7 servings per quart

Stuffing for poultry: about 5 quarts

Sugar for tea or coffee: ¾ pound

Tea: 3 ounces

Turkey, to roast: 18 to 20 pounds, ready to cook

### Cooking in Quantity

■ Do as much cooking and preparation as possible in advance.

Cookies, cakes, pies, breads, candies, spaghetti sauces, lasagna, and other good freezers can be made and frozen well ahead of time. Leave the frosting of cakes and the baking of pies for the last day. The same rules that govern home freezing apply here: Don't try to freeze sandwiches or other foods containing hard-cooked egg whites, cream cheese, mayonnaise.

Salad dressings, gelatin salads and desserts can be made a day or two before. (This allows adequate time for congealing.) The ingredients for stuffings can be prepared, but not combined.

■ It may be hard to mix highly seasoned foods in enormous quantities and have them mixed evenly. Plan to mix these in small amounts.

■ Don't crowd roasts in pan or pans in oven. It not only affects time and temperature, but interferes with heat currents, affecting the behavior of the roasts themselves.

Use meat thermometers if possible. Two pieces of meat in the oven at the same time take longer to roast than a single roast the size of one of them, but not as long as a single roast the size of the two pieces combined. For example, one 5-pound roast may take 2½ hours, one 10-pound roast may take 5 hours; two 5-pound roasts in the oven together will probably take about 3 hours.

Plan to take roasts out of the oven 30 to 40 minutes before serving time. They will hold their heat until cut and will carve better if allowed to stand a few minutes at room temperature before carving. Carving can begin about 20 minutes before serving time with the cut meat returned to a warming oven in quantities sufficient to make 10 or 20 servings. Cover meat to keep tender and juicy.

■ Under- rather than over-season. Salt and pepper can be added at the table, but they can't be removed, and tastes in seasoning vary greatly.

■ Be sure you have good tools ready ahead of time. Nothing can be more frustrating at the last minute than to find you do not have a good can opener, a sturdy bottle opener, or good sharp knives.

### Storing in Quantity

■ Because of unusual quantities, longer preparation times, and greater strain on refrigeration facilities, be especially careful to keep foods under refrigeration as much of the time as possible. This is good insurance against food poisoning. Cool foods before refrigerating. Spread out such foods as cooked poultry until cool, then pack in deep containers.

■ Plan ahead, clearing as much refrigerator space as possible, and have the proper containers ready for storage. Turn the refrigerator to the coldest setting possible without actually freezing.

■ To store sandwiches, stack them in containers, cover with a damp cloth, and then with foil or a polyethylene wrap to prevent drying.

■ And don't forget that even those groceries that don't require refrigeration, do require space. Make room for them.

### Serving in Quantity

■ Be scrupulously clean about all kitchen, preparation, and serving areas, facilities, and tools. Don't let people with colds handle the food.

■ Keep hot foods hot. Plan cooking, warming, and "keep hot" space ahead. If a steam table is not available, improvise by putting pans of vegetables into a large roasting pan filled with hot water.

■ Keep salad materials cold and fresh. For individual salads consider preparing about half of the salads just before serving time and the rest as the first are being served.

■ Cut cakes, pies, etc., ahead of time to facilitate serving.

### OVEN-BARBECUED STEAKS

  8 pounds round steak, cut ¾ inch thick
  ¼ cup cooking oil
  1 large onion, sliced
  2 cups ketchup
  1 cup cider vinegar
  ¼ cup firmly packed brown sugar
  3 cups water
  ¼ cup prepared mustard
  2 tablespoons Worcestershire
  1 teaspoon salt
  ¼ teaspoon pepper

Trim off fat around edge of meat and cut steak into 25 serving pieces. Brown on both sides in hot oil in skillet. Put in shallow baking pans. Brown onion lightly in drippings remaining in skillet. Add remaining ingredients, bring to boil, and simmer for 5 minutes. Pour over meat, cover with foil if baking pans have no lids, and bake in preheated slow oven (325°F.) for 2 to 2½ hours. Skim off any accumulated fat. Serve meat with the gravy. Makes 25 servings.

### DIFFERENT BEEF BIRDS

16 pounds round steak, cut thin
    Salt and pepper to taste
  2 pounds carrots
  2 pounds small onions
    All-purpose flour
  2 cups shortening
  5 chicken-bouillon cubes
  4 cups boiling water

Cut beef into 100 pieces about 2 by 4 inches. Sprinkle with salt and pepper. Scrape carrots and cut into thin strips. Peel onions and slice. Place 2 carrot strips and 1 onion slice on each piece of meat. Roll meat crosswise to make individual rolls. Fasten with toothpicks. Dip rolls into flour; brown in melted shortening; place in baking pans. Dissolve bouillon cubes in boiling water; pour into vessel in which meat was browned; then pour over meat. Cover. (Use aluminum foil if pans do not have covers.) Bake in preheated moderate oven (350°F.) for 1 hour, or until tender, adding more water if needed. Then uncover and brown birds for 15 minutes. Makes 100 birds, or 50 servings.

## CHILI CON CARNE

- 4 pounds ground beef
- 2 pounds lean pork, ground
- 6 cups chopped onions
- ¼ cup diced celery
- 8 cups (four 1-pound cans) tomatoes
- 4 cups (two 1-pound cans) tomato purée
- 16 cups (eight 1-pound cans) kidney beans, undrained
- ¼ cup salt
- ½ cup chili powder

Brown meats in shallow pans in broiler. Pour off drippings into heavy kettle. Add onion and celery to drippings and cook for 5 minutes. Add meat and remaining ingredients and cook, uncovered, over low heat for about 2 hours, stirring frequently. Serve in bowls. Makes 25 servings, 2 cups each.

## SWEDISH MEATBALLS

- 2 eggs
- 2 cups milk
- 1 cup fine dry bread crumbs
- ⅓ cup minced onion
  Butter or margarine
- 4 teaspoons salt
- 1 teaspoon pepper
- 3 pounds ground beef
- 1 pound ground pork
- ¼ cup water

Beat eggs; add milk and crumbs and let stand for a few minutes. Brown onion in 2 tablespoons butter. Combine crumb mixture, onion, and other ingredients except water. Mix well and shape into about 100 one-inch balls. Brown in butter, add water, cover, and simmer for 20 minutes. Makes 25 servings.

■ **Variation**—To make these with a cream gravy: After browning meatballs, pour off all but 2 tablespoons fat; sprinkle ¼ cup all-purpose flour over meatballs. Add 3 cups milk and 1 cup light cream. Cover; simmer for 20 minutes.

## BONELESS BAKED HAM

- 2 10-pound boneless skinned ready-to-eat hams
- 1 pound (2¼ cups) brown sugar
  Pear juice (optional)
  Whole cloves

Heat hams in preheated slow oven (300° F.) for 2¼ hours. Remove hams; glaze with brown sugar, mixed with a little pear juice if desired, and stud with cloves. Increase heat to hot (400°F.) and return hams to oven for about 15 minutes to brown. Plan to take hams from oven at least 20 minutes before serving, to allow time for slicing. Lower heat to 300°F. to keep slices warm. Cover slices if they must be kept for more than a few minutes. Makes 50 servings.

## HAM LOAF IN RAISIN SAUCE

- 1½ tablespoons all-purpose flour
- 1½ cups firmly packed brown sugar
- ¾ teaspoon ground cloves
- 3 cups seedless raisins

- 2½ cups packaged corn-flake crumbs
- 6 eggs, beaten
- 3 cups milk
- ⅓ cup each of minced onion and green pepper
- 3 pounds ham, ground
- 1½ pounds lean pork, ground
- 1½ pounds veal, ground
- 4 teaspoons salt
- 1 teaspoon pepper

Mix first 4 ingredients and sprinkle evenly over bottoms of 2 greased baking pans (13 x 9 x 2 inches). Mix remaining ingredients lightly but thoroughly and divide between pans. Press down lightly but firmly. Bake in preheated slow oven (325°F.) for about 1½ hours. Let stand for a few minutes; then turn out and cut each into 12 squares. Makes 24 servings.

## BRUNSWICK STEW

- 2 tablespoons salt
- 1 teaspoon pepper
- 4 frying chickens (3½ pounds each), cut up
- ½ cup shortening
- 4 cups chopped onions
- 2½ quarts water
- 9⅓ cups (four 1-pound, 3-ounce cans) tomatoes
- ¼ cup Worcestershire
- 4 packages (10 ounces each) frozen Lima beans
- 4 cups (two 1-pound cans) okra
- 4 packages (10 ounces each) frozen cut corn
- 2 cups dry bread crumbs (not dry packaged kind)

**Chicken Salad**

Season chicken. Heat shortening in large skillet and brown chicken on all sides. Remove chicken to large kettle and brown onion lightly in drippings remaining in skillet. Add onion to chicken with next 3 ingredients. Cover, bring to boil, and simmer, covered, for 45 minutes. Add beans and okra; simmer for 10 minutes. Add corn and crumbs and simmer for 10 minutes longer. Season if necessary. Makes 25 servings.

### CHICKEN HAWAIIAN

6 onions, sliced
3 quarts sliced celery
¾ cup shortening
14 cups (seven 1-pound cans) bean sprouts, undrained
2½ quarts finely diced cooked chicken
12 chicken-bouillon cubes
2¼ quarts hot water
¾ cup soy sauce
¾ cup cornstarch
1½ cups cold water
Salt and pepper to taste
Hot packaged precooked rice
Chow-mein noodles

Cook onion and celery in shortening in large kettle for 10 minutes. Add bean sprouts, chicken, and bouillon dissolved in hot water. Bring to boil and simmer for 5 minutes. Add soy sauce. Stir in cornstarch blended with cold water. Cook, stirring, until thickened. Season and serve on rice and noodles. Makes 25 servings.

### CHICKEN ALEXANDRIA

6 cups packaged precooked rice
Salt
6 cups water
1 cup butter or margarine
1 cup all-purpose flour
5 cups hot chicken bouillon
4 cups hot milk
2 teaspoons steak sauce
Seasoned salt
Pepper
6 cups diced cooked chicken
4 cans (4 ounces each) chopped mushrooms with liquid
2 cans (4 ounces each) pimientos, chopped
½ cup chopped parsley
1 medium onion, minced
1½ cups soft stale bread cubes, buttered

Prepare rice as directed on label with 1

**Baked Beans**

tablespoon salt and water. Melt butter and blend in flour. Stir in liquids and cook, stirring, until thickened. Add steak sauce, seasoned salt, and pepper to taste. Mix with rice and remaining ingredients except crumbs. Pour into shallow baking dishes and top with crumbs. Bake in preheated hot oven (400°F.) for 10 minutes, or until piping hot. Makes 25 servings.

## CHICKEN TETRAZZINI

1½ pounds spaghetti
1 onion, minced
1 garlic clove, minced
2 tablespoons butter or margarine
4 cans each of cream-of-chicken and mushroom soups
2 teaspoons steak sauce
4 cups milk
1½ pounds sharp Cheddar cheese, shredded
2½ quarts diced cooked chicken
1 can (4 ounces) pimientos, chopped
⅓ cup chopped parsley
Pepper, paprika

Cook and drain spaghetti; rinse in hot water and put in shallow dishes, filling them about one-third full. Cook onion and garlic in butter for 5 minutes. Add soups, steak sauce, milk, and half of cheese. Cook until smooth, stirring. Add chicken, pimiento, and parsley; mix well. Add pepper to taste. Pour over spaghetti, mixing lightly. Sprinkle with remaining cheese and a little paprika. Bake in preheated moderate oven (375°F.) for about 30 minutes. Makes 25 servings, about 1 cup each.

## CHICKEN SALAD

3 quarts diced cooked chicken
12 hard-cooked eggs, diced
¼ cup chopped parsley
1½ cups finely diced celery
½ cup chopped sweet pickle
2 teaspoons salt
½ teaspoon pepper
¼ cup fresh lemon juice
5 cups mayonnaise or salad dressing
Salad greens
¾ cup toasted slivered blanched almonds
Paprika

*Fruit Punch*

*Golden Glow Cake*

Mix all ingredients well except last 3. Serve on greens with a sprinkling of nuts and paprika. Makes 25 servings, about ⅔ cup each.

### TURKEY PIE WITH PASTRY CRUST

- 1 turkey (12 pounds, ready-to-cook), cut into quarters
  Salt
- 1 yellow onion, sliced
- 3 bunches of celery
- 2 pounds small white onions
- 3 pounds potatoes
- 3 bunches of carrots
- 3 packages (10 ounces each) frozen peas
- 2 cups margarine
- 2 cups all-purpose flour
  Pepper
  Special Pastry

Put washed turkey in kettle and cover with hot water. Add 1 tablespoon salt, yellow onion, and a few celery tops. Bring to boil and simmer, covered, for 1½ hours, or until tender. Reserve broth. Cool meat and separate from skin and bones. Cut meat into attractive slices and pieces. Peel and cook white onions. Peel potatoes and carrots; cut potatoes into 1-inch cubes and carrots into 1-inch pieces. Cook together until tender. Cut celery into 1½-inch pieces and cook. Cook peas. Melt margarine. Blend in flour. Add 4½ quarts turkey broth. Cook until thickened. Season to taste. Add vegetables and turkey and heat thoroughly. Allowing about 1½ cups per serving, dish onto plates and top with squares of Special Pastry. Makes 25 servings.

### Special Pastry

Sift 2½ quarts sifted all-purpose flour and 5 teaspoons salt. Cut in 3½ cups lard in coarse pieces. Mix 5 egg yolks with ¾ cup water; stir into dry mixture. Add more water if necessary. Roll out to ⅛-inch thickness and cut into 3-inch squares. Brush with egg white and prick with fork. Bake on cookie sheets in preheated hot oven (400°F.) for 15 to 20 minutes.

### TUNA À LA KING

- 2 cups thinly sliced celery
- ½ cup chopped green pepper
- 1 can (4 ounces) chopped mushrooms, drained
- ¾ cup butter or margarine
- 1¼ cups all-purpose flour
- 2 teaspoons salt
- ¼ teaspoon pepper
- 2 quarts milk
- ¼ pound Cheddar cheese, diced
- 1 can (4 ounces) pimientos, chopped
- 1 package (10 ounces) frozen mixed vegetables, cooked
- 3 cans (6½ ounces each) tuna
- 25 Baking-Powder Biscuits (page 1524)

Cook first 3 ingredients in the butter for 5 minutes. Blend in flour and seasonings. Gradually add milk and cook, stirring, until thickened. Add remaining ingredients except Baking-Powder Biscuits and

heat well. Serve on hot split biscuits, ½ cup per serving. Makes 25 servings.

### Chicken or Turkey à la King

In recipe above, use 4 cups diced cooked chicken or turkey instead of tuna.

### ITALIAN SPAGHETTI AND MEATBALLS
**Meatballs:**

- 3 pounds each of ground beef and ground pork
- 4 cups minced onions
- 6 garlic cloves, minced
- 1 cup chopped parsley
- 3 cups grated Parmesan cheese
- 3 cups fine dry bread crumbs
- 6 eggs
- 3 tablespoons salt
- 2 teaspoons pepper

**Sauce and Spaghetti:**

- 5 cups chopped onions
- 10 garlic cloves, minced
- ½ cup cooking or olive oil
- 17½ cups (five 1-pound, 12-ounce cans) tomatoes
- 5 cups water
- 1 cup chopped parsley
- ½ teaspoon crumbled dried basil
- 2½ teaspoons crumbled dried thyme
- 3 tablespoons salt
- 1 teaspoon pepper
- 1 teaspoon crushed dried red pepper
- 5 cans (6 ounces each) tomato paste
- 4 pounds spaghetti
  Grated Parmesan cheese

Mix all ingredients for meatballs, adding a little water if too dry. Shape into 50 balls, allowing about ⅓ cup for each ball. Put balls, one layer deep, in 3 pans (13 x 9 x 2 inches). Bake in preheated very hot oven (450°F.) for about 30 minutes. Put balls and drippings in roasting pan.

To make sauce: Cook onion and garlic in oil for 5 minutes. Add all ingredients except last 2; simmer, covered, for 30 minutes. Pour over balls and bake, covered, in preheated moderate oven (350°F.) for about 1½ hours. Serve over hot cooked spaghetti; serve cheese in separate bowls at tables. Makes 25 servings.

### MEAT SPAGHETTI SAUCE

- 3 cups (6 medium) minced onions
- 6 garlic cloves, minced
- ⅓ cup cooking oil
- 1½ pounds each of ground beef and pork
- 14 cups (four 1-pound, 12-ounce cans) tomatoes
- ¾ cup chopped parsley
- 2 cans (15½ ounces each) tomato purée
- 3 green peppers, chopped
- 1½ teaspoons each of dried thyme and basil
- 3 tablespoons salt
- ¾ teaspoon pepper

In 12-quart kettle cook onion and garlic in oil until golden. Add meat and cook until lightly browned, stirring to break up meat. Add remaining ingredients and simmer, uncovered, for 4 hours, or until thick, stirring frequently. Makes 5½

quarts, or 25 servings. Keep refrigerated or frozen in plastic containers until ready to use. (Simmering sauce in 2 kettles will reduce cooking time.)
**Note:** For 25 servings use 4 pounds spaghetti.

## SALADS AND VEGETABLES

### JELLIED CRANBERRY AND ORANGE SALAD

- 1¾ cups orange-flavored gelatin dessert
- ¼ teaspoon salt
- 6 cups hot water
- 2 pounds raw cranberries
- 1 pound (2 large) unpeeled oranges
- 1½ cups sugar
  Salad greens
  Mayonnaise

Dissolve gelatin and salt in hot water. Chill until slightly thickened. Force cranberries and oranges through food chopper, using medium blade; mix with sugar and fold into gelatin. Pour into shallow pans to a depth of 1¼ inches. Chill until firm. Cut into squares and serve on greens with a garnish of mayonnaise. Serve with poultry or cold meats. Makes 25 servings.

### COLD POTATO SALAD

- 7 pounds new potatoes
- 1 onion, minced
- ½ cup salad oil
- ¼ cup vinegar
- 1 tablespoon salt
- ½ teaspoon pepper
- 3 cups thinly sliced celery
- ½ cup minced pimiento
- ½ cup chopped parsley
- 4 hard-cooked eggs, diced
- 2 cups mayonnaise or salad dressing

Cook potatoes in jackets; peel and slice while warm. Mix next 5 ingredients and pour over potatoes. Cool, and add remaining ingredients. Serve with greens if desired. Makes 25 servings, about ¾ cup each.

### MACARONI SALAD

- 1½ pounds elbow macaroni
- 1 cup sliced green onions
- 3 cups thinly sliced celery
- 2¼ cups (3 medium) shredded raw carrots
- ¾ cup chopped parsley
- 1 can (4 ounces) pimientos, chopped
- 3 cups mayonnaise
- 2¼ teaspoons salt
- 2 tablespoons prepared mustard
- 3 tablespoons vinegar

Cook and drain macaroni; rinse in hot water and cool. Add next 5 ingredients. Mix remaining ingredients and add to first mixture. Chill. Makes 25 servings, about ¾ cup each.

### JELLIED TOMATO-JUICE SQUARES

- 10 envelopes unflavored gelatin
- 14 cups (two 46-ounce cans and one 19-ounce can) tomato juice
- 2 small onions, sliced
- 2 bay leaves

4 celery stalks
8 whole cloves
2 teaspoons powdered mustard
½ cup sugar
1 teaspoon salt
1 cup vinegar

Soften gelatin in 3 cups cold tomato juice. Simmer remaining juice with other ingredients except vinegar for 5 minutes. Strain. Dissolve gelatin in hot juice. Add vinegar. Pour into shallow pans and chill for about 3 hours, or until firm. Serve on lettuce leaves. Pass mayonnaise. Makes 50 servings.

### CABBAGE AND GREEN-PEPPER SLAW
4½ pounds cabbage
2 small green peppers
½ cup chopped stuffed olives
2 cups mayonnaise
Salt and pepper to taste

Wash cabbage and shred or chop. Wrap in towels or moisture-proof paper and chill. Chop peppers and add with olives to mayonnaise. Chill. When ready to serve, mix cabbage, dressing, and seasonings. Makes 25 servings, about ½ cup each.

### MARINATED CUCUMBERS
6 to 8 cucumbers
1 cup vinegar
½ cup water
¼ cup chopped parsley or dill
6 tablespoons sugar
1 teaspoon salt
¼ teaspoon pepper

Peel and slice cucumbers very thin. Add remaining ingredients. Refrigerate for at least 2 hours before serving. Makes 2 quarts, or 25 servings.

### SCALLOPED POTATOES
14 pounds medium potatoes
¾ cup all-purpose flour
3 tablespoons salt
1 teaspoon pepper
1½ cups margarine
2½ quarts hot milk

Peel potatoes and slice thin. Cook in boiling water for 2 minutes. Drain. Alternate layers of potatoes and flour in greased shallow baking pan. Stir seasonings and margarine into hot milk. Pour over potatoes. Bake, uncovered, in preheated moderate oven (350°F.) for 1¼ hours, or until potatoes are tender. Makes 50 servings.

### CREAMED POTATOES AND PEAS
18 pounds (50) medium potatoes
8 10-ounce packages frozen peas (or two 40-ounce packages, if available)
1½ cups margarine, softened
1½ cups all-purpose flour
1 tablespoon salt
3 quarts milk

Scrub potatoes; cook in boiling salted water until tender. Peel; cut into halves. Cook frozen peas in small amount of boiling salted water until barely tender. Meanwhile, cream together margarine, flour, and salt. Heat milk. Stir in marga-rine-flour mixture slowly, stirring constantly until smooth. Boil for 1 minute. Add potatoes and peas. Set, covered, over simmering water to keep hot until served. Add a little hot milk if sauce becomes too thick. Allow 2 pieces of potato and ¼ cup peas for each serving. Makes 50 servings.

### SCALLOPED CORN
10 cups (five 1-pound cans) whole-kernel corn
Undiluted evaporated milk
1½ cups butter or margarine
1 onion, minced
4 cups finely broken unsalted plain crackers
1½ teaspoons salt
¼ teaspoon pepper
½ cup fine cracker crumbs

Drain corn liquid into saucepan and add enough evaporated milk to make 3 cups. Heat liquid with 1¼ cups butter and the onion. Pour over broken crackers. Add corn and seasonings and pour into shallow baking dishes. Melt remaining butter and mix with fine crumbs. Sprinkle on mixture. Bake in preheated moderate oven (375°F.) for about 30 minutes. Makes 25 servings, about ⅓ cup each.

### BAKED BEANS
4 pounds dried pea beans
6 quarts water
1½ to 2 pounds lean salt pork
2 onions, minced
4 teaspoons salt
2 cups light molasses
1 tablespoon powdered mustard
¼ cup sugar

Cover washed beans with the water, bring to boil, and boil for 2 minutes. Cover and let stand for 1 hour; then cook until tender. Drain, reserving liquid. Score rind of pork and cut off thin slices of pork. Put half of slices in pots or covered roasting pans. (When baking, cover pans with foil if lids are not available.) Put beans in pots and top with remaining pork and scored rind. Mix 1 quart bean liquid and remaining ingredients; pour over beans. Add enough more liquid to cover beans. Cover; bake in preheated slow oven (300°F.) for 6 to 8 hours. Uncover during last hour. Makes 25 servings, 1 cup each.

### HOT CRANBERRY PEARS TO SERVE WITH HAM
50 canned pear halves
3½ cups (two 1-pound cans) whole-cranberry sauce

Drain pears. Place on cookie sheets with sides or in shallow pans. Pile ½ tablespoon cranberry sauce in each pear cavity. Heat in preheated slow oven (300° F.) for about 20 minutes while hams are being cut. Makes 50 servings.

## BREADS

### CORN BREAD
3 cups sifted all-purpose flour
4 tablespoons baking powder
½ cup sugar
2 tablespoons salt
6 cups yellow cornmeal
4 eggs, well beaten
3 cups undiluted evaporated milk
2 cups water
1 cup margarine, melted

Sift first 4 ingredients. Stir in cornmeal. Combine last 4 ingredients and add to first mixture. Stir only until dry ingredients are dampened. Pour into 2 greased pans (13 x 9 x 2 inches) and bake in preheated hot oven (425°F.) for about 20 minutes. Cut each into 12 pieces.

### BAKING-POWDER BISCUITS
5 cups sifted all-purpose flour
2 tablespoons baking powder
2½ teaspoons salt
1 cup shortening
About 1¾ cups milk

Sift dry ingredients into large bowl. Cut in shortening until mixture resembles coarse meal. Add milk and mix until soft dough is formed. Turn out on lightly floured board and knead for 30 seconds. Roll ½ inch thick; cut into 2-inch squares.* Bake in preheated hot oven (450°F.) for 12 to 15 minutes. Makes 42.

* To serve with Tuna à la King, page 1523, cut biscuits into 2½-inch squares and allow 1 per serving. Makes 26.

### PAN ROLLS
2 packages active dry yeast or 2 cakes compressed yeast
1 cup water*
1 cup milk, scalded
1 cup butter or margarine
⅔ cup sugar
1½ teaspoons salt
2 eggs, beaten
8 cups sifted all-purpose flour
Melted butter or margarine

Sprinkle yeast into water. *Use very warm water (105°F. to 115°F.) for dry yeast; use lukewarm (80°F. to 90°F.) for compressed. Let stand for a few minutes, then stir until dissolved. Pour hot milk over butter, sugar, and salt. Cool to lukewarm; add yeast, eggs, and half of flour. Beat well. Add enough more flour to make a dough that will not stick to bowl. Turn out on floured board and knead lightly. Put in greased bowl, cover, and let rise until doubled, about 1½ hours. Punch down and turn out on board. Shape into 50 balls and put close together in greased shallow pans. Let double, about 30 minutes. Brush with melted butter and bake in preheated hot oven (425°F.) for 20 minutes. Makes 50.

## PARKER HOUSE ROLLS

Use recipe for Pan Rolls, page 1524. Roll raised dough to ¼-inch thickness; cut with floured 2¾-inch cutter. With handle of wooden spoon, make a crease in each circle to one side of center; flatten smaller half of round slightly by rolling handle of spoon toward edge. Brush with melted butter; fold thicker half over thinner half; press edges together. Put on greased cookie sheets and let rise until doubled, about 30 minutes. Bake in preheated hot oven (400°F.) for 15 minutes. Makes 50.

 **DESSERTS**

## LEMON FLUFF DESSERT

    2 tall cans (14½ ounces each) undiluted evaporated milk
    2 boxes (3 ounces each) lemon-flavored gelatin
    ½ cup fresh lemon juice
    1⅓ cups sugar
    5 cups graham-cracker crumbs

Chill milk for at least 3 hours. Dissolve gelatin in 3 cups hot water. Chill until thickened; then beat until fluffy. Fold in lemon juice and sugar. Beat milk until thick and fold into gelatin mixture. Sprinkle half of crumbs into two pans (13 x 9 x 2 inches); pour in gelatin mixture and sprinkle remaining crumbs on top. Chill until firm. Cut each into 12 squares. Makes 24 servings.

## BUTTERSCOTCH RAISIN PUDDING

    4 cups evaporated milk
      Water
    6 eggs, separated
    2 cups firmly packed brown sugar
    ⅔ cup quick-cooking tapioca
    ½ teaspoon salt
    2 cups seedless raisins
    ⅓ cup butter or margarine
    4 teaspoons vanilla extract

Combine evaporated milk and 6 cups water in top part of large double boiler. Heat to scalding. Beat egg whites until foamy; gradually add ¾ cup brown sugar and beat until stiff. Set aside. Mix remaining brown sugar, the tapioca, salt, and raisins in top part of double boiler. Beat egg yolks with ⅔ cup water; add to tapioca mixture and stir into milk. Cook, stirring, over boiling water for 5 minutes. Stir quickly into meringue. Add butter and vanilla and mix well. Cover with wax paper and cool, stirring once or twice during first 15 minutes. When thoroughly cool, chill. Makes 25 servings, about ⅝ cup each.

## APPLE CRISP

    15 cups (six 1-pound, 4-ounce cans) apple slices
    ¼ cup fresh lemon juice
    3 cups sifted all-purpose flour
    3 cups firmly packed brown sugar
    1 teaspoon salt

    1 tablespoon ground cinnamon
    1½ cups butter or margarine
      Cream

Put apples in baking pan, making layer about 1½ inches deep. Sprinkle with lemon juice. Combine next 4 ingredients and cut in butter. Sprinkle over apples, covering well. Bake in preheated moderate oven (375°F.) for 35 minutes. Serve with cream. Makes 25 servings, about ⅔ cup each.

## ANGEL DELIGHT

    4 cups (two 1-pound cans) crushed pineapple
    8 ounces marshmallows, cut fine, or 8 ounces miniature marshmallows
    2 bottles (8 ounces each) maraschino cherries
    2 envelopes unflavored gelatin
    2 cups milk
    1½ cups chopped blanched almonds
    4 cups heavy cream
    2 angel cakes (10-inch size)

Mix undrained pineapple, marshmallows, and cherries including juice. Let stand in refrigerator for 6 hours, or overnight. Soften gelatin in 1 cup milk; heat, stirring, until gelatin is dissolved. Add 1 cup cold milk and chill until slightly thickened. Add fruit mixture and nuts. Whip cream and fold into mixture. Chill until ready to serve. Cut each cake into 12 to 16 wedges; put on plates; top with mixture. Makes 24 to 32 servings.

## DEEP-DISH CHERRY PIES

**Pastry:**

    4 cups sifted all-purpose flour
    2 teaspoons salt
    1⅓ cups lard
      About ¼ cup ice-cold water

**Filling:**

    10 cups (five 1-pound cans) pitted red sour cherries
    4 cups sugar
    ¼ cup cornstarch
    ¼ teaspoon salt
      Juice of 1 lemon

To make the pastry, sift flour and salt. Cut in lard until mixture resembles coarse meal. Gradually add ice water, mixing with fork until mixture can be shaped into a ball. Divide dough into halves and roll out each piece to ⅛-inch thickness on lightly floured board. Cut into 3-inch squares with pastry wheel or knife and bake in preheated very hot oven (450°F.) for about 15 minutes. For filling, drain cherry juice into saucepan. Heat juice to boiling. Mix sugar, cornstarch, and ¼ teaspoon salt; sift into juice, stirring constantly. Cook, stirring, until clear and thickened. Add lemon juice and cherries. Heat through. Serve hot or cold with a square of pastry on top, and whipped cream if desired. (For 25 servings, whip 2 cups heavy cream. Or use commercial whipped topping.) Makes 25 servings.

## GINGERBREAD

    5 cups sifted all-purpose flour
    2 teaspoons baking powder
    2 teaspoons each of baking soda and salt
    2 teaspoons each of ground cinnamon and ginger
    1 teaspoon ground cloves
    1 cup shortening
    1 cup sugar
    4 eggs
    2 cups water
    2 cups molasses
      Lemon Sauce or
      Amber Whipped Cream

Sift dry ingredients together. Cream shortening and sugar until light. Add eggs, one at a time, beating well after each addition. Add dry ingredients alternately with combined water and molasses and beat until smooth. Pour into 2 greased baking pans (13 x 9 x 2 inches). Bake in preheated moderate oven (350°F.) for about 35 minutes. Serve hot with Lemon Sauce or with Amber Whipped Cream. Makes about 50 servings.

## Lemon Sauce

    10 cups sugar
    1⅓ cups cornstarch
    1 teaspoon salt
    4 quarts water
      Juice and grated rind of 12 lemons
    1 cup butter or margarine

Blend sugar, cornstarch, and salt in kettle. Add water. Cook, stirring, until thick and clear. Add juice, rind, and butter. Bring to boil again and remove from heat. Serve warm or cold. Makes 50 servings, 3 tablespoons each.

## Amber Whipped Cream

Mix 4 cups heavy cream, 1⅓ cups firmly packed light brown sugar, and 1 teaspoon vanilla extract. Chill for 1 hour; then whip until stiff. Allow 2 tablespoons per serving. Makes 50 servings.

## GOLDEN GLOW CAKE

    1 cup shortening
    5 cups sifted cake flour
    3 cups sugar
    6 teaspoons baking powder
    2 teaspoons salt
    2 cups milk
    2 teaspoons vanilla extract
    4 eggs
      Confectioners' sugar
      Fudge Sauce, Butterscotch Sauce, or ice cream

Put shortening in bowl. Sift flour, sugar, baking powder, and salt into bowl with shortening. Add 1⅓ cups milk and the vanilla. Mix until dry ingredients are moistened; then beat for 2 minutes at medium speed in electric mixer, or 300 strokes by hand. Add remaining milk and eggs; blend and beat for 2 minutes at medium speed, or 300 strokes, scraping bowl and beaters thoroughly. Divide batter between 2 pans (13 x 9 x 2 inches) lined on bottom with wax paper. Bake in preheated moderate oven (375°F.) for about 30 minutes. Cool slightly, turn out on racks, and peel off paper. Sprinkle with confectioners' sugar, if desired. Serve with Fudge Sauce, Butterscotch Sauce, or ice cream.

### Fudge Sauce

Melt 12 ounces (12 squares) unsweetened chocolate in 3 cups milk over low heat, stirring constantly. Beat until smooth. Add 1 teaspoon salt, 6 cups sugar, and ¾ cup light corn syrup; cook, stirring, for 5 minutes. Add ⅓ cup butter or margarine and 1 tablespoon vanilla extract. Serve warm or cold on ice cream, cream puffs, or plain cake. Makes 2 quarts, or enough for 50 servings.

**Note:** This sauce keeps well in the refrigerator and can be reheated.

### Butterscotch Sauce

In heavy kettle mix 3 pounds (6¾ cups) light brown sugar, 3 cups corn syrup, 1 cup butter or margarine, and ¾ teaspoon salt. Bring to full boil, stirring until sugar is dissolved. Add 3 cups undiluted evaporated milk and 1 tablespoon vanilla extract. Serve warm or cold. Makes about 10½ cups, or enough sauce for 50 servings.

> *The dessert recipes which follow are also suitable for food sales. For sales, foods should be neatly labeled as to contents and number of servings.*

### CHOCOLATE NUT FUDGE

24 ounces (two 12-ounce packages) semisweet chocolate pieces
1 cup margarine
1 jar (any size) marshmallow cream
1 tall can (14½ ounces) evaporated milk
4½ cups sugar
2 cups chopped nuts
1 tablespoon vanilla extract

Put first 3 ingredients in large bowl. In heavy kettle put milk and sugar. Bring to a rolling boil and cook rapidly, stirring vigorously, for exactly 9 minutes (mixture scorches easily). Pour over ingredients in bowl and mix well. Beat with electric mixer or rotary beater only until well blended. Stir in nuts and vanilla and spread into buttered pan (1 x 10 x 15 inches). Cool, score, and let stand for 12 to 24 hours. Cut and wrap. Makes 5 pounds.

### REFRIGERATOR OATMEAL COOKIES

¾ cup granulated sugar
3½ cups firmly packed light brown sugar
1½ cups margarine, melted
4 eggs, beaten
2 cups quick-cooking oats
4 cups sifted all-purpose flour
2 teaspoons baking soda
2 teaspoons ground cinnamon
½ teaspoon salt
1 cup chopped nuts
2 cups seedless raisins

Mix sugars and margarine. Add eggs and

oats. Stir in flour sifted with soda, cinnamon, and salt. Add nuts and raisins and mix well. Pack into 2 loaf pans (9 x 5 x 3 inches) lined with wax paper. Chill thoroughly. When ready to bake, turn out of pans and remove paper. Slice ¼ inch thick; put on ungreased cookie sheets. Bake in preheated moderate oven (350°F.) for 10 minutes. Makes 5 dozen cookies.

### CHOCOLATE BROWNIES

12 ounces (12 squares) unsweetened chocolate
2 cups butter
1 dozen eggs
6 cups sugar
4 teaspoons vanilla extract
1 teaspoon salt
3½ cups sifted all-purpose flour
5 cups chopped walnuts

Melt chocolate and butter together. Beat eggs until thick. Gradually beat in sugar. Add to chocolate mixture. Add vanilla, salt, and flour; beat. Fold in nuts. Bake in 3 greased pans (1 x 10 x 15 inches) in preheated moderate oven (325°F.) for 25 to 30 minutes. Cool; cut contents of each pan into 35 pieces. Makes 105.

### FROSTED DATE-NUT BARS

½ cup butter or margarine
1 cup sugar
2 eggs
½ cup each of dark corn syrup and molasses
4 cups sifted all-purpose flour
½ teaspoon each of salt and baking soda
3 teaspoons baking powder
1 cup milk
2 teaspoons vanilla extract
2 cups each of chopped nuts and dates
Confectioners'-Sugar Frosting

Cream shortening and sugar. Add eggs, syrup, and molasses; beat until light. Sift dry ingredients and add alternately with milk, beating until smooth. Add vanilla and fold in nuts and dates. Pour into 2 greased pans (13 x 9 x 2 inches). Bake in preheated moderate oven (350°F.) for about 25 minutes. Cool slightly in pan and spread with a thin coat of frosting. Cool thoroughly. Cut contents of each pan into 30 bars. If made for a crowd, serve with ice cream or fruit. Makes 60 servings.

### Confectioners'-Sugar Frosting

Mix 2 cups confectioners' sugar with enough water or milk to make of spreading consistency.

### POPCORN BALLS

2 cups sugar
⅔ cup light corn syrup
⅔ cup water
½ cup margarine
2 teaspoons salt
1½ teaspoons vanilla extract
6 quarts popped corn

Mix sugar, corn syrup, water, margarine, and salt in saucepan. Cook until mixture becomes brittle when a small amount is

dropped into cold water (270°F. on a candy thermometer). Add vanilla and stir. Pour slowly over popped corn and mix well. Grease fingers with margarine and shape mixture into popcorn balls. Makes 2 dozen medium popcorn balls. For larger amounts, make single recipe as many times as needed.

## BEVERAGES

### HOT COFFEE
**(Made with instant coffee)**

Empty 1 jar (2 ounces) instant coffee into large kettle. Add 7 quarts boiling water. Keep hot. Makes 42 cups.

### HOT COFFEE
**(Made in kettle)**

Have 1 pound coffee, ground coarse. It will measure about 5½ cups. Divide into 2 lots and tie each loosely in a double thickness of cheesecloth, allowing plenty of room for coffee to swell. Bring 7½ quarts water to boil in large kettle. Drop in bags of coffee, cover, and reduce heat until water barely bubbles. Let bags remain in water for 10 to 12 minutes. Do not boil. Remove bags and serve. Makes 40 cups.

### HOT TEA

Bring 7½ quarts water to boil in large kettle. Tie 1¼ cups (3 ounces) tea loosely in cheesecloth. Drop into water, turn off heat, cover, and steep for 5 minutes; remove bag. Have more boiling water ready. If serving from a buffet table, extra-strong tea can be made in the kitchen and diluted when served. Use 1¼ cups tea as above, and only 3¾ quarts boiling water. Steep as directed. Keep tea in a warm place but not over a hot range unit. Fill a hot teapot with the strong tea and put on the serving table with a pot of boiling hot water. The server can then dilute the tea as desired while pouring. Makes 40 cups.

### HOT COCOA

In kettle mix 1¾ cups cocoa, 1 cup sugar, and ⅛ teaspoon salt. Gradually add 2 cups cold water and bring to boil, stirring. Boil for 3 minutes, or until thickened. Add 4½ quarts hot milk and mix well. Just before serving, beat well. Makes 4½ quarts.

### CONCORD PUNCH

4 cups boiling water
8 teaspoons tea
1 cup sugar
4 cups grape juice
Juice of 8 lemons
Juice of 4 oranges
2 bottles (12 ounces each) ginger ale
Orange and lemon slices

Make double-strength tea by pouring boiling water over tea. Let steep for 5 minutes and strain. Add sugar and stir to dissolve. Pour over ice cubes in punch bowl. Add grape juice, lemon and orange juice, and ginger ale. Garnish with orange and lemon slices. Makes about 1 gallon, or twenty-four 5-ounce servings.

### FRUIT PUNCH
2 cups boiling water
4 teaspoons tea
2 cups sugar
1 cup fresh lemon juice
1 cup fresh orange juice
2 cups pineapple juice
2 quarts water
  Lemon slices
  Maraschino cherries

Make double-strength tea by pouring boiling water over tea. Let steep for 5 minutes and strain. Add sugar and stir to dissolve. Cool. Add lemon, orange, and pineapple juices and 2 quarts water. To serve, pour over block of ice in punch bowl; garnish with fluted lemon slices and maraschino cherries. Makes about 1 gallon, or twenty-four 5-ounce servings.

### PARTY PUNCH
2 cups boiling water
4 teaspoons tea
2 cups sugar
2 cups water
2 tablespoons crushed mint leaves
3 cups fresh orange juice
1 cup raspberry or loganberry juice
1 cup fresh lemon juice
2 quarts water
1 bottle (12 ounces) ginger ale
  Orange and lemon slices
  Fresh mint sprigs

Make double-strength tea by pouring boiling water over tea. Let steep for 5 minutes and strain. Boil sugar with 2 cups water for 5 minutes. Add crushed mint leaves. Cool, and strain. Combine tea, mint syrup, fruit juices, and 2 quarts water. Just before serving add ginger ale. Pour over block of ice in punch bowl; garnish with orange and lemon slices and sprigs of fresh mint. Makes about 5 quarts, or thirty 5-ounce servings.

### CRANBERRY-APPLE PUNCH
4 cups cranberry juice
3 cups apple juice
½ cup fresh lemon juice
1 lemon, thinly sliced
1 cup pineapple chunks
1 bottle (29 ounces) soda water

Combine cranberry, apple, and lemon juices. Add lemon slices and pineapple chunks. Chill thoroughly. To serve, pour over ice in punch bowl and add soda water. Makes about 3 quarts, or twenty 5-ounce servings.

### CHAMPAGNE AND SAUTERNE PUNCH
2 cups sugar
2 cups fresh lemon juice
5 cups fresh orange juice
2 bottles (4/5 quart each) sauterne, chilled
1 bottle (4/5 quart) champagne, chilled

1 lemon, sliced
1 orange, sliced

Combine sugar and juices and stir until sugar dissolves. Chill thoroughly. Just before serving, add wine and pour over ice in punch bowl. Add champagne and garnish with lemon and orange slices. Makes about 5½ quarts, or thirty-five 5-ounce servings.

### RUM PUNCH
¾ cup fresh lemon juice
2¼ cups fresh orange juice
3 cups white rum
  Crushed ice
3 bottles (28 ounces each) ginger ale, chilled
  Oranges, sliced
  Maraschino cherries

Combine juices with rum and chill thoroughly. Just before serving, pour over crushed ice and add ginger ale. Garnish with orange slices and cherries. Makes about 5 quarts, or thirty 5-ounce servings.

### PORT PUNCH
3 cups fresh orange juice
1½ cups fresh lemon juice
1½ cups chilled port
  Crushed ice
3 bottles (28 ounces each) ginger ale, chilled
3 oranges, sliced

Combine juices with wine and chill. Just before serving, pour over crushed ice and add ginger ale. Garnish with orange slices. Makes about 5 quarts, or thirty 5-ounce servings.

**QUENELLE**—A dumpling made of fish or meat forcemeat, bound with eggs, and generally poached in boiling salted water or stock. The word "quenelle" is thought to have come from the German *knödel*, "dumpling."

Small quenelles are used as a garnish; larger ones are served as a separate dish.

### PIKE QUENELLES
½ cup water
¾ cup butter or margarine
½ cup all-purpose flour
¼ teaspoon salt
2 eggs
1 pound pike
  Salt, pepper, and grated nutmeg
2 egg whites
½ cup heavy cream

Heat water and ¼ cup butter in saucepan until butter is melted and water boils. Add flour and salt, and stir briskly until mixture leaves the sides of the pan, forming a ball. Remove from heat and beat in eggs, one at a time. Continue beating until mixture is smooth; cool. Remove bones and force fish through finest blade of food chopper 3 or 4 times. Work ground fish with wooden spoon until smooth. Beat in cooled pastry mixture. Add salt, pepper, and nutmeg to taste. Beat in gradually, one at a time, the egg

whites, ½ cup softened butter, and cream. Chill overnight. Next day, shape quenelles with a pastry tube, in a dessert spoon by leveling pastry and sliding it into a buttered skillet, or by rolling paste into cylinders. Cover with boiling salted water and simmer for 10 minutes, or until done. Remove and drain. Serve plain or with a lobster or shrimp sauce. Makes 4 to 6 servings.

### CHICKEN QUENELLES
½ cup water
¾ cup butter or margarine
½ cup all-purpose flour
¼ teaspoon salt
2 eggs
2 cups finely ground cooked chicken
  Salt, pepper, and grated nutmeg
2 egg whites
½ cup heavy cream
  Melted butter or margarine

Heat water and ¼ cup butter in saucepan until butter is melted and water boils. Add flour and salt, and stir briskly until mixture leaves the sides of the pan, forming a ball. Remove from heat and beat in whole eggs, one at a time. Continue beating until smooth. Cool. Work chicken with wooden spoon until smooth. Beat in cooled pastry mixture. Add salt, pepper, and nutmeg to taste. Gradually beat in egg whites, one at a time, ½ cup softened butter, and the cream. Chill overnight. Next day, shape the quenelles with a pastry tube, or in a dessert spoon by leveling pastry and sliding it into a buttered skillet, or by rolling paste into cylinders. Cover with boiling salted water and simmer for 10 minutes, or until done. Remove and drain. Serve at once with melted butter. Makes 4 to 6 servings.

**QUICHE**—A savory baked custard tart thought to have originated in Lorraine, a province of eastern France bordering on Germany, although Alsace, the neighboring province, also lays claim to being the home of the true quiche. The word quiche is derived from the French-German dialect spoken in these regions and can be traced back to the German word *kuchen*, "cake."

The best-known quiche, Quiche Lorraine, is one made with eggs, bacon, cheese, and cream, baked in a pastry shell. It is always eaten as hot as possible. Any quiche makes an excellent luncheon or supper dish, or it can be served in the traditional way as a hot hors-d'oeuvre.

### QUICHE LORRAINE WITH CREAM CHEESE
8 ounces cream cheese
½ cup heavy cream
3 egg yolks
1 egg

**Quiche Lorraine
with Swiss Cheese**

¼ teaspoon freshly ground pepper
¼ teaspoon salt
6 slices of bacon
Pastry for 1-crust 8-inch pie, unbaked

Beat cream cheese with next 5 ingredients until smooth and blended. Cut bacon into 1-inch pieces and cook until lightly browned and almost crisp. Arrange in bottom of pastry-lined pie pan. Pour cheese mixture over bacon. Bake in preheated hot oven (400°F.) for 20 minutes. Reduce heat to moderate (350°F.) and bake for 10 minutes longer, or until puffed and golden-brown. Let stand for 2 or 3 minutes before cutting into wedges. Makes 4 to 6 servings.

### QUICHE LORRAINE WITH SWISS CHEESE

1½ cups (6 ounces) grated imported
    Swiss cheese
8 slices of crisp bacon, crumbled
Pastry for 1-crust 9-inch pie, unbaked
3 eggs
1 cup heavy cream
½ cup milk
½ teaspoon salt
¼ teaspoon pepper
Dash of cayenne
¼ teaspoon powdered mustard

Sprinkle cheese and bacon into pastry-lined pie pan. Beat remaining ingredients together and pour over cheese. Bake in preheated moderate oven (375°F.) for 45 minutes, or until firm and browned. Cut into wedges and serve hot. Makes 6 servings.

### LOBSTER QUICHE

Pastry for 1-crust 9-inch pie, unbaked
2 tablespoons finely chopped green
    onions
2 tablespoons butter
1¼ cups diced canned or fresh-cooked
    lobster
1 tablespoon freshly snipped dill
4 eggs, slightly beaten
2 tablespoons dry white wine
½ teaspoon salt
¼ teaspoon pepper
1¼ cups heavy cream, scalded

Line a 9-inch pie pan with pastry. Flute the edge, prick bottom with a fork, line with foil, and fill with beans or rice. Bake in preheated hot oven (400°F.) for 8 minutes. Remove foil and beans and bake for about 3 minutes longer. Reduce oven heat to moderate (375°F.). Meanwhile, sauté onions in butter and spread in partly cooked shell; top with lobster and dill. Combine the eggs, wine, salt, pepper, and cream; pour into shell. Bake for 25 to 30 minutes, or until set.

**QUINCE**—The round to pear-shape fruit of a tree of the same name. When ripe the fruit is rich yellow or greenish-yellow with a strong odor, hard flesh. Its taste is so tart and astringent that it cannot be eaten raw. Quinces are full of natural pectin and are used for making marmalade, jellies, jams, fruit paste, butters, preserves, and syrups.

Quince trees are usually small (fifteen to twenty feet high) and gnarled with many crooked branches. Sometimes the tree takes a bush form. The quince tree has been cultivated for over 4,000 years, and it still greatly resembles its ancient ancestor. Quinces are a native of western Asia and reached the Mediterranean countries quite early. The quince was given mythological significance by the Greeks and Romans, who considered it sacred to the Goddess of Love. If you gave a quince to someone of the opposite sex it was considered to be an engagement token.

The Romans used the quince in ways other than the ceremonial. The quince blossoms were made into perfume, and the fruit formed the base of a hair dye. But early Greeks and Romans also knew that the sacred fruit could be eaten in many ways. There is a 12th-century translation from the Greek which gives directions for quince honey: "Take quynces ripe and pare and heve hem smal,/And al for smal, but kest away the core,/In honey thene upboile hem, lese and more/De pepur (or ginger) with yt boiling." Translated into more modern English this means to peel and cut up the fruit, discarding the core, and boil in honey, adding pepper or ginger.

Roman recipes for quinces included a kind of reduced wine, fish sauces, sauces for minced meat, and quince purée. Apicius, the Roman who wrote the 1st century cook book that has come down to us as *The Art Of Cooking*, gives a recipe for keeping quinces fresh: "Choose faultless quinces with their twigs and leaves, and put them in a receptacle, and pour over honey and defrutum [a reduced wine]: you will keep them for a long time."

Many modern American uses of quinces are based on these early classical recipes, for quinces in jams and jellies are most popular. The English and Germans have sometimes been more inventive, serving roast quince, quince pie, and quince honey. Spaniards, Portuguese, and Latin Americans make quinces into a sweet paste. It is eaten with cream and other soft cheeses, an excellent flavor combination.

The early American colonists had developed a taste for quinces, and the settlers of Massachusetts wrote home for quince kernels almost immediately after arriving in this country. The fruit spread throughout the country. John Bartlett, a 19th century bibliographer and historian, saw quinces growing in Mexico and in a report of his experiences commented: "There are two varieties of the quince here, one hard and tart like our own, the other sweet and eatable in its raw state, yet preserving the rich flavor of the former. The Mexicans gathered and ate them like apples, but I found them too hard for my digestive organs." It is exactly this difficulty which makes it necessary to cook quinces. They are most often pared, cored, seeded, then stewed like apples or made into a preserve of some kind.

*Availability*—October to December. Quinces are easily bruised and must be handled carefully.

*Purchasing Guide*—Select quinces with a greenish-yellow or pale-yellow color. Avoid fruit with spots or bruises; punctures indicate worms.

*Storage*—Store in a cool, dark, dry place.

*Caloric Value*

☐ 3½ ounces, raw = 57 calories

### BAKED QUINCES

Wipe, quarter, core, and peel quinces. Put in a deep casserole and sprinkle with sugar, allowing 2 tablespoons for each quince. Add ½ inch water, and 1 sliced orange, if desired, for each 4 quinces. Bake in preheated slow oven (300°F.) for 2 hours, or until tender and deep red in color. Cool before serving.

### QUINCE GINGER MARMALADE

6 pounds quinces
2 cups water
Juice and grated rind of 4 lemons
2 tablespoons fresh gingerroot
¼ teaspoon salt
Sugar

Pare quinces; cut into small pieces. Cook in water in large preserving kettle for 15 minutes. Add lemon rind and juice, gingerroot, and salt. Boil for 15 minutes. Measure and add an equal amount of sugar. Boil until quinces are translucent and deep red in color. Makes about 4 pints.

**Note:** If fresh gingerroot is unavailable, use preserved or crystallized gingerroot and ½ teaspoon ground ginger.

### QUINCE JELLY WITHOUT PECTIN

3 pounds ripe quinces
Water
3 cups sugar

Remove cores and blossom and stem ends from quinces. (Do not peel.) Slice quinces. Measure, and for each quart add 3 cups water. Put in kettle, bring to boil, and simmer for 45 minutes. Drain through damp cotton flannel, jelly bag, or 4 layers of cheesecloth. (For greater yield of juice, twist the two ends of the bag in opposite directions until most of the juice is extracted. Then strain through clean, damp cotton flannel or jelly bag. Do not squeeze or press.) Measure juice. There should be 4 cups. If not quite enough, add small amount of water to make up the amount. Put juice in large kettle and bring to boil. Add sugar and stir until dissolved. Boil rapidly until mixture sheets from a spoon. Pour into hot sterilized jars, and seal. Makes about four ½-pint jars.

**RABBIT**—A small furry mammal of the rodent family, the rabbit has large eyes, long ears, long strong hind legs and feet, and a short tail. It differs most significantly from its close relative the hare in its burrowing habits and in the fact that the young of rabbits are born naked, blind, and helpless whereas hares are born furred and able to see.

Rabbits have an average weight of three pounds and are sixteen to eighteen inches long. In addition to being hunted in their wild state they are bred for food, for their skins, and as pets.

Rabbit meat is practically all white, is fine-grained, and mild-flavored. It can be prepared in many of the ways in which chicken is prepared. Young animals can be panfried, broiled, and roasted. Older animals can be braised and fricasseed.

*Availability and Purchasing Guide*—Fresh rabbit, whole or cut into pieces, is available ready-to-cook in weights from 1½ to 3 pounds. Frozen rabbit is also available.

Look for firm, plump meat, light in color. Avoid any meat with stringy or tough appearance.

*Storage*—Refrigerate immediately.
- ☐ Refrigerator shelf, raw: 2 days
- ☐ Refrigerator shelf, cooked and covered: 1 to 2 days
- ☐ Fresh, prepared for freezing; or frozen, refrigerator frozen-food compartment: 1 week
- ☐ Fresh, prepared for freezing; or frozen, freezer: 2 to 3 months

Do not refreeze once thawed. Use within 2 days of thawing.

*Caloric Values*
- ☐ Domesticated, 3½ ounces, raw = 162 calories
- ☐ Wild, 3½ ounces, raw = 135 calories

*Basic Preparation*—Wear rubber gloves when handling wild rabbits to avoid tularemia. They should be bled and eviscerated immediately. Skin as soon as possible after cleaning.

☐ **To Freeze**—Wash thoroughly and wrap tightly, whole or cut into pieces, in moisture- vapor-proof material excluding as much air as possible. Seal.

### WILD RABBITS

2 rabbits (1 to 1½ pounds each)
3 cups water
1 cup vinegar
2 tablespoons salt
1 teaspoon pepper
3 tablespoons mixed
whole spice
1 Bermuda onion, sliced
1 carrot, diced
3 slices of bacon, diced
2 tablespoons butter or margarine
1 tablespoon sugar
3 tablespoons all-purpose flour
3 gingersnaps
½ cup dairy sour cream

Cut rabbits into 4 to 6 pieces. Wash in cold water several times. Remove excess skin and wash again. Dry on paper towels. Prepare a marinade of the water, vinegar, seasonings, onion, and carrot; pour over rabbit in a glass or earthen jar. Refrigerate for 2 or 3 days. Remove rabbit from marinade and dry on paper towels. Strain marinade and reserve. Brown bacon with the butter in a Dutch oven or skillet with a lid. Add the rabbit and brown well. Cover and simmer for 1 hour. Sprinkle sugar over rabbit and allow to caramelize. Add the flour, 2 cups marinade, and gingersnaps. Simmer for 20 minutes. Stir in the sour cream and simmer for another 10 minutes. Taste for seasoning. Makes 4 to 6 servings.

### JUGGED RABBIT

    2 rabbits, about 3 pounds
      each, cut up
    2 carrots, diced
    1 onion, stuck with 3 cloves
    6 garlic cloves, peeled
    1 bay leaf
    6 peppercorns
    2 cups coarsely chopped celery
    2 cups dry red wine
      Water
    3 tablespoons shortening
    1 tablespoon tomato purée
    1 teaspoon salt
    ½ cup all purpose flour
    8 slices of crisp bacon
    8 whole mushrooms, sautéed
    2 tablespoons minced parsley

Put meat into a big bowl with carrots, onion, garlic, bay leaf, peppercorns, celery, and wine. Add water to cover and allow to marinate for 3 days. Remove pieces of meat from marinade and pat dry. Brown in shortening in a deep kettle. Add marinade, tomato purée, and salt. Simmer gently, covered, for about 2 hours, or until meat is tender. Remove meat and keep warm. Blend flour and ½ cup water. Stir into sauce. Bring just to a boil. Strain through a fine sieve. Add pieces of meat. Bring to a boil again. Serve garnished with bacon and mushrooms and sprinkled with parsley. Makes 6 to 8 servings.

### RABBIT STEW

    1 rabbit, about 3 pounds,
      cut up
    ½ cup all-purpose flour
    3 tablespoons butter
    1 cup diced celery
    2 onions, sliced
    1½ teaspoons seasoned salt
    1 teaspoon salt
      Dash of pepper
    1 bay leaf
    4½ cups water
    4 cups dry red wine
    2 cups diced peeled carrots
    4 potatoes, peeled and diced
    1 can (4 ounces) sliced
      mushrooms, drained

Dredge meat with flour and brown on all sides in butter in kettle. Add next 6 ingredients, 4 cups water, and the wine. Bring to boil, cover, and simmer for 2 hours, or until meat is almost tender. Add carrots and potatoes; simmer for about 30 minutes longer. Add mushrooms. Thicken with ¼ cup flour and remaining water, blended. Makes 4 servings.

**RACCOON or COON**—A North American carnivorous mammal found throughout the United States and on the Pacific Coast from Alaska to South America. The common raccoon is a heavily built animal, about three feet long, blackish-gray in color with a pointed snout and a bushy tail striped black and white. It makes its home in trees, descending at night to feed, often on the banks of ponds and streams. Raccoons feed on a great variety of things, including fruits, green corn, fish, frogs, birds, small animals, and occasionally poultry. Raccoons are related to the South American kinkajou and the Asian panda.

Much used for food during America's pioneer days, they are still considered good game by many people. The meat is dark and the fat strong in flavor and odor. A dressed animal without head or feet weighs from five to fourteen pounds. Roasting is the preferred method of cooking young raccoons. Older ones should be braised or stewed. To improve the flavor of a dressed raccoon and to remove some of the gamy taste, the dressed carcass should be wrapped tightly in wax paper and refrigerated from four to seven days at a temperature as near 35° F. as possible.

*Caloric Value*

☐ 3½ ounces, roasted = 255 calories

### ROAST RACCOON WITH SWEET-POTATO STUFFING

    1 dressed raccoon, 4 to 5 pounds
    4 teaspoons salt
    3 cups mashed sweet potatoes
    ¾ cup seedless raisins
    2½ cups soft bread crumbs
    1¾ cups peeled diced apples
    ¼ cup corn syrup
    ¼ cup butter or margarine, melted
    ¼ teaspoon pepper

From the raccoon, remove the waxy nodules, commonly referred to as "kernels," from under each front leg and on either side of the spine in the small of the back. Wash meat thoroughly and dry. Remove part of the fat, leaving just enough to cover the carcass with a thin layer of fat. Sprinkle 1 teaspoon salt inside body. Fill with mixture of 2 teaspoons salt and remaining ingredients except pepper. Skewer the vent by inserting several toothpicks through the skin from side to side. Lace with string, tying the ends securely. Fasten both the forelegs and the hind legs with toothpicks and string. If there are any lean parts on the outside of the body, fasten a small piece of the surplus fat to this part with a toothpick. Sprinkle with remaining salt and the pepper. Put on side on greased rack in shallow baking pan and roast in preheated slow oven (325°F.) for 45 minutes per pound. Turn when half done. Makes 6 to 8 servings.

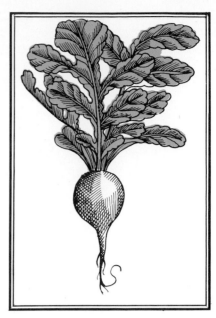

**RADISH**—The pungent fleshy root of a hardy annual plant, *Raphanus sativus*, which is widely valued as a salad vegetable. Apparently it is native to the temperate regions of Asia, and it has been cultivated in China, Japan, and India for thousands of years. The name radish is derived from the Latin word for "root," *radix*.

Radishes come in many shapes and colors: round, long, or oblong, and white, pink, red, yellow, purple, or black. Their taste varies from mild to peppery. Depending on the variety, they can be from one inch to two or more feet long and weigh up to several pounds apiece. The oriental radishes are by far the largest, and since they are coarse in flavor and texture, are most often cooked or pickled.

*Availability*—Radishes are available year round. Peak season for red globe radishes, the most common variety, is May through July.

The long tapering varieties, both white- and red-skinned, are mild in flavor and at their peak from July through October.

The longer oval winter radishes, red, white, or black in color and about 6 inches long, are in season from December through February.

*Purchasing Guide*—Look for smooth, well-formed, firm radishes. The condition of the leaves is not always an indication of quality. Radishes are marketed in bunches or, with their tops removed, in small plastic bags.

*Storage*—Remove leaves and rootlets and wash thoroughly. Refrigerate.

☐ Refrigerator shelf or vegetable compartment: about 1 week
Radishes cannot be frozen.

*Caloric Values*

☐ Common, 3½ ounces, raw = 17 calories

Veal and Pork Ragout

☐ Oriental, 3½ ounces, raw = 19 calories

**Basic Preparation**—Wash. Be sure all leaves and rootlets have been removed.

Radishes may be cut in attractive ways to use on a relish plate or to garnish salads.

### RADISH SALAD

    2 cups sliced red
      or white radishes
      French dressing
      Salt and pepper
      Chopped parsley

Marinate radishes in French dressing. Add salt and pepper to taste. Before serving, drain and sprinkle thickly with parsley. This radish salad can be added to any potato or green-vegetable tossed salad to give color and texture as well as flavor. Makes 4 servings.

**RAGOUT**—A French word for a stew made from meat, poultry, or fish, with or without vegetables. It is derived from *ragoûter*, "to stimulate the taste." The word has come directly into English, without the accent, and as an English word, ragout is most often used in reference to well-seasoned meat and vegetable stews cooked in thick rich sauces, usually brown.

### VEAL AND PORK RAGOUT

    1½ pounds boneless stewing veal
    1½ pounds boneless pork shoulder
        All-purpose flour
      3 tablespoons butter or margarine
      1 onion, chopped
      1 cup hot water
      ½ cup dry red wine
      1 tablespoon salt
      ½ teaspoon pepper
      2 parsley sprigs
      ½ bay leaf
      1 garlic clove, minced
        Veal bone, if desired
      4 to 6 small potatoes, peeled and
        quartered
      ½ pound mushrooms, halved
      1 can (1 pound) onions, drained
      1 can (1 pound) tiny carrots, drained
      ½ cup frozen peas

Cut meat into 1½-inch cubes. Dredge with flour and brown on all sides in butter. Add onion and brown a few minutes longer. Add next 8 ingredients. Bake, covered, in preheated moderate oven (350°F.) for 1½ hours. Remove bone, and add potatoes, mushrooms, and enough water to almost cover. Return to oven; cook for 40 minutes. Add onions, carrots, and peas; cook for 20 minutes. Makes 6 to 8 servings.

### LAMB RAGOUT IN CARROT-POTATO RING

    2 cups cubed roast lamb
    2 tablespoons lamb fat
    8 small onions, quartered
    1½ cups water
    ½ teaspoon salt

Dash of pepper
Flour
4 medium potatoes
4 medium carrots
1 tablespoon margarine
⅓ cup hot milk
Salt and pepper

Brown lamb in fat. Add onions and cook until lightly browned. Add water, ½ teaspoon salt, and dash of pepper. Bring to boil; cover and simmer for 30 minutes, or until onions are tender. Thicken gravy with a paste of a little flour blended with cold water. Cook potatoes and carrots together in boiling salted water until tender. Drain and mash. Add margarine, milk, and salt and pepper to taste. Beat until light and fluffy. Heap in ring around edge of deep 9-inch pie pan. Fill center with lamb mixture. Reheat, or keep warm in oven if necessary. Makes 4 servings.

**RAISE, TO**—The culinary process of making a food light and porous by the action of yeast. A yeast dough is placed in a warm spot, thus activating the yeast and producing a gas which expands, or raises, the dough. The dough literally rises in the bowl. When the dough rises until doubled in volume, it is ready to be shaped. After shaping, the dough is usually allowed to rise a second time until doubled in volume; then it is ready for baking.

**RAISIN**—The name given to several varieties of grapes when they are dried, either naturally in the sun, or by artificial heat. When grapes are dried, their skins wrinkle, they have a higher sugar content, and a flavor quite different from that of fresh grapes.

The word raisin comes from the Latin word *racemus* meaning "a cluster of grapes or berries." It is thought that the Egyptians were the first to notice that grapes left on the vine lost moisture and became sweeter. Thus dried, they kept better than when fresh.

Varieties of grapes dried to make raisins run from dark bluish-brown to golden. The two most popular varieties are muscats and sultanas. When the fruit is ripe it is picked and spread out on trays to dry in the sun. The golden sultanas are not dried in the sun, but dehydrated indoors and given a sulfur treatment. This preserves their golden color.

Raisins are good for snacks, eaten out-of-hand. They also mix well with nuts. In cooking they can be added to cereals, rice puddings, cookies, cakes, muffins, stuffing, salads, and rolls. They are an indispensable part of mince pie and fruitcake.

***Availability and Purchasing Guide***—Golden and dark (bluish- or reddish-brown) raisins are available year round seedless, seeded (the seed is removed after drying), and in clusters (grapes dried on the stem in large bunches to make fancy table raisins).

***Storage***—Store in a cool, dry place. In hot weather, refrigerate. If refrigerated, raisins will keep indefinitely.

***Nutritive Food Values***—Raisins contain a variety of vitamins and minerals, especially iron. Their natural sugar content makes them an excellent sweet for children since they do not cause dental caries.
- 3½ ounces, uncooked = 289 calories
- 3½ ounces, cooked with sugar added, fruit and liquid = 213 calories

***Basic Preparation***—Add 1 cup water to every cup raisins. Cover and simmer for 10 minutes. Sugar is not necessary. Raisins combine better with other ingredients if they are first cooked in boiling water for 5 minutes, then drained.

### HAM NUGGETS IN RAISIN SAUCE

⅓ cup raisins
2 cups water
1 cup firmly packed dark brown sugar
2 tablespoons cornstarch
Dash of salt
¼ teaspoon ground ginger
2 tablespoons cider vinegar
2 cups chunky nuggets baked ham (¾ pound)
2⅔ cups (one 6-ounce package) wide noodles, cooked

Cook raisins in water for 5 minutes. Combine brown sugar, cornstarch, salt, ginger, and vinegar; add to water and raisins and cook until slightly thickened. Add ham; heat thoroughly. Put drained hot noodles in heated shallow baking dish or deep platter; pour ham and sauce over center. Makes 4 servings.

### RAISIN-NUT SANDWICHES

Put 1 cup seeded raisins and ¼ cup nuts through food chopper. Moisten with mayonnaise. Spread between slices of buttered bread.

### RAISIN BREAD

2 packages active dry yeast or 2 cakes compressed yeast
1 cup water*
2 cups boiling water
2 cups seedless raisins
½ cup soft butter or margarine
¼ cup firmly packed brown sugar
2 eggs
2 tablespoons ground coriander
3 teaspoons salt
¼ cup wheat germ
1 cup nonfat dry milk crystals
9½ cups sifted all-purpose flour

*Use very warm water (105°F. to 115° F.) for dry yeast; use lukewarm (80°F. to 90°F.) for compressed yeast. Sprinkle yeast or crumble cakes into water in large bowl. Let stand for a few minutes, then stir until dissolved. Pour boiling water over raisins and let stand until lukewarm. Add yeast and remaining ingredients except 5 cups flour; mix well. Add remaining flour; mix well and turn out on floured pastry cloth or board. Knead until smooth and satiny. Put in greased bowl; turn once, cover, and let rise until doubled, about 1 hour. Punch down and let rise for 30 minutes. Shape into 3 loaves and put in greased loaf pans (9 x 5 x 3 inches). Let rise until doubled, about 45 minutes. Bake in preheated moderate oven (350°F.) for about 50 minutes. Makes 3 loaves.

### RUMANIAN RAISIN COMPOTE

2 cups golden raisins
1 cup water
1 cup honey
Grated rind of 1 lemon
½ cup pine nuts

Soak raisins in water to cover for 1 hour; drain. Boil together water and honey for 2 to 3 minutes. Add raisins and lemon rind; simmer for 10 minutes over low heat. Skim with slotted spoon as needed. Add pine nuts to raisins. Chill thoroughly before serving. Makes 4 to 6 servings.

### RAISIN PIE

2 cups seeded raisins
1 cup water
½ cup corn syrup
¼ cup cornstarch
¼ teaspoon salt
Pastry for 1-crust, 9-inch pie and lattice topping, unbaked

Wash raisins; drain. Add water; simmer for 10 minutes. Add corn syrup mixed with cornstarch and salt; cook for 3 minutes, stirring constantly. Cool; pour into pastry-lined pie pan; arrange strips of pastry over top. Bake in preheated hot oven (425°F.) for about 20 minutes. Makes 6 servings.

## CHOCOLATE DROPS

½ cup soft butter or margarine
1 cup sugar
1 egg and 1 egg yolk
3 ounces (3 squares) unsweetened chocolate, melted
½ cup milk
½ teaspoon vanilla extract
1¾ cups sifted all-purpose flour
½ teaspoon each of baking soda and baking powder
¼ teaspoon salt
1 cup seedless raisins
1 cup chopped walnuts
Chocolate Frosting

Cream butter and sugar until light. Add egg and egg yolk, chocolate, milk, and vanilla and mix well. Sift flour with soda, baking powder, and salt; add to butter mixture. Fold in raisins and nuts. Drop from teaspoon onto greased cookie sheets. Bake in preheated moderate oven (375° F.) for 12 minutes. Top with Chocolate Frosting. Makes 4 dozen.

### Chocolate Frosting

Cream 3 tablespoons butter with 1 cup confectioners' sugar, 2 tablespoons cocoa, 1½ tablespoons cold coffee, and ½ teaspoon vanilla extract.

### RAISIN-NUT PINWHEELS

1 cup soft butter or margarine
½ cup sugar
1 egg
2 cups sifted all-purpose flour
1 teaspoon baking powder
1 cup dairy sour cream
Raisin-Nut Filling

Cream butter and sugar until light. Beat in egg. Add sifted dry ingredients alternately with sour cream, beating until smooth. Chill overnight. Roll one fourth of dough at a time on well-floured board or pastry cloth to form a rectangle (10 x 6 inches). Dough will be soft. Keep in refrigerator until ready to use. Spread with one fourth of Raisin-Nut Filling and roll up from 10-inch side. Cut into 12 pieces and put 3 inches apart on greased cookie sheet. Bake in preheated moderate oven (350°F.) for about 15 minutes. Repeat until all ingredients are used. Makes 4 dozen cookies.

### Raisin-Nut Filling

Mix 1 cup chopped nuts, ¼ cup raisins, ¾ cup orange marmalade, ¼ cup sugar, and 1 teaspoon ground cinnamon.

### RAISIN-FILLED COOKIES

**Cookie Dough:**
½ cup sugar
½ cup shortening
1 egg
½ cup milk
2½ cups sifted all-purpose flour
¼ teaspoon salt
2 teaspoons baking powder
1 teaspoon vanilla extract

**Filling:**
1 teaspoon all-purpose flour
½ cup sugar

½ cup water
1 cup ground raisins

To make dough, add ingredients in order given. Chill dough.

To make filling mix flour and sugar; add water and raisins, stirring carefully. Cook until thick. Let cool. Place between two thinly rolled cookies. Bake in preheated moderate oven (350°F.) for 15 minutes, or until browned. Makes 3 dozen.

### RAISIN SPICE CAKE

1 cup firmly packed brown sugar
1 cup seeded raisins
1¼ cups water
½ cup shortening
1 teaspoon ground cinnamon
½ teaspoon each of ground nutmeg and allspice
2 cups sifted all-purpose flour
1 teaspoon each of baking soda and baking powder
½ teaspoon salt

Boil sugar, raisins, water, shortening, and spices for 5 minutes. Chill. Sift flour, baking soda, baking powder, and salt together; stir into first mixture. Pour into greased loaf pan (9 x 5 x 3 inches) lined with wax paper. Bake in preheated moderate oven (350°F.) for 55 to 60 minutes. Turn out onto cake rack; remove paper; cool. Makes 1 loaf cake.

### IRANIAN RAISIN CAKE

1 cup sifted all-purpose flour
½ cup sugar
½ teaspoon baking powder
5 medium eggs
½ teaspoon vanilla extract
1 cup raisins
¼ cup sliced blanched almonds
¼ cup sliced pistachio nuts

Mix flour, sugar, and baking powder together thoroughly. Beat eggs slightly, add vanilla, and combine with dry ingredients. Add raisins and nuts. Pour into greased loaf pan (9¼ x 5¼ x 2¾ inches). Bake in preheated moderate oven (350° F.) for about 35 minutes, or until firm. Cool thoroughly and cut into very thin slices.

### SPICED RAISINS

2 cups firmly packed light brown sugar
1 teaspoon ground allspice
½ teaspoon each of ground ginger and cloves
1 cup water
2 cups raisins (golden, seeded or seedless)
1½ cups granulated sugar

Cook brown sugar, spices, and water until 232°F. registers on candy thermometer, or until a small amount of syrup dropped into very cold water spins a 2-inch thread when dropped from fork or spoon. Stir in raisins; cook for 2 minutes. Remove from heat and put pan in bowl of warm water while working. Drain raisins, ½ cup at a time, on paper towel and roll in granulated sugar. When thoroughly cool,

store in covered jar. Makes 2 pounds.

### SPICY JELLIED RAISINS

1 envelope unflavored gelatin
¼ cup cold water
¼ cup vinegar or liquid from sweet pickles
1½ cups liquid from canned fruit
6 whole cloves
½ cup seedless raisins

Let gelatin stand in cold water for 5 minutes. Combine vinegar, fruit liquid, and cloves; boil for 5 minutes. Remove cloves and stir in gelatin. Pour into loaf pan; chill until partially congealed. Add raisins; chill until firm. Cut into 1-inch cubes. Makes 6 to 8 servings.

### RAISIN, APPLE, AND NUT RELISH

1 tablespoon prepared mustard
1 cup sugar
⅓ cup cider vinegar
⅔ cup water
⅛ teaspoon ground allspice
2 cinnamon sticks
1 piece of whole gingerroot
4 medium cooking apples
½ cup seedless raisins
¼ cup chopped nuts

In saucepan blend mustard and sugar. Add vinegar, water, and spices. Bring to boil and simmer for 10 minutes. Pare apples, core, and cut each apple into eighths. Cut each eighth into quarters crosswise. Remove cinnamon and ginger from hot mixture. Add apples, raisins, and nuts; bring to boil and simmer for 10 minutes. Cool. Serve with poultry or ham. Makes about 3 cups.

**RAMEKIN or RAMEQUIN**—A French word which originally referred to toasted cheese but has developed two different meanings: 1) A certain type of cheese tart or tartlet and 2) an individual baking dish in which food is baked and served. The word ramekin comes from the Flemish *rammeken* which means "a little bit of cream."

In modern culinary usage, the cheese dish called a ramekin is a pastry filled with a creamy mixture of cheese, eggs, milk, or cream. Ramekins are eaten hot or warm, never cold. They can be made in one- or two-bite sizes, and are an excellent hors-d'oeuvre.

Ramekin dishes are usually white, with straight fluted sides, resembling miniature soufflé dishes.

### RAMEKINS

Standard pastry made with 2 cups flour
½ pound Swiss cheese, grated (2 cups)
1 tablespoon all-purpose flour
3 eggs, well beaten
1 cup light cream
Salt and pepper

Line ramekin with pastry dough rolled to ⅛-inch thickness. Chill. Dredge cheese with flour. Place cheese on pastry. Beat together eggs, cream, and salt and pepper to taste. Pour over cheese—the pans should not be more than three quarters full. Bake in preheated hot oven (425° F.) for 15 to 25 minutes, depending on size of the ramekin. Serve hot or warmed up. Makes eight 4-inch ramekins.

## RAMPION

**RAMPION**—A bellflower, *Campanula rapunculus,* which grows wild in Europe and is sometimes cultivated for its edible tuberous root. The root, about a foot in length, looks like a long white radish. It and the tender young leaves of the plant are used raw in salads and cooked as vegetables.

**RAREBIT**—Another name for Welsh rabbit, a popular cheese dish.

**RASPBERRY**—The fruit of a bush of the *Rubus* genus which is a member of the rose family. Raspberries grow wild in woods and are also cultivated. The berry is made up of many small drupelets. In contrast to blackberries, which retain their stems or receptacles when the fruit is picked, the stem of a raspberry separates from the berry and remains on the plant. Raspberries may be red, purple, black, or amber in color. They are a delicately flavored fruit and can be eaten raw either plain or with cream, and can be used for jellies, jams, puddings, pies, etc. Berries of any color can be used interchangeably in recipes and can also be used in most strawberry recipes.

**Availability**—Fresh raspberries are available from June through November, with July the peak month. They are also canned and frozen in syrup, and are available as raspberry jam and apple-raspberry sauce.

**Purchasing Guide**—Select berries that are bright, fresh, plump, well-shaped, and solid in color. Avoid wet or leaky berries. A stained container is an indication of overripe or damaged berries.

**Storage**—Sort berries and refrigerate. Use as soon as possible.

☐ Refrigerator shelf: 1 to 2 days
☐ Fresh, prepared for freezing; or frozen, refrigerator frozen-food compartment: 2 to 3 months
☐ Fresh, prepared for freezing, or frozen, freezer: 1 year
☐ Canned, kitchen shelf: 1 year

**Nutritive Food Values**—A fair source of iron and vitamin C.

☐ Fresh red, 3½ ounces, raw = 57 calories
☐ Fresh black, 3½ ounces, raw = 73 calories
☐ Canned red, 3½ ounces, water pack, solids and liquid = 35 calories
☐ Canned black, 3½ ounces, water pack, solids and liquid = 51 calories
☐ Frozen red, 3½ ounces, sweetened, unthawed = 98 calories

**Basic Preparation**—Wash berries just before using. Do not allow berries to soak in water.

☐ **To Freeze**—Use firm ripe berries. Wash in ice water quickly without bruising berries. Spread berries in a single layer on a cookie sheet and freeze until firm. Pour into freezer container. Seal, and freeze.

Or add ¾ cup sugar to every 4 cups berries. Stir gently until sugar is partly dissolved. Spoon into containers, allowing ½-inch headspace. Freeze.

Or pour berries into freezer container. Cover with cold syrup made by cooking 4 cups water with 6 cups sugar; allow ½-inch headspace. Seal.

### RASPBERRY PUDDING

2 cups raspberry juice
¼ cup sugar (about)*
1 cinnamon stick
¼ teaspoon salt
¼ cup cornstarch
  Red food coloring (optional)
  Cream

Bring juice, sugar, cinnamon stick, and salt to a boil. Mix the cornstarch in a small amount of cold water and stir into the hot juice. Bring mixture to a quick boil and remove from heat as soon as it thickens. Add a few drops of red food coloring if necessary. Pour into pudding dish or individual glasses. Sprinkle the top with additional sugar to keep a skin from forming. Chill. Serve with cream. Makes 4 servings.

*Sugar should be used to taste, depending on tartness of juice. The pudding should be tart rather than sweet.

### FROZEN CHEESE AND RASPBERRY DESSERT

2 cups creamed cottage cheese
  Juice of 1 lemon
1 cup sugar
2 cups dairy sour cream
2 packages (10 ounces each) frozen raspberries, partially thawed

Turn refrigerator control to coldest setting. Force cheese through food mill or fine sieve. Add lemon juice and sugar and beat until smooth. Add sour cream and mix well. Pour into refrigerator tray and freeze until firm. Cut into serving pieces and serve with raspberries. Makes 8 servings.

### RASPBERRY CREAM PIE

6 cups raspberries
  Water
⅔ cup sugar
3 tablespoons cornstarch
  Dash of salt
  Pastry for 1-crust 9-inch pie, baked

1 cup heavy cream, whipped
  Mint sprigs

Mash 2 cups berries and force through sieve; add water to make 1½ cups. Mix sugar, cornstarch, and salt; add to sieved berries. Cook, stirring constantly, for 5 minutes, or until thickened. Cool. Reserve a few berries for garnish. Put remaining berries in baked pie shell. Pour on cooked cornstarch mixture. Chill. Garnish with whipped cream, reserved berries, and mint. Makes 6 to 8 servings.

### FRESH RASPBERRY PASTRIES

2 cups fresh raspberries
5 tablespoons sugar
1 teaspoon fresh lemon juice

**Fresh Raspberry Pastries**

**Raspberry Cream Pie**

1 cup sifted all-purpose flour
¼ teaspoon salt
½ teaspoon baking powder
⅓ cup butter or margarine
3 tablespoons cold water
½ cup heavy cream, whipped
5 whole fresh raspberries

Wash raspberries and mix with 3 tablespoons sugar and the lemon juice. Chill until ready to use. Sift flour with salt, baking powder, and 1 tablespoon sugar. Add butter and cut it in until mixture resembles coarse meal. Add water and mix only until all flour is moistened. Turn out on lightly floured board. Shape into a ball. Roll into a circle ⅛ inch thick. Cut into circles with 3-inch cookie cutter (scalloped edge is attractive). Bake on ungreased cookie sheets in preheated hot oven (425°F.) for 12 to 15 minutes, or until lightly browned. Cool on a wire rack. When ready to serve, place a pastry circle on a plate. Cover with 2 tablespoons drained raspberries and 1 tablespoon of the whipped cream which has been sweetened with remaining sugar. Cover with another pastry circle and top with additional berries and whipped cream. Garnish each with a whole fresh raspberry. Makes 5 servings.

### RASPBERRY PEACH GLACÉES
2 egg whites
⅛ teaspoon salt
½ teaspoon cream of tartar
½ cup sugar
⅛ teaspoon almond extract
1 pint peach ice cream
Raspberry Sauce

Have egg whites at room temperature; beat with rotary or electric beater until foamy. Add salt and cream of tartar and beat until just stiff enough to stand in peaks. Gradually add sugar and continue beating until very stiff. Add almond extract. Spoon 4 small mounds onto lightly buttered unglazed brown paper on cookie sheet; flatten each mound to make a thin base about 1½ inches in diameter. With a pastry tube or spoon, surround bases with more meringue to height of 2 inches, leaving center unfilled. Bake in preheated slow oven (250°F.) for 1¼ hours. Transfer paper to a damp board; remove meringues. When cold, fill with ice cream and top with Raspberry Sauce. Makes 4 servings.

### Raspberry Sauce
1 pint raspberries
Water
¼ cup sugar
1 tablespoon cornstarch
Few drops of fresh lemon juice

Mash and sieve berries; add water to make 1 cup. Add sugar and cornstarch, mixed. Cook until thickened, stirring constantly. Add lemon juice. Cool; chill.

**RATATOUILLE**—The word is French and describes a stew or casserole which most frequently contains a well-seasoned combination of eggplant, zucchini, tomato, and green pepper. Occasionally meat is added.

### RATATOUILLE
2 garlic cloves, minced
1 onion, sliced thin
½ cup cooking or olive oil
1 medium eggplant, diced
3 medium zucchini, sliced
1 green pepper, sliced
3½ cups (one 29-ounce can)
   Italian-style tomatoes
1 teaspoon dried oregano or basil
   Salt and pepper to taste

Sauté garlic and onion in oil until clear. Add eggplant and toss. Add zucchini and pepper and cook for 10 minutes. Add remaining ingredients and simmer, covered, for 30 minutes. Uncover and simmer for 30 minutes longer. Makes 6 servings.

**RAVIGOTE**—A well-seasoned classic French sauce consisting of green herbs, butter, and tarragon vinegar added to béchamel sauce. The name is derived from the French *ravigoter,* "to revive, refresh."

Ravigote sauce is served with hot or cold fish, meat, poultry, and vegetables. For a recipe see page 1620.

**RAVIOLI**—Shells or cases of noodle dough filled with meat, chicken, cheese, or spinach.

Although the word ravioli is Italian, this type of food preparation is by no means a uniquely Italian dish. It occurs under different names in the cookery of many lands. The Chinese know ravioli as *won ton,* the Jews as *kreplach,* and the Russians as *pelmeni.* It all goes to show that ravioli, filled one way or another, make an excellent dish.

Ravioli dough is not difficult to prepare if the liquid is added to the flour

until the dough cleans the bowl but is not sticky. The dough should then be kneaded to develop gluten strands which will make the dough elastic. Let the dough rest for 30 minutes before rolling as this will also help develop gluten strands. The dough should be rolled as thinly as possible on a pastry cloth or board using as little flour as possible. Extra flour makes the dough tough. The filling must be thick and pasty, not wet, or the dough around the filling will absorb moisture and become sticky. The filling should be thick enough to be shaped into balls with the fingers or a spoon. Once the filling has been placed on the dough, the edges of the dough should be moistened with water to prevent the ravioli from opening during cooking. The ravioli should be dried only for a short time, about 2 hours, before cooking. Uncooked ravioli can be frozen successfully. The ravioli should be dried slightly, then packed into freezer containers with a layer of freezer paper between each two layers of ravioli. Cover and seal. When ready to prepare, cook the ravioli only from the frozen state as defrosting makes them difficult to handle. Remove cooked ravioli from the cooking liquid with a slotted spoon and serve with hot sauce or hot sautéed buttered bread crumbs and Parmesan cheese.

Canned beef or cheese ravioli is available in most food stores. Frozen cheese, beef, or spinach ravioli is available in Italian food stores and some general food stores.

### RAVIOLI
2 cups sifted all-purpose flour
½ teaspoon salt
2 eggs, slightly beaten
6 tablespoons lukewarm water
   Hamburger Filling
2 cups spaghetti sauce
   Grated Parmesan cheese

Sift flour and salt. Add eggs and stir with a fork until thoroughly mixed. Gradually add lukewarm water and stir until mixture forms a smooth ball. Turn out on lightly floured board and knead for a few minutes, or until smooth and elastic. Put in bowl and sprinkle with a little flour. Cover and let stand for 30 minutes. Roll out half of dough on lightly floured board to an oblong 10 x 16 inches. Put small teaspoons of Hamburger Filling about 2 inches apart on the dough. Roll out remaining dough and brush with water. Put dough, moistened side down, over the hamburger. Press edges of dough firmly around each teaspoon of filling. With a sharp knife or a pastry jagger cut ravioli into 2-inch squares. Set aside and let dry for 2 hours. Drop ravioli into boiling salted water and cook for 15 minutes, or until ravioli are tender. Put

ravioli in a shallow casserole, cover with hot spaghetti sauce, and sprinkle with Parmesan cheese. Bake in preheated moderate oven (375°F.) for 25 minutes, or until sauce is bubbly. Makes 6 servings.

### Hamburger Filling
¾ pound ground beef
½ teaspoon salt
⅛ teaspoon pepper
1 tablespoon grated Parmesan cheese
2 parsley sprigs, chopped
1 egg, slightly beaten
1 tablespoon fine dry bread crumbs
2 teaspoons grated onion

Cook beef, stirring with a fork, until it loses its red color. Drain off fat. Add remaining ingredients. Mix well and cool.

### RAVIOLI ITALIAN STYLE
**Dough:**
3½ cups sifted all-purpose flour
3 egg yolks
1½ teaspoons salt
⅔ cup water, about

**Meat or Cheese Filling:**
6 quarts beef or chicken bouillon or water
   Tomato Sauce
1 cup grated Parmesan cheese

Put flour on a pastry board or in a bowl. Make a well in the center. Put egg yolks, salt, and water into the center of the flour. Stir carefully with a fork until liquid is mixed into flour, forming a soft dough. Knead dough on the board until all flour is incorporated. Continue kneading in a little additional flour until dough becomes smooth and elastic, about 10 minutes. Cover dough with a bowl and let stand for 30 minutes.

Cut dough into 4 pieces and roll out each piece on lightly floured board into the same size sheet. Cover sheets of dough with a towel while rolling to prevent drying. Brush 2 of the sheets lightly with water. On the 2 brushed sheets put small balls of the filling about 1½ inches apart. Cover filled sheets with 2 remaining sheets, pushing the dough tightly around each ball of filling. Cut into 2-inch squares. Put ravioli on a lightly floured towel. Sprinkle lightly with flour and let stand for 30 minutes. Cook ravioli in boiling bouillon for 7 to 10 minutes. Remove with a slotted spoon. Put a layer of ravioli into a serving bowl. Spoon some Tomato Sauce over the ravioli and sprinkle with grated Parmesan cheese. Continue layering until bowl is filled. Makes 8 servings.

### Meat Filling
⅔ cup ground cooked ham or prosciutto
1 cup ground cooked white meat of chicken
1 cup ground cooked veal
2 egg yolks
1½ teaspoons salt
1 tablespoon olive oil
1 tablespoon grated Parmesan cheese
   Salt and pepper

*Ravioli Italian Style*

Combine all ingredients and blend well into a smooth paste. Shape mixture into small balls the size of a large olive.

### Cheese Filling
¾ pound ricotta cheese
1 tablespoon chopped parsley
2 tablespoons grated Romano cheese
1 egg yolk, beaten
  Salt to taste

Combine all filling ingredients and put small spoonfuls about 2 inches apart on the dough. Prepare as instructed in recipe.

### Tomato Sauce
1 can (6 ounces) tomato paste
1½ cups water
5 ripe tomatoes, peeled and diced
¼ cup olive oil
1 garlic clove
¼ cup butter or margarine
¼ teaspoon crumbled dried basil
¼ teaspoon crushed red pepper
  Salt and pepper to taste

Blend tomato paste with water. Add tomatoes, oil, and garlic. Simmer for 25 minutes, stirring occasionally, or until sauce is reduced to one-third of its original amount. Remove garlic and put mixture through a food mill, or whirl in a blender. Add remaining ingredients, season with salt and pepper, and continue simmering until sauce is reduced to half its original volume.

**RECIPE**—When applied to cooking, a recipe is a formula for preparing a dish. In old-fashioned usage the words "receipt" or "rule" were often used to mean the same thing.

A recipe is made up of two major parts: the list of ingredients and the directions for preparing the dish. In reading and interpreting recipes there are certain points to bear in mind:

1. Read the recipe through thoroughly, making sure you understand what the ingredients are and the method to be used.

2. Before beginning the dish, make sure you have all the ingredients. A good plan is to collect them before beginning.

3. If you are making the dish for the first time, do not alter any ingredients or procedures. If you are an experienced cook, after you have made the dish once, you may want to alter it as far as the seasonings, method of serving, etc., are concerned.

4. Generally speaking, it is unsafe to double or triple recipes, especially cakes and candies. The cooking time, texture, or consistency of the resulting product may be changed.

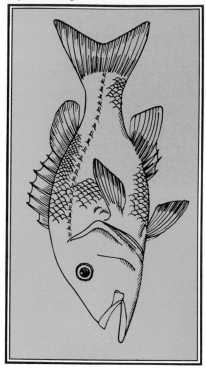

**RED SNAPPER**—A salt-water fish of a family that includes gray snapper, mutton-fish, schoolmaster, and yellowtail. These fishes are caught in the South Atlantic and the Gulf of Mexico. The market weight ranges from two to fifteen pounds although snappers weighing as much as twenty pounds have been caught.

All varieties are considered lean fishes, with juicy meat and a delicate flavor. They can be panfried, steamed, poached, or broiled, and are particularly delicious baked.

*Availability and Purchasing Guide*—Available year round fresh and frozen, whole, and as steaks and fillets.

Fresh fish should have bright, clear bulging eyes; gills that look and smell clean; scales that are shiny and lie close to the skin; and firm flesh with some spring to it when pressed with a finger.

*Storage*—Fresh fish is very perishable. Wrap snapper in moisture-proof paper or place in tightly covered container in coldest part of refrigerator.

Keep frozen snapper solidly frozen until ready to use. Once thawed, use immediately. Do not refreeze.

☐ Fresh, refrigerator shelf, raw: 1 to 2 days

☐ Fresh, cooked; or frozen, refrigerator shelf: 3 to 4 days

☐ Fresh, refrigerator frozen-food com-partment, prepared for freezing, raw: 2 to 3 weeks

☐ Fresh, refrigerator frozen-food compartment, prepared for freezing, cooked: 3 to 4 weeks

☐ Frozen, refrigerator frozen-food compartment: 2 months

☐ Fresh, prepared for freezing, raw or cooked; or frozen, freezer: 1 year

*Caloric Value*

☐ 3½ ounces, raw = 93 calories

*Basic Preparation*

☐ **To Poach**—Cut fillets into serving-size portions. Or use steaks. Put fish in a wire basket or on a plate. If plate is used, it should be tied in a piece of cheesecloth. Lower the fish into boiling salted water and simmer for 10 minutes, or until fish flakes easily with a fork. Serve with any desired sauce such as tomato, drawn butter, egg, etc.

☐ **To Steam**—Sprinkle both sides of fillets or steaks with salt. Put in a well greased steamer pan and steam over boiling water for 10 to 12 minutes, or until fish flakes easily with a fork. Serve with sauce as listed above.

☐ **To Panfry**—Cut fillets into serving-size portions. Dip into flour and season on both sides with salt and pepper. Panfry in hot butter or margarine until browned on both sides and fish flakes easily with a fork. Serve with lemon wedges, if desired.

☐ **To Broil**—Cut fillets into serving-size portions. Or use steaks. Sprinkle on both sides with salt and pepper. Put fish on a preheated greased broiler pan about 2 inches from the heat, skin side up, if skin has not been removed from fillets. Brush fish with melted butter or margarine. Broil for 5 to 8 minutes on each side, or until lightly browned, and fish flakes easily with a fork, basting with butter after turning.

☐ **To Bake Whole Fish**—Wipe fish with damp cloth. Rub inside and out with salt. Put in a greased shallow baking pan. Brush with melted butter or margarine and, if desired, lay 3 slices of bacon over top. Bake in preheated moderate oven (350°F.) for 40 to 60 minutes, or until fish flakes easily with a fork. Baste with melted butter several times during the baking.

☐ **To Bake Fillets or Steaks**—Cut fillets into serving-size portions. Or use steaks. Sprinkle on both sides with salt and pepper. Dip each piece into a mixture of twice as much melted butter as fresh lemon juice. Put in a greased shallow baking pan. Bake in preheated moderate oven (350°F.) for 25 to 30 minutes, or until fish flakes easily with a fork. Sprinkle with paprika.

☐ **To Freeze**—Eviscerate fish and wash well. Cut as desired into steaks or fillets or leave whole. Dip pieces of fish into a solution of ¼ cup salt to 4 cups water for 20 to 30 seconds. Wrap in moisture-vapor-proof wrapping, excluding as much air as possible. Seal.

### RED SNAPPER STEAKS WITH SHRIMPS
    2 pounds red snapper steaks
      Salt and pepper to taste
    4 tablespoons butter or margarine
      Few parsley sprigs, chopped
    1 small carrot, minced
    1 celery stalk, minced
    ¼ teaspoon dried basil
    1 cup Rhine wine
    ¼ pound raw shrimps, shelled and
      cleaned
    1 lemon, sliced

Wipe fish with a damp cloth and season on both sides with salt and pepper. Melt 2 tablespoons of the butter and use to brush the inside of a shallow baking dish. Arrange fish in dish. Top with parsley, carrot, and celery. Sprinkle with basil and add wine. Bake in preheated moderate oven (350°F.) for 20 minutes. Mince shrimps and sauté in remaining butter for 3 minutes, or until lightly browned, stirring constantly. Pour over fish and bake for 10 minutes longer, or until fish flakes easily with a fork. Garnish with lemon slices. Makes 4 servings.

### BAKED RED SNAPPER, FLORIDA STYLE
    1 whole red snapper, 5 to 7 pounds
    1 medium onion, minced
    1 green pepper, minced
    1 garlic clove, minced
      Bacon fat
    2 cups soft stale-bread crumbs
      Chopped fresh dill or dill seed
    3 eggs, beaten
    6 slices of bacon
  1½ cups red wine
    3 tablespoons all-purpose flour
    ½ cup tomato paste
      Salt and pepper
      Chopped parsley

Have fish cleaned and split with head left on. Sauté onion, green pepper, and garlic in 3 tablespoons bacon fat for 5 minutes. Add crumbs and season with chopped fresh dill to taste. Stir in eggs. Stuff fish with the mixture and sew or secure opening with toothpicks. Put fish in a greased shallow baking pan and arrange bacon slices on it. Pour in 1 cup red wine. Bake in preheated hot oven (400°F.) for about 35 minutes, or until fish flakes easily with a fork. Remove fish to a hot platter. Blend flour into drippings in pan. Add remaining wine and tomato paste. Cook, stirring constantly, until smooth and thickened. Season to taste with salt, pepper, and parsley. Serve with the fish. Makes 6 to 8 servings.

### RED SNAPPER AMANDINE
Panfry 2 pounds red snapper fillets, cut into serving-size portions, as directed in To Panfry (at left). Put cooked fillets

in a shallow baking dish. Put ¾ cup sliced almonds in a skillet with ¾ cup butter. Cook, stirring, until golden-brown. Pour over fish and sprinkle with the juice of 1 lemon. Put in preheated moderate oven (375°F.) for 5 minutes to heat and blend flavors. Makes 4 servings.

**REDUCE, TO**—As a culinary process, the phrase means to cook a liquid until a certain amount of it is cooked away, thus concentrating the flavor in, and thickening the consistency of, that which remains.

Reducing is most commonly done in sauces, stews, and syrups. It is one of the simplest cooking processes; all it requires is that one watches to make sure that there is not *too* much evaporation.

**REINDEER**—Any of several varieties of deer of the genus *Rangifer* that live in Arctic and subarctic Europe, Asia, and America. The American variety is called caribou. Their chief characteristics are large hoofs and the possession of crescent-shape antlers in both sexes, which is not usual with deer. However, the antlers of the male reindeer are much larger than those of the female and present a most imposing sight. In the winter their fur is long and grayish-brown on the body while the neck, hindquarters, and belly are white. In the summer the animal becomes a darker gray and brown. The winter furs are especially prized because of their thickness and softness. The meat is sweet, dark red, with clear white fat.

Reindeer have been domesticated and used as a source of food and as draft animals. They are still an essential part of the economy of Laplanders.

Reindeer meat is highly prized in all Scandinavian countries and wherever reindeer are raised. Fresh or smoked, it is excellent. Its flavor is much more delicate than that of other venison, but it is apt to be tough and should be well hung. Reindeer meat can be prepared like any venison. In Scandinavia the meat is often marinated first and then pot-roasted. The sauce usually contains cream.

*Availability*—Frozen reindeer imported from Norway is available as leg steaks, backs, rump roast, and boneless stew meat in specialty food stores in a very limited area of the Northeast. Canned reindeer meatballs in brown gravy are also available imported from Norway.

### NORWEGIAN REINDEER POT ROAST WITH MUSHROOMS, TOMATOES, GRAPES, AND PINEAPPLE
5-pound roast of reindeer, boned and rolled
4 cups dry red wine
1 large onion, sliced
1 celery stalk
10 peppercorns
1 tablespoon salt
2 bay leaves
½ pound salt pork or bacon, cut into slices
½ cup butter
1 cup dairy sour cream
½ cup heavy cream, whipped

Garnish:

1 pound mushroom caps, sautéed in butter
6 tomatoes, cut into halves and grilled
½ pound dark-blue grapes, stemmed
1 cup chopped pineapple, sautéed in butter

Place meat in deep bowl. Combine wine, onion, celery, peppercorns, salt, and bay leaves. Pour over meat and marinate for 24 to 48 hours. Turn meat several times. Drain and wipe dry. Strain marinade and reserve. Lard meat with salt pork, or wrap larding around meat, tying with string. Heat butter in large heavy casserole or Dutch oven. Brown meat on all sides. Reduce heat as low as possible. Pour half of marinade over meat. Simmer, covered, for 2 to 3 hours (depending on toughness of the meat), or until meat is tender. To test for doneness, lift meat and test with a skewer; it should not draw blood. Baste occasionally during cooking time with pan juices; if necessary, add a little more marinade. When done, transfer meat to hot platter and keep hot. Remove string and salt pork or bacon. Make gravy by swirling sour cream in pan in which meat was cooked, but do not boil. If necessary, thicken gravy with a little flour mixed with water to a smooth paste. Begin with 1 tablespoon and cook for 2 or 3 minutes over lowest possible heat. Add whipped cream to finished gravy and spoon a little over meat on platter. To garnish, surround meat with mushroom caps in rows and alternate mounds of grilled tomatoes, grapes, and pineapple. The arrangement should be decorative. Serve remaining gravy separately. Serve with browned potatoes. Makes 6 to 8 servings.

**RELISH**—As a verb "to relish" means "to enjoy," and when the word relish is used as a culinary term it can be, and is, applied to a wide range of foods and food preparations served as accompaniments to add zest, flavor, and variety to the main dishes of a meal. Olives and such vegetables as celery, radishes, cucumbers, carrots, and cauliflower, when served raw, are one major type of relish.

A second major type includes such widely used condiments as ketchup and chutney, and all the other savory foods prepared from mixed chopped vegetables or fruits, either uncooked, pickled, or preserved.

Many commercially prepared relishes are available. When making preserved relishes at home it is important to cook them in an enamelware, glass, or stainless-steel container which will not discolor the food, and to stir the preparation almost constantly to prevent burning.

### APPLE RELISH
12 apples, peeled and chopped
1 onion, chopped
2 green peppers, seeded and chopped
1 cup sugar
2 cups cider vinegar
1 lemon, sliced thin and seeded
1½ teaspoons each of salt and ground ginger
1 cup seeded raisins

Combine all ingredients in a large saucepan and cook for 2 hours, stirring occasionally, until mixture is thick. Spoon mixture into hot sterilized jars, seal, and cool. Makes about 2 quarts.

### BEET AND CABBAGE RELISH
4 cups chopped peeled cooked beets
4 cups shredded raw green cabbage
1 cup grated fresh horseradish
1 cup sugar
1 teaspoon each of red pepper, white pepper, and salt
1 tablespoon powdered mustard
2 cups cider vinegar

Combine all ingredients and mix well. Cook for 20 minutes, stirring occasionally. Spoon mixture into hot sterilized jars, seal, and cool. Makes about 2 quarts.

### CORN AND PEPPER RELISH
7 cups corn cut from cobs
2 cups chopped cabbage
2 green peppers, chopped
2 sweet red peppers, chopped
1 cup each of sugar and water
4 cups cider vinegar
1 tablespoon each of celery seed and whole pickling spice
2 tablespoons salt

Mix all ingredients and cook for 30 minutes, stirring frequently to prevent sticking. Pack into hot sterilized jars; partially seal; process in hot-water bath for 20 minutes; complete seals. If closures are self-sealing type, do not tighten after processing. Makes about 6 pints.

### QUICK CORN RELISH
1⅓ cups cooked whole-kernel corn
½ cup finely diced celery
1 tablespoon chopped green pepper
3 tablespoons wine vinegar
2 tablespoons brown sugar
½ teaspoon salt
⅛ teaspoon each of pepper and ground turmeric
1 tablespoon chopped canned pimiento

Combine all ingredients except pimiento in saucepan and mix well. Heat thoroughly. Add pimiento. Cool, and refrigerate. Makes 2 cups.

### CRANBERRY-FILBERT RELISH

2½ cups (one 1-pound, 4-ounce can) crushed pineapple
2 cups sugar
1 pound (4 cups) cranberries
2 oranges
½ cup seedless raisins
½ cup chopped candied gingerroot
½ cup chopped toasted filberts

Drain pineapple. Measure juice and add enough water to make 2 cups. Add sugar to liquid and bring to boil, stirring until sugar is dissolved. Add cranberries and cook for 5 minutes. Grate rind of 1 orange. Remove segments of both oranges. Add grated rind, segments, raisins, and gingerroot to cranberry mixture. Simmer, stirring frequently, for 25 minutes, or until thick. Add nuts and pour into hot sterilized ½-pint jars; seal immediately. Makes about 6 jars.

### CRANBERRY PEAR RELISH

1 pound cranberries
4 hard pears
1 lemon
¼ cup honey
1 cup sugar
Dash of salt

Wash cranberries; peel and core pears. Force with lemon and rind through food chopper, using medium blade. Stir in honey, sugar, and salt. Cover and chill. Keeps for 1 to 2 weeks in refrigerator. Makes 1 quart.

### SWEET CUCUMBER RELISH

8 large ripe cucumbers
¼ cup salt
4 sweet red peppers, seeded and cored
4 large onions, quartered
1½ tablespoons each of celery seeds and mustard seeds
2½ cups sugar
1½ cups white vinegar

Peel cucumbers and slice into crock or glass bowl. Add salt and mix well. Let stand overnight in refrigerator. Drain and force through coarse blade of food chopper with peppers and onions. Put in kettle; add remaining ingredients. Bring to boil and cook, uncovered, stirring occasionally, for about 30 minutes. Pack into hot sterilized jars and seal. Makes 3 pints.

### CUCUMBER PICKLE RELISH

12 large cucumbers, unpeeled and sliced
Salt
6 onions, sliced
2 cups cider vinegar
1 cup sugar
1 teaspoon each of ground cinnamon, ginger, and mace
½ teaspoon each of white pepper and ground turmeric
1 teaspoon celery seeds

Cover cucumbers with salt. Let stand for 1½ hours. Drain, and add remaining ingredients. Cook for 10 to 15 minutes, or until onions are tender. Spoon mixture into hot sterilized jars. Makes 8 pints.

### LIME RELISH

12 limes
1½ cups sugar
1 cup vinegar
½ cup water

Wash limes and soak them in water to cover for 24 hours. Drain, cover with fresh water, and cook for 15 to 20 minutes, or until limes are just easily pierced. Drain. Cool; cut limes into eighths. Remove seeds. Cook remaining ingredients for about 15 minutes, or until syrupy. Spoon limes into hot sterilized jars and cover with syrup. Seal and cool. Makes 2 pints.

### PEACH RELISH

16 medium peaches
1 cup raisins
1½ cups firmly packed light brown sugar
¾ cup cider vinegar
1 teaspoon ground cinnamon
½ teaspoon ground cloves
2 teaspoons mustard seeds
½ cup coarsely chopped nuts

Peel, pit, and slice peaches. There should be 8 cups. Combine in kettle with remaining ingredients except nuts. Bring to boil and cook, uncovered, for 45 minutes, or until thick, stirring frequently. Add nuts and cook for 2 minutes. Fill hot sterilized jars and seal. Makes 3 pints.

### PEACH-TOMATO RELISH

6 large peaches
6 ripe tomatoes
1 cup ground onions
1 cup diced green peppers
1 small hot red pepper
2 cups firmly packed light brown sugar
1 cup cider vinegar
¾ teaspoon salt
2 tablespoons mixed pickling spices, tied in cheesecloth bag

Peel and pit peaches and cut into small pieces. Peel tomatoes and cut into ½-inch pieces. There should be 4 cups of each. Combine with other ingredients in kettle. Bring to boil and cook, uncovered, for 1 to 1½ hours, or until thick, stirring frequently. Fill hot sterilized jars and seal. Makes 3 pints.

### PEAR RELISH

16 pounds (about 8 quarts) pears, peeled, cored, and quartered
2 dried hot peppers or ½ teaspoon cayenne
8 sweet green peppers
1 quart dill pickles
2 quarts chopped onions
2 cups salt
4 cups sugar
3 tablespoons all-purpose flour
2 teaspoons ground turmeric
¼ cup powdered mustard
2 quarts cider vinegar

Grind pears, peppers, pickles, and onions in food grinder, using medium blade. Mix with salt and let stand overnight. In the morning drain off liquid; cover pulp with cold water and drain again. Combine remaining ingredients, stir until smooth, and boil for 5 minutes. Add pear mix-

ture; boil for 5 minutes, stirring constantly. Pour into hot sterilized jars and seal. Makes about 8 quarts.

### RHUBARB-ONION RELISH

2 pounds rhubarb
2 pounds small white onions
4 cups firmly packed brown sugar
1 cup cider vinegar
2 teaspoons salt
1 tablespoon each of ground cinnamon and ginger
1 garlic clove
1 tablespoon mixed pickling spice

Cut rhubarb into ½-inch pieces, using all of stalks up to 2 inches below the leaves. Do not peel. There should be 2 quarts rhubarb. Peel and slice onions. There should be 1 quart. Put rhubarb, onions, sugar, vinegar, salt, cinnamon, and ginger in kettle. Tie garlic and pickling spice in a small cheesecloth bag. Add to mixture. Bring to boil and simmer, uncovered, for 20 minutes, or until rhubarb is tender, but not mushy. Remove cheesecloth bag. Pack into hot sterilized jars and seal. Makes about 3 pints.

### GREEN-TOMATO RELISH

2 quarts chopped green tomatoes (4 to 5 pounds)
2 medium onions, chopped
2 quarts cold water
½ cup salt
1½ cups white vinegar
½ cup boiling water
1½ cups sugar
1½ teaspoons celery seeds
1 tablespoon mustard seeds
½ teaspoon each of ground turmeric and cinnamon
¼ teaspoon powdered mustard

Combine tomatoes and onions with water and salt in crock or bowl; soak for 3 hours. Drain and rinse thoroughly with cold water. Combine remaining ingredients and boil for 3 minutes. Add tomatoes and onions, bring to boil, and simmer, uncovered, for 10 minutes. Pack into hot sterilized jars and seal. Makes 2 or 2½ pints.

**Note:** For a colorful addition, tuck in red-pepper strips among the green tomatoes and white onions.

### SPICY APPLE AND TOMATO RELISH

6 medium onions
2 sweet red peppers, seeded
6 medium apples (about 2 pounds), peeled and chopped
8 large ripe tomatoes (about 3 pounds), peeled and chopped
1 celery stalk, minced
1½ cups raisins
4 cups white vinegar
2 tablespoons ground ginger
5 tablespoons mustard seeds
3 pounds (6¾ cups) brown sugar
2 tablespoons salt

Force onions and peppers through fine blade of food chopper. Put in large kettle with remaining ingredients; bring to boil and cook, stirring frequently, for 2 hours, or until mixture thickens. Pack into hot sterilized jars and seal. Makes 4 pints.

### CHUCK'S BARBECUE SAUCE RELISH
- 3 garlic cloves, minced
- 1 cup malt vinegar
- 2 teaspoons each of pepper and chili seasoning
- 2 tablespoons powdered mustard
- 2 cups ground onions
- 2 quarts ground tomatoes
- ¼ cup each of Worcestershire and sugar
- 1 tablespoon salt

Mix all ingredients; cook until thick, stirring frequently. Pour into hot sterilized jars and seal. Makes 3 pints.

### FRUIT-TOMATO RELISH
- 12 pounds large ripe tomatoes
- 6 medium peaches
- 6 medium pears
- 2 large onions
- 3 cups sugar
- 3 tablespoons salt
- 1½ cups finely diced celery
- 4 cups white vinegar
- 2 tablespoons mixed pickling spices

Peel tomatoes, peaches, pears, and onions; chop fine. Add sugar, salt, celery, and vinegar. Tie spices in a piece of cheesecloth; add. Bring to boil and simmer, uncovered, for 1 to 1½ hours. Remove spice bag. Pack into hot sterilized jars and seal. Makes 5 pints.

### HARVEST RELISH
- 3 cups shredded cabbage
- 1 tablespoon minced onion
- ¼ cup vinegar
- ½ teaspoon salt
- 1 cup chopped raw cranberries
- ½ cup diced celery
- ½ cup orange marmalade
- ¼ cup salted peanuts, coarsely chopped

Mix all ingredients except nuts. Chill for several hours. Add nuts. Makes 6 servings.

### HOT DOG AND HAMBURGER RELISH
- 3 pounds (about 10) medium green tomatoes
- 4 medium red apples
- 3 sweet red peppers
- 4 onions, peeled
- 1½ tablespoons salt
- 1½ teaspoons each of pepper and ground cinnamon
- ¾ teaspoon ground cloves
- 2½ cups sugar
- 2 cups white vinegar

Wash tomatoes and remove stem ends. Core apples; do not peel. Remove cores and seeds from peppers. Force apples and all vegetables through coarse blade of food chopper. Combine remaining ingredients and bring to boil in kettle. Add vegetables and simmer, uncovered, for 30 minutes, or until thick, stirring occasionally. Pack into hot sterilized jars and seal. Makes 4 or 5 pints.

### MINT RELISH
- ½ cup fresh mint leaves
- 3 large apples, cored
- 1½ cups raisins
- 12 ripe tomatoes
- 2 red peppers, seeded
- 4 large onions, peeled
- 2 tablespoons white mustard seeds
- ½ cup salt
- 2 cups sugar
- 6 cups cider vinegar

Put mint, apples, raisins, tomatoes, peppers, and onions through coarse blade of food chopper. Add remaining ingredients. Mix well and store the mixture in a crock for 10 days, stirring occasionally. Pour into sterilized jars, seal, and store. Makes about 3 quarts.

### RED-HOT SAUCE RELISH
- 10 pounds (about 30) ripe tomatoes
- 8 medium onions
- 2 hot red peppers
- 1 cup cider vinegar
- 1 cup sugar
- 1 teaspoon ground cinnamon
- 1½ tablespoons salt

Wash and quarter tomatoes; peel and quarter onions; seed peppers and cut into pieces. Cook together until soft; rub through sieve. Add remaining ingredients and boil until mixture begins to thicken. Reduce heat and simmer, stirring frequently, until quite thick. Pour into hot sterilized jars and seal. Makes about 5 pints.

### SPICED TOMATO RELISH
- 1 quart peeled and chopped ripe tomatoes, drained
- 1½ cups finely chopped celery
- 1 cup finely chopped onion
- 1 apple, chopped
- 2 tablespoons prepared horseradish
- 2 tablespoons salt
- 2 tablespoons mustard seeds
- ⅓ cup firmly packed brown sugar
- ¼ teaspoon each of ground cloves and powdered mace
- ½ teaspoon ground cinnamon
  Dash of cayenne
- 1½ cups vinegar

Mix all ingredients thoroughly. Cover and refrigerate. If too juicy, drain off some liquid. Makes about 1½ quarts.

**RÉMOULADE, RÉMOLADE**—A highly seasoned classic French sauce based on a blend of mustard, flour, water, oil, and vinegar with other seasonings. It is served cold with fish and seafood, cold meats, poultry, and vegetable salads. For a recipe see page 1622.

**RENDER, TO**—To melt down or try out meat fat, especially pork, in order to separate the portions of lean or connective tissues from the clear fat. Rendering is done in a heavy pan over low heat. If the rendered fat is to be stored for later use it should be strained and refrigerated. The crisp bits of connective tissue left after the fat has been rendered are known as cracklings. Cracklings from rendering chicken or goose fat are sometimes called greben or grebenes. They are

excellent when added to mashed potatoes or to chopped liver dishes. Diced salt pork is often rendered for making chowders. The fat is used for browning the onion and the crisp cracklings added to the chowder just before serving.

Bacon cracklings are available canned as a cocktail snack.

**RENNET**—A combination of two inorganic enzymes or ferments, rennin and pepsin, obtained from the membranes of the stomachs of young mammals. The best quality is that from an animal so young that it has received no other food than milk, the most desirable coming from a calf's stomach. Rennet's chief importance from a food standpoint is its property of coagulating milk and its widest food use is in the manufacture of cheese. Available commercially are packaged rennet-custard desserts in powder form in vanilla, chocolate, maple, lemon, orange, and raspberry flavors. Tablets in vanilla flavor are also available. These desserts are easily digested and are used for children and invalids as well as a basis for other desserts.

**RHUBARB**—A hardy perennial plant of the genus *Rheum* native to northern Asia and now grown chiefly for its thick succulent leaf stalks. The plant has large clumps of broad green leaves, up to two feet across, growing on thick fleshy red and green leaf stalks which average twelve to eighteen inches in length, but can be much longer.

There are many varieties of rhubarb, but the only important distinction in the edible types is between forced or hothouse rhubarb and field rhubarb. The first usually has slender pink to light red stalks with yellow-green leaves and the second deep red stalks and green leaves.

Only the leaf stalks of the rhubarb are edible. Leaves and root contain a substance that can sometimes be poisonous. But the stalks are so delicious in pies that rhubarb has also been known as pie plant. Stewed rhubarb and desserts of many kinds, as well as jam and wine, are equally delicious.

Rhubarb is extremely popular in northern Europe and in the Scandinavian countries. Apart from the fact that it is easily grown, it is also the first fresh fruit of the year and the harbinger of summer's bounty.

Like so many other plants, rhubarb crossed the Atlantic Ocean with the colonists, but it wasn't until the late 18th century that it was used much. The early Indians cooked the stalks like asparagus, and the new Americans learned from them to prepare the plant for eating.

*Availability*—Fresh rhubarb is available from February to August with the peak season in May and June.

Rhubarb is also available canned and frozen.

*Purchasing Guide*—Rhubarb is sold by the bunch, or by weight. Select fresh, firm, large, crisp, straight stalks with bright dark-red or cherry color. Rhubarb may be field grown or forced. The forced variety is lighter in color and has yellowish-green leaves. Avoid wilted, oversized, or very thin stalks.

□ 1 pound = 2 cups cooked

*Storage*—Fresh rhubarb is perishable. Refrigerate and use as soon as possible.

□ Fresh, refrigerator shelf, uncooked: 1 to 3 days
□ Fresh, cooked; or canned, opened, refrigerator shelf: 4 to 5 days
□ Fresh, prepared for freezing; or frozen, refrigerator frozen-food compartment: 2 to 3 months
□ Fresh, prepared for freezing; or frozen, freezer: 1 year
□ Canned, kitchen shelf: 1 year

*Nutritive Food Values*—Fair source of vitamin A.

□ Fresh, 3½ ounces, cooked, with added sugar = 141 calories

*Basic Preparation*—Wash; remove leaves and stem ends. If tender, do not peel. Cut stalks into inch-long pieces. Add only enough water to cover and cook until just tender. Stir in sugar to taste. Cool, and serve warm or chilled.

□ **To Freeze**—Use tender red crisp stalks. Trim stems and cut into 1-inch lengths. Wash and pack into freezer containers.

Cover with cold syrup made by cooking 3½ cups sugar with 4 cups water. Allow ½-inch headspace. Seal.

Rhubarb can also be packed into containers without syrup, or can be mixed with sugar, 1 cup to 4 cups rhubarb, and spooned into freezer containers, allowing ½-inch headspace.

### BAKED ROSY RHUBARB

Cut 1 pound unpeeled rhubarb into 1-inch lengths. Mix in shallow baking dish with 1 cup sugar and ¼ cup water. Bake in preheated moderate oven (350°F.) for 35 minutes, or until rhubarb is just tender. Chill; serve. Makes 4 servings.

### RHUBARB TANGY FRESH APPLESAUCE

Diced fresh rhubarb added to the apples when making fresh applesauce gives it a rosy red color and a tangy flavor.

### FRESH RHUBARB BETTY

    6 cups diced fresh rhubarb
1¼ cups sugar
2½ tablespoons quick-cooking tapioca
    1 teaspoon grated lemon rind
    1 tablespoon grated orange rind
    ¼ teaspoon salt
2⅔ cups soft bread crumbs
    ⅓ cup melted butter or margarine
    1 teaspoon vanilla extract

Combine first 6 ingredients and set aside. Mix bread crumbs with melted butter and vanilla. Fill 1½-quart casserole with alternate layers of rhubarb and bread crumbs, having rhubarb as the bottom layer and bread crumbs as the top layer. Cover and bake in preheated hot oven (400°F.) for 25 minutes. Remove cover and bake until crumbs are brown, about 10 minutes. Serve warm. Makes 6 to 8 servings.

### RHUBARB FLUMMERY

1½ pounds rhubarb
1½ cups water
    ½ cup sugar
    ¼ teaspoon vanilla extract
    3 tablespoons cornstarch
       Heavy cream

Cut rhubarb into ½-inch slices. Add water and sugar and simmer until mushy. Add vanilla. Mix cornstarch with a little cold water; stir into rhubarb. Cook, stirring constantly, for 5 minutes, or until thickened. Serve warm or chilled with cream, a little extra sugar if desired, and butter cookies. Makes 4 servings.

### JELLIED RHUBARB

Drain 1 cup sweetened cooked rhubarb and add water to the liquid to make 1 cup; heat to boiling and pour over ½ box (3-ounce size) lemon-flavored gelatin; stir until dissolved. Cool; then chill until syrupy. Stir in rhubarb. Chill until firm. Makes 2 servings.

### TANGY RHUBARB ICE

    2 cups cooked rhubarb

1¼ cups water
    ½ cup sugar
    ⅛ teaspoon salt
    1 envelope unflavored gelatin
       Juice of 1 lemon
       Few drops of red food coloring

Crush and strain rhubarb. Add 1 cup water, the sugar, and salt; heat. Soften gelatin in ¼ cup water. Add lemon juice, rhubarb mixture, and red coloring. Freeze until firm in crank-type freezer, or in refrigerator until firm 1 inch from edge of tray. Put into a cold bowl and beat with rotary beater until fluffy. Return to tray and freeze until firm. Makes 4 servings.

### RHUBARB AND STRAWBERRY PIE

       Standard pastry for 2-crust 9-inch pie, unbaked
    1 cup sugar
    ¼ cup all-purpose flour
    ¼ teaspoon salt
    2 cups diced rhubarb
    1 pint strawberries, hulled
    2 tablespoons butter

Roll a little more than half of pastry ⅛ inch thick and line 9-inch pie pan. Mix sugar, flour, and salt and sprinkle a small amount in pastry-lined pan. Combine remaining sugar mixture with rhubarb and berries. Put in pie pan and dot with butter. Roll remaining pastry ⅛ inch thick. Put on pie, trim edges and flute. Cut a few slits for steam to escape. Bake in preheated hot oven (425°F.) for 40 to 50 minutes.

### RHUBARB-APPLE PIE

Add ¼ cup sugar and 2 cups diced fresh rhubarb to the apples of a deep-dish apple pie for an extra flavor boost to this old-time favorite.

### BAKED RHUBARB MERINGUE

    2 pounds fresh rhubarb
1½ cups sugar
    5 tablespoons quick-cooking tapioca
    ¼ teaspoon salt
    ½ teaspoon grated lemon rind
    ¼ cup butter or margarine
       Meringue

Wash rhubarb and cut into 2-inch lengths. Combine sugar, tapioca, salt, and lemon rind. Add to rhubarb. Toss and place in a 6-cup casserole. Dot with butter. Cover and bake in preheated moderate oven (350°F.) for 25 minutes. Remove cover, stir mixture to blend in melted butter, and bake for 25 minutes longer, or until rhubarb is tender. Cover with Meringue and bake in slow oven (325°F.) for 20 minutes, or until brown. Makes 6 to 8 servings.

#### Meringue

    2 egg whites
       Dash of salt
    3 tablespoons sugar

Combine egg whites and salt and beat until soft peaks are formed. Gradually add sugar and continue beating until stiff.

Spread over rhubarb and bake according to directions given above.

### FRESH RHUBARB FRUIT PUNCH

To give fruit punch extra flavor and color, too, add rhubarb to the fruit juices. Cook diced fresh rosy rhubarb in enough water to cover until soft. Strain, and cool.

### RHUBARB AND STRAWBERRY JAM

1 quart rhubarb, cut into ½-inch pieces
1 quart strawberries, cut into pieces
4 cups sugar

Mix fruit and sugar and let stand for 1 hour. Bring to boiling point and cook rapidly for about 30 minutes, or until thick. Stir frequently to prevent burning. Turn into hot fruit jars and seal, or put in jelly glasses and seal with paraffin. Makes about four 8-ounce glasses.

### RHUBARB AND STRAWBERRY JELLY

2 pounds fresh rhubarb
1 cup water
1 quart fresh strawberries
1 package (2½ ounces) powdered pectin
5 cups sugar

Wash rhubarb and cut into 1-inch pieces. Place in a saucepan with water. Cover and bring to boiling point. Simmer until rhubarb is tender, 5 to 8 minutes. In the meantime, wash and cap strawberries. Mash and place in a jelly bag along with cooked rhubarb. Let juice drip into a bowl. Measure 4 cups juice. Mix juice and pectin together in a saucepan. Place over high heat and stir until mixture comes to a hard boil. Stir in sugar and bring to a full rolling boil. Boil hard for 1 minute, stirring constantly. Remove from heat and skim off foam with a metal spoon. Pour into sterilized jars, leaving ½ inch of space at top of each jar. Seal at once with paraffin. Cool, and cover jars with lids. Makes about 4 pints.

**RICE**—An annual cereal grass the seed of which provides the chief source of food for half the world's population.

Although wheat, barley, and millet were domesticated before it, rice is an ancient grain. Its wild ancestor has been identified as *Oryza sativa,* a semiaquatic marsh grass native to India and southeast Asia. Most cultivated rice, known as aquatic rice, is grown in marshy or flooded lands, the sort of terrain found throughout much of the southern Orient and southeastern United States. It can also be grown, but with a lesser yield of lower quality, in areas with a long growing season and a great deal of steady rainfall. This type is called hill rice. (American wild, or Indian, rice is not a member of the true rice family at all, but is an aquatic perennial grass, *Zizania aquatica.* It has never been successfully domesticated for large-scale cultivation, although it has a long history of use by the Indians, and is considered a culinary delicacy today.)

Rice is a giving food. It will grow where wheat hesitates to grow. It yields much more per acre than wheat or corn. Where wheat or barley must be ground first, rice can be eaten as a grain, eliminating the need for elaborate tools, mills, yeasts, and baking ovens. Rice is a highly nutritious and easily digested food, too. Almost all of it is completely assimilated. When milled so that only the husks are removed, producing "whole" or "brown" rice, eighty-eight per cent of it is nutrients: about eight per cent protein and seventy-nine per cent carbohydrates (chiefly starch) with very small amounts of fat. The peoples who rely on rice as a mainstay of their diet always eat it in this state since further milling reduces its food value.

The grain seems to invite controversy. The fight over the proper way to cook it—covered or uncovered, in lots of water or a little, stirred or unstirred—is still being fought. The didactic tone of those instructing others on how to cook rice is evident in the voice of Charles Gayarré, a gourmet writing in the 1880's about an old southern cook: "Who but Valentin knew how to bake rice in an iron pot? I say *iron,* because it must be nothing else, and that rice must come out solid, retaining the exact shape of the pot, with a golden crust about its top and sides."

In modern processing, rice when harvested goes to a drying plant where hot air is blown through it to "cure" it and reduce its moisture content, assuring good keeping quality. The first step in the milling process is the removal of the husk, leaving what is known as "natural brown rice." If the milling is carried further the next step involves the grinding away of several outer layers of the grain. This results in white rice. It also produces such by-products as rice bran and rice polishings, used mainly as stock feeds. In the next step all broken particles and any foreign seeds or defective grains are screened out, leaving clean white rice. Finer particles of broken rice are used in making beer. Larger broken particles are sometimes mixed with whole grains for extremely low-cost table rice, where economy is the main factor. Years ago rice was given a coating of talc or glucose, which is why old recipes say "wash rice until the water runs clear." Nowadays this is not necessary. Rice no longer requires washing when it comes from a package.

Brown rice is rich in the vitamins of the B complex, thiamine, niacin, and riboflavin, and in iron and calcium. It is higher in many of these vitamins and minerals than enriched, parboiled, or other processed rice.

*Availability and Purchasing Guide*—Packaged rice is available year round. The varieties include *brown rice,* which has a nutlike flavor and requires a comparatively long cooking time; and *short-* and *long-grain* white rice. Most rice is short grain unless the package specifically states otherwise. When cooked, short-grain rice is moister and more tender than long-grain rice, which cooks more quickly and is drier and fluffier. Carolina and Honduras types are long-grain rices.

*Parboiled white rice* is a long-grain rice parboiled, steamed, and dried, a process designed to retain many of the nutrients otherwise lost in milling. It takes longer to cook than regular rice. *Precooked rice* is long-grain rice that has been cooked, rinsed, and dried, and requires only a short heating period before serving. *Enriched rice* has had iron and B vitamins added to it.

Other rice products are available. Spanish rice, chicken and rice dinners, soup, and pudding are available in cans. Fried rice is included in frozen Chinese dinners. Mixes are available for rice pudding and for a rice and vermicelli product with meat, cheese, or vegetable flavoring. Regular, quick-cooking, and ready-to-eat rice cereals are also available. There is a waxy rice flour which is used by persons allergic to wheat flours. It has also found use as a stabilizer in frozen sauces and gravies.

☐ 1 cup regular rice = 3 cups cooked
☐ 1 cup parboiled rice = 4 cups cooked
☐ 1 cup brown rice = 4 cups cooked
☐ 1 cup precooked rice = 2 cups cooked

*Storage*—Store in covered container in a cool dry place. Rice will keep almost indefinitely.

*Nutritive Food Values*—Rice contains some calcium and iron, and the B-complex vitamins thiamine, riboflavin, and niacin. Brown rice is richer in these minerals and vitamins than the other types of rice.

☐ Brown rice, 3½ ounces, cooked = 119 calories
☐ White rice, all types, 3½ ounces, cooked = 109 calories
☐ Parboiled white rice, 3½ ounces, cooked = 106 calories
☐ Rice, granulated, breakfast cereal, 3½ ounces, cooked = 50 calories
☐ Rice flakes, 3½ ounces = 390 calories
☐ Rice, puffed, 3½ ounces = 399 calories

# How to Cook Superbly: Rice
### by Helen Evans Brown

**Rich Rice Pudding**

**Mexican Rice**

**Purée of Rice with Rice Balls**

**Rice Pudding**

The Indians and Chinese are probably born knowing how to cook rice perfectly, but it's an art that doesn't come as easily to many of us. However, we can learn to cook it so that each grain is separate and dry, yet tender, not gummy or sticky. There are several ways to accomplish this and good cooks have been known to come to blows over which is the right one. I think perhaps you should decide for yourself, so I'll give you several recipes for cooking plain rice. But before we begin I should warn you that there are even more kinds of rice than there are ways of cooking it. In this country, long-grain rice from Louisiana and Texas is usually the most satisfactory, as it cooks into fluffy white grains, but short-grain rice from California is fine for puddings and soups. Then there is Spanish-

type rice, which has a short plump grain, Patna rice from India, with a long narrow grain, Japanese rice, Chinese rice, Italian rice, hundreds of rices; not counting wild rice, which isn't a rice at all, but a grass. There's also parboiled rice, which is uncooked but is treated to preserve the food values lost in polishing, and precooked rice, which is quick to prepare. Most white rice today is lightly milled so that it retains its natural qualities. Brown rice has only the husks removed. Most rices may be cooked the same way, but some require a longer cooking time than others. Long-grain Louisiana rice was used in these recipes, so if you are using other varieties, start testing for tenderness sooner, and if necessary, cook longer. In these recipes the rice was not washed first, but if you

prefer to do it that way, go ahead.

### TO TEST FOR TENDERNESS
The easiest way is to taste. Scoop out a few grains and bite into them. The grains should have no hardness in the center. As soon as the grains are tender all through but still firm, the rice is done.

### RICE MEASUREMENTS
A pound of rice measures 2¼ cups; 1 cup rice weighs about 6¾ ounces; ¼ pound rice is a heaping ½ cup. Rice increases in bulk a little over three times when cooked. Allow 1 cup rice for each 3 to 6 servings, depending upon whether it is an accompaniment to meats and vegetables or the basis of a one-dish meal.

**Poires à l'Imperatrice**

**Italian Rice and Peas**

### EQUIPMENT

You won't need any special equipment when cooking rice recipes. The usual casseroles, skillets, saucepans, molds, measures, spoons, double boiler, rotary beater, and strainer are all that will be necessary.

### BASIC PREPARATION

☐ **To Boil**—Add 1 teaspoon salt to 8 cups rapidly boiling water in a large pot, then slowly dribble in 1 cup rice. Do not cover and do not stir. Start testing at about 15 minutes (18 minutes is usually right for long-grain; 15 minutes for short-grain). Drain rice and then rinse in hot water and put in a warm oven to dry out more, or serve as is. I find that rice cooked this way, then rinsed in cold water and put overnight in the refrigera-

tor in an uncovered dish, becomes marvelously dry. It reheats easily in double boiler or in a lightly buttered casserole in a preheated moderate oven.

☐ **To Cook Oriental Style**—Add ½ teaspoon salt to 2 cups rapidly boiling water, then slowly add 1 cup rice. Shake pot to level rice, cover, and reduce heat as low as possible. Cook for 18 to 25 minutes. Don't remove cover until first testing.

☐ **To Bake**—Set oven at slow (300°F.). Put ½ teaspoon salt, 1 cup rice, and 1 tablespoon butter in a 1½- or 2-quart casserole. Pour on 2 cups rapidly boiling water, cover, and put in the oven for 30 minutes. Turn off oven, remove cover, put a folded paper towel over the top of the casserole, and leave the oven door open to dry out rice. Bouillon may be

used in place of water, in which case butter and salt could be eliminated.

☐ **To Toast**—Distribute 1 cup uncooked rice as evenly as possible on a cookie sheet and put in preheated hot oven (400°F.) for 6 to 10 minutes, or until golden-brown, stirring occasionally so that it will color evenly. Proceed exactly as for Baked Rice, above. Rice may also be toasted before boiling or steaming.

■ **Variations for Plain Rice**—Either of the following, added to cooked rice, gives it added interest. To each 3 cups cooked rice (1 cup uncooked), add:

*1 cup mushrooms* which have been sliced and sautéed in 3 tablespoons butter for 6 minutes.

*½ cup slivered almonds* which have been stirred over heat with 3 tablespoons butter until golden.

# Rice Cook Book

*Rice, economical and versatile,
is delicious in savory casseroles, tasty side dishes,
salads, and piping hot puddings.*

## SOUPS

### PURÉE OF RICE

½ cup chopped onion
2 tablespoons butter or margarine
½ cup chopped carrot
2 tablespoons uncooked rice
3 cups bouillon, preferably chicken
1 cup cream, light or heavy
  Salt and pepper
  Rice Balls

Cook onion in butter until golden. Add carrot, rice, and bouillon and bring to a boil. Turn heat low and simmer for 30 to 40 minutes, or until rice is very soft. Strain, pressing rice and vegetables through a strainer, or whirl smooth in a blender (you'll have to do this in two batches). Return to pot, add cream, and season to taste. Serve with Rice Balls or croutons. Makes 4 servings.

■ Variations—This may be seasoned with 1 to 3 teaspoons curry powder, or with 2 tablespoons minced chives, or ½ cup cooked sorrel, chopped fine, or with anything else that appeals to you. Make up your own version, and serve it hot or cold.

### Rice Balls

Mix ¾ cup cooked rice with 2 tablespoons butter, 1 egg yolk, 2 tablespoons grated Parmesan cheese, ¼ teaspoon salt, and a dash of cayenne. Cook, stirring, over low heat for 4 minutes, then cool. Form into tiny balls, roll them in 2 tablespoons all-purpose flour, then dip into slightly beaten egg. Fry in deep hot fat (370°F. on a frying thermometer) until golden-brown and crispy. Drain on paper towels.

### GREEK RICE SOUP

6 cups seasoned chicken broth*
⅓ cup uncooked rice
2 eggs
3 tablespoons fresh lemon juice
  Salt and pepper

Heat broth, add rice, and cook for 20 minutes. Beat eggs well, then beat in about ½ cup of the hot liquid. Add lemon juice and pour into the remaining liquid and rice. Mix well, correct seasoning, and serve hot. Makes 6 servings.

*If you don't have chicken broth, make some by covering 3 pounds of chicken backs, wing tips, and necks with 2 quarts boiling water; add 2 teaspoons salt and an herb bouquet, and simmer for 1½ hours, or until reduced to 6 cups. Strain, and discard bones. Chill, and remove hardened fat on top.

## MAIN DISHES

### SHRIMP AND RICE JAMBALAYA

4 slices of bacon, diced
1 medium onion, minced
½ medium green pepper, diced
2 cups chicken bouillon
½ cup ketchup
2 tablespoons brown sugar
1 package (10 ounces) frozen shelled shrimps, cooked
1 cup finely diced cooked ham
2 tablespoons cornstarch
3 tablespoons cold water
  Salt and pepper to taste
  Hot cooked rice

Cook bacon until crisp. Remove bacon, and cook onion and pepper in the fat for 5 minutes. Add next 3 ingredients. Simmer, covered, for 15 minutes. Cut shrimps into pieces. Add with ham to first mixture. Heat well; thicken with blended cornstarch and water; season; serve on rice. Makes 4 servings.

### HAM- AND RICE-STUFFED PEPPERS

4 large green peppers
2¾ cups boiling water
1 cup uncooked rice
1 medium onion, minced
2 tablespoons butter or margarine
½ pound process American cheese, diced
1 cup diced cooked ham
2 tablespoons minced parsley
  Salt and pepper

Cut peppers into halves crosswise. Remove seeds. Cook peppers in 2 cups of the boiling water for 5 minutes. Drain, reserving liquid. Cook rice until tender; drain. Sauté onion in hot butter for 5 minutes. Add remaining water and diced cheese. Stir until blended. Add ham, rice, parsley, and salt and pepper to taste. Fill pepper halves. Put on rack in skillet with 1½ cups pepper liquid in bottom. Simmer, covered, for about 15 minutes. Makes 4 servings.

### HAM-CHEESE RICE BAKE

1 small onion, minced
6 tablespoons butter or margarine
3 tablespoons all-purpose flour
1 teaspoon salt
⅛ teaspoon pepper
½ teaspoon powdered mustard
1 teaspoon Worcestershire
2 cups milk
½ pound sharp Cheddar cheese
½ cup diced cooked ham
1 cup (one 8-ounce can) peas, drained
4 cups hot cooked rice
3 tablespoons fine dry bread crumbs

Cook onion in 4 tablespoons of the butter for 5 minutes. Blend in flour and seasonings. Add milk. Cook, stirring constantly, until thick and smooth. Dice half of cheese and add to mixture. Stir until blended. Add ham and peas. Slice remaining cheese. Put half of rice in shallow baking dish. Cover with layer of sliced cheese; pour half of hot mixture over top. Repeat. Sprinkle with crumbs; dot with remaining butter. Bake in preheated hot oven (400°F.) for 20 minutes, or until lightly browned and bubbly. Makes 4 to 6 servings.

### Tuna-Cheese Rice Bake

In Ham-Cheese Rice recipe, in place of ham, add 1 can (7 ounces) tuna, drained and flaked, to hot mixture with the peas. Pour over rice and proceed with rest of recipe as directed.

### RICE AND PORK CASSEROLE

4 pork chops
  Salt and pepper to taste
2 chicken bouillon cubes
2 cups hot water
1 cup uncooked rice
½ green pepper, chopped
2 green onions, sliced
1 tomato, peeled and diced
  Paprika

Brown chops and put in shallow baking dish. Season with salt and pepper. Dissolve bouillon cubes in water; pour over chops. Add next 4 ingredients. Sprinkle top with pepper and paprika. Cover tightly, with foil if cover is not available, and bake in preheated moderate oven (350°F.) for about 1 hour. Makes 4 servings.

### BAKED RICE, PORK, AND CABBAGE

¾ pound boneless lean pork
½ cup uncooked rice
1½ teaspoons salt
¼ teaspoon pepper
8 cabbage leaves
1 small onion, minced
1 tablespoon cooking oil
1 can (10½ ounces) tomato soup
¾ cup water

Cut pork into ½-inch cubes and mix with rice, salt, and pepper. Cook cabbage leaves in boiling salted water until limp. Fill each leaf with about ⅓ cup of the meat mixture and roll up loosely. Put seam side down in baking dish. Cook onion in oil for 5 minutes. Add soup and water; mix well, and pour over cabbage rolls. Bake, covered, in preheated moderate oven (375°F.) for about 1½ hours. Makes 4 servings.

### BAKED TURKEY AND RICE

1½ cups packaged precooked rice
1½ cups boiling water
¾ teaspoon salt
2 tablespoons instant minced onion
1 teaspoon curry powder
2 cups diced cooked turkey
6 olives, sliced
1 can (10½ ounces) cream-of-mushroom soup
½ cup milk
½ cup grated Cheddar cheese
¼ cup corn-flake crumbs

Prepare rice with water and salt as directed on the label. Add onion and curry powder; put in shallow baking dish. Cover with turkey and sprinkle with olives. Mix soup and milk; pour over top. Sprinkle with cheese and crumbs. Bake in preheated moderate oven (350°F.) for about 30 minutes. Makes 6 servings.

### BOK YOU GUY

1 frying chicken (about 2½ pounds),
　cut up
1½ cups water
3 tablespoons soy sauce
3 tablespoons cornstarch
1 cup rice, cooked
½ cup seedless raisins
½ cup peanuts
　Flaked coconut

Simmer chicken in water with soy sauce
for 45 minutes, or until tender. Thicken
liquid with cornstarch mixed with a little
cold water. Combine hot rice and raisins;
sprinkle with peanuts and coconut. Serve
with chicken and gravy. Makes 4 servings.

### SPANISH CHICKEN WITH RICE

1 frying chicken (about 2½ pounds),
　cut up
　Salt
3 tablespoons olive oil
1 large onion, chopped
1 garlic clove, minced
1 medium green pepper, chopped
2⅓ cups (1-pound, 3-ounce can) tomatoes
⅓ cup sherry
¼ teaspoon pepper
　Pinch of ground saffron
½ teaspoon paprika
2 whole cloves
1 crumbled bay leaf
1 cup water
1¼ cups uncooked long-grain rice
1 cup cooked peas
1 pimiento, cut up

Season chicken with salt. Brown in oil.
Add onion, garlic, and green pepper, and
brown for about 5 minutes longer. Add
remaining ingredients except rice, peas,
and pimiento; simmer, covered, for 15
minutes. Add rice, bring to boil, stirring
constantly. Cover, and simmer for about
30 minutes. Garnish with peas and pimiento. Makes 4 to 6 servings.

### BAKED RICE AND CHEESE

1 cup uncooked rice
1 small onion, minced
6 tablespoons butter or margarine
3 tablespoons flour
1 teaspoon salt
⅛ teaspoon pepper
½ teaspoon powdered mustard
1 teaspoon Worcestershire
2 cups milk
½ pound sharp Cheddar cheese
3 tablespoons fine dry bread crumbs

Cook and drain rice. Cook onion for 5
minutes in 4 tablespoons butter. Blend
in flour and seasonings. Gradually add
milk and cook, stirring constantly, until
thickened. Dice half of cheese and add
to mixture, stirring until blended. Slice
remaining cheese. Put half of rice in
shallow 1½-quart baking dish. Cover
with layer of sliced cheese; pour half of
hot mixture over top. Repeat. Sprinkle
crumbs on top and dot with remaining
butter. Bake in preheated hot oven (400°
F.) for 20 minutes. Makes 4 to 6 servings.

### Meat-Cheese Rice

Add ½ to ¾ cup slivered luncheon meat
or cooked ham or tongue to hot cheese
mixture before pouring over rice.

### Vegetable-Cheese Rice

Top first rice layer with 1 cup cooked cut
green beans, asparagus, or cooked peas;
add remaining ingredients.

### Fish-Cheese Rice

Add 1 can salmon (7¾ ounces) or tuna
fish (7 ounces), drained and flaked, to
hot mixture before pouring over rice.

## SALADS

### RICE AND SEAFOOD SALAD

1 cup uncooked rice
¼ cup salad oil
1 tablespoon vinegar
1½ teaspoons salt
½ teaspoon pepper
1 cup cooked green peas
¼ cup each of chopped pimiento,
　chopped parsley, and minced onion
2 tablespoons chopped green pepper
1 cup cooked flaked crabmeat
1 cup shelled and deveined cooked
　shrimps
1 cup cooked flaked lobster
⅔ cup mayonnaise
1 tablespoon fresh lemon juice
　Salad greens
　Black olives

Cook rice until tender according to package directions. In the meantime combine
oil, vinegar, and salt and pepper to make
a French dressing. Drain rice and toss
immediately with French dressing; cool.
Gently mix in vegetables, crabmeat,
shrimps, and lobster; chill. Just before
serving time combine mayonnaise with
lemon juice. Fold into salad. Pile pyramid fashion on salad greens and decorate
with black olives. Makes 8 servings.

### CHEESE-AND-BACON RICE SALAD

1 cup uncooked rice
2 cups boiling water
1½ teaspoons salt
⅛ teaspoon pepper
6 bacon strips, cooked crisp
2 tablespoons bacon fat
¼ cup mayonnaise
½ cup chopped sweet pickles
¼ pound sharp Cheddar cheese,
　cut into ½-inch cubes
1 cup thinly sliced radishes
3 green onions, sliced
½ green pepper, chopped

Cook rice in the water with salt and
pepper until tender. Drain. Crumble
bacon; add with remaining ingredients to
warm rice. Serve at once, or chill and
serve on salad greens. Makes 4 to 6
servings.

### MAIN-DISH RICE SALAD

1½ cups packaged precooked rice
1½ cups boiling water
¾ teaspoon salt
2 tablespoons powdered mustard
2 tablespoons cold water

1½ teaspoons sugar
2 tablespoons wine vinegar
¼ cup cooking oil
½ green pepper, chopped
1 cup diced cooked ham
½ cup cooked peas
　Chopped parsley
　Salad greens

Prepare rice with boiling water and salt
as directed on the label. Mix next 4 ingredients and gradually beat in oil. Stir
lightly into warm rice. Cool; add next 3
ingredients. Add more salt if necessary.
Sprinkle with parsley and serve with
greens. Makes 4 servings.

### ITALIAN RICE SALAD WITH VEAL

3½ pounds veal cut from the leg
4 celery stalks
　Olive oil (about 1½ cups)
1 carrot
10 anchovy fillets
½ sour pickle
2 cans (7 ounces each) tuna fish
1 cup dry white wine
2 garlic cloves
　Salt, pepper, crumbled dried thyme
2 egg yolks
1½ cups uncooked rice
2 carrots, chopped
1 cup dried celery
6 green onions, sliced
1 red onion, chopped
½ green pepper, chopped
12 each of ripe and green olives,
　chopped
¼ cup minced parsley
　Tarragon vinegar

Simmer veal, celery stalks, ½ cup olive
oil, next 6 ingredients, and seasonings to
taste for about 3 hours. When tender,
cool in pot. Remove meat and purée
mixture in a blender, or force through
a food mill. Season to taste with salt, pepper, and thyme. Beat egg yolks. Stir in ½
cup oil, a few drops at a time. When
thickened, beat in puréed mixture. Cook
and cool rice. Add chopped carrots, diced
celery, green and red onion, green pepper, olives, and parsley. Dress to taste
with remaining oil, vinegar, and additional salt and pepper, if desired. Add a
little purée. Serve veal sliced very thin,
with the purée as a sauce, and with the
rice salad. Garnish with artichokes and
pimientos if desired. Makes 8 servings.

### FRENCH RICE SALAD

1 cup uncooked rice
　Oil and vinegar
　Salt and pepper
½ pound Bel Paese cheese, cubed
12 radishes, sliced
2 tablespoons chopped walnuts
　Handful of watercress, chopped

Cook rice; while still warm, dress to
taste with oil, vinegar, salt, and pepper.
Chill, add other ingredients, and serve.
Makes 4 servings.

## MEAT ACCOMPANIMENTS

### ITALIAN RICE AND PEAS

½ cup chopped onion
3 tablespoons butter or margarine
1½ cups shelled peas*
½ cup chopped cooked ham (optional)
1 cup uncooked rice
3 to 5 cups chicken or beef bouillon
2 tablespoons grated Parmesan cheese

Cook onion in 2 tablespoons butter until golden. Add peas, cook for 1 minute, then add ham (if used) and rice. Cook, stirring, over low heat until the rice becomes golden; then add 3 cups bouillon. Cover, turn heat low, or put in preheated moderate oven (350°F.), and cook until the rice is tender, adding more bouillon if necessary, and stirring lightly with a fork to prevent sticking. This will take from 18 to 30 minutes. The liquid should be absorbed, the rice tender but not mushy. Stir in 1 tablespoon butter and the cheese and serve at once, garnished with a little pimiento if desired. Makes 4 to 6 servings.

*Frozen peas may be used; add when rice is half cooked.

**Note:** This dish is excellent to take the place of a vegetable and farinaceous dish, as it is a combination of both. Add ham and it becomes a main dish.

### SURPRISE RICE CROQUETTES

2 cups cooked rice
½ cup grated cheese
1 egg, well beaten
2 teaspoons prepared mustard (optional)
1 teaspoon salt
⅛ teaspoon white pepper
1 tablespoon melted butter or margarine
½-inch cubes of your favorite cheese
Fine bread crumbs
Fat for frying

Mix rice and grated cheese. Add egg, seasonings, and melted butter. Blend well. Cover each cube of cheese with the rice mixture. Form into croquettes or balls. Roll in bread crumbs. Fry in deep fat or oil heated to 365°F. on frying thermometer for 5 minutes, or until light brown. Drain on absorbent paper. Serve with meats or as a main dish with tomato sauce. Makes 12 to 14 croquettes depending on size.

### SAUTÉED BROWN RICE AND MUSHROOMS

1 medium onion, minced
¼ green pepper, minced
¼ cup butter or margarine
1 can (3 ounces) mushroom stems and pieces, drained
3 cups cooked brown rice
¾ teaspoon salt
⅛ teaspoon pepper
½ teaspoon chili powder

Cook onion and green pepper in butter for 5 minutes. Add remaining ingredients. Cook until lightly browned, stirring gently. Makes 4 servings.

### CURRIED RICE

2½ cups boiling water
1 teaspoon salt
1¼ cups uncooked rice
¼ cup butter or margarine
1½ teaspoons curry powder
1 package (10 ounces) frozen peas
1 pimiento, cut into strips

Mix first 5 ingredients in Dutch oven or covered casserole. Bake, covered, in preheated hot oven (400°F.) for about 45 minutes. Cook and drain peas; mix lightly into rice with fork. Top with pimiento strips. Good with roast lamb, poultry, or pork. Makes 6 servings.

### VIENNESE RICE

1 small onion, minced
3 tablespoons butter or margarine
1 cup uncooked rice
Salt and pepper to taste
2 cups hot consommé
1 cup canned peas, heated
1 teaspoon paprika

Brown onion lightly in 1 tablespoon of the butter. Add rice and cook until glazed. Season with salt and pepper. Add consommé, bring to boil, and simmer, covered, until rice is done. Consommé should be entirely absorbed. With a fork, carefully stir in peas. Add remaining butter and sprinkle with paprika. Makes 4 or 5 servings.

### FRIED RICE

½ cup minced onion
3 tablespoons cooking oil
6 cups cooked rice
½ cup cooked ham, chicken, pork, or shellfish
¼ cup water chestnuts and/or bamboo shoots
Sliced or chopped mushrooms
1 tablespoon soy sauce
2 eggs, slightly beaten
Salt and pepper to taste

Cook minced onion in oil until it colors slightly. Add rice and cook, stirring, over low heat for 2 or 3 minutes; then add meat and water chestnuts slivered into matchlike pieces or chopped. Sliced or chopped mushrooms may be added with any of the above, or used alone. Mix well, then add soy sauce, eggs, and seasonings. Cook, stirring, over low heat until the egg is cooked. This will take only 2 or 3 minutes. Put into a bowl, pack down, then unmold on a hot dish. If you wish, sprinkle over the top some chopped green onions or some of the same meat, slivered, that is used in the rice. Makes 6 servings, or twice as many if used as one of the dishes in a Chinese meal.

**Note:** This versatile Chinese recipe is wonderful for using up bits of cooked ham, shrimps, pork, chicken, mushrooms, or such. It makes a good main dish for luncheon or supper. Without the additions, it is a good accompaniment for broiled chicken, pork chops, meat loaf, or seafood.

### INDIAN KITCHREE

1 onion, chopped
3 tablespoons butter or margarine
1 cup uncooked rice
1 cup dried lentils
5 to 7 cups water
Salt
1 teaspoon each of pepper and ground coriander
¼ teaspoon each of ground caraway, cloves, and cardamom
½ teaspoon ground cinnamon

Cook onion in butter until soft. Add rice and lentils and cook, stirring, for 2 minutes, then add 5 cups water. Bring to a boil, then turn heat low, and simmer for 10 minutes. Add salt to taste and the spices. Cover and continue to cook until rice and lentils are tender, adding liquid if necessary, and stirring occasionally. Makes 6 servings.

**Note:** 2½ teaspoons curry powder and ½ teaspoon ground pepper may be substituted for the pepper, coriander, caraway, cloves, cardamom, and cinnamon in this recipe.

### MEXICAN RICE

1 cup minced onions
⅓ cup oil, preferably olive
1 cup uncooked rice
1 teaspoon salt
1 tablespoon chili powder
3 to 4 cups tomato juice (part may be bouillon)
½ cup sliced chorizo (Spanish sausage)
½ cup sliced sautéed mushrooms (optional)

Cook onions in oil for 2 or 3 minutes. Add remaining ingredients. Bring to boil; cover and simmer for 18 to 25 minutes, or until rice is tender. Makes 4 to 6 servings.

### YELLOW RICE

1 cup uncooked rice
2 tablespoons butter or oil
1 teaspoon salt
Pinch of ground saffron, or 1 teaspoon ground turmeric, or 2 teaspoons ground curry powder
3 to 4 cups boiling water or bouillon

Cook rice in butter until opaque. Add salt and seasonings and 3 cups of the liquid. Cover and cook for 16 to 20 minutes, or until the rice is tender. After 18 minutes, stir lightly and add more liquid if necessary. Makes 3 or 4 servings.

**Note:** If whole saffron is used, pound fine in a mortar or steep in ¼ cup of the liquid for 10 minutes, then strain off liquid and use.

## BREADS

### RICE PANCAKES

Mix well 1 egg, 1 cup pancake mix, and 1½ cups milk. Stir in 1 cup cooked rice.

Fry on hot well-greased griddle until browned on both sides. Serve at once with butter and syrup. Makes about 3 dozen 3-inch pancakes.

### RICE WAFFLES

Beat until smooth 4 cups biscuit mix, 3⅓ cups milk, 2 eggs, and ¼ cup cooking oil. Add 2 cups cooked rice. Cook on hot waffle iron. Serve hot with butter and syrup. Makes 10 waffles, 11 x 6 inches.

### NEW ORLEANS RICE FRITTERS

½ package active dry yeast or ½ cake compressed yeast
½ cup water*
1½ cups very soft cooked rice
3 eggs, beaten
1¼ cups sifted all-purpose flour
¼ cup sugar
½ teaspoon salt
¼ teaspoon ground nutmeg
Fat for deep frying

Sprinkle or crumble yeast into water. *Use very warm water (105°F. to 115°F.) for dry yeast; use lukewarm (80°F. to 90°F.) for compressed. Let stand for a few minutes, then stir until dissolved. Mash rice grains and cool to lukewarm. Stir into yeast mixture and mix well. Cover and let rise overnight. Next morning, add eggs, flour, sugar, salt, and nutmeg and beat until smooth. Let stand in a warm place for 30 minutes. Drop by tablespoonfuls into deep hot fat (360° F. on a frying thermometer) and fry until golden-brown, about 3 minutes. Serve sprinkled with confectioners' sugar or sugar mixed with ground cinnamon. Makes 2 dozen.

## DESSERTS

### OLD-TIME RICE PUDDING

½ cup uncooked rice (not processed)
½ cup sugar
½ teaspoon salt
½ teaspoon ground nutmeg
2 quarts milk
¾ cup raisins

Mix rice, sugar, salt, and nutmeg in a shallow 2½-quart baking dish. Add 1 quart of the milk. Then, to prevent spilling, add second quart of milk after placing dish in the oven. Bake in preheated moderate oven (325°F.) for 2½ hours, stirring twice during first hour. Stir the brown crust into pudding several times during the remainder of baking. Add raisins 30 minutes before pudding is done. Then allow crust to form again. Serve with cream if desired. Makes 6 to 8 servings.
**Note:** Can be made with brown rice.

#### Butterscotch Rice Pudding

In Old-time Rice Pudding recipe, substitute 1 cup firmly packed brown sugar for the white. Omit raisins. Serve cold.

#### Date Rice Pudding

In Old-time Rice Pudding recipe, substitute ¾ cup chopped pitted dates for the raisins.

### CUSTARD RICE PUDDING

½ cup rice, cooked
3 eggs, beaten
½ cup sugar
¼ teaspoon salt
1 teaspoon vanilla extract
1½ teaspoons grated lemon rind
½ cup raisins
3½ cups milk
Ground nutmeg

Mix all ingredients except nutmeg. Pour into shallow baking dish and sprinkle with nutmeg. Set in pan of hot water and bake in preheated slow oven (300° F.) for about 1½ hours. Serve warm or cool. Makes 6 servings.

### WALNUT-RICE FRITTERS

1 cup sifted all-purpose flour
1 teaspoon baking powder
1 teaspoon salt
3 eggs, slightly beaten
½ cup milk
2 tablespoons cooking oil
2 cups cooked brown rice
½ cup chopped walnuts
Fat for deep frying
Maple syrup

Sift dry ingredients into a bowl. Add eggs, milk, and oil; beat until smooth. Stir in rice and nuts. Drop by teaspoonfuls into deep hot fat (365°F. on a frying thermometer) and fry until golden-brown and done. Serve very hot with syrup. Makes about 22.

### SWEET SCRAMBLED RICE

¼ cup raisins
¼ cup rum
1 cup uncooked rice
¼ teaspoon salt
Sugar (about 1¼ cups)
3 cups milk
2 tablespoons chopped nuts
Grated rind of 1 lemon
1 egg, beaten
½ cup butter
Ground cinnamon

Soak raisins in rum for several hours. Cook rice, salt, and 1 cup sugar in the milk in top part of double boiler over boiling water for 30 minutes, or until rice is tender and milk is absorbed, stirring occasionally. Add raisins, nuts, lemon rind, and egg. Melt butter in skillet, add rice mixture, and cook, letting brown crusts form. Turn and brown remainder. Sprinkle with sugar and cinnamon. Makes 4 to 6 servings.

### PEARS CONDÉ

About 3½ cups (one 1-pound, 13-ounce can) pear halves or
6 fresh pears
2 cups water
2⅓ cups sugar
2 teaspoons vanilla extract
4 cups boiling water

¾ cup uncooked rice
2 cups milk
¼ teaspoon salt
2 tablespoons butter
4 egg yolks
1 cup heavy cream, whipped

You may use either canned or fresh pears for this French dessert. If fresh are used, select 6 firm ones and leave whole. Make a syrup by combining the water, 2 cups sugar, and 1 teaspoon vanilla. Bring to a boil, add pears, and cook, turning, for 3 minutes, or until skins loosen. You will probably have to do 3 at a time. Remove from syrup. When cool enough to handle, peel off skins, cut pears into halves, and remove stems and cores. Return to syrup and simmer for about 7 minutes, or until a toothpick slips in easily. Drain; you can use the syrup again. Pour boiling water over rice and allow to stand for 10 minutes, then drain. Put 2 cups milk in the top part of a double boiler and scald (cook over direct heat until tiny bubbles form around the edge). Remove from heat, add the rice, salt, ⅓ cup sugar, and the butter. Cover, put over hot water, and cook for 1 hour, or until the rice is tender. Remove from heat. Beat egg yolks and 1 teaspoon vanilla until well mixed, add a little of the hot rice, and mix well; then combine with remaining rice. Taste and add more salt and sugar if needed; mix well. Butter a 3- or 4-cup mold, or a ring mold if you have it, and pack in the rice. Chill, and unmold. Surround with poached pears and garnish with whipped cream. If ring mold is used, put cream in center. Makes 6 servings.

### RICE PUDDING

Prepare rice as in Pears Condé, above; instead of molding, put in a baking dish, brush top with 1 tablespoon heavy cream, and brown under broiler. Serve warm or cold.

### RICH RICE PUDDING

Prepare rice as in Pears Condé; instead of molding, cool mixture slightly, add ¼ cup raisins that have been heated in ¼ cup sherry, then drained, ¼ cup candied fruit, and 1 cup heavy cream, whipped. Put into serving dish; chill. Sprinkle top with slivered almonds and mint sprigs if desired. Makes 6 servings.

### RICE À L'IMPÉRATRICE

3 cups boiling water
½ cup uncooked rice
2 cups milk
1- inch piece of vanilla bean or 1 teaspoon vanilla extract
1 envelope unflavored gelatin
2 tablespoons cold water
3 egg yolks
⅓ cup sugar
¼ teaspoon salt
½ to ¾ cup slivered candied fruit
3 tablespoons kirsch or other liqueur

Ham-and-Rice-stuffed Peppers

Italian Rice Salad with Veal

1 cup heavy cream, whipped
Additional candied fruit and whipped cream (optional)

Pour boiling water over rice and let stand for 5 minutes. Drain. Put rice into a heavy pan with 1¼ cups milk. Bring to a boil, turn heat low, and simmer without stirring until the rice is tender, 30 to 40 minutes. Heat ¾ cup milk with vanilla bean. In the meantime, soften gelatin in cold water and beat egg yolks with sugar and salt. Pour a little of the hot milk into the egg mixture, then combine both mixtures and the gelatin. Heat, stirring, until it begins to thicken. Add rice and chill. Soak candied fruit (mixed peels) in kirsch (or any liqueur or rum or brandy). When the rice starts to set, mix in the fruits and the whipped cream and pour into a 1½-quart mold. Chill until set, and unmold in a fancy dish. Garnish with candied cherries and strips of angelica and more whipped cream, if desired. Makes 6 servings.

### POIRES À L'IMPÉRATRICE

Halves of canned pears may be used for this, although the classic version calls for poaching fresh pears in vanilla syrup (see Pears Condé, page 1552). Make the Rice à l'Impératrice (page 1552) but pour it into a 6-cup ring mold. Chill and unmold on a round dish. Arrange pears around the edge, having them small end up, like a crown, and fill the center with sweetened whipped cream. Decorate with mint sprigs, candied cherries, and angelica. Makes 6 servings.

### PINEAPPLE RICE PUDDING

Mix 2 cups cooked rice, 2 tablespoons sugar, dash of salt, and 1 can (1 pound, 14½ ounces) crushed pineapple. Chill; fold in 1 cup heavy cream, whipped. Chill. Makes 6 servings.

**Marshmallow Pineapple Rice Pudding**
Use recipe above. Add 16 halved marshmallows to first mixture. Proceed as directed. Garnish with maraschino cherries.

---

## Rice Casseroles
### by Shirley Sarvis

If you dress hot rice as you dress a salad, you show off those pearly grains. You toss the rice with a seasoned butter or oil dressing, lightly and gently, as if the grains were leaves of lettuce. The coating dressing carefully seasons each grain; it cloaks each grain to keep it separate and shapely. Then, if you join that rice with a chosen vegetable and meat or other protein, you have a resplendent dinner dish. It can be termed a casserole, but it is much more elegant than the casserole title connotes.

This is the exalted treatment rice takes in the six party casseroles that follow. Dressed rice leads as the axis ingredient; the other participants are chosen to surround and enhance rice or to stand compatibly on their own, out of competition.

All these casseroles have in common particular boons for entertaining. 1) Each will carry practically the total menu because it includes protein, vegetable, and rice. 2) Each allows you to fit casserole preparation into party preparation: assemble the casserole in steps, leaving just the finishing for serving time (do a part of the casserole as you have time; in most cases, the various parts of a dish are quite independent of the others); or assemble entirely ahead, and heat in time for serving. 3) Each is suitable for serving at the table or from the buffet.

When you make these casseroles do not overcook the rice; cook it just until tender. But don't fear rice cookery as an absolutely critical operation. If you use long-grain rice it will allow you a good bit of cooking time leeway during which the grains will stay tender and separate, yet not limply soft. And in these recipes, the butter or oil dressing helps guard rice against overcooking and merging of grains.

When timing the baking of the casseroles, be sure to consider the thickness and speed of heating of your casserole container.

### MENU

PORK-AND-PEPPER CASSEROLE WITH
FRUITED BLACK-BEAN SAUCE
SALAD OF BOSTON LETTUCE,
WATERCRESS, AND
SIEVED HARD-COOKED EGG
HOT BUTTERED CORN BREAD
APPLE CRISP WITH BROWN SUGAR
CRUMB TOPPING AND CHEESE SLICE
OR
WARM STREUSEL-TOPPED
APPLE PIE, CHEESE

### PORK-AND-PEPPER CASSEROLE WITH FRUITED BLACK-BEAN SAUCE

*This casserole admittedly takes a little time to prepare, but it is simple to do in parts and assemble entirely ahead.*

4½ pounds pork loin, boned and cut
into ½-inch-thick slices (or ½-inch-thick boneless pork chops for 6)
Salt and pepper
Marinated Pepper Strips
Pimiento Rice
Fruited Black-Bean Sauce

In a large skillet, over medium heat, brown pork slices on both sides; season with salt and pepper to taste. Cover and cook over low heat for ten minutes. Arrange, slightly overlapping, over about half the bottom area of a shallow casserole (about 15 x 12 inches). Remove Pepper Strips from marinade and arrange alongside pork chops. Spoon Pimiento Rice into remaining part of casserole. Pour about half the Fruited Black-Bean Sauce over the pork chops. Cover casserole loosely with foil. Bake in preheated moderate oven (375°F.) for 20 minutes, or until heated through. Reheat remaining sauce and pass at table. Makes 6 servings.

**Marinated Pepper Strips**
Cut 4 green peppers into lengthwise strips ⅜ inch wide. Marinate for 1 hour in a mixture of 6 tablespoons olive oil, 2 tablespoons red wine vinegar, and 1 garlic clove, split. Turn occasionally.

**Pimiento Rice**
Cook 1½ cups rice as directed on the package. Toss lightly with 2 tablespoons melted butter, 1 tablespoon dry sherry, and about ½ teaspoon salt. Add 1 can or jar (4 ounces) sliced pimientos; 1 can (4 ounces) water chestnuts, thinly sliced; and 3 tablespoons grated onion. Mix lightly.

**Fruited Black-Bean Sauce**
In a saucepan combine 1 can (about 11 ounces) black-bean soup, undiluted; ½ cup dry red wine; ⅓ cup cherry or strawberry jam (or currant jelly); 1 tablespoon Worcestershire; ½ teaspoon celery salt; and ⅛ teaspoon ground ginger. Cook over low heat, stirring occasionally, until blended and slightly thickened, about 10 minutes.

### MENU

CLAM PILAF CASSEROLE
DILL-PICKLE SALAD
SOURDOUGH OR
DARK RYE BREAD, BUTTER
CHOCOLATE CAKE WITH CHOCOLATE
ICING AND RASPBERRY-JELLY
FILLING

### CLAM PILAF CASSEROLE

*The rice must almost pop as it browns well before baking. Just before serving the casserole, sprinkle toasted almonds as a border strip around the top.*

1 cup uncooked rice
1½ tablespoons vegetable oil

4 slices of bacon, diced
⅔ cup chopped celery
1 small onion, finely chopped
½ large green pepper, chopped
2 cans (7½ ounces each) chopped
  clams with liquid
1 cup chicken broth
1 cup chopped tomatoes (peeled and
  seeded fresh, or well-drained canned)
½ can (6 ounces) tomato paste
¼ cup dry vermouth
1 tablespoon fresh lemon juice
1 teaspoon brown sugar
  About ¼ teaspoon each of salt and
  pepper
¼ teaspoon each of ground ginger,
  crumbled dried thyme, and tarragon
½ small garlic clove, minced or mashed
1 can (2¼ ounces) sliced black olives,
  drained
½ cup toasted sliced almonds*

In a large heavy skillet, sauté rice in oil over medium heat, stirring, until rice is evenly and well browned. Remove to a 2- to 2½-quart casserole. In skillet, cook bacon slowly until some fat accumulates; add celery, onion, and green pepper, and sauté until limp. Drain off any excess fat. Add remaining ingredients except almonds; add to rice and mix lightly but thoroughly. Bake, uncovered, in preheated moderate oven (350°F.) for 45 minutes, or until rice is just tender. Sprinkle with toasted almonds. Makes 6 generous servings.

*To toast almonds, sprinkle on baking sheet, put in preheated moderate oven (350°F.) until lightly browned; shake or stir occasionally.

### DILL-PICKLE SALAD
6 cups broken mixed salad greens:
  iceberg lettuce, romaine, and a
  soft-leaf lettuce (pack loosely to
  measure)
3 tablespoons chopped parsley
1 to 1½ whole dill pickles, halved
  lengthwise and thinly sliced
  crosswise
  Dill Dressing

Place salad greens, parsley, and dill pickles in a chilled salad bowl. Toss lightly with just enough Dill Dressing to moisten. Makes 6 servings.

#### Dill Dressing
Shake or beat together ¼ cup salad oil, 1 tablespoon each of tarragon vinegar and red wine garlic vinegar, ¼ teaspoon each of ground dillweed and celery salt, ⅛ teaspoon freshly ground pepper, and a pinch of cayenne. Let stand for 30 minutes. Shake again before using.

### MENU
PUREÉD CARROTS IN CHICKEN
BROTH, OR SHELLFISH AND
SLICED GREEN ONIONS IN BROTH
LAYERED SPINACH CURRY CASSEROLE
CONDIMENTS
FRENCH BREAD  CARDAMOM BUTTER
CHILLED FRESH FRUIT, OR

### MELON WITH LEMON SHERBET AND CHOPPED GINGER

### LAYERED SPINACH CURRY CASSEROLE
*You can assemble this casserole the day before the party. If you do this, allow about 45 minutes for heating rather than 30.*

  Spinach Layer
1½ cups rice, cooked as directed on the
  package
  Currant Curry Seasoning
  Salt
  Spiced Browned Lamb Cubes
  Condiments

Spread Spinach Layer over bottom of buttered 2½-quart casserole with cover. Mix rice with Currant Curry Seasoning, add salt to taste, and arrange in a layer over spinach. Top with Spiced Browned Lamb Cubes. Cover and bake in preheated moderate oven (350°F.) for 30 minutes, or until heated through. Serve on large heated dinner plates. Pass condiments. Makes 6 servings.

#### Spinach Layer
Cook 2 packages (12 ounces) of frozen chopped spinach according to package directions; drain well. Mix in 1½ teaspoons grated fresh gingerroot (or 1 teaspoon ground ginger) and ¼ teaspoon salt.

#### Currant Curry Seasoning
In a small saucepan or skillet, melt 6 tablespoons butter. Stir in about 2 teaspoons curry powder, and cook, stirring, for about 1 minute. Add 1 medium onion, minced or grated, and sauté until limp. Stir in ½ cup dried currants and ¼ cup dry sherry; simmer for 5 minutes.

#### Spiced Browned Lamb Cubes
Brown 2 pounds lean boneless tender lamb (round-bone lamb chops, boned and trimmed), cut into 1-inch cubes, over medium heat in a small amount of shortening. When almost brown, sprinkle with ½ teaspoon salt and ¼ teaspoon each of ground cinnamon and cardamom.

#### Condiments
Thick banana slices, brushed with fresh
  lemon juice
Fresh tomatoes, peeled, seeded, and
  coarsely chopped
Finely chopped green peppers
Toasted flaked or shredded coconut
Lemon wedges
Toasted slivered or sliced almonds

### MENU
BLUE CHEESE-AND-RICE HOT SALAD
CHILLED TOMATO SLICES
SESAME SEED CRACKERS
FRESH FRUIT CUP

### BLUE-CHEESE AND RICE HOT SALAD
*Any leftovers of this casserole are delicious chilled and served as a luncheon rice salad.*

1 cup rice, cooked as directed on the
  package
2 tablespoons each of melted butter
  and fresh lemon juice
½ teaspoon powdered mustard
4 green onions with part of green tops,
  finely sliced
3 hard-cooked eggs, pressed through
  a coarse sieve
1 cup dairy sour cream
2 cans (2½ ounces each) sliced black
  olives, drained, or 1 cup pitted black
  olives
4 ounces firm cold blue cheese, cut
  into ½-inch cubes

Toss together lightly but thoroughly the rice, butter, lemon juice, and mustard. Add onions, eggs, sour cream, and olives; mix gently. Lightly toss in blue cheese. Turn into a 1½-quart casserole; cover and bake in preheated moderate oven (350°F.) for about 30 minutes. Just before serving you can garnish the casserole top with sieved hard-cooked egg yolk or hard-cooked egg wedges and a few whole olives. Makes 4 to 6 servings. **Note:** When you combine ingredients, it is important to add the cold and firm blue cheese cubes last of all, just before baking, so that they will remain as distinctive little nuggets of melted cheese throughout the baking.

■ **Variation**—For most meals, make this casserole just as it is written. But for an occasion when you want to be more elaborate, add artichoke hearts and crabmeat: before baking, tuck into the top of the casserole large pieces of fresh or canned crabmeat (about ½ pound) and 1 package (9 ounces) frozen artichoke hearts, cooked just until tender and drained, or a 9-ounce can artichoke hearts, drained. Cover and bake as directed.

### MENU
HAM JAMBALAYA
TOMATO-CUMIN CHUTNEY
SPINACH SALAD
LEMON, OLIVE-OIL DRESSING
PEACH ICE CREAM WITH FROZEN
SLICED PEACHES, OR
LEMON MERINGUE PIE

The cold Tomato-Cumin Chutney is so right with this casserole it is almost imperative. But if you should have to sacrifice this completing condiment, keep the cumin taste in some evidence by substituting ⅛ teaspoon crushed cuminseed for the ground ginger in the rice. Garnish the finished casserole with parsley sprigs and overlapping fresh mushroom slices.

The accompanying salad might be fresh spinach leaves and broken Boston lettuce lightly dressed with olive oil, fresh lemon juice, salt, and pepper. The wine: a chilled white table wine with a touch of sweetness. Dessert: peach ice cream with frozen sliced peaches, or lemon meringue pie.

### HAM JAMBALAYA
About 1¾ pounds cooked smoked ham, cut into ¾-inch chunks (4 cups ham chunks)
2 tablespoons butter or margarine
1 large green pepper, finely chopped
1 medium onion, finely chopped
1½ cups thinly sliced celery
½ pound sliced fresh mushrooms
1 can (4½ ounces) chopped black olives (optional)
1¼ cups uncooked rice
2 tablespoons cooking oil
1⅔ cups hot chicken broth
6 tablespoons dry sherry
1 teaspoon Worcestershire
¼ teaspoon crumbled dried thyme
⅛ teaspoon ground ginger
½ cup chopped fresh parsley

In a large skillet, cook ham, covered, in butter for about 10 minutes; remove cover and sauté for 5 minutes more. Stir in green pepper, onion, celery, mushrooms, and olives. In a large skillet, sauté rice in oil over medium heat, stirring, until rice loses translucence and begins to brown. Reduce heat, and stir in hot chicken broth, sherry, Worcestershire, thyme, and ginger. Stir in ham and vegetable mixture. Turn into 2½-quart casserole; cover and bake in preheated moderate oven (375°F.) for 30 minutes. Remove cover and gently stir in parsley. Bake, uncovered, for 10 minutes more, or until rice is just tender. Makes 6 generous servings.

### TOMATO-CUMIN CHUTNEY
In a saucepan, over low heat, sauté ½ teaspoon whole cuminseed, ¼ teaspoon each of ground nutmeg and whole mustard seed, and ⅛ teaspoon crumbled crushed red chili peppers in 1 tablespoon cooking oil, stirring, until seeds begin to pop. (If you prefer a hotter chutney, use more crushed red peppers.) Add 1 can (1 pound, 12 ounces) peeled solid-pack tomatoes and half a lemon, cut in quarters. Simmer for 15 minutes, stirring frequently. Stir in ½ cup sugar and ⅓ cup raisins. Simmer, stirring frequently, until thickened, for about 40 minutes. Allow to cool. Chill. Makes about 2 cups.

## MENU
ROSEMARY CHICKEN WITH
TANGERINE RICE
ROMAINE
HERBED SOUR-CREAM DRESSING
HOT BUTTERFLAKE ROLLS
CARAMEL CUSTARD

You use only the white part of the green onions in the casserole. Slice green part to use as garnish. Have the topping avocados, apricots, and green onions at room temperature when you arrange them on the chicken, and they will warm sufficiently from the heat of the casserole.

### ROSEMARY CHICKEN WITH TANGERINE RICE
4 to 4½ pounds frying chicken pieces (split breasts, legs, thighs)
About ½ cup fresh tangerine or orange juice
Seasoned flour: ¾ cup all-purpose flour, 1½ teaspoons salt, ½ teaspoon ground ginger, ¼ teaspoon pepper
About 4 tablespoons each of butter or margarine and cooking oil
Rosemary-Wine Seasoning
1¾ cups rice, cooked as directed on the package
Tangerine Butter
6 green onions, sliced
1 package (10 ounces) frozen peas, thawed just enough to separate
1 can (4 ounces) pimientos, sliced
2 avocados, peeled and cut into lengthwise wedges about ½ inch thick
1 can (29 ounces) whole apricots, drained

Wash and dry chicken pieces; dip into tangerine juice, then dust lightly with seasoned flour. In a large skillet, brown chicken over medium heat in 3 tablespoons each of butter and oil for about 20 minutes (add more butter and oil if necessary). Add Rosemary-Wine Seasoning, cover loosely, and allow to simmer for 15 to 20 minutes, or until chicken is tender and liquid evaporated. Toss rice gently with Tangerine Butter, then fold in green onions, the peas, and pimientos. Spread rice over bottom of shallow casserole or baking pan (13 x 9 x 2 inches). Arrange chicken in single layer over rice. Cover and bake in preheated moderate oven (375°F.) for 20 minutes; remove cover and bake for 10 minutes more, or until heated through. Pile chicken in the center. Decorate with avocado and whole apricots; sprinkle with green part of onions. Makes 6 to 8 servings.

#### Rosemary-Wine Seasoning
Crush 2 to 2½ tablespoons dried rosemary into ⅔ cup dry vermouth and 3 tablespoons water; allow to stand in warm place for 1 hour.

#### Tangerine Butter
Combine 2 tablespoons melted butter, 6 tablespoons frozen tangerine (or orange) juice concentrate, 1 tablespoon dry vermouth, about 1 teaspoon salt, ¼ teaspoon pepper, and a dash of ground cinnamon (optional).

### HERBED SOUR-CREAM DRESSING FOR ROMAINE
2 cups dairy sour cream
4 teaspoons tarragon vinegar
1 teaspoon scraped onion
1 teaspoon celery salt
½ teaspoon dried thyme, finely crushed between fingers
¼ teaspoon each of dried oregano and sweet basil, finely crushed
¼ teaspoon celery seed
Pinch of garlic powder
Dash of cayenne

Mix all ingredients together thoroughly; chill for 1 hour. Makes about 1 pint dressing. (Store any unused dressing in refrigerator.)

**RICE FLOUR**—Ground rice made principally from the rice broken during milling. It cannot be used in breadmaking but is used commercially for making ice creams and confections. It is also widely used by the Chinese in making rice cookies, etc. Another use is by persons on allergy diets. It can be purchased in health-food stores or stores selling oriental products.

**RICE, TO**—To press a vegetable, especially a potato, through a heavy sievelike utensil which reduces it to ricelike pellets.

**ROAST, TO**—The phrases "to roast" and "to bake" both refer to a method of cooking by exposing food to dry heat. It can be the enclosed heat of an oven or the open heat of a fire. If an open fire is used, the food to be roasted can be placed on a spit, or buried in hot ashes. Usage determines whether we say "roast" or "bake," and in general roasting is used in reference to the cooking of meats, baking to other foods. There are, however, exceptions: the commercial process of removing the excess moisture from coffee, cocoa, etc., is called "roasting"; and we speak of roasted chestnuts and roasted corn on-the-cob. On the other hand, we say "baked ham."

Whichever word is used, roasting is one of the oldest methods of cooking in the world, if not *the* oldest and most universal. Since it does not necessarily call for a pot or pan, it was easier for primitive man than boiling or frying. The earliest roasting was probably of two kinds: foods were buried in hot ashes or placed on sticks or spits. Spit roasting used to be much more common than it is now. In colonial days, the huge fireplace of every kitchen normally contained a spit. Oven roasting was done in an oven in the wall off the fireplace.

Nowadays, oven roasting is the method most often used, in a range oven, in top-stove ovens, or in portable electric ovens. However, electric rotisseries are popular for both indoor and outdoor cooking. Rotisserie roasting is the modern equiva-

*A pork roast served with candied yams, glazed white onions, and spiced pears.*

lent of spit roasting.

Poultry and the tender cuts of meat or "roasts" are the foods most often selected for roasting. A large shallow pan and a rack are the best equipment. The rack allows the heat to circulate under and around the roast. A broiler pan and a cake rack can be used. Helpful but not essential are: a bulb-handled baster, a pair of large metal tongs, and a meat thermometer.

Wipe the meat with a damp cloth and dry thoroughly. If the meat is too lean, it may be larded with a larding needle or by pushing strips of bacon or salt pork into it with an ice pick or a knitting needle. Season with salt and pepper, or don't season, as you prefer. Some claim that salting draws the juices out of the

roast and that it is better done halfway through the cooking when the outside of the meat has been seared. The uncooked roast may be seasoned with garlic slivers, herbs, and spices by making tiny incisions in the surface of the meat and inserting the seasoning with the point of a knife.

Put the meat, fat side up, on the rack in the pan. Give lean meats, such as veal, lamb, poultry, or birds which have not been larded, a covering of either rubbed-on butter or olive oil, slices of bacon, salt pork, or suet. The fat will baste the meat and prevent it from drying out; this will make the roast more tender.

Insert the shaft of the meat thermometer into the thickest part of the meat. It must *not* touch bone, fat, or gristle.

If the roast is slender, insert it on a slant. For a bird, insert the meat thermometer into the thickest part of the thigh. If the bird is stuffed, place it in the center of the stuffing.

Generally speaking, low temperatures of 300°F. to 350°F. are best for roasting meats since these temperatures keep the meat juicy and tender. However, roasting directions in the individual recipe should be followed.

Cook a roast to about 10° under the meat-thermometer temperature you want, since the meat continues cooking after it has been taken out of the oven. This is particularly important if rare meat is desired. Remove the meat from the oven, stand it on a heated platter or carving board, and let it stand at room temperature for 15 to 25 minutes, depending on the size of the roast. The meat will go on cooking inside, but the connective tissues and juices will have time to settle from the softening which has taken place during cooking, and the meat will be easier to carve.

## ROCK CORNISH HEN or CORNISH GAME HEN

**ROCK CORNISH HEN or CORNISH GAME HEN**—A small fowl with small bones and all white meat. It was developed from the Cornish hen, an English breed of domestic fowl with a pea comb, very close feathering, and a compact, sturdy body. Rock Cornish hens weigh from one-half to one and a quarter pounds and are good broiled or roasted.

*Availability and Purchasing Guide*—Available year round frozen whole, unstuffed or with wild-rice stuffing.

### Storage

☐ Refrigerator frozen-food compartment: 4 to 5 weeks
☐ Freezer: 6 months

#### GLAZED ROASTED STUFFED ROCK CORNISH HENS

6 frozen Rock Cornish hens
  Pecan Stuffing
½ cup butter, melted
  Salt and pepper to taste
1 cup beef bouillon
2 tablespoons cornstarch

Thaw Cornish hens. Stuff with Pecan Stuffing; secure with toothpicks and tie legs together. Put in shallow roasting pan; pour butter over birds. Sprinkle with salt and pepper. Roast in preheated hot oven (425°F.) for 1 to 1¼ hours, basting twice with drippings in pan. When done, glaze with hot bouillon thickened with cornstarch mixed with a little cold water. Makes 6 servings.

#### Pecan Stuffing

1 medium onion, chopped
½ cup chopped celery
½ cup butter or margarine
1 teaspoon salt
½ teaspoon paprika
5 cups diced stale bread
1½ cups chopped pecans
½ cup chopped parsley

Sauté onion and celery in butter for about 5 minutes. Add salt and paprika. Mix lightly with remaining ingredients.

## ROCKFISH

**ROCKFISH**—The name given to a large genus, *Sebastodes,* of salt-water food fish found along the Pacific coast from California to Alaska. The fish is sometimes mistakenly called the rock cod. Among the best known and most valuable rockfish are the black fish, bocaccio, rasher, red rockfish, Spanish flag, yellow-backed rockfish, and the yellowtail rockfish. The skin varies in color from dark gray to bright orange and the meat from almost a pure white to a deep pink. The texture and flavor of the meat of all the species seem to be the same: texture is firm and when cooked, it is white and flaky, resembling crabmeat; flavor also resembles crabmeat and the fish is often steamed and used for salads, etc., just as crabmeat is. Baking and oven-steaming are favorite methods of preparation. The steamed fish is good with such sauces as Newburg, cheese, herb butter, etc.

*Availability*—Year round, sold fresh, whole, and dressed, or as fillets.

*Storage*—See Red Snapper, page 1540.

*Caloric Value*

☐ 3½ ounces, oven-steamed = 107 calories

*Basic Preparation*—See Red Snapper, page 1540.

☐ To Oven-Steam—Wipe fish fillets with damp cloth. Sprinkle lightly with salt and put in a casserole. Cover and bake in preheated moderate oven (350°F.) for 30 minutes, or until fish can be shredded easily with a fork.

#### CURRIED ROCKFISH SALAD

Oven-steam 1 pound rockfish fillets (see above). Chill fish, and shred. Add 2 cups diced celery and mayonnaise to moisten. Season with salt, pepper, and curry powder to taste. Serve in lettuce cups. Makes 6 to 8 servings.

#### ROCKFISH EN PAPILLOTE

4 shallots, chopped
¼ cup chopped mushrooms
  Butter or margarine
¼ cup all-purpose flour
1 cup white wine
1 cup heavy cream
1 egg yolk
  Salt and pepper
6 large mushrooms
1½ pounds rockfish, cut into serving pieces
6 shrimps, cooked, shelled, and cleaned

Sauté shallots and mushrooms in ¼ cup butter for 5 minutes. Blend in flour, wine, and cream. Cook, stirring constantly, until smooth and thickened. Beat in egg yolk and season to taste with salt and pepper. Chill. Cut heart-shape pieces of foil about 11 x 8½ inches, allowing one sheet for each of the 6 servings. Sauté 6 mushrooms lightly in 1 tablespoon butter. Spread a little chilled mixture on one-half of foil heart, put a piece of fish on it, and top with a mushroom and a shrimp. Add about ½ cup more mixture. Fold foil and double-fold the edges, crimping firmly. Bake in preheated very hot oven (450°F.) for about 15 minutes. Serve in the foil. Makes 6 servings.

**ROE**—Fish eggs still enclosed in the thin natural membrane in which they are found in the female fish are called roe or hard roe. Roe is taken from many species of fish and is now available in food stores year round in most sections of the country. Shad roe is perhaps the most popular and best known. However, the fish industry is marketing large quantities of roe in fresh, frozen, and canned forms from many different fish including alewife, herring, cod, mackerel, mullet, salmon, shad, and whitefish. The size of roe varies with the fish. Shad roe is usually from five to six inches long, about three inches wide, and an inch or more thick. The canned variety is somewhat smaller in size.

Sturgeon roe is so scarce that it is widely reserved for the making of caviar, which is hard roe, salted down. A large part of the salmon and whitefish roe is also used for this purpose.

Soft roe or milt is the male fish's reproductive gland when filled with secretion, or the secretion itself. It has a soft creamy consistency and the vein must be removed before cooking.

Hard roe has a grainy texture when cooked. It can be poached, broiled, or baked.

*Nutritive Food Values*—A source of protein.

☐ Cod and shad, 3½ ounces, cooked = 126 calories
☐ Canned cod, haddock, or herring, 3½ ounces, solids and liquid = 118 calories

*Basic Preparation*—Before cooking hard roe, the membrane holding the eggs together should be pricked with a needle to prevent its bursting. The roe should be cooked slowly and gently to prevent excessive drying.

#### DEVILED ROE

1½ pounds roe
1½ teaspoons prepared mustard
1 teaspoon anchovy paste
1 tablespoon Worcestershire
  Dash each of cayenne and crushed rosemary leaves
1 tablespoon butter, melted
3 tablespoons dry sherry
3 drops Angostura bitters
4 slices of hot buttered toast
  Parsley sprigs

Put roe in saucepan and cover with boiling water. Bring to boil and simmer, covered, for 15 minutes. Drain, and cut roe into 1-inch pieces. Blend remaining ingredients except toast and parsley. Arrange toast on an ovenproof platter. Dip roe pieces into mixture and arrange on the toast. Put in preheated hot oven (400°F.) for 5 minutes to heat. Garnish with parsley. Makes 4 servings.

### ROE EN CASSEROLE

1½ pounds roe
 1 cup dry sauterne
 1 bay leaf
 2 whole cloves
 3 peppercorns
 6 tablespoons butter or margarine
 2 tablespoons all-purpose flour
 1 cup milk
   Salt and pepper
 1 teaspoon grated onion
   Few parsley sprigs, minced
 1 tablespoon fresh lemon juice
 1 cup toasted soft-bread crumbs
   Paprika

Put roe in saucepan. Add sauterne, bay leaf, cloves, and peppercorns. Bring to boil, cover, and simmer for 15 minutes. Drain, and break roe into pieces with fork. Put a layer in 1½-quart casserole. Melt 2 tablespoons butter and blend in flour. Gradually add milk and cook, stirring, until thickened. Season with salt and pepper to taste. Sprinkle roe lightly with salt and pepper, onion, parsley, lemon juice, and crumbs. Pour some of white sauce over crumbs. Continue making layers until all ingredients are used, ending with crumbs. Dot with remaining butter and sprinkle with paprika. Bake in preheated moderate oven (350°F.) for 20 minutes, or until browned. Makes 4 servings.

**ROLL**—The word is derived from the Latin *rotulus,* a diminutive of *rota,* "wheel," and its most common food usage is as a description of varieties of bread made in the form of small pointed, oval, or round cakes, and generally intended to be eaten for breakfast or dinner.

The word roll is also used to describe other roll-shape or rolled-up foods, for example: jelly rolls, veal rolls, etc.

**ROLL, TO**—The phrase is used to describe several culinary processes: 1) The flattening of dough into a thin sheet with a rolling pin, as for cookies or piecrust; 2) the shaping of foods such as ground meat, cookie dough, candy, etc., into round balls; 3) the coating of foods with flour or dry crumbs, chopped nuts, parsley, paprika, etc.; 4) the shaping of foods into long tubular shapes which are then sliced, as the dough for refrigerator cookies; 5) the crushing of cookies or crackers into fine crumbs with a rolling pin.

**ROMAINE**—One of the principal types of lettuce, also known as Cos lettuce. Romaine has a long narrow cylindrical head with stiff leaves and a broad rib. The leaves are dark green on the outside, becoming greenish-white near the center. Romaine is a flavorful and crisp lettuce and it lends itself excellently to tossed salads of mixed greens.

**ROOT BEER**—The bottled beverage generally called root beer nowadays is a non-alcoholic drink containing carbonated water, sugar, caramel coloring, and a combination of natural and artificial flavorings.

Originally, however, root beer was a beverage made by the fermentation of an infusion of roots, barks, and such herbs as sarsaparilla, sassafras, spruce, wild cherry, spikenard, wintergreen, and ginger with sugar and yeast. The action of the yeast on the sugar produced a small percentage of alcohol and the effervescence was caused by the action of the carbon dioxide. A root-beer flavoring or extract is sold in packages in very limited areas.

**ROSEFISH**—Also known as a redfish, this is a salt-water food fish, *Sebastes marinus,* found in the northern coastal waters of Europe and America. When mature it reaches a length of about eleven inches, weighs between three quarters and one pound, and is a bright rose-red or orange-red in color. It may be marketed as an ocean perch. The fish is fatty, with firm flesh and a bland flavor which makes it suitable for preparation with a variety of sauces.

*Availability*—Available year round fresh whole or filleted and as frozen fillets, plain, or breaded and fried.

*Purchasing Guide*—See Red Snapper, page 1540.

*Storage*—See Red Snapper, page 1540.

*Caloric Values*

☐ Fresh, 3½ ounces, panfried = 227 calories
☐ Frozen, breaded and fried, 3½ ounces, reheated = 319 calories

*Basic Preparation*—See Red Snapper, page 1540.

### SESAME-BAKED ROSEFISH

 2 pounds rosefish fillets, fresh or frozen
   Salt
   Melted butter or margarine
 3 cups soft bread crumbs
 ¼ teaspoon pepper
 ¼ cup sesame seed, toasted in 350°F. oven for 10 minutes
 ½ teaspoon thyme

If frozen fillets are used, thaw until they can be separated. Put in shallow baking dish. Sprinkle with salt and cover with ¼ cup melted butter. Mix 1 teaspoon salt, ⅓ cup melted butter, and remaining ingredients. Spread on fish. Bake in preheated moderate oven (375°F.) for about 30 minutes. Makes 6 servings.

### ROSEFISH MARINARA

 2 pounds rosefish fillets, fresh or frozen
 ¼ cup cooking oil
 ½ cup minced celery
 1 garlic clove, minced
 ½ teaspoon each of salt, sugar, and dried basil
 ¼ teaspoon cayenne
 1 teaspoon dried oregano
 ¼ cup chopped parsley
3½ cups (one 29-ounce can) tomatoes

If frozen fillets are used, thaw until they can be separated. Heat oil in large skillet. Add celery and cook for 2 or 3 minutes. Add remaining ingredients except fish and simmer, uncovered, for about 25 minutes. Separate fillets and put in another large skillet. Add water to cover. Put lid on skillet and bring to boil. Simmer for 5 to 10 minutes, or until fish flakes easily with a fork. Serve with the hot marinara sauce, and with rice, if desired. Makes 6 servings.

### ROSEFISH BAKED IN PAPRIKA SAUCE

 2 pounds rosefish fillets, fresh or frozen
 1 teaspoon salt
   Dash of pepper
 1 teaspoon paprika
 2 tablespoons fresh lemon juice
 1 teaspoon grated onion
 ¼ cup butter or margarine, melted

If frozen fillets are used, thaw until they can be separated. Put in a single layer, skin side down, in shallow baking dish. Mix remaining ingredients and pour over fish. Bake in preheated moderate oven (350°F.) for about 25 minutes, or until fish flakes easily with a fork. Makes 6 servings.

## ROSE HIP

**ROSE HIP**—The fleshy, swollen red seed capsule of any of various roses, but especially of the wild rose. The capsules are rich in vitamin C and are used commercially in making a vitamin C concentrate sold in health-food stores. They are also sold dried whole, cut, and powdered. Excellent jelly and jam can be prepared from fresh rose hips.

### ROSE-HIP JAM

3 cups fully ripe rose hips
1 orange
1 lemon
1 cup water
1½ cups sugar

Remove the stiff hairs from calyx end of rose hips, split open, and scrape out the seeds. Wash hips and measure 1½ cups. Cut peel from orange and lemon in thin slivers. Add to the water and boil for 5 minutes. Add sugar and stir until dissolved. Add the juice from the orange and lemon and the rose hips. Cover and simmer for 15 minutes. Uncover and cook until hips are clear and transparent and syrup is thick. Pour into hot sterilized jars; seal. Makes about two ½-pint jars.

**ROSEMARY (Rosemarinus officinalis)**—A perennial evergreen shrub which grows wild in southern Europe and is cultivated throughout the rest of Europe and the United States. It reaches a height of from four to five feet, and has branching stems which bear long thin dark-green leaves with grayish undersides and a strongly aromatic smell. The leaves, fresh or dried, are used as an herb seasoning.

Rosemary can flavor many dishes. It may be added to fruit cups and various soups, almost any hearty meat or poultry, fish stuffings and creamed seafood dishes, cheese sauces and eggs, herb breads and stuffings, many sauces and marinades, fruit salads, and vegetables such as lentils, mushrooms, peas, potatoes, spinach, and squash.

Rosemary is not limited to culinary endeavors, however. Its sweet smell adds to toilet water and potpourri. It can be used in making wines and cordials, too.

Rosemary, like all herbs, is at its best when fresh. If bought dried, it should be crumbled before using to release the rosemary's full flavor.

### BROILED FRESH ALBACORE

¼ cup olive oil
¼ cup salad oil
1 bay leaf
   Pepper to taste
½ teaspoon salt
½ teaspoon crumbled dried rosemary
   Juice of 1 lemon
6 albacore steaks, ½ pound each,
   1 inch thick
   Lemon wedges or Hollandaise Sauce
   (page 1621)

Combine all ingredients except fish and lemon wedges, and blend thoroughly. Marinate albacore steaks in mixture, turning occasionally, for 1 to 3 hours. Grill fish over charcoal or in preheated broiler. Baste with remaining marinade. Cook for 8 to 10 minutes, turning once with spatula. Remove to hot dish and serve with lemon wedges. Makes 6 servings.

### LAMB CHOPS WITH ARTICHOKES

2 large or 4 medium artichokes
4 cups water
2 tablespoons fresh lemon juice
   or vinegar
   Salt and pepper to taste
3 to 4 tablespoons olive oil
6 lamb chops, trimmed of excess fat
2 garlic cloves, minced
1 teaspoon dried rosemary
2 cups (one 16-ounce can) stewed
   tomatoes

Trim artichokes of tough outer leaves by tearing them off. Trim stem down to ½ inch. Cut off tops of artichokes with sharp knife, leaving about ½ inch of leaves. Have ready in a bowl the water acidulated with the lemon juice. Cut trimmed artichokes into quarters, remove chokes, and cut into eighths if large. Drop trimmed artichokes into acidulated water to prevent darkening. Parboil in salted water. Heat olive oil and brown lamb chops. Pour off excess fat. Arrange artichoke slices around the meat; add salt, pepper, garlic, and rosemary and cover with tomatoes. Cover and simmer over low heat for about 30 minutes, or until meat and artichokes are tender. If sauce is too thin, cook, uncovered, for 5 to 10 minutes until sufficiently reduced. Makes 4 to 6 servings.

### FLORENTINE PORK ROAST ARISTA

1 loin of pork (3 to 4 pounds)
3 garlic cloves, halved
1 tablespoon crumbled dried rosemary
   or 2 tablespoons fresh rosemary
   leaves
3 whole cloves
   Salt and pepper to taste
   Red or white dry wine

Trim pork of excess fat. Wet garlic and roll in rosemary. Cut 3 pockets in meat by inserting pointed knife and making each hole large enough to hold a garlic clove. Insert garlic cloves and whole cloves into these pockets; rub meat with salt and pepper. Place on rack in roasting pan with an equal mixture of water and wine, which should be about 2 inches deep. Cook in open pan in preheated slow oven (300°F.). Baste occasionally. Allow 45 minutes of roasting time per pound. Cool in its own juice. The meat should be moist. Serve with cold, not chilled, green beans or broccoli, dressed with a simple French dressing. Makes 6 to 8 servings.
**Note:** This dish can be made successfully with other roasting cuts of pork, with leg of veal, boned rump of veal, and with leg of lamb. Traditionally, Pork Arista is served cold, but it is also good hot.

### ROSEMARY CHICKEN IN CREAM

1 large frying chicken, cut into pieces
¼ cup all-purpose flour
1 teaspoon salt
¼ teaspoon pepper
1 teaspoon crumbled rosemary leaves
2 cups (about) light cream
   Hot milk
   Chopped parsley

Coat chicken pieces with next 4 ingredients, mixed together. Put in a shallow baking dish. Almost cover the chicken with the cream. Bake, uncovered, in preheated slow oven (325°F.) for about 2 hours. Turn the chicken pieces after the first hour. If the gravy is too thick, add a little more light cream. At serving time, put the chicken pieces on a heated serving dish and keep warm. Stir enough hot milk into the gravy to make it of desired consistency and pour over chicken. Sprinkle with parsley. Makes 4 servings.

### VEAL ROSEMARY

2 tablespoons cooking oil
2 tablespoons butter or margarine
1½ pounds boned veal shoulder, cut
   into 1-inch cubes
1 onion, chopped
2 tablespoons all-purpose flour
1 teaspoon crumbled rosemary leaves
2 cups (one 16-ounce can) tomatoes
½ cup dry white wine
1 cup chicken bouillon
   Salt and pepper
¼ pound mushrooms, sliced

Heat oil and butter in heavy skillet. Add veal and onion and cook until browned. Stir in flour and rosemary. Add tomatoes, wine, and bouillon. Bring to boil, stirring constantly. Season with salt and pepper to taste. Add mushrooms and pour into 2-quart casserole. Cover and bake in preheated moderate oven (350°F.) for 1 hour, or until veal is tender. Good with rice or mashed potatoes. Makes 4 to 6 servings.

## HASHED OR HOME-FRIED POTATOES WITH ROSEMARY

Add 1 to 2 teaspoons crumbled dried rosemary, or more to taste, to hashed or home-fried potatoes as they are cooking.

**ROSETTE**—A type of waffle or fried cake made of a thin batter of milk, eggs, and flour, fried in deep fat. Rosettes may be made in a skillet, but preferably they are prepared by dipping a specially shaped rosette iron into the batter and then immersing the iron in the hot fat. As it becomes crisp, the rosette is lifted from the iron and allowed to fry until crisp and brown. A rosette iron consists of a long handle onto which various shapes, such as butterflies, flowers, and rings, are screwed. It may also be a timbale-shape iron. Rosettes can be prepared ahead of time and, after draining on absorbent paper, can be stored in an airtight container. After frying they can be sprinkled with confectioners' sugar or granulated sugar mixed with ground cinnamon. They can also be served as a nonsweet appetizer and can be sprinkled with garlic or celery salt.

To achieve thin crusty rosettes, chill the batter for at least two hours before frying. While the fat is heating, let the rosette iron heat too. In this way the rosettes will not stick to the iron and will come off easily.

### ROSETTES

- 2 eggs, well beaten
- ¼ teaspoon salt
- 1 cup sifted all-purpose flour
- 1 cup milk
- 2 tablespoons cooking oil
- Fat or oil for deep frying

Beat together all ingredients except fat with a rotary egg beater until smooth and well blended. Chill for 2 hours. Heat fat until 375°F. registers on a frying thermometer. Dip rosette iron into batter until the mold is about three-fourths covered. Do not allow the batter to come above the top of the iron or it will be difficult to remove the rosette. Dip the covered mold into the hot fat. Fry for 25 to 30 seconds. With a fork loosen the rosette and let it float in the fat and fry until brown on both sides. Drain on absorbent paper. Dip rosette iron again into batter and continue frying. Makes about 36 rosettes.

**Note:** For a sweet rosette add 1 tablespoon sugar to the batter.

**ROSEWATER**—This is an essence distilled from rose petals, and it carries the delicious scent and flavor of the flower.

Rosewater has been known for thousands of years to the countries of the East. It was used for religious ceremonies, such as the purification of temples and mosques, and even for Christian baptism. It also had extensive cosmetic uses.

In the kitchen, rosewater makes an admirable flavoring, used instead of vanilla, almond, and other extracts, or sometimes in conjunction with these. Oriental cookery has always relied on rosewater, and many of the poetic desserts and confections of India, Iran, and Turkey are flavored with it. Victorian cookery made much use of it, and the French do so to this day.

Rosewater can be bought, imported from France or Near Eastern countries like Lebanon, in specialty food stores and shops where Arab groceries are sold.

### TURKISH DREAMS

- ⅓ cup melted butter or margarine
- 4 round shredded-wheat biscuits
- ½ cup honey
- ¼ cup sugar
- ¼ cup water
- ⅛ teaspoon salt
- ⅔ cup chopped nuts
- 2 teaspoons rosewater

Pour melted butter over biscuits in shallow baking dish. Bake in preheated hot oven (425°F.) for about 20 minutes. Bring remaining ingredients except flavoring to boil. Add flavoring and spoon over biscuits. Serve warm or cool. Makes 4 servings.

### SOUR-CREAM DEVONSHIRE PEARS

- 7 to 12 (one 1-pound, 13-ounce can) pear halves
- Juice of 1 orange
- Juice of ½ lemon
- ¼ teaspoon ground ginger
- 1 cinnamon stick
- 3 whole cloves
- 1 cup currant jelly
- Red food coloring
- 1 cup heavy cream
- ½ cup dairy sour cream
- 2 tablespoons sugar
- 2 tablespoons rosewater

Drain pears, reserving syrup. In saucepan mix syrup with orange and lemon juices and spices. Let stand for 1½ hours. Add pears and simmer until thoroughly heated. Cool; chill. Beat jelly until smooth. Add small amount of red coloring and 3 tablespoons liquid from chilled pears. Remove pears to serving dish and cover with the jelly mixture. Whip heavy cream until stiff. Fold in remaining ingredients and spoon in a circle on pears. Makes 8 servings.

### RUSSIAN CREAM

- 1 cup light cream
- ¾ cup sugar
- 1½ teaspoons unflavored gelatin
- 2 tablespoons rosewater
- 1 cup dairy sour cream
- Frozen fruit

Heat light cream and sugar in top part of double boiler until lukewarm. Add gelatin softened in 1 tablespoon cold water; stir until dissolved. Remove from heat and cool. Add rosewater. Fold in sour cream beaten to a smooth fluffy consistency. Pour into individual molds. Refrigerate for 3 to 4 hours. Unmold and serve with partially thawed frozen fruit. Makes 4 servings.

### INDIAN RAVO

- ½ pound almonds
- Butter
- ¼ pound seedless raisins
- 4 cups milk
- 1 cup sugar
- ¼ pound cream of wheat
- 2 tablespoons rosewater
- ½ teaspoon each of ground nutmeg and cardamom

Blanch almonds and slice; fry in butter until golden. Fry raisins lightly, leaving them soft. Drain. Heat milk with sugar, add cream of wheat, and cook until thickened. Then add rosewater. Last of all, mix in thoroughly nutmeg and cardamom without letting the mixture boil and remove from heat at once. Pour into a flat serving dish and sprinkle top with reserved almonds and raisins. Serve hot. Makes 6 servings.

### EAST INDIAN ROSE PUDDING

- 1 cup almonds, blanched
- 2 tablespoons butter or margarine
- ¾ cup seedless raisins
- 4 cups milk
- 1 cup sugar
- ¾ cup quick-cooking farina
- 2 tablespoons rosewater
- ½ teaspoon each of ground nutmeg and cardamom

Slice almonds and brown in butter. Add raisins and sauté lightly. Heat milk with sugar in saucepan. Stir in farina and cook until thickened, stirring frequently. Remove from heat and add flavoring and spices. Pour into serving dish and top with reserved almonds and raisins. Serve warm. Makes 6 servings.

### OLD-FASHIONED ROSEWATER SUGAR COOKIES

- 1 cup butter or margarine
- Sugar (about 1¾ cups)
- 2 eggs
- 4½ cups sifted all-purpose flour
- 1 teaspoon each of baking soda, baking powder, and salt
- 1 cup dairy sour cream
- 1 tablespoon rosewater

Cream butter with 1½ cups sugar until fluffy. Add eggs, one at a time, beating well after each addition. Add sifted dry ingredients alternately with sour cream, mixing after each addition until smooth. Blend in rosewater. Wrap in wax paper and chill overnight, or until firm enough to roll. Roll on floured board to about ¼-inch thickness and cut with 3-inch cookie cutter; put on ungreased cookie sheets. Sprinkle with sugar; bake in preheated moderate oven (375°F.) for 12 minutes, or until browned. Makes about 5 dozen cookies.

## ROTISSERIE

**ROTISSERIE**—There are several meanings for this French word which implies both roasting and rotating. It may be a stationary or portable appliance used to cook foods by rotating them in front of or over a source of heat. Or it may be a shop where meats are roasted and sold. Or again, it may be that part of a restaurant kitchen where the roasting is done by *rôtisseurs,* chefs especially trained in the art of roasting, broiling, and even frying.

Any turning spit that was ever used by primitive man to cook the day's hunt over a campfire was a rotisserie. So were the spits that stood near or in the fireplaces of castles and inns from the Middle Ages on, where flesh and fowl were roasted for the lord and his household, and for travelers. Before electricity, the turning of the spit was done either by the patient hands of apprentices or women.

Rotisserie roasting allows air to circulate around the food as it cooks, and it subjects the food to direct heat. Both factors make for a deliciousness of flavor that cannot be duplicated. This unique flavor is the reason for the popularity of the modern rotisserie.

Before using any rotisserie, the manufacturer's instructions for use should be carefully read.

**ROUX**—A French culinary term for a mixture of flour and fat cooked together and used to thicken soups and sauces. The flour and fat are cooked before the liquid is added to them in order to give them a certain color and taste and, above all, to avoid the raw, pasty taste that insufficiently cooked flour has.

There are three kinds of *roux:* brown, blond, and white.

*Brown roux* is used to thicken rich brown sauces for red meats. Flour and such fats as butter, pork, drippings, etc., are cooked together until the mixture turns an even light-brown color. The cooking must be done very slowly and gently and the mixture has to be stirred frequently, for if the flour burns, it will not thicken properly. Brown *roux* can be refrigerated and frozen.

*Blond roux* is a pale gold color, and is made with butter only. It is cooked for less time than the brown variety, and it is used to thicken the sauces used in lighter dishes, such as fish, chicken, veal, etc. It too can be refrigerated and frozen.

*White roux* is also only made with butter, but it is cooked for a shorter time than the blond and must be stirred constantly. It is used for cream and other white sauces.

All *roux* should be made in a heavy-bottomed saucepan that will hold the heat well and evenly, to allow slow cooking. Aluminum tends to discolor a white sauce, so it is better to use an enamelware, copper-bottomed, stainless steel, heatproof glass, or copper pan for a white *roux.*

Purists of French cooking make their *roux* from clarified fats, that is fats that have been melted down and strained to remove any gritty particles, or in the case of butter, the milk casein. These particles burn easily during cooking and taste bitter, whereas a clarified fat gives a suave, satin-smooth *roux.*

**RUE** (*Ruta graveolens*)—The leaves of this small perennial plant have limited use as a culinary herb because they are very bitter. Great care should be taken in picking rue for the grayish-green leaves are thick and covered with a nonhairy bloom which rubs off when touched. It sometimes causes a severe rash. The plant itself grows up to two feet, is evergreen, and has pretty four-petaled bright yellow flowers.

Rue can be used in the kitchen in small amounts. Chicken broth takes its flavor well, as do minced chicken or mushroom canapés. The Europeans make sandwiches of rue leaves, either minced or whole, and buttered brown bread.

Rue's bitterness is an addition to beef, lamb, kidney, or chicken stews, and it may be mixed sparingly with cottage or cream cheese. Rue can be included in salad dressings or it can be sprinkled over boiled potatoes. Discretion, and always discretion, is the key word in the use of rue.

**RUM**—Rum is an alcoholic beverage distilled from the fermented products of sugar cane. Rum was an important part of early American commerce: in the famous triangle trade of colonial days, slaves were brought from Africa to the West Indies and sold for molasses which was then carried to New England where distilleries produced the rum which was in its turn the medium of exchange for more slaves in Africa.

There are three chief kinds of rum. The oldest type is Jamaican rum. This was the rum known to our ancestors, heavy, dark, full-bodied, and usually aged in wood. Cuban rum is a relatively modern refinement of this. Dry and light-bodied, Cuban-type rum has only been produced since the last part of the 19th century. It is also distilled in Puerto Rico and the Virgin Islands. More aromatic rums than either the Jamaican and Cuban are produced throughout the Caribbean area.

Historically, rum has been popular in the United States. In the early days it was sometimes mixed with molasses and called blackstrap, or mixed with cider and called stonewall. Rum was equally popular in England, where in the British Navy a tot of rum is issued to sailors at sea to this day.

Rum is used in many mixed drinks and as a flavoring in many foods. In cooked foods the alcoholic content evaporates and the flavor alone remains.

### ITALIAN RUM CAKE

3 eggs
1 cup sugar
3 tablespoons cold water
2 teaspoons vanilla extract
1 cup sifted all-purpose flour
2 teaspoons baking powder
Topping
Garnishes

Beat eggs until light. Gradually beat in the sugar. Keep on beating until mixture is thick and pale in color. If possible, use an electric beater at high speed for 6 minutes. Stir in water and vanilla. Sift flour with baking powder. Fold into batter. Bake in greased and floured 9-inch springform pan in preheated moderate oven (350°F.) for 30 minutes, or until cake tests clean. Cool in pan while making the Topping.

Pour topping over cooled cake in pan and chill until serving time. To serve, remove cake from pan and garnish with orange segments, glacé cherries, and rosettes of whipped cream. Makes 8 to 12 servings.

### Topping

1 envelope unflavored gelatin
¼ cup cold water
2 cups hot milk
¾ cup sugar
4 egg yolks, lightly beaten

⅓ cup dark rum
1 large orange
1 cup heavy cream

Soften gelatin in cold water. Stir in hot milk and sugar. Cook over low heat until mixture is hot and gelatin dissolved. Mixture must *not* boil. Gradually pour over egg yolks, stirring constantly. Stir in rum. Set pan in bowl of cracked ice and stir constantly until mixture cools and begins to set. Peel orange and separate into segments. Fold orange segments and cream into custard.

### NORWEGIAN RUM CREAM

2 eggs, separated
6 tablespoons sugar
1½ tablespoons unflavored gelatin
3 tablespoons cold water
2 cups heavy cream, whipped
¼ cup rum

Beat egg yolks and sugar together over very low heat until smooth and slightly thickened. Cool. Soak gelatin in cold water for 5 minutes. Put gelatin over very low heat and stir until dissolved. Add to egg-yolk mixture. Cool. Fold in whipped cream, rum, and egg whites beaten until stiff but not dry. Pour mixture into lightly oiled 1½-quart mold. Chill until firm. Unmold and serve with sweetened berries or with small nut cookies. Makes 6 to 8 servings.

### SPARKLING RUM PUNCH

½ fresh pineapple, sliced
½ cup sugar
¼ cup water
1 cup fresh lemon juice
2 cups fresh pineapple juice
5½ cups light rum
2 cups sliced fresh strawberries
2 quarts chilled club soda

Cover pineapple with sugar and water. Let stand until sugar is dissolved. Add lemon juice, pineapple juice, and rum. Chill for several hours. Pour mixture into a large bowl. Add strawberries and soda. Add a small block of ice. Makes 20 servings.

### DAIQUIRI

For one serving combine 1 tablespoon fresh lime juice with 1 teaspoon sugar and 2 ounces white rum in a cocktail shaker with cracked ice. Shake until well blended. Strain and pour into a cocktail glass.
**Note:** Can be shaken with 1 raw egg white for a smooth drink with a foamy topping.

#### Frozen Daiquiri

Prepare the same mixture as above, shaking the mixture with shaved ice. Serve unstrained with short straws. This mixture can also be whirled in a blender with shaved ice. Pour mixture into a cocktail glass filled with shaved ice and serve immediately.

## RUSSIAN COOKERY —by Princess Alexandra Kropotkin — Russia is an immense country that stretches over the European and Asiatic continents. It is about 7,000 miles from the Russian western frontier with Poland to the eastern one at the end of Siberia, on the Pacific Ocean. From north to south the distances in Russia range up to 3,000 miles. A country so vast offers not only an enormous variety of landscapes, climates, and foodstuffs, but also of populations. The USSR, or Union of Soviet Socialist Republics, has some seventy major nationalities within her borders. These have any number of subdivisions, each in its turn with different ways of preparing this or that dish.

Besides these purely Russian variations, the French influence, which imprinted itself under Catherine the Great (r. 1762-1796), is very apparent. Catherine was a great Francophile, a friend of Voltaire with whom she corresponded regularly. She imported French chefs and followed French recipes with true gastronomical fervor. Most of the sauces so popular with the Russians are of French origin.

Catherine the Great also brought with her some German methods of food preparation. The word *forshmak,* "a warm appetizer," is one of the reminders of this influence. The word has become a permanent part of the Russian language. Roast goose, such a tremendous favorite with Russians at all times, probably can also be attributed to German influence. Of course Russians have a silly joke about a goose; they say it is "too much for one and not enough for two." But they love the bird, stuffed with *kasha* (cooked buckwheat groats) and served with some kind of salad on the side. A favorite is cabbage cut into eighths, put up like sauerkraut, with whole apples fermented in the barrel with the cabbage. These are called *marinovony e iabloki,* that is, "pickled apples." Some Russian delicatessens in this country carry them.

Earlier Russian rulers were also responsible for bringing foreign influences to bear upon Russian food. One of the first to do so was Ivan the Terrible (r. 1533-1584), who sent for Italian architects to build additions within the Kremlin. With them came a sizeable contingent of Italian workmen. It is to the Italians of those distant days that the Russians owe the sherbets, ice creams, and fancy pastries of which they are so inordinately fond to this day.

Besides the French, German, and Italian influences, still a fourth was introduced during the reign of Peter the Great (r. 1682-1725) whose eyes turned to the west and who was the founder of Russian naval power. He lived surrounded by Dutchmen, whom he regarded as the greatest of ship builders, and many of the vegetable dishes and spiced honey-cakes found in Russian cookery go back to his days.

Persian and Turkish accents have percolated into Russia through the Caucasus. Hence the *shashlik* and its variations (skewered broiled mutton, or lamb, served at times with mushroom caps alternating, or tomato slices); also the pilafs. These dishes have become so familiar in Russian menus that the average Russian just considers them part of his own food tradition, without a thought of where they originated.

Poland was part of Imperial Russia for so long that any number of Polish recipes have become incorporated in the Russian food pattern; the famous soup, *borsch,* is said to be of Polish origin. Besides whatever German dishes came in with Catherine the Great, certain German ways of preparing food infiltrated through the Baltic provinces which were part of Russia.

The habit of *zakuska,* or cocktail appetizer, is said to have arrived with Rurik, the Scandinavian prince who became the first Czar of Russia. In 862 A.D. he was invited to "rule and make laws." With him came many fellow Scandinavians. Actually *zakuska* in Russian means the "bite-down." You take your tiny glassful of vodka, drink it, no sipping ever, then "bit it down" with a bit of herring, or whatever appetizer you may fancy.

The usual *zakuska* in a private home consists of just one dish, herring. That is standard. Perhaps there may be a second dish, probably a few slices of sausage, or maybe pickled mushrooms, or a small salad of some kind. Black bread invariably accompanies *zakuski* and, in fact, is part of any dinner. A dish of sweet butter goes along with the *zakuski.*

After the *zakuska* course comes a large tureen of soup. Nearly always the soup has a chunk of meat in it and any vegetables that are available; carrots, cabbage, and turnip are the most usual; minced dill for sprinkling. The meat will be taken from the soup and placed on a separate dish. Sauerkraut, with freshly grated carrot and a few drops of olive or cooking oil, often accompanies the meat. This is the cheapest and easiest of so-called salads, and on winter days one sees it on every table.

The most usual complement to the soup is a big pot of baked *kasha.* This may be varied by a dish of pearl barley, possibly a *pirog,* a nonsweet pastry filled with fish, eggs, or cabbage. *Pirozhki,* little pastries with fillings similar to those of *pirogi,* are reserved, in homes, for meals when guests are present.

After the soup, the dessert, for an everyday home dinner, is very simple. It is probably *kissel,* a fruit purée thickened with cornstarch, or maybe a fruit compote, or possibly some store-prepared pastry.

Generally speaking, pastries are more likely to be eaten with the inevitable tea with the *samovar* which comes later, when homemade jam also appears. The jam is added to the cup of tea (with no milk), or taken from a tiny saucer which is placed to the left of each person, next to the cup of tea. The saucer measures about two and a half inches across and the name for it is *bliudechko.* You put some jam on it, not much, then take tiny half teaspoonfuls, put them in your mouth, and then take a sip of tea.

Russians, all Russians, have a real complex about jam. Only homemade jam, the way Russians make it, is right. Every berry must remain whole and be quite separate in the heavy syrup. No such thing as a mixed-up mass of fruit, however tasty, can be tolerated.

Russian jam is delicious; it is taken with tea and is not for spreading. A great number of Russians living in exile in this country make their own jam. They grumble, however, at the quality of various fruits, at the strawberries in particular, for Russian strawberries are far more aromatic than those grown here. Raspberries, and gooseberries as well, are excellent and very popular and easy to get in Russia.

Tea is the most universal beverage, morning, noon, and night. Coffee was only for the sophisticated in the days before the Czar was ousted. Today coffee is far more widely known and it is drunk in many private homes. But tea is still the more usual drink. The Navy quaffs tea, laced with rum.

*Kvass,* a slightly fermented drink made from either white or dark rye bread, accompanies many meals. Foreigners rarely take to *kvass.* There is, however, a perfectly delightful fruit *kvass,* which should be imitated in this country. This is made from cranberries or lingonberries, which are very common in Russia, with sometimes a small amount of raspberries. The beverage is very slightly fermented. Served well chilled, it is delightfully refreshing.

Breakfast in Russia, called *utrennii chai,* morning tea, isn't much of a meal. Bread, usually white, small sweet rolls, sweet butter, and maybe a couple of soft-boiled eggs, make the meal. Lunch is *zavtrak.* For a home lunch, or even in a cafeteria, unless this is your main meal, one dish of fish, or pot-cheese cakes, maybe a small salad, perhaps some *kasha,* or new potatoes in the spring, make up the menu. Many people drink milk with lunch, especially if the meal is eaten at home.

*Obed,* dinner, is the main meal, at whatever hour it is consumed; this, today, varies according to work schedules. With or without guests, if no salad is served with the meat course, a separate vegetable course follows the meat. This may be meat taken from the soup, or maybe a lighter soup will be served, with chicken in some form or other to follow, or perhaps the delicious little hazel hens, *riabchiki,* quickly roasted, with a salad, may follow the soup.

*Riabchiki,* infinitely tastier and more succulent than American Rock Cornish hens, abound in Russia. They are quite small and have a very slight gamy flavor. They are never stuffed, just roasted quickly and served at once.

Very young small spring chickens, either steamed or quick-roasted, served with a gooseberry sauce, always rate high acclaim. They are truly delicious, if you can get the chickens young enough. Game of all kinds has always been extremely

popular in Russia, particularly woodcock. With woodcock, or wild duck which is also very popular, go pickled cherries or preserved lingonberries. Also a chestnut purée, when available, made from fresh or dried chestnuts.

There are certain rules to be followed when a guest at a party dinner. Russians are incredibly hospitable and someone will drink your health during the outset of the *zakuska* period, saying *Za vashe zdorove* (your health). The person toasted must down his, or her, drink, then get another one and respond with *Za vashe* (your). Bottoms up, always. The prolonged toasting may make people quite intoxicated. To counteract this, thoughtful hostesses provide a platter of sliced Swiss cheese, for a good bite of this cheese is the old cavalry receipt for staying sober. Take the cheese after every drink and hope there are not too many toasts.

If the host is fairly affluent, there will be caviar in some form or other with the *zakuski.* Caviar always was a luxury. Nowadays in Soviet territory caviar seems to be less expensive. The top kinds are still in the luxury class, the *Malossol,* lightly salted, large grained, and very slightly smoked; next come several grades of smaller-grained caviar, smokier, and saltier than the *Malossol.* There is also pressed caviar, black, excellent on open-face sandwiches. This is very popular in present-day Russia. Comparatively inexpensive, it appears at the buffets which are usual in all large theaters and hotels.

All caviars must be served in a bowl, surrounded with ice and lemon wedges. Most plebian of all caviars is the red one, made of salmon roe. If it is large grained and not too salty, quite a few people in the United States like it. Very few Russians do. To serve this caviar to its best advantage, a little sour cream with finely snipped chives should accompany the caviar in a separate bowl. Like other kinds of caviar this too must be served ice cold. It makes a good cocktail snack, with split, lightly toasted English muffins. In fact, these should accompany all types of caviar. They are best left unbuttered.

Besides the usual vodka, a party spread requires two other vodkas, to be drunk from the same kind of thimble-size glasses. These vodkas are *Zubrovka,* a yellowish, herb-infused vodka, very aromatic and just as strong as ordinary vodka; and *Riabinovka,* a distillate of mountain-ash berries, slightly pinkish in color and a great favorite with the ladies. They think it less dangerous than ordinary vodka, which it certainly is not.

# RUSSIAN COOK BOOK

*Culinary influences from many lands
have produced a rich and varied
cuisine: caviar and herring
appetizers; borsch with sour cream;
fish with delicate cream sauces;
stroganoff and shashlik; pirogi
and tart fruit purées.*

# ZAKUSKI
## (Appetizers)

### ANCHOVIES ON EGG SLICES

Cut rounds of pumpernickel bread the size of a slice of hard-cooked egg. Spread the bread lightly with unsalted butter. Cover each round with a slice of egg. Lay 2 thin strips of anchovy crosswise across the egg. Russians like the Norwegian anchovies that come in small wooden casks. They are difficult to clean and bone. Ordinary anchovy fillets taken from a can, drained of the oil, and cut down the middle, serve just as well.
**Note:** This is the simplest of all Russian appetizers.

### SELYODKA
#### (Herrings)

2 large or 3 small herring fillets*
Mustard Dressing
Vegetable Garnish

Cover herring with Mustard Dressing and decorate with Vegetable Garnish. Makes 4 to 6 servings. *Scandinavian Matjes herring can be used; it is skinned and boned, and sold in fillets. Schmaltz herring is favored in Russia, but preparing it is plenty of trouble: it must be soaked first in cold water for a couple of hours, and then in cold tea or milk for another 3 hours. After this the fish is skinned, boned, and filleted. If using large herrings, split each into 2 pieces.

#### Mustard Dressing

2 tablespoons olive oil
1 tablespoon sharp prepared mustard
1 teaspoon sugar, diluted in 1 teaspoon water

Stir oil into mustard, drop by drop. Add sugar and water. Mix well. Let stand for 15 minutes. Pour over fillets.

#### Vegetable Garnish

This is simply slices of cold boiled potato, sliced cooked beet, and a peeled and sliced dill pickle. Arrange around the herring fillets.

### SALAT OLIVIER
#### (Olivier Salad)

*A very popular zakuska dish with quite a tradition behind it. It was created by the Czar's French chef and first served to his royal master; the Czar was so delighted that he ordered the salad to be named for his ingenious chef.*

1 whole breast of chicken, cooked*
3 medium-size potatoes, boiled and peeled
2 small dill pickles, peeled and cut into thin slices
1 teaspoon Worcestershire
3 tablespoons mayonnaise
2 hard-cooked eggs, cut into 6 wedges
6 large olives
1 tomato, cut into 6 slices

Trim off all skin and fat from the chicken. Slice meat into very thin strips. The potatoes should be firm enough to be sliced into even ¼-inch slices. Add pickles. Mix Worcestershire into mayonnaise. Combine it very carefully with the chicken, potatoes, and dill pickles, lifting with a fork to avoid breaking. Pile the salad onto an oval *zakuska* dish. Decorate with 6 egg wedges, 6 olives, and 6 slices of tomato. Makes 6 servings.
*This is best made with breast of cold boiled chicken, although roast chicken can be used. Some gourmets prefer cold duck.

### IKRA IZ BAKLAZHANOV
#### (Eggplant Caviar)

*This is a favorite summer zakuska, all vegetable. It is also used as an accompaniment to meat dishes. The dish comes from the Ukraine.*

1 large eggplant
2 small onions, minced
¼ cup olive or cooking oil
¼ cup tomato purée or 1 cup (about) tomato sauce
2 teaspoons fresh lemon juice
2 teaspoons salt
Pepper
Dash of garlic salt (optional)

Drop the whole eggplant into a pot of boiling water. Cook for about 20 minutes. Drain and cool sufficiently to handle. Cut off stem end and remove skin. Cut into halves lengthwise and chop very fine. Simmer the onion in a little of the oil in a large heavy skillet for 10 minutes without browning. Add the chopped eggplant, tomato purée, and remaining oil. Cook slowly for 10 minutes, stirring constantly. Cook very slowly, covered, for about 30 minutes longer, stirring occasionally. Some eggplants are drier than others and may require a little more oil or even a teaspoon of water. When the eggplant has the required thick and moist consistency, add lemon juice, salt, a dash of pepper, and garlic salt, if desired. Serve well chilled. Makes 6 servings.

### SALAT IZ TELIATINI S OGURTSAMI
#### (Veal and Cucumber Salad)

½ cup mayonnaise
½ cup dairy sour cream
1 teaspoon Worcestershire
2 cups cold diced veal
1 cup diced peeled cucumbers
½ cup diced dill pickles
1 cup diced peeled tart apples
2 cups diced cold cooked potatoes

Mix mayonnaise, sour cream, and Worcestershire. Add remaining ingredients and toss very carefully with fork. Serve very cold. Makes 6 servings.

### SALAT IZ TSVETNOI KAPUSTI S VINOGRADOM
#### (Cauliflower and Grape Salad)

*This recipe comes from the Caucasus.*

1 small head cauliflower
Salt
1 ripe tomato, cubed
½ cup thinly sliced unpeeled cucumber
1 tart-sweet unpeeled apple, sliced
½ cup seedless grapes or halved grapes with seeds removed
½ cup (about) French dressing
Lettuce

Break cauliflower into flowerets. Cook in salted water for about 15 minutes, or until tender. Cool in the water. Drain well and mix with remaining ingredients except lettuce. Chill. Serve on lettuce leaves. Makes 4 to 6 servings.

### SALAT IZ KRASNOI I BELOI REDISKI
#### (Red and White Radish Salad)

1 bunch of young red radishes
1 bunch of white radishes, scraped
½ cup grated raw young carrots
½ cup dairy sour cream
Sugar and salt to taste
Lettuce leaves
Chopped parsley
Fresh dill (optional)

Trim red radishes; cut off roots and green leaves. Slice red and white radishes very thin. Combine vegetables, reserving a small amount of carrot to trim the salad when served. Mix sour cream with sugar and salt. Add vegetables; stir well. Make a mound of the salad in a salad bowl. Trim with lettuce leaves and small mounds of carrot. Sprinkle with finely chopped parsley, and dill if to your taste. Serve chilled. Makes 4 servings.

### KARTOFELNII SALAT S VECHINOI I VISHNIAMI
#### (Potato Salad with Ham and Cherries)

*The cherries in Russia would be likely to come from Vladimir, a central Russian province whence come the best cherries in the world, large, red, and so juicy that when you bite, you have to hold a napkin under your chin to catch the juice.*

2 cups cold sliced potatoes
½ cup finely shredded celery
½ cup minced peeled apple
½ cup pitted fresh sweet cherries
1 cup shredded cooked ham
Cider vinegar and salad oil
Salt and pepper to taste
Celery stalk

Mix potatoes with celery and apple. Add cherries. In this country canned light sweet cherries, pitted and well drained, make an agreeable substitute. Add ham. Mix a vinegar and oil dressing and add to salad. Amount of salt depends on the saltiness of the ham. Taste before adding. Add pepper at the last moment. This salad is always served with a small celery stalk with leaves laid across the top of the salad, and a few additional cherries around the salad. Serve chilled. Makes 4 to 6 servings.

### VINAIGRETTE S SYOMGOI
#### (Salmon Vinaigrette)

½ pound smoked salmon slices

2 cold potatoes, diced
1 tablespoon capers
1 tablespoon minced onion
¼ cup sliced pitted green olives
1 tablespoon chopped scallions
1 tablespoon vinegar
2 tablespoons salad oil
1 teaspoon prepared mustard
  Pepper to taste
  Fresh dill sprigs (optional)

Cut smoked salmon into even strips. Mix salmon, potatoes, capers, onion, olives, and scallions carefully with a fork. Arrange in a dish and cover with the dressing, made by mixing vinegar with oil, mustard, and pepper. Don't stir into the salad; it will run down and the potatoes and salmon will stay in better shape. Chill before serving. Garnish with dill. Makes 4 to 6 servings.

### GRIBY V SMETANE
#### (Mushrooms in Sour Cream)
1 pound large mushrooms, thickly sliced
3 tablespoons sweet butter
1½ tablespoons all-purpose flour (about)
1 cup dairy sour cream
1 teaspoon fresh lemon juice
  Salt and pepper
  Minced dillweed (optional)

Cook mushrooms in hot butter for 7 minutes, stirring frequently with wooden spoon. Stir in flour. Cook over moderate heat for 5 more minutes. Stir in sour cream and lemon juice. Cook for 10 minutes, stirring frequently, until sauce is of the consistency of heavy cream. The water content of mushrooms varies, and if the sauce appears too thin, stir in a little more flour, ½ teaspoon at a time. If too thick, thin down with a little hot water. Season lightly with salt and pepper. Sprinkle with dill. Serve warm, not bubbling hot. Makes 8 servings.

**Note:** The mushrooms may also be put in a 1-quart baking dish, sprinkled with grated cheese, and lightly browned under the broiler.

### FORSHMAK DRAGOMIR
Forshmak Dragomir *is distinguished from plain Forshmak by the omission of herring and ground boiled meat.*

2 small onions, chopped
3 tablespoons butter or margarine
1 tablespoon all-purpose flour
½ cup consommé
½ cup dairy sour cream
2 drops of hot pepper sauce
1 teaspoon Worcestershire
2 cooked potatoes, peeled and thinly sliced
2 cups cooked ham, cut into thin strips
2 small dill pickles, thinly sliced
1 cup grated sharp Cheddar cheese

Simmer onions in 1 tablespoon of the butter until soft but not brown. Add flour. Cook, stirring constantly, for 5 minutes. Stir in consommé, sour cream, hot pepper sauce, and Worcestershire.

Continue cooking for 10 minutes over low heat, stirring with wooden spoon. Sauté potatoes in remaining butter for 5 minutes. Mix all ingredients except cheese with onion sauce, using a fork to mix. Do not break potatoes. Place in shallow 1-quart baking dish and cover with grated cheese. Bake in preheated very hot oven (450°F.) for 10 to 15 minutes. Makes 4 to 6 servings.

## SOUPS

*Russians love soups and dinner isn't dinner without soup. The heartier soups so favored in Russia are not exactly suited to American tastes, but various beet soups, such as* borsch, *are highly popular in this country. Some of these soups are very easy to make.*

### UKRAINSKI BORSCH
#### (Ukrainian Borsch)
*This soup is a complete meal in itself.*

2 pounds soup meat
½ pound lean smoked pork
  Water
1 bay leaf
6 peppercorns
1 garlic clove
1 bunch of soup greens
8 medium-size beets
1 cup shredded cabbage
2 large onions, chopped
3 large potatoes, peeled and halved
6 tomatoes, peeled, seeded, and chopped
1 cup cooked navy beans
1 tablespoon vinegar
1 teaspoon sugar
5 frankfurters, sliced
1 tablespoon all-purpose flour
1 tablespoon butter
  Dairy sour cream

Put soup meat and pork in deep kettle. Cover with 2½ quarts of water. Bring to boil and cook for about 15 minutes. Skim; add bay leaf, peppercorns, garlic,

and soup greens which should include a carrot, celery, a leek, some parsley, and a parsley root. Simmer, covered, for 2 hours.

Cook 7 of the beets, unpeeled, in the soup or separately. Peel remaining beet and grate. Mix with 3 tablespoons water. This is for coloring, to be added at the last moment. When the beets are tender, peel and dice. Add beets to soup with cabbage, onions, and potatoes. Discard soup greens or cut them up and return to kettle. Add tomatoes, navy beans, vinegar, and sugar. Cook for another hour. Add frankfurters 20 minutes before serving. Skim off excess fat. Cut meat into serving pieces. Thicken soup with flour browned in the butter; bring to a boil. Add beet juice drained from raw beet for red color. Serve very hot in large soup plates, with side plates for meat. A bowl of dairy sour cream accompanies the soup. Makes 3 quarts.

### BORSCH POPROSHCHE
#### (Very Quick Borsch)
*This is admirable either hot or cold.*

2 cans (10½ ounces each) consommé
1 can (13¾ ounces) beef bouillon
  Water
1 large cabbage leaf (optional)
1 teaspoon vinegar
  About 2 cups (one 1-pound can) shoestring beets
1 teaspoon (scant) sugar (optional)
½ cup dairy sour cream
  Salt and pepper to taste
  Chopped dill or parsley

Cook consommé, bouillon, 1 cup water, and cabbage leaf for about 20 minutes. The cabbage leaf gives a special flavor, but it is not necessary. Discard cabbage leaf and add vinegar, beet juice drained from beets, half of beets, and sugar if beet juice and beets have not sweetened soup sufficiently. Be very careful not to oversweeten. If you do, add a few drops of fresh lemon juice. Cook over medium

heat for about 15 minutes. Stir sour cream with about 2 tablespoons water; cream must be at room temperature. Add a little at a time to soup. Heat but do not boil. If the soup is to be served cold, do not add sour cream before chilling. Instead add sour cream just before serving. Season with salt and pepper and sprinkle hot or cold soup with chopped dill. Makes about 2 quarts.

**Note:** For *Vatrushki,* open-face tarts filled with cottage cheese and egg that go with every kind of *borsch,* see page 1572.

### SOLDATSKIE SHCHI
### (Soldiers' Sauerkraut Soup)

2 pounds beef flank
  Water
1 bay leaf
2 tablespoons each of minced dill and parsley
2 carrots, sliced
1 turnip, diced
2 celery stalks, diced
3 large potatoes, peeled and diced
1½ pounds sauerkraut
2 onions, chopped
2 tablespoons bacon fat
1 tablespoon all-purpose flour
  Polish sausage (kielbasa) or 4 frankfurters

Put beef in deep kettle. Cover with 2 quarts of water; add bay leaf, dill, and parsley. Bring to a boil. Simmer, covered, for 1 hour, skimming as needed. Add vegetables. Continue simmering for 1 more hour. Rinse sauerkraut with cold water; drain well. Sauté onions in hot bacon fat for 5 minutes; add sauerkraut. Cook slowly, covered, for 20 minutes. Add to soup. Mix flour with a little cold water until smooth and stir into soup. Cook sausage and cut into 1-inch pieces. Add to soup and simmer for 15 minutes. Skim off excess fat before serving. Garnish with additional minced parsley and dill, or dill alone. Serve with sour cream and plenty of rye bread on the side. Makes about 2 quarts.

### RUSSIAN STURGEON CHAMPAGNE SOUP

*This is the super gourmet soup, reserved for special party occasions. There are no substitutes for the ingredients.*

  Water
1 cod's head and bones
1 small bay leaf
4 white peppercorns
2 celery stalks, sliced
1 small parsley root
2 small onions, chopped
2 pounds cod or haddock
1 teaspoon salt
1 pound fresh sturgeon, skinned, boned, and cut into 6 slices
1 cup dry champagne
  Minced scallions or chives
  Lemon wedges, seeded

Add water to cover the fish head and bones, bay leaf, peppercorns, celery, parsley root, and onions. Bring to a boil and simmer for 1 hour. Skim, add cod,

and simmer, covered, for 1 more hour, adding an extra cup of water and the salt. Line a fine sieve with a piece of cheesecloth. Strain fish stock into a clean kettle. Bring stock to a boil. Add sturgeon. Reduce heat and simmer, covered, over lowest possible heat for 20 minutes. Heat the champagne in a small pan until lukewarm. Add to the soup just before serving. To serve, first place 1 piece of sturgeon into each plate; then add soup. The fish must be handled with great care to keep the pieces whole. A dish of minced young scallions, surrounded by lemon wedges, accompany this soup. Makes about 1½ quarts.

### RASSOLNIK S YACHMENEM
### (Soup with Pickles)

*A very popular home soup*

2 tablespoons medium barley
3 cups water
4 cups (three 10½-ounce cans) consommé
2 cups (one 13¾-ounce can) chicken broth
2 cups diced potatoes
3 tablespoons butter or margarine
1 large onion, minced
1 veal kidney or 5 lamb kidneys, trimmed and sliced
1 tablespoon all-purpose flour
2 small dill pickles, thinly sliced
½ cup dairy sour cream, at room temperature
2 tablespoons minced parsley
  Pepper to taste

Cook barley in the water for about 1 hour. Drain and reserve. In deep kettle combine consommé and chicken broth. Add potatoes and cook until half tender. Heat butter and cook onion in it until soft but not brown. Add kidney and cook, stirring constantly, for 3 minutes. Stir in flour and cook for 3 minutes. Add pickles, barley, and kidneys to soup mixture. Bring to boil. Lower heat and simmer, covered, for 15 minutes. Pour sour cream into large soup tureen. Add a few teaspoons of soup and beat vigorously to prevent curdling. Pour remaining soup over mixture. Sprinkle with parsley and pepper. Makes 2 quarts.

### IABLOCHNII SUP
### (Apple Soup)

*This soup, most popular of all fruit soups in Russia, came originally from Poland. Poland was part of Russia for long, long years and many dishes of Polish origin became part of Russian everyday fare.*

6 large tart apples
3 cups water
1 cup sugar
1 cup dairy sour cream
2 cups light red wine (claret or rosé)
1 tablespoon fresh lemon juice
  Ground cinnamon (optional)

Peel and core apples. Reserve peels. Stew apples in 2 cups of the water until soft. Put stewed apples through sieve. In an-

other pan cook peels in the remaining water, strain, and add to apple purée. Add sugar and sour cream at room temperature, and mix well until quite smooth. Slowly add wine and lemon juice. Serve chilled. If desired, dust very lightly with ground cinnamon. Makes about 2 quarts.

## PIROGI OR PIROZHKI

*Pirogi and their infant brothers pirozhki are savory and plump turnovers made from a dough filled with meat, fish, or vegetable mixture. Pirogi and pirozhki are served with borsch or a meat broth. Pirogi are substantial eating and they make good entrées.*

*The dough used can be plain pastry, although for a big pirogi a yeast dough is preferable since it will be elastic enough to stretch around the filling which must be piled in a high mound. Pirozhki can also be very successfully made from a standard cream-cheese pastry.*

### CABBAGE PIROZHKI

5 cups chopped green cabbage (about 1¼ pounds)
2 tablespoons salt
2 onions, chopped
¼ cup butter or margarine
2 hard-cooked eggs, chopped
1 tablespoon minced dill or parsley
  Standard pastry made with 2 cups flour, unbaked, or Raised Dough for Pirozhki (page 1570)

Mix cabbage with salt and let stand for 15 minutes. Squeeze juice out of cabbage. Put cabbage into a colander and pour boiling water over it. Let drain for 30 minutes. Sauté onions in the butter. Add cabbage and cook slowly for 30 minutes. Do not brown mixture. Add eggs and dill. Cool. Roll pastry ⅛ inch thick and cut pastry into 12 pieces, each 4 x 5 inches. Put filling on half of each piece. Moisten edges with water and fold other half of dough over filling; seal edges. Bake on greased and floured cookie sheet in preheated moderate oven (375°F.) for 25 to 30 minutes, or until *pirozhki* are brown. Makes 12 *pirozhki*.

**Note:** If preferred, put filling into an 8-inch pie pan lined with pastry. Adjust top and bake in preheated hot oven (425°F.) for 25 minutes. Cut into wedges. Makes 6 to 8 servings.

### LIVER PIROZHKI

1 pound calf's liver, cut into thin slices
1 slice of salt pork
1 large onion, chopped
1 thick slice of day-old bread, crust removed
1 tablespoon mixed grated nutmeg and pepper

Vinaigrette s Syomgoi

Teliachia Grudinka s Sousom
iz Tsuetnoi Kapusty,
Kreretok, i Limona

Kompot iz Narezanykh Popolam
Grush i Vishen

1 tablespoon butter
3 tablespoons Madeira
1 tablespoon rum
   Standard pastry made with 2 cups flour, unbaked, or Raised Dough for Pirozhki (below)

Have liver at room temperature. Cut salt pork into 1-inch cubes. Put pork, liver, and onion in heavy pan, cover, and cook over high heat. Stir frequently with a spoon. Cook until liver is brown. Chop the liver and discard the salt pork. Put liver through the meat grinder twice. Soak bread in a little water. Squeeze dry and add to liver. Add nutmeg and pepper, butter, wine, and rum. Mix until very smooth. Chill. Roll, cut, and fill pastry pieces as directed in Cabbage *Pirozhki*. Bake on greased and floured cookie sheet in preheated hot oven (425°F.) for 15 minutes. Lower heat to moderate (350° F.) and bake for another 15 to 20 minutes. Makes 12 *pirozhki*.

### MEAT AND ANCHOVY PIROZHKI

1 onion, chopped
2 tablespoons butter or margarine
1½ cups ground cooked beef
¼ cup thick gravy
2 anchovy fillets, minced
1½ teaspoons minced parsley
1 teaspoon minced dill
1 hard-cooked egg, chopped
   Standard pastry made with 2 cups flour, unbaked, or Raised Dough for Pirozhki (below)

Sauté onion in butter until golden. Add meat and cook for 5 minutes. Add next 5 ingredients. Cool. Roll, cut, fill, and bake pastry as directed in Cabbage *Pirozhki* (above). Makes 12 *pirozhki*.
**Note:** If preferred, put filling into a 9-inch pie pan lined with pastry. Adjust top and bake in preheated hot oven (425°F.) for 25 minutes. Cut into wedges. Makes 6 to 8 servings.

### RAISED DOUGH FOR PIROGI OR PIROZHKI

1 envelope active dry yeast or 1 cake compressed yeast
¼ cup water *
½ cup butter or margarine
1 cup lukewarm milk
1 teaspoon salt
2 teaspoons sugar
4½ to 5 cups sifted all-purpose flour
3 eggs, slightly beaten

*Use very warm water (105°F. to 115° F.) for dry yeast; use lukewarm water (80°F. to 90°F.) for compressed. Sprinkle dry yeast or crumble cake yeast into water. Let stand for a few minutes, then stir until dissolved. Add butter to milk and stir until butter is melted. Add dissolved yeast, salt, and sugar. Beat in 1 cup of the flour. Beat in eggs and then beat in remaining flour until a soft dough is formed. Knead the dough on a lightly floured board until smooth and elastic. Put dough into a greased bowl. Grease the top and let rise in a warm place until doubled in bulk. Punch down and roll into a *pirog* 14 x 18 inches, or into 12 *pirozhki*, each 4 x 5 inches.

## FISH

### SYOMGA S SOUSOM IZ IKRI
### (Salmon Steaks with Caviar Sauce)

2 salmon steaks, 1 inch thick
   Salt and pepper
   Cooking oil
¼ cup butter or margarine
¼ cup all-purpose flour
1½ cups light cream
2 egg yolks
1 teaspoon fresh lemon juice
2 tablespoons caviar *

Rub salmon steaks with a little salt and plenty of pepper; brush with oil. Broil for 8 minutes on each side. When turning steaks, brush unbroiled side with oil. Make cream sauce with butter, flour, and cream; do not season. Beat hot sauce into egg yolks mixed with lemon juice. When fish steaks are broiled, add caviar to the sauce; season to taste with salt. Pour over salmon steaks. Serve at once. Makes 2 servings.
*The caviar in this recipe can perfectly well be good red caviar, large grained and not too salty.

### FILE KAMBALI SO
### SLIVKAMI I LUKOM
### (Fillets of Flounder with Sweet Cream and Scallions)

2 pounds flounder fillets
   Salt
¼ cup fresh bread crumbs
1½ tablespoons butter
1½ cups light cream
¼ cup minced scallions
   Pepper

Sprinkle fillets with salt; let stand for 1 hour. Dry thoroughly with absorbent paper. Cut each fillet across into 3 or 4 pieces, depending on size of fillet. Sauté bread crumbs in hot butter for 5 minutes, add cream, and cook for 5 more minutes. Put fillets in cream and bread-crumb sauce. Add scallions and a little pepper and simmer gently for 10 to 15 minutes. Makes 6 servings.
**Note:** Use a saucepan or casserole that can go to the table. Serve small new potatoes and a plain cucumber salad with this dish, which is a luncheon favorite in Russia.

### PECHENNAIA RYBA
### V SLIVKAKH S SHAFRANOM
### (Porgies Baked in Saffron Cream)

½ teaspoon ground saffron
1 tablespoon water
3 pounds porgies
   Salt and pepper to taste
3 tablespoons all-purpose flour
4 tablespoons butter or margarine
½ cup milk
1½ cups dairy sour cream
   Fine dry bread crumbs

Soak saffron in the water for 30 minutes. Wash fish and pat dry; season inside with salt and pepper. Season 2 tablespoons of the flour with salt and pepper. Coat fish with it. Heat 3 tablespoons of the butter. Cook fish in it for about 4 minutes. Turn and cook for 4 minutes longer. Make a white sauce from the remaining flour, remaining butter, and milk. Strain saffron through a fine sieve and add liquid to white sauce. Stir in sour cream. Put fish in greased shallow baking dish. Pour sauce over it. Sprinkle with bread crumbs. Bake in preheated hot oven (400°F.) for about 10 minutes, or until top is golden-brown. Makes 6 servings.
**Note:** Serve with a salad of cooked green peas and diced fresh cucumber dressed with a very light French dressing.

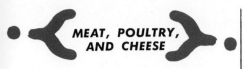

## MEAT, POULTRY, AND CHEESE

### BIF STROGONOV
### (Beef Stroganoff)

1½ pounds top sirloin of beef
1 teaspoon salt
1 teaspoon pepper
3 tablespoons butter or margarine
1 tablespoon all-purpose flour
1 cup beef bouillon
1 teaspoon (scant) hot prepared
   mustard
2 small onions, sliced
3 tablespoons dairy sour cream, at
   room temperature

Remove all fat and gristle from meat. Cut into narrow strips 2 inches long and ½ inch thick. Sprinkle meat strips with the salt and pepper. Melt 1½ tablespoons of the butter. Blend in flour. Stir in bouillon and bring to boil. Stir in mustard. Cook, stirring constantly, until thick and smooth. Heat remaining butter in another saucepan. The butter must be very hot. Brown meat and onions quickly on all sides. Add sour cream to mustard sauce. Bring to boil. Add meat and onions to sauce. Cover saucepan and keep hot for 20 minutes, either over pilot light or on asbestos plate set over lowest possible heat. The mixture must be kept hot, but must not simmer. Before serving, heat through over high heat for about 3 minutes. Makes 3 or 4 servings.

### SVINYE KOTLETY S SOUSOM
### IZ CHERNOSLIV ILI
### KISLYKH VISHEN
### (Breaded Pork Chops with Prune or
### Sour-Cherry Sauce)

6 pork chops, trimmed of fat
   All-purpose flour mixed with a little
   salt
   Fine dry bread crumbs
2 tablespoons butter
1 cup puréed prunes or cherries
1 teaspoon grated lemon rind
½ teaspoon ground cinnamon
¼ teaspoon ground cloves
½ cup water (about)
½ cup port

Drop chops into boiling salted water. Reduce heat and simmer for 15 minutes. Drain chops and dry. Cool. Dust with lightly salted flour and roll in bread crumbs. Sauté chops in hot butter for 5 minutes on each side. Cook gently for 20 minutes, turning once. If using prunes, they should be soaked, well cooked, pitted, and put through a coarse sieve. Canned pitted sour cherries are also good. They should be stewed, finely chopped, and sweetened with 2 tablespoons sugar. Add lemon rind, spices, and the water to purée if it seems too thick. Heat and add wine. Bring to boil. Pour over chops and serve very hot. Makes 6 servings.

### TELIACHIA GRUDINKA S SOUSOM
### IZ TSVETNOI KAPUSTY,
### KREVETOK, I LIMONA
### (Breast of Veal with Cauliflower, Shrimps,
### and Lemon Sauce)

4-pound breast of veal
3 to 4 cups boiling salted water
3 onions, sliced
1 carrot, sliced
4 parsley sprigs
   Grated rind of ½ lemon
2 tablespoons butter or margarine
   Pepper to taste
   All-purpose flour
2 tablespoons fresh lemon juice
½ cup dry white wine
1 pound medium-size shrimps, cooked
   and shelled
1 medium cauliflower, broken into
   flowerets and cooked
½ cup cooked peas
   Parsley

Cut meat into pieces as for stew. Drop meat into boiling salted water. Bring to a rolling boil and cook for 3 minutes. Add onions, carrot, parsley sprigs, lemon rind, butter, and pepper. Simmer, covered, for 1 to 1½ hours, or until veal is tender. Remove veal from broth and keep warm. Strain broth and heat. Thicken with flour mixed with a little water to a smooth paste. Add lemon juice and simmer for about 5 minutes. Add veal, wine, and shrimps. Heat through thoroughly.

Arrange veal and shrimps in deep serving platter. Top with sauce. Garnish with parsley. If desired, surround veal and shrimps with cooked cauliflowerets and peas. Makes 6 servings.

### SHASHLIK

*Shashlik*, which comes from the Caucasus, is almost as well known nowadays outside Russia as in Russia. True classic *shashlik* permits only pieces of fine lamb, or mutton, threaded on long skewers, broiled and served at once. The real secret of fine *shashlik* is an overnight soaking in pomegranate juice. Nothing else is as good. This is easy in the Caucasus where every backyard has its own pomegranate tree. The juice from the fruit also makes a wonderful salad dressing. Pomegranate juice can be bought bottled here in gourmet food stores. If pomegranate juice is unavailable, a vinegar and wine mixture is a reasonably satisfactory replacement. To obtain fresh pomegranate juice, cut pomegranate into halves and press out juice on a reamer.

3-pound leg of lamb, boned
1 onion, chopped
1 garlic clove, crushed
⅔ cup vinegar and ½ cup red wine or
   1½ cups fresh or bottled
   pomegranate juice
   Salt to taste
½ cup cooking oil
   Pepper to taste

Cut lamb into pieces about 1½ inches thick and 2 inches square. Trim off all fat. Save some of the fat and cut into thin slices. Place pieces of lamb in bowl. Add onion and garlic, mix well, and set aside. Dilute vinegar with ⅓ cup water. Add wine and salt. Bring to boil, cool, then pour over lamb pieces. When using pomegranate juice, do not heat, just pour juice over meat. Put in cool, not cold, place for 4 hours.

Dry each piece of lamb carefully. Brush pieces of meat with oil. Thread meat onto long *shashlik* skewers with a slice of lamb fat between each 2 pieces of meat. Use about 4 pieces per skewer. A cube of bread at the end of the skewer keeps the meat from sliding off when handled. Brush the bread with oil. Sprinkle with pepper. Broil for 12 to 20 minutes under very high heat, until lamb is cooked through. Turn once and baste with juice that has run off.

The correct way to serve *shashlik* is to slip meat off skewer onto a hot plate for each person being served. Makes 6 servings.

### SIBIRSKIE PELMENI
### (Siberian Dumplings)

*In Siberia every housewife makes these dumplings in great big batches, wraps them in a cloth, and puts them out on the windowsill to freeze. When needed, some are taken in, defrosted, then cooked in boiling water. Actually pelmeni are the Russian form of Italian ravioli, with a different dough and quite different filling.*

2 cups sifted all-purpose flour
1 teaspoon salt
3 egg yolks
½ cup (about) water
   Filling
1 egg white

Sift flour and salt together. Mix with egg yolks and enough water to make a stiff paste. Knead well on lightly floured board and set aside for 1 hour. Roll out as thin as possible on lightly floured board. Cut either rounds or squares of pastry 3 or 3½ inches across. Put 1 heaping teaspoon of Filling on each piece of pastry. Moisten edges of pastry with slightly beaten egg white; fold over to form crescents, or triangles if pastry is cut into squares. Pinch edges together. If possible, chill overnight in refrigerator. Drop *pelmeni*, a few at a time, into a large kettle of boiling water. Cook at a rolling boil for 15 minutes; they will float to top when done. Remove with slotted spoon, and drain. Place on a hot platter and serve very hot. In Siberia a bowl of mild vinegar goes with the *pelmeni*, but drawn butter may suit your taste better. Makes about 20.

### Farsh Dlia Sibirskikh Pelmenei
### (Pelmeni Filling)

¾ pound beef round, ground
2 ounces beef suet
1 onion, chopped

2 tablespoons water
½ teaspoon salt
¼ teaspoon pepper

Put beef, suet, and onion through fine blade of food chopper. Beat in water, salt, and pepper. Use mixture in *pelmeni*. Makes about 1¾ cups filling.

### VATRUSHKI
### (Cheese and Egg Tart)

1 pound dry pot cheese
1 tablespoon dairy sour cream
½ teaspoon sugar
1 teaspoon salt
2 eggs, slightly beaten
  Pastry made with 2 cups flour, unbaked
1 egg yolk

Beat or sieve cheese. Add sour cream, sugar, salt, and eggs. Mix thoroughly and set aside to chill for 30 minutes. Line 8 or 9 round tart pans (3½ inches in diameter) with pastry. Fill with cheese mixture. Have cheese smooth on top. Brush with egg yolk mixed with a little water. Bake in preheated hot oven (425° F.) for 15 minutes; lower heat to moderate (350°F.) and bake for 15 minutes longer. Serve warm. Makes 8 to 9 *vatrushki*.

■ **Other Fillings**—Sauté scallions in butter; mix with cooked rice and 2 tablespoons dairy sour cream to each 1 cup rice.

Mix chopped cooked carrots and minced chives with enough thick white sauce to make a thick mixture. Flavor with a dash of ground nutmeg.

Sauté chopped mushrooms and onions in butter and mix with cooked or baked buckwheat groats.

### SYRNIKI
### (Fried Cheese Cakes)

*Skim-milk cottage cheese and farmer's cheese are also suited to this recipe; the latter does not need to be sieved.*

1 pound very dry pot cheese
½ teaspoon salt
2 eggs, lightly beaten
½ cup all-purpose flour
  Butter
  Dairy sour cream
  Fresh dill, minced

Put cheese through food mill or sieve, or pound smooth. Beat in salt, eggs, and flour until thoroughly mixed and very smooth. Chill for 2 hours. To shape, use a little dough at a time, keeping remainder in refrigerator. With floured hands, shape dough into flat round 2-inch cakes. Fry over medium heat in hot butter for 10 minutes. Lower heat and cook for another 10 to 15 minutes. Turn cakes once during each frying time to brown on both sides. Serve with sour cream and dill. Makes 10 to 12 cakes, depending on size.

■ **Variation**—Add 1 more tablespoon all-purpose flour to basic mixture. Pat mix-

ture into greased shallow baking dish. Sprinkle with fine bread crumbs and dot with butter. Bake in preheated moderate oven (375°F.) for 20 to 30 minutes, or until browned. Serve with a creamed vegetable or as a dessert with a fruit compote.

# VEGETABLES

*Vegetables are served chiefly as a separate course or as special salads accompanying boiled or roast meat. They also come to table as part of the* zakuski *course, the appetizers. Northern districts of Russia rely on root vegetables during the cold months, and the first fresh lettuce, dressed with sour cream, is greeted as a veritable* praznik, *a real holiday treat.*

### SALAT IZ MORKOVI I KISLOI KAPUSTY
### (Carrot and Sauerkraut Salad)

In Russia this is a favorite winter salad to serve with meat or fish.

Drain 2 cups sauerkraut thoroughly, and chill. Shred raw carrots fine or grate them on a coarse grater until you have 1 cup. Mix the carrots with sauerkraut and 2 tablespoons of olive or salad oil. Makes 4 servings.

### SALAT IZ REPY I OGURTZOV
### (Turnip and Cucumber Salad)

*The younger the turnips, the better this salad will be. The best cucumbers to use for this and for other Russian salads are the small sweet cucumbers usually sold here for pickling.*

3 cups sliced cooked white turnips
2 cups sliced cucumbers
  Fresh lemon juice
1 cup Sour-Cream Dressing

Have turnips chilled. Peel cucumbers and slice them about ½ inch thick. Squeeze a little lemon juice over the turnips. Mix the turnips, cucumbers, and Dressing together. Makes 6 servings.

**Note:** Russians like to eat this salad with baked fish or broiled fish.

### SOUS IZ SMETANY
### (Plain Sour-Cream Dressing)

1 teaspoon salt
¼ teaspoon pepper
1 teaspoon sugar
1 tablespoon salad or olive oil
1 tablespoon vinegar
1 cup dairy sour cream

Mix together all the ingredients except sour cream. Let stand for 5 minutes, then add 2 tablespoons of the cream and stir hard until well mixed. Add the remainder of the cream and stir until smooth. If the cream is very thick, use 1 tablespoon of water with it, or you can add a little more of the vinegar if it isn't too sharp. Makes about 1 cup.

### KARTOFEL' S ANCHOUSAMI
### (Scalloped Potatoes with Anchovies)

2 onions, chopped
  Butter
8 anchovy fillets, drained and finely minced (or more to taste)
6 cups cooked potatoes, sliced
1½ cups dairy sour cream
  Salt and pepper
  Fine dry bread crumbs

Sauté onions in 2 tablespoons of the butter. Add anchovies and cook for 2 minutes. Butter an ovenproof dish. Spread it with a layer of potatoes, moisten with a little of the sour cream, then add a layer of the anchovies and onions. Sprinkle lightly with salt and pepper. Repeat until dish is full. Top with bread crumbs and 1 tablespoon melted butter. Brown in preheated medium oven (350°F.) for 30 minutes. Makes 6 servings.

**Note:** Serve with a bland green salad.

### SVEZHIYE PODZHARENNYYE OGURTZY
### (Braised Cucumbers)

4 small cucumbers *
  Salt
2 tablespoons butter
1 small onion, chopped
2 tablespoons all-purpose flour
¼ cup dairy sour cream
  Pepper and grated nutmeg

Peel cucumbers and cut each one lengthwise into 4 slices. Remove some of the seeds. Sprinkle cucumbers lightly with salt and let stand for 20 minutes. Dry well with a towel. Heat 1 tablespoon butter; add cucumbers and sauté for 15 to 20 minutes. Sauté onion in remaining butter until golden-brown. Add flour to onion and cook for 5 minutes; then add cucumbers. Stir in sour cream. Boil up once. Season with freshly ground pepper to taste and a dash of nutmeg. Simmer for 5 minutes. Makes 4 to 6 servings.

*The cucumbers should be young and firm, with small seeds.

**Note:** Serve these with roast lamb.

### SPARZHA ZAPECHENNAYA S
### SUKHARYAMI I SLIVKAMI
### (Asparagus Baked with Bread Crumbs and Cream)

2 pounds asparagus
  Sugar and salt to taste
1 cup soft bread crumbs
  Butter
1 tablespoon fresh lemon juice
  Pepper
1 cup light cream

Cook asparagus until just soft, adding a little sugar as well as salt to the water in which you cook the asparagus. Drain for 1 hour. Cut off stalks, leaving only the really soft parts. Place these in a buttered ovenproof dish. Use a dish you can serve at table. Sauté bread crumbs in 3 tablespoons butter. Sprinkle the lemon juice on the asparagus; dust with pepper and cover with half the bread crumbs. Add cream; cover with rest of bread crumbs. Bake in preheated hot oven (400°F.) for 15 minutes. Makes 6 servings.

### OLAD'I S LUKOM
### (Baked Onion Dumplings)

6 large onions
1 tablespoon butter
2 cups consommé
Salt and pepper
Standard pastry made with 2 cups flour

With a thin skewer pierce the onions carefully in 3 or 4 places. Put in cold salted water and bring to a boil. Drain onions and put them in a pot with the butter and consommé. Bring to a boil and simmer until tender. The onions must remain whole. When they are done, drain them thoroughly for 1 hour. Dry in a towel and dust them with salt and pepper to taste. Wrap onions in pastry squares rolled to ⅛-inch thickness as you would wrap an apple for apple dumplings. Refrigerate for 30 minutes. Bake in preheated hot oven (425°F.) for 20 minutes. Serve very hot. Makes 6 servings.

**Note:** Personally I consider this one of our finest Russian contributions to vegetable cookery. They are absolutely wonderful with roast lamb.

### PERTZY FARSHIROVANNYE TIORTOI MORKOV'YU
### (Green Peppers Stuffed with Grated Carrots)

*This is a favorite dish from the Caucasus.*

4 green peppers
2½ cups grated carrots*
2 tablespoons grated onion
4 tablespoons butter
Salt and pepper
3 tablespoons fine dry bread crumbs
2 tablespoons grated cheese

Scald the peppers for about 10 minutes; cut off tops, scoop out seeds and white membrane. Mix the grated carrots and onion with 2 tablespoons softened butter and 1 tablespoon bread crumbs. Season with salt and pepper to taste. Stuff peppers with this mixture and top stuffing with remaining bread crumbs and cheese. Dot with remaining butter. Put in well-buttered baking dish and bake in preheated moderate oven (350°F.) for 30 to 40 minutes. Serve from dish in which baked. Makes 4 servings.

*Corn, freshly grated or canned, may be substituted for the carrot. In this case add a little water to moisten the corn.

### GRECHNEVAIA KASHA
### (Buckwheat Porridge)

*The basic Russian cereal. Since in America buckwheat groats are usually sold packaged, package directions may be followed for cooking.*

1 cup large-grained buckwheat groats *
1 tablespoon butter

5 cups boiling water (about)
Salt to taste

In skillet cook groats in hot butter over medium heat for 10 minutes, stirring constantly. Transfer groats to 2-quart casserole. Add boiling water to cover, and salt. Bake, covered, in preheated hot oven (400°F.) for 15 minutes. Lower heat to moderate (350°F.) and stir. Replace cover and continue to cook for 45 minutes, or until groats are tender, adding a little more water if necessary. Makes 6 to 8 servings.

*If large-grained groats are not available, use medium groats.

## SAUCE

### SOUS IZ KHRENA
### (Horseradish Sauce)

1 tablespoon mayonnaise
1½ cups dairy sour cream
½ cup freshly grated horseradish*
1 teaspoon salt
2 teaspoons sugar
1 tablespoon vinegar*

Mix all ingredients until smooth. Put into serving bowl and chill for at least 6 hours. Makes about 1½ cups.

*If using bottled horseradish omit vinegar.

**Note:** This is a very popular sauce for boiled or braised meat or fish.

### SPETSIALNI RUSSKI SOUS DLIA ZHARENOI GOVIADINI
### (Special Russian Sauce for American Pot Roast)

Prepare pot roast as usual but it should be well browned. When there is plenty of dark gravy in kettle, skim off fat and thicken with a flour-and-water paste.

Add 2 tablespoons minced pitted green olives and 2 tablespoons of juice from any spiced fruit such as peaches, pears, or plums to gravy. Bring to boil. Just before serving, add dark rum to taste. Don't let gravy boil after rum is added.

## DESSERTS

### KISSEL

*The best known Russian dessert, which is a fruit purée thickened with cornstarch or potato flour, chilled, and served with cream. The consistency of kissel should be thinner and softer than that of a gelatin dessert. This form of fruit porridge is not exclusive to Russia, but is also popular in all of Scandinavia. Kissel is an excellent dessert, especially when made with cranberries or other tart berries. Any ripe berries, frozen berries, or canned berries can be used for kissel. Frozen or canned berries need not be sweetened.*

Defrost frozen berries. Or cook any ripe berries with water to cover until fruit is tender. Sweeten to taste. Strain berries through food mill or sieve. The purée should be of the consistency of heavy cream. Measure purée. For each cup of purée, allow 2 to 3 teaspoons cornstarch or potato flour, depending on thickness desired. Blend cornstarch with a little water to make a smooth paste. Reheat purée. Stir in starch. Cook over medium heat, stirring constantly, until purée is thickened and clear. Pour into glass serving dish and chill thoroughly. Serve with heavy cream. Allow ½ to ¾ cup *kissel* for each serving.

### KHVOROST
### (Twigs)

3 eggs
3½ cups sifted all-purpose flour
½ cup water
3 tablespoons gin, rye whisky, or rum
Sugar
½ teaspoon salt
Fat for deep frying
Ground cinnamon or nutmeg *

Beat eggs into flour, one at a time. Add water, gin, ¼ cup sugar, and salt. Knead dough on floured board until blended. Let stand for 15 minutes. Roll out very thin on lightly floured board. Cut into strips (7 x 1½ inches). Cut a small lengthwise slit 1 inch from one end of each strip. Twist the other end of strip through this slit, so you have a loop. Heat fat until you see a faint bluish smoke (375°F. on a frying thermometer). Drop 8 or 10 loops into oil together. Cook for about 2 minutes, or until slightly browned. Remove *khvorost* with slotted spoon and drain well on paper towels. Serve piled on a hot platter. Sprinkle generously with sugar and cinnamon. Makes 18 to 20.

* Cinnamon is used most often in Russia.

### KOMPOT IZ NAREZANYKH POPOLAM GRUSH I VISHEN
### (Pear Halves and Cherry Compote)

Use cooked fresh or canned pear halves and cooked fresh or canned pitted sweet cherries in equal quantities. Combine fruit syrups. Add ¼ teaspoon vanilla extract and 2 drops of almond extract for each 1 to 1½ cups syrup. Pile cherries in middle of a glass serving dish. Arrange pear halves around them. Pour over just enough syrup to cover fruits. Chill thoroughly. Serve with plain heavy cream and thin plain cookies.

### KOMPOT IZ APELSIN I CHERNOSLIV
### (Prune-Orange Compote)

In glass serving dish combine cooked pitted prunes and fresh orange sections.

Sprinkle with grated orange peel. Moisten with a little fresh orange juice or water in which the prunes were cooked. Sweeten to taste. Chill before serving.

### RUSSKII IABLOCHNII PIROG
#### (Apple Pie)

    8  large apples, peeled, cored, and
         thinly sliced
    ½  cup raisins
    ½  cup (or more) sugar
    3  tablespoons dry wine
 1½  teaspoons grated orange rind
    ¼  cup finely ground blanched almonds
    ½  teaspoon almond extract
    2  tablespoons currant jelly
         Standard pastry for 2-crust 9-inch pie,
         unbaked

Combine apples, raisins, sugar, wine, orange rind, almonds, and almond extract. Cook over low heat for 15 minutes, stirring constantly. If apples are dry add a couple of tablespoons of water. Stir in jelly when mixture is thick and apples are done; cool. Fill pastry-lined pie pan with mixture and cover with top crust. Cut two small slits in top crust. Bake in preheated moderate oven (375°F.) for 45 to 60 minutes. Serve warm. Makes 6 to 8 servings.

### IABLOCHNII KREM
#### (Cream of Apples)

*This is usually a company dessert. It should be made in a mold of fancy shape.*

 2½  pounds cooking apples, cored
         Water
    2  egg whites
    2  envelopes unflavored gelatin
    1  tablespoon grated lemon rind
    ½  cup sugar
    1  teaspoon vanilla extract
    2  tablespoons rum
    1  cup heavy cream

Cook apples in ½ cup water until tender. Add more water if apples are dry, but liquid should be almost all absorbed when apples are done. Put apples through food mill or coarse sieve. There should be 3 cups thick apple sauce. Cool. Beat egg whites until stiff. Fold into cooled apple pulp and beat again until quite stiff. Soften gelatin in ½ cup cold water. Let stand for a few minutes. Add ½ cup boiling water and the lemon rind. Chill until mixture begins to set. Combine with apple mixture; add sugar, vanilla, and rum. Whip cream until it holds soft peaks. Fold cream into apple mixture. Pour into a well-chilled 2-quart mold. Chill for at least 4 hours. Unmold and serve with a rum-flavored thin custard sauce. Makes 8 servings.

### CHERRY OR BLUEBERRY VARENIKI

Pitted cherries or fresh blueberries are used in fruit *vareniki*. The same dough as used for Siberian Pelmeni (page 1571) is used. Dust fruit with very small amount of well-sugared all-purpose flour. Add ½ teaspoon almond extract to cherry mix-

ture. Proceed as with Pelmeni, 1 heaping teaspoon of fruit on each portion of dough. Drop not more than 6 *vareniki* at a time into a kettle of boiling water. Serve hot with a bowl of sugar, dish of fruit juice, and some sweet cream.

### GUREEVSKAIA KASHA
#### (Guriev Pudding)

*A very old traditional Russian dessert.*

    2  cups shelled walnuts
    3  cups milk
    3  cups light cream
    ½  teaspoon salt
    ¾  cup semolina or farina
    ½  cup sugar
    ½  cup seedless raisins,
         chopped
    ½  teaspoon almond extract
    1  cup mixed candied fruits,
         coarsely chopped
         Apricot jam
         Fine bread crumbs
         Sugar

Put walnuts through a nut grinder, pound in a mortar, or whirl in a blender. Pour milk and cream into shallow pan, an enamelware pan preferably. Bring mixture to a boil and sprinkle in the semolina. Cook for 7 minutes, stirring constantly with a wooden spoon. Remove from stove and add sugar, nuts, raisins, and almond extract. Put a layer of the cooked semolina in a bowl and top it with some of the chopped fruit. Repeat until there are 6 layers, with candied fruit on top. Spread a little apricot jam on top of each layer of semolina. (The jam is a substitute for the milk skins which is the authentic Russian ingredient for this dessert. The milk is cooked very slowly and as soon as a skin forms it is taken off and laid on a plate. This classic way of making Guriev Pudding is definitely not to the American taste.) Sprinkle with bread crumbs and sugar. Serve warm. Makes 8 servings.

**Note:** Glacé fruits, apricots, cherries, peaches, pears, etc., are even better than plain sugared candied fruit.

**RUTABAGA**—A root vegetable which belongs to the Mustard family and is closely related to cabbage, cauliflower, Brussels sprouts, kale, kohlrabi, mustard, and turnips. Rutabaga is larger than the turnip, has smooth yellowish skin and flesh, and smooth leaves. The flesh has a typical sweet flavor. There are white varieties of rutabaga, but the yellow is the best known.

Rutabagas are also known as Swedish turnips or swedes, and the name comes from a Swedish word. It is a cold-weather vegetable and one of the staple crops of northern Europe, where it has nourished countries through wars and famines. As recently as World War II, many would

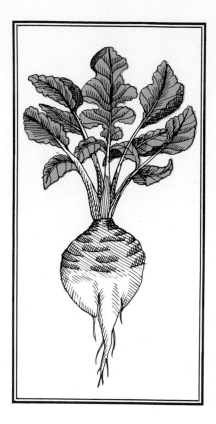

not have survived without rutabagas.

Rutabagas are admittedly not one of the more delicate vegetables. But well cooked, they add nourishment and robustness to winter meals. They can be cooked in any way turnips are cooked.

*Availability and Purchasing Guide*—In season from July to April. Look for smooth, firm roots that are heavy for their size. Some may be coated with a thin layer of paraffin to prevent spoilage.

*Storage*—Store in a dry, well-ventilated place, about 55°F., or refrigerate. Rutabagas will keep for about 1 month.

*Nutritive Food Values*—Some vitamin A and a small amount of vitamin C.

☐  3½ ounces, boiled and drained =
       35 calories.

*Basic Preparation*—Wash and pare; slice or dice.

☐  **To Boil**—Cook, covered, in 1 inch of boiling salted water for 25 to 40 minutes, or until tender. Drain; add butter or margarine; season with salt and pepper.

A teaspoon of sugar added to cooking water improves the flavor. Rutabagas are good creamed with minced onion or chives and a dash of Worcestershire.

☐  **To Freeze**—Cook rutabagas as above; mash. Cool, and spoon into freezer containers, allowing ½-inch headspace.

Can also be cut raw into cubes or slices. Scald in boiling water for 3 minutes. Chill in ice water. Drain; pack in freezer containers with ½-inch headspace. Seal.

## RUTABAGA WITH SALT PORK

4 cups cubed rutabaga
¼ pound salt pork, finely chopped
1 onion, minced
Salt and pepper to taste

Cook rutabaga in boiling water until tender. Fry pork until brown and crisp; add onion and cook for a few minutes longer. Add drained rutabaga. Cook for 5 minutes, stirring often to brown cubes slightly. Season with salt and pepper. Makes 4 to 6 servings.

## RUTABAGA AU GRATIN

6 tablespoons butter or margarine
¼ cup all-purpose flour
2 cups milk
1 cup shredded sharp Cheddar cheese
Salt and pepper to taste
4 cups diced cooked rutabaga
½ cup soft bread crumbs

Melt ¼ cup butter and stir in flour. Gradually stir in milk. Cook over low heat, stirring constantly, until smooth and thick. Add cheese and stir until melted. Season with salt and pepper. Pour sauce over rutabaga in 1½ quart shallow baking dish. Mix crumbs with remaining butter and sprinkle over top. Bake in preheated hot oven (400°F.) for about 15 minutes. Makes 6 servings.

## MASHED RUTABAGA WITH ONION

1 medium rutabaga
2 onions
2 tablespoons butter or margarine
½ teaspoon salt
¼ teaspoon pepper

Cook rutabaga and onions in small amount of boiling salted water until tender. Drain. Mash; add butter and seasonings and beat well. Makes 4 to 6 servings.

**RYE**—A hardy annual cereal grass, *Secale cereale,* closely allied to wheat. It grows from four to six feet high and looks very much like wheat growing in the fields. Rye is the fifth most important cereal crop in the United States. The seeds are used to make flour, malt liquors, whisky, Holland gin, and a Russian drink, *kvass.*

Rye is also used as an animal fodder. Rye flour is usually mixed with wheat flour to make rye breads. These are especially popular with people of central and northern European and Slavic origin, countries where rye bread is a basic food. Pumpernickel bread, the heavy dark loaf, is made of all rye flour.

Rye can be grown in colder and damper climates than can wheat. It is thought that rye may have grown as a weed in parts of Asia where wheat was cultivated thousands of years ago. Ancient civilizations in warm climates, such as the Egyptian, did not seem to grow rye,

but there are early traces of the grain in cold northern Europe. During Roman times it flourished in central Europe. Countries that could grow wheat easily looked down on its harsher cousin, rye. Theoprastus, a Roman naturalist who probably lived in the 3rd or 4th century B.C., thought that if wheat was planted on poor soils it would turn into rye.

This feeling by wheat eaters that rye was somehow inferior carried over into England. Part of the reason may be that rye flour was traditionally a part of the bread that was eaten by the poor.

The early Americans who came to New England found rye to be a more successful crop than wheat. Corn, grown first by the Indians, was the most important food of these early settlers, and the staple bread, known as rye'n'Injun, was made from rye flour and cornmeal. The Puritans, according to an 18th-century writer, were fond of saying: "Brown bread and the Gospel is good fare."

Rye flour can be used alone or combined with wheat flour. The rye flour makes a stickier and less-elastic dough than wheat. It is used to make breads, rolls, muffins, crackers.

*Availability*—Rye flour is available in food stores and health-food stores. It is sold as dark, light, medium, or unspecified rye flour. Rye grits and cream of rye are also available, as are rye wafers.

*Storage*—Whole rye flours or any other whole-rye products which contain the rye germ should be refrigerated.

☐ Refrigerator shelf: 6 months

*Nutritive Food Values*—A source of energy with small amounts of protein, potassium, and B vitamins.

☐ Whole-grain, 3½ ounces = 334 calories

☐ Light flour, 3½ ounces = 357 calories

☐ Medium flour, 3½ ounces = 350 calories

☐ Dark flour, 3½ ounces = 327 calories

☐ Wafers, whole-grain, 3½ ounces = 344 calories

## FINNISH BREAD

1½ cups hot water
1 tablespoon sugar
1 tablespoon salt
2 tablespoons margarine
½ cup water *
1 package active dry yeast or 1 cake compressed yeast
3 cups rye flour
2½ cups (about) unsifted all-purpose flour

Measure hot water into a large mixing bowl. Stir in sugar, salt, and margarine. Cool to lukewarm. Measure ½ cup water into small warm bowl. *Use very warm water (105°F. to 115°F.) for dry yeast; use lukewarm (80°F. to 90°F.) for com-

pressed. Sprinkle or crumple yeast into water. Let stand for a few minutes, then stir until dissolved. Add yeast mixture and rye flour to first mixture. Beat until smooth. Add 2 cups all-purpose flour and mix well. Add enough additional flour to make a soft dough. Turn out onto lightly floured board and knead until smooth and elastic, 8 to 10 minutes. Place in greased bowl, turning to grease all sides. Cover; let rise in warm place, free from draft, until doubled in bulk, about 45 minutes. Punch dough down; divide into halves. Shape into 2 loaves. Place in greased loaf pans (9 x 5 x 3 inches). Cover; let rise in warm place, free from draft, until doubled in bulk, about 40 minutes. Bake in preheated hot oven (400°F.) for about 30 minutes, or until done. Serve warm with honey. Makes 2 loaves.

## RYE-HONEY COOKIES

2 cups honey
1 cup rye flour
1 cup cake flour
1 teaspoon ground ginger

Heat honey until liquid. Sift together rye flour, cake flour, and ginger. Place flour in skillet and heat gently. The flour must not change color in any way. Gradually stir flour into hot honey. Beat vigorously with a large spoon until the dough clears the spoon. Cool until stiff enough to roll. Roll the dough paper-thin on floured board and cut into 2-inch rounds. Bake on greased cookie sheets in preheated moderate oven (350°F.) for 10 to 12 minutes, or until well browned. Makes about 8 dozen cookies. **Note:** This is a hard, chewy, flat cookie.

## SWEDISH RYE COOKIES

1 cup sifted all-purpose flour
1 cup sifted rye flour
½ teaspoon salt
¾ cup soft butter
½ cup sugar
2 teaspoons grated orange rind

Sift together all-purpose flour, rye flour, and salt. Cream butter and sugar thoroughly with orange rind. Mix in flour until smooth dough forms. Wrap in wax paper or aluminum foil and chill until easy to handle: for 2 hours in refrigerator or 30 minutes in freezing compartment. Divide dough into halves; roll out between sheets of wax paper or aluminum foil to ⅛-inch thickness. Cut with floured 2½-inch doughnut cutter. Put on ungreased cookie sheet and prick with fork several times. Bake in preheated slow oven (325°F.) for 8 to 10 minutes. Watch carefully; these burn easily. Makes 4 dozen.

**SABAYON**—A dessert sauce or simple dessert made of sugar, beaten eggs or egg yolks, and wine or liqueur or orange and lemon juice and grated rind. A variation containing whipped cream is also made. Sabayon is actually the French name for the Italian zabaglione or Austrian weinschaum. For a Sabayon recipe see page 1629.

**SABLEFISH**—A salt-water fish found in Pacific waters, it is also called the coalfish or skil. This fish resembles the black ocean cod or hake. It is a flat fish with oyster-white meat and a delicate flavor and can be broiled, baked, sautéed, or poached. It is also commercially kippered or smoked and may be marketed as "kippered" or "smoked cod" or "Alaskan smoked black cod." Smoked sablefish, served like smoked salmon, is excellent for appetizers and can be cooked in any of the ways smoked haddock is cooked.

**Availability**—Generally available on the West Coast only, fresh, whole and in steaks and fillets; and smoked or kippered.

**Purchasing Guide**—See Red Snapper, page 1540.

**Storage**—See Red Snapper, page 1540.

**Nutritive Food Values**—Good source of protein and fat.

☐ Fresh, 3½ ounces, raw = 190 calories

**Basic Preparation**—See Red Snapper, page 1540.

Smoked sablefish can be broiled as fresh sablefish is. Brush with oil first. Serve with lemon quarters.

**BAKED SABLEFISH CREOLE**

2-pound piece of fresh sablefish
   Salt and pepper
½ cup red wine
1 medium onion, chopped
1 garlic clove, minced
¼ cup butter or margarine
1 can (1 pound) tomatoes
   Chopped parsley

Put fish in buttered shallow baking dish and sprinkle with salt and pepper. Add wine. Bake in preheated hot oven (400°F.) for about 25 minutes, basting several times with the wine in the bottom of the dish. Cook onion and garlic in the butter for 2 or 3 minutes. Add the tomatoes and simmer for 15 to 20 minutes. Season to taste and serve poured around the fish. Top with parsley. Makes 4 to 6 servings.

**SACCHARIN**—A crystalline chemical used alone or in combination with other chemicals to add sweetness to foods without the addition of sugar. Believed to be the first of the artificial sweeteners, it is very sweet, 250 to 300 times as sweet as sugar. It has a slight aftertaste of bitter almond and sometimes leaves a dryness in the throat. Since it has no food value, it is useful in both diabetic and low-calorie diets.

**SADDLE**—In culinary usage the word is applied to a meat cut, most often of venison, mutton, or lamb, taken from below the last ribs to the legs on both sides and including the loins. It is a luxurious cut and may be roasted either bone-in or boned.

The term "saddle of hare," found in English literature, refers to a cut extending from the base of the hare's shoulder to the tail.

## SAFFLOWER or BASTARD SAFFRON

**SAFFLOWER or BASTARD SAFFRON**—An Old World herb, *Carthamus tinctorius,* resembling a thistle, with large vivid red or orange flowers. Native to the East Indies, it is cultivated in southern Europe and in Egypt. The flowers are used as the basis of a dye widely used in the Orient for dyeing silks and cottons.

An edible oil is expressed from the white seeds which remain when the blossoms fade. Safflower oil is light, flavorless, and colorless. It does not solidify under refrigeration as do many other oils so it is good for salad dressings and marinades, as well as for frying and other recipes in which oil is an ingredient. Safflower oil is available in food stores.

**SAFFRON**—A small crocus, *Crocus saturis,* with purple flowers. There are three deep orange-yellow stigmas, or filaments, in the center of each tiny blossom. These are aromatic when dried, with a pungent taste, and they are used to add flavor and color in cooking. The stigmas are so tiny they must be picked by hand, and it takes at least 4,000 of them to produce one ounce of saffron, which accounts for its high price. They are dried in a kiln, either loosely or between paper-covered boards. As a cooking spice, saffron comes either in the shape of the dried filament shreds or it is ground. Saffron colors any food a bright yellow.

Saffron appears to have come from the Near East. Its name would bear this out, for it is an adaptation of the Arabic word *za'faran,* "yellow."

Since antiquity, the deep-yellow color of saffron and its aromatic properties have been used for dyeing, for flavoring foods, and for medicinal purposes. As early as 4,000 B.C., the Assyrians used it as a medicine, and so did the Egyptians, who also anointed their royalty with saffron-tinted oil. In the Song of Solomon (4:14) in the Bible, saffron is mentioned as one of the chief spices. The gods and goddesses of the ancient Greeks were dressed in saffron-colored robes. Greeks and Romans made saffron into a fragrant essence which was sprinkled in streets and theaters to sweeten the air, and also used as a personal cosmetic.

The Roman legions introduced saffron into England. It became tremendously popular there both as a dyestuff and as a food flavoring. A 14-century cook book lists saffron as an ingredient in more than half its recipes. At first saffron was grown in monastery and manor gardens, but by the 16th century it had become a commercial crop for export.

The different varieties of saffron have varying degrees of pungency: Italian saffron, for instance, is stronger than the Spanish saffron which is imported into the United States.

Either whole or ground, saffron should be used with discretion, not because of its price, but because a little saffron goes a very long way. It gives a distinctive color to breads and cakes, and is much in favor with rice dishes, especially those of Spain, Italy, the Near East, and India, where saffron is much used. Saffron also enhances cream soups, sauces, potatoes, and veal and chicken dishes.

*Availability*—Whole or ground Spanish saffron is available in some food stores, in gourmet stores, and in stores catering to people of Mediterranean descent. Most drugstores also carry it.

### SAFFRON VEAL

⅛ to ¼ teaspoon whole or ground saffron (amount depends on taste)
1 tablespoon hot water
2 pounds veal steak, cut into ½-inch strips
¼ cup butter or margarine
½ teaspoon salt
¼ teaspoon pepper
1 tablespoon instant minced onion
¼ cup hot bouillon
2 cups light cream
1 tablespoon cornstarch
1 tablespoon hot water

Soak saffron in hot water. Trim all fat and gristle off meat. Melt butter in skillet. Cook veal strips in it for about 2 minutes, or until browned on all sides. If whole saffron is used, strain and use liquid. Add saffron, salt, pepper, and minced onion to veal. Stir in bouillon. Cook, covered, over lowest possible heat for 35 minutes, or until veal is tender. Stir frequently and check for moisture; add a little more bouillon if necessary to prevent scorching. Add cream. Mix together cornstarch and water to make a smooth paste. Stir into meat. Cook, stirring constantly, until sauce is thickened and smooth. Serve very hot with buttered noodles or rice. Makes 6 servings.

### SAFFRON RICE

¼ teaspoon ground saffron
2 tablespoons boiling water
⅛ teaspoon garlic powder
¼ teaspoon white pepper
1 teaspoon salt
3 tablespoons cooking oil
2½ cups boiling chicken broth or bouillon
1 cup uncooked long-grain rice
¼ cup seedless raisins
3 tablespoons shredded blanched almonds

Dissolve saffron in the boiling water and put in saucepan with next 5 ingredients. Bring to a boil. Stir in rice and raisins. Bring again to a boil and put in 1-quart casserole. Cover and bake in preheated moderate oven (350°F.) for 45 minutes, or until rice is tender. Stir in almonds 10 minutes before rice is done. Makes 6 servings.

**Note:** This rice dish is good with chicken, lamb, shrimps, or other seafood.

### SAFFRON TEA BREAD

2 cups sifted all-purpose flour
2 teaspoons baking powder
1 teaspoon salt
½ cup shortening
¼ teaspoon baking soda
⅛ teaspoon ground saffron
2 teaspoons grated lemon rind
¾ cup sugar
2 large eggs
¾ cup water
2 tablespoons fresh lemon juice

Sift first 3 ingredients together and set aside. Mix shortening with next 3 ingredients. Gradually blend in sugar. Beat in eggs, one at a time. Mix water and lemon juice and add to mixture alternately with sifted dry ingredients. Beat for a half minute. Pour into well greased, lightly floured loaf pan (9 x 5 x 3 inches). Bake in preheated moderate oven (350°F.) for 1 hour, or until done. Cool in pan for 10 minutes. Turn out onto a rack to finish cooling. Let stand overnight before slicing. Good with cream cheese.

**SAGE (Salvia officinalis)**—There are over 500 varieties of this popular herb growing in temperate zones throughout the world. The fresh or dried leaves are widely used in cooking for their aromatic bitter taste. Dalmatian sage, grown in Yugoslavia and imported in great amounts into this country, is one of the best varieties of the plant. In addition to the imported Dalmatian sage and the common garden sage *(Salvia officinalis)*, other varieties are white sage, Cyprus sage, *Salvia horminum* (another garden variety), meadow sage, pineapple sage, and clary sage. Not of culinary or medicinal value is the unrelated purple sage or sagebrush, which grows profusely on the western plains of the United States.

The garden sage, long grown in New England, is generally one to two feet high, with grayish leaves and bluish or purplish flowers. Clary sage, usually called only clary, is taller with unusually large leaves. Dalmatian and pineapple sage are especially mild, and the pineapple has a pineapple fragrance.

The name "sage" comes through French from the Latin *salvus,* meaning "safe, whole, or healthy." Since its earliest usage as a medicinal plant it has been said to lengthen and strengthen life. An Arabian proverb, also well known in England, asks "How can a man die who has Sage in his garden?" This question has been answered most eloquently by an 18th-century Englishman, Sir John Hill, who summed up the properties of sage in *Virtues of British Herbs* in 1662. "Sage," said Sir John, "will retard the rapid progress of decay that treads upon our heels so fast in the latter years of life . . . and prevent absolutely that sad depression of spirits, which age often feels and always fears." It will, in answer to the Arabian question, "make the lamp of life, so long as nature lets it burn, burn brightly."

Another of the reasons for sage's popularity and value lay in its culinary use. It was one of the most popular of medieval herbs, flavoring pottage, salads, poultry stuffings, and meat pies.

Accustomed to the many uses and the goodness of sage as a seasoning, it is no surprise that the colonists early brought the plant to this country. Its flavor went well with pork, the colonists' chief meat, as well as in stuffing for their poultry and game. The Shakers began the growing and commercial packaging of the popular herb; America's huge meat-packing industry made and still makes much use of it in sausages. Today, sage rates as the most popular of the seasoning herbs and is one of the most important ingredients in prepared poultry seasoning. Its use does not have to be limited to stuffing and pork products, however; it also adds flavor to cheese, fish, poultry, salad dress-ings, chowders, cream soups, and such vegetables as Brussels sprouts, carrots, eggplant, Lima beans, onions, peas, and tomatoes.

Ground fresh sage is available, as are cut dried leaves and stems of sage, which are also known as sage "tea," and whole dried sage leaves. Since fresh sage has a superb flavor, it is well worth growing it or buying it fresh.

### SAGE-CHEESE APPETIZER
1 package (8 ounces) cream cheese
¼ teaspoon salt
5 or 6 leaves fresh sage, minced, or
¾ teaspoon ground dried sage

Blend all ingredients thoroughly. Chill overnight in refrigerator. Spread on crackers, thin toast, or Melba toast. Makes 1 cup.

### CHICKEN LIVERS WITH SAGE
Thread small skewers alternately with chicken livers, bacon slices, and dry or fresh sage leaves. Broil as usual. Season with salt and pepper when done. Allow 3 or 4 chicken livers, 2 bacon slices, and a few leaves of sage for each serving.
**Note:** This is one of the happiest flavor combinations, especially when made with fresh sage.

### SAGE STUFFING
9 cups toasted soft bread crumbs
1½ teaspoons salt
1 tablespoon ground sage
½ teaspoon pepper
1 chicken bouillon cube, dissolved in ½ cup hot water
½ cup instant minced onion
1 cup butter or margarine, melted

Mix all ingredients together. Use to stuff a 10- to 12-pound ready-to-cook turkey. Makes about 8 cups stuffing.

**SAGO**—A starch extracted from the pithy trunks of various tropical palms, among them the sago palm. It is basic food in the southwest Pacific where sago meal is used for making thick soups, biscuits, and puddings. In the United States it is occasionally used for thickening puddings and sauce.

To make sago, the palm trees are felled and the trunk is cut into pieces. Then the bark is taken off and the inner portion soaked in water to remove the starch. The pulpy paste that results is dried and used as sago meal. When the paste is rubbed through a sieve, pearl sago results. Sago flour is also made from the sago meal. Small and large pearl sago is available in health-food and specialty food stores.

When used for cooking, pearl sago must be soaked for 1 hour before use.

Soak each ¼ cup pearl sago in ½ cup water until water is absorbed.

**SAKE**—The national alcoholic drink of Japan. Made by fermenting rice, its character lies somewhere between western beers and wines. It is yellowish-white and is often drunk warm.

**SALAD**—The first salads were edible herbs or plants dressed only with salt. The word "salad," in fact, derives from the Latin word for salt, *sal.* Salt was the universal preservative, and vegetables could be kept the year round with some sort of salt dressing. From this simple beginning, salads have expanded to include a wide variety of ingredients: fruits, vegetables, herbs, meat, cheese, and fish, cooked or uncooked. There is everything from a simple lettuce salad to a chef's salad which is a main dish full of meats and cheeses. Salads are usually eaten cold, but there are hot salads, such as hot potato salad.

Depending on their ingredients, salads may be the main course of a meal or one of its accompaniments. Regional and individual tastes dictate when an accompanying salad is served. Most often a salad is served with or after the main course. But on the West Coast, the salad is served first. This, in fact, is done in some European countries as well, where the hors-d'oeuvre often consist of a vegetable salad of some sort.

Whatever the ingredients of the salad and whenever it is served, authorities agree that it should have a moist dressing: oil and vinegar, mayonnaise, or variations of these ingredients.

### TO MAKE A GOOD SALAD
■ **Storing Lettuce**—Rinse under running water, drain well, wrap in foil or other moisture-proof wrap, and refrigerate.
■ **Preparing Greens**—Be sure they are really dry so that dressing will adhere evenly. Wrap washed salad greens in a clean kitchen towel. Store in refrigerator for at least 30 minutes. This will make them crisp and dry.
■ **Using Fruits**—Fruits that become dark after being cut up (apples, bananas, pears) should be placed in a dressing or fruit juice as soon as they are cut. Others should have dressing added just before serving.
■ **Adding Dressing**—In most cases dressing should be added just before serving. Avoid using too much or you will have a limp wilted salad, and much of a salad's visual appeal lies in its crispness.

# salad
# cook book

*Main-dish salads; shimmering jellied salads;*
*tempting side-dish salads; refreshing fruit salads;*
*and a collection of dressings to top them off.*

## MAIN-DISH SALADS: MEAT, FISH, AND POULTRY

### CLASSIC CHEF'S SALAD
Assorted greens
Strips of ham or tongue, Swiss cheese, and turkey or chicken
Sliced cucumbers
Radish roses
Hard-cooked eggs
French Dressing (page 1622)
Salt and freshly ground pepper

Have ingredients in separate dishes, and allow the family members or guests to help themselves. Other ingredients such as anchovies, artichoke hearts, small sardines, olives, red-onion rings, or cauliflowerets may be used.

### BRUSSELS CHEF'S SALAD
1 pint fresh, or 1 package (10 ounces) frozen, Brussels sprouts, cooked
1½ cups cooked ham strips
3 cups cooked chicken strips
1 cup diced process Swiss cheese
½ cup chopped celery
3 cups torn lettuce
¼ cup cider vinegar
½ cup salad oil
¾ teaspoon paprika
1 teaspoon salt
¼ teaspoon pepper
2 tablespoons sugar

Combine cooked Brussels sprouts, ham, chicken, cheese, celery, and lettuce; toss lightly. Chill. Mix remaining ingredients; blend or shake well. Before serving, combine mixtures; toss lightly, but thoroughly. Makes 6 servings.

### ORANGE CHEF'S SALAD
½ bunch of watercress
½ head each of lettuce and romaine
1½ cups orange sections
1 cup diced unpeeled apples
1½ cups slivered cooked chicken
½ cup diced sharp Cheddar cheese
⅔ cup French Dressing (page 1622)

Tear salad greens into bite-size pieces. Add remaining ingredients and toss lightly. Makes 4 to 6 servings.

### FRENCH BEEF SALAD
Thinly sliced cold cooked beef
Thinly sliced tomatoes
Sliced onion
Sliced cooked potatoes
Pitted ripe olives
Vinaigrette Sauce (page 1622)
Hard-cooked eggs, quartered
Chopped parsley

Arrange first 4 ingredients in alternating layers in a salad bowl. Garnish with olives and pour Vinaigrette Sauce over top. Add quartered eggs and sprinkle with parsley.

### MINTED LAMB AND POTATO SALAD
2 cups of small thin slices of cold roast lamb
2 cups sliced cooked potatoes
¾ cup French Dressing (page 1622))
1 tablespoon finely shredded mint leaves
1 tablespoon minced green onion
1 teaspoon instant minced onion
Seasoned salt and pepper to taste
Salad greens

Mix all ingredients except greens. Chill for 1 hour and serve on greens. Makes 4 servings.

### LAMB, CUCUMBER, AND TOMATO SALAD
2 cups diced cooked lamb
1 cucumber, thinly sliced
2 tomatoes, diced
1 apple, diced
4 cups broken lettuce, romaine, and chicory
Salt and pepper to taste
Dairy sour cream

Mix all ingredients except sour cream. Moisten with cream; toss. Makes 4 servings.

### VEAL SALAD WITH MARINATED BROCCOLI
Mix 2 cups each of diced cooked veal, diced apple, and sliced celery with ⅓ cup well-seasoned French Dressing (page 1622). Season to taste; chill. Pour ⅓ cup dressing over 1 bunch of warm cooked broccoli; cool, then chill. Serve with the veal. Makes 4 to 6 servings.

### RICE SALAD HORTENSE
1 cup uncooked rice
Mustard Dressing (page 1623)
1 large sweet red pepper or ½ green pepper, diced
1½ cups cold cooked ham, diced
1 cup cold cooked peas
2 tomatoes, peeled and sliced
Chopped parsley

Cook rice; while still warm add Mustard Dressing. When cool, add pepper, ham, peas, and tomatoes. Sprinkle with parsley. Makes 4 to 6 servings.

### FRANKFURTERS AND HOT-POTATO SALAD
3 tablespoons bacon fat
1½ tablespoons all-purpose flour
1 tablespoon sugar
1 teaspoon salt
⅛ teaspoon pepper
½ cup water
⅓ cup vinegar
5 cups sliced cooked potatoes
1 small onion, minced
Chopped parsley
8 frankfurters

Heat fat; add flour, sugar, and seasonings; stir in water and vinegar. Cook until slightly thickened. Add potatoes, onion, and parsley. Heat well. Cut several diagonal gashes, ¼ inch deep, in frankfurters. Brown lightly in a little fat. Arrange on salad. Makes 4 servings.

### SALADE PARISIENNE
1 cup each of cooked green beans, peas, and cauliflower
3 raw carrots, shredded
½ cup sliced raw mushrooms
½ cup diced cooked chicken livers
½ cup diced cooked shrimps

**Dressing:**
1 teaspoon prepared mustard
⅓ cup olive oil
Salt and pepper
Vinegar
Dash of sugar
1 tablespoon heavy cream

Mix vegetables, chicken livers, and shrimps. To make dressing, put mustard in small bowl and gradually beat in oil. Season and add vinegar to taste. Add sugar and cream. Pour over first mixture and toss well. Makes 4 servings.

### MEAT AND VEGETABLE SALAD
1 cup diced cooked meat (beef, lamb, or pork)
1 bunch of watercress (leaves only), chopped
1 cup diced cooked potatoes
1 cup diced cooked beets
2 large unpeeled red apples, diced
1 sweet pickle, minced
¼ cup capers
Dressing as in Salade Parisienne, above
Salt and pepper to taste

Mix all ingredients and chill thoroughly. Makes 6 servings.

### SALMAGUNDI SALAD WITH SALAMI AND LIVERWURST
2 cups diced cooked potatoes
3 hard-cooked eggs, diced
1 cup diced celery
1 tablespoon minced onion
½ cup cubed hard salami
½ cup cubed liverwurst
½ cup cubed sharp Cheddar cheese
1 cup shredded cabbage
¼ cup olive oil
Salt and pepper
½ cup mayonnaise
Salad greens
Paprika

Mix first 8 ingredients. Add olive oil, and salt and pepper to taste. Mix lightly but well. Add mayonnaise. Serve salad on greens with a sprinkling of paprika. Makes 4 servings.

### SHRIMP SALAD
2 cups cooked cleaned shelled shrimps
⅓ cup sliced sweet pickles
1 small onion cut in rings
½ cup French Dressing (page 1622)
Salad greens

Mix all ingredients except greens. Chill. Serve on greens. Makes 4 servings.

### JAPANESE SHRIMP AND EGG SALAD
½ cup uncooked rice
1 tablespoon instant minced onion
1 cup well-seasoned French Dressing (page 1622)
1 package (10 ounces) frozen shrimps, cooked
4 hard-cooked eggs
Salad greens
3 sweet gherkins, chopped
2 tablespoons ketchup
1 tablespoon capers

Cook and drain rice. Add onion, ½ cup French Dressing, shrimps, and 2 eggs,

**Salmagundi Salad          Apple Glacé with Honey Cream Cheese          October Salad with Ginger Mayonnaise Dressing**

diced. Mix lightly with fork, and chill. Put on greens in bowl. Sprinkle pickles around edge. Grate separately whites and yolks of 2 eggs. Sprinkle whites next to pickles and put yolks in center. Serve with remaining ½ cup Dressing mixed with ketchup and capers. Makes 4 to 6 servings.

### AVOCADO HALVES WITH SPICED SHRIMPS

1 pound fresh jumbo shrimps
1 heaping teaspoon pickling spice
2 large ripe avocados
1 cup dairy sour cream
½ teaspoon salt
1 tablespoon fresh lemon juice
1 pimiento, diced

Cook shrimps with spice in boiling water. Drain shrimps, shell, and devein. Chill. Halve avocados and remove seeds. Spoon shrimps into hollows of avocados. Mix remaining ingredients and serve as dressing for shrimps and avocados. Makes 4 servings.

### FRESH GRAPEFRUIT SHRIMP SALAD

1½ cups fresh grapefruit sections
2 cups cooked shrimps, deveined
1 cup diced celery (white part only)
1 tablespoon fresh lemon juice
1 tablespoon heavy cream
¼ cup mayonnaise
¼ teaspoon each of salt and white pepper
Salad greens

Combine grapefruit, shrimps, and celery. Mix together lemon juice, cream, mayonnaise, and salt and pepper. Add to first mixture and toss. Serve on a bed of salad greens. Makes 4 servings.

### LOBSTER SALAD TROPICALE

1 cup diced cooked lobster meat
1 grapefruit in segments
1 avocado, sliced
½ cup slivered toasted almonds
½ cup mayonnaise
1 teaspoon horseradish
Dash of cayenne
Salt
Salad greens

Mix lightly first 4 ingredients. Mix next 3 ingredients and fold into first mixture.

Add salt to taste. Serve on greens. Makes 4 servings.

### CURRIED ROCK-LOBSTER SALAD

Salt
4 frozen rock-lobster tails (about 6 ounces each)
1 cup thinly sliced celery
2 tablespoons thinly sliced blanched almonds, toasted
Mayonnaise (about ¾ cup)
1½ teaspoons curry powder
Juice of 1 lemon
Pepper
Stuffed olives, paprika

Bring 1½ quarts water to boil with 1 teaspoon salt. Add lobster tails and bring to boil. Simmer for 7 minutes if frozen and 5 minutes if thawed. Drain; cool. With kitchen scissors cut under membrane of lobster, leaving outer hard shell intact. Remove meat and reserve shells. Chill meat; dice; add celery and nuts. Mix ½ cup mayonnaise with curry powder and lemon juice. Combine two mixtures. Season to taste with salt and pepper. Pile into reserved shells. Garnish with remaining mayonnaise, slices of stuffed olives, and paprika. Makes 4 servings.

### CELERY AND CRABMEAT SALAD

2 cups cold cooked crabmeat
1½ cups diced green celery
¼ cup diced green pepper
1 teaspoon salt or salt to taste
¼ teaspoon pepper
1 tablespoon fresh lemon juice
3 to 4 tablespoons mayonnaise
Lettuce or 3 ripe avocados

Flake crabmeat and mix lightly with celery, green pepper, salt, pepper, lemon juice, and mayonnaise. Serve on lettuce or pile into cavities of ripe avocados. Makes 6 servings.

### TUNA-FISH SALAD

2 cans (7 ounces each) tuna, drained and flaked
1 cup diced celery or cucumber
Juice of 1 lemon
Cooked Sour-Cream Dressing (page 1588) or mayonnaise
Salad greens

Mix first three ingredients. Add Cooked Salad Dressing to moisten. Chill; serve on greens. Makes 4 servings.

■ **Variations**—Add one or more of the following to the above recipe: 2 chopped hard-cooked eggs; ¼ cup diced pickles or stuffed or ripe olives; 2 tablespoons pickle relish; 1 chopped pimiento; ½ cup cooked peas or cut green beans.

#### Salmon Salad

Use recipe for Tuna-Fish Salad, substituting 1 can (1 pound) salmon, drained and flaked, for the tuna fish. The same variations can also be used.

### SALADE NIÇOISE

Crisp salad greens
Hard-cooked eggs, sliced
Anchovy fillets
Sliced cold potatoes
Olive oil
Vinegar
Sliced peeled tomatoes or tiny cherry tomatoes
Thin green-pepper rings
Tuna fish
Tiny ripe olives
Cold cooked green beans
Capers
Onion rings
Vinaigrette Sauce (page 1622)
Fresh basil (optional)

Arrange greens on a large round or oval platter. Arrange slices of egg on the greens and top slices with a curled anchovy. Add potatoes, marinated in oil and vinegar, and remaining ingredients, except last 2. Serve with Vinaigrette Sauce seasoned with basil, if desired. **Note:** This salad can be a whole meal at lunch or a first course at a buffet supper, followed by a ragout or stew.

### PERFECT CHICKEN SALAD

1 roasting chicken (5 to 6 pounds), quartered
Salt
1 onion, sliced
2 whole cloves
1 celery stalk
1 parsley sprig
Pepper
Mayonnaise (preferably homemade, see page 1621)
Bibb lettuce or romaine
Cucumber
Capers
Toasted walnut halves

Cook the chicken in salted water to cover, together with the onion, cloves, celery, and parsley. The white meat should take ⅓ less time to cook than the dark; remove it when it is tender, leaving the dark meat for an additional period. Cool the chicken and remove skin. Cut the white meat into long pieces (about 1 x 2 inches) and dice the dark meat. Season to taste with salt and pepper. Toss the chicken with Mayonnaise. Arrange on a salad plate with bibb lettuce at one end and crisp sliced cucumber at the other. Spoon more Mayonnaise over the chicken. Garnish with the capers and walnuts. Makes 4 servings. Suggested accompaniments: tiny buttered rolls, a fruit tart, and a chilled white wine.

### CHINESE CHICKEN SALAD

3 cups diced cooked chicken
1 cup drained canned bean sprouts
1½ cups sliced celery
⅛ teaspoon pepper
½ cup French Dressing (page 1622)
2 tablespoons soy sauce
¾ cup mayonnaise
Salad greens
Ripe olives

Mix first 5 ingredients, and chill. When ready to serve, blend soy sauce and mayonnaise. Stir into first mixture and serve on greens with a garnish of olives. Makes 4 to 6 servings.

⬤⬤⬤⬤⬤⬤⬤⬤⬤⬤⬤⬤
**MAIN-DISH SALADS: EGGS AND CHEESE**
⬤⬤⬤⬤⬤⬤⬤⬤⬤⬤⬤⬤

### HOT CHEESE-POTATO SALAD

6 medium potatoes, cooked and diced
1 cup diced celery
1 small onion, minced
⅓ cup vinegar
2 teaspoons salt
¼ teaspoon pepper
1 teaspoon powdered mustard
2 hard-cooked eggs, chopped
⅓ cup liquid bacon fat
2 cups (½ pound) grated sharp Cheddar cheese

Mix all ingredients except cheese. Put in shallow broilerproof baking dish and sprinkle with cheese. Broil until golden-brown and bubbly. Makes 6 servings.

### MACARONI, CHEESE, AND SOUR CREAM SALAD

2 cups small seashell macaroni
1 pound cottage cheese
⅓ cup chopped green pepper
½ cup chopped chives or green onions
⅓ cup sliced radishes
⅓ cup French Dressing (page 1622)
1 cup dairy sour cream
2 tablespoons fresh lemon juice
¼ teaspoon powdered mustard
Seasoned salt and pepper

Cook macaroni according to package directions. Add cottage cheese, green pepper, chives, radishes, and French Dressing. Mix well, and chill. Just before serving fold in sour cream, lemon juice, and mustard. Season to taste. Makes 6 servings.

### EGG-SALAD-STUFFED TOMATOES

4 large tomatoes
6 hard-cooked eggs
Salad dressing
1 can (3 ounces) deviled ham
Salt and pepper
Lettuce
Capers

Cut a slice from stem end of each unpeeled tomato. Scoop out pulp; turn tomatoes upside down to drain. Chop eggs, add tomato pulp, and moisten with salad dressing. Add deviled ham, and salt and pepper to taste. Fill tomato shells with mixture. Serve on lettuce, with a garnish of capers. Makes 4 servings.

### BEAN AND CHEESE SALAD

1 cup dried white beans, washed and drained
4 cups water
1 tablespoon instant minced onion
½ green pepper, chopped
1 cup sliced celery
1 cup diced sharp Cheddar cheese
½ cup mayonnaise
1 tablespoon cider vinegar
½ teaspoon prepared mustard

Cover beans with water, bring to boil, and boil for 2 minutes. Cover pan and let stand for 1 hour; then cook until tender, adding more liquid if necessary. Drain, cool, and chill. Toss beans with onion, green pepper, celery, and cheese. Blend mayonnaise with vinegar and mustard. Add to bean mixture. Mix well, and chill. Makes 4 servings.

## MAIN-DISH SALADS: JELLIED

### JELLIED TOMATO-HAM SALAD

2 envelopes unflavored gelatin
½ cup cold water
2 cups sieved cooked tomatoes
1 onion, grated
1 teaspoon sugar
Salt and pepper to taste
5 blanched almonds
10 green-pepper strips
1 cup minced cooked ham
1 teaspoon prepared mustard
½ cup cold cooked rice
1 teaspoon salad dressing
2 tablespoons dairy sour cream
½ pound cream cheese
2 tablespoons chopped green pepper
2 tablespoons chopped celery

Soak gelatin in cold water for 5 minutes. Simmer tomatoes, onion, sugar, and seasonings for 5 minutes; mix with gelatin and stir until dissolved. Cool, and pour into a quart measure or pitcher, but do not allow to harden. Lightly oil 5-cup ring mold; in bottom of mold, arrange almond halves alternating with green-pepper strips. Pour a little tomato mixture over almonds and green pepper almost to cover them; chill until firm. Fill mold with remaining tomato mixture and chill again until firm. Mix remaining ingredients. Press on firm tomato layer. Chill; unmold. Makes 6 servings.

### TUNA AND SALMON MOLD

2 envelopes unflavored gelatin
1 tablespoon steak sauce
1¾ cups canned tomato juice
Water
¾ cup mayonnaise
1 cup dairy sour cream
1 teaspoon grated lemon rind
⅓ cup chopped stuffed olives
1 green onion, chopped
1½ cups diced celery
1 can each of salmon and tuna fish (7 ounces each)
Salt and pepper
Fresh dill
Lemon wedges
Paprika

Mix 1 envelope of the gelatin with the steak sauce and ¾ cup of the tomato juice. Heat, stirring to dissolve gelatin. Add remaining tomato juice, and pour into 1½-quart mold. Chill until firm. In top part of a double boiler, soften remaining gelatin in ½ cup water. Dissolve over hot water. Stir in mayonnaise and sour cream. Add lemon rind, olives, onion, celery, salmon, and tuna. Season to taste with salt and pepper. Put on top of jellied tomato. Chill until firm. Gar-

nish with dill and lemon wedges generously sprinkled with paprika. Makes 6 servings.

### CRABMEAT SALAD

2 envelopes unflavored gelatin
1 cup cold water
½ teaspoon salt
Hot pepper sauce
¼ cup fresh lemon juice
2 cups mayonnaise
2 teaspoons instant minced onion
1 cup chopped celery
2 cans (6½ ounces each) crabmeat or 2 packages (6 ounces each) frozen crabmeat, thawed
Salad greens
Pimiento strips
Crabmeat for garnish
1 pimiento-stuffed olive slice (optional)

Soften gelatin in water. Heat gently, stirring, until gelatin is dissolved. Add seasonings, lemon juice, mayonnaise, and onion. Beat with rotary beater until blended. Chill until slightly thickened. Fold in celery and flaked crabmeat. Pour into 5-cup fish mold or other mold and chill until firm. Unmold on greens and garnish with pimiento and crabmeat. If fish mold is used, put olive slice in eye position. Makes 6 to 8 servings.

#### Lobster Salad

Omit crabmeat; use 2 cans (6½ ounces each) lobster or 2 cups lobster meat in the above recipe.

### JELLIED CABBAGE SALAD

1 envelope unflavored gelatin
1 cup water
1 cup liquid from pickled beets
2 cups shredded cabbage
1 tablespoon prepared horseradish
Salt and pepper
Salad greens

Soften gelatin in ¼ cup cold water; dissolve in ¾ cup boiling water. Add beet liquid. When beginning to set, add cabbage and horseradish; season to taste with salt and pepper. Pour into 4 molds and chill until set. Unmold on salad greens. Makes 4 servings.

## SIDE-DISH SALADS

### TOSSED SALADS

Wash one or more greens thoroughly, using a wire basket if you have one. Choose from a variety of greens such as romaine, iceberg, bibb or Boston lettuce, chicory, watercress, endive, spinach, dandelion greens, escarole, or Chinese cabbage. Drain greens well and dry on a clean dish towel. Greens can be washed and dried ahead of time and stored in plastic bags in the refrigerator. Use a wooden bowl if available, but in any case use a bowl large enough to toss the salad in. If you like a hint of garlic in your salad, split a clove and rub bowl with the cut side. Tear greens into bite-size pieces and put into bowl. Dribble oil

over greens and toss lightly but thoroughly to coat each leaf. Use any favorite oil such as olive, safflower, corn, or other vegetable oil, or a combination of oils. Then add a few chopped fresh herbs such as thyme, marjoram, or basil, or a pinch of dried herbs. Minced chives and/or parsley can also be added. Season with cracked, freshly ground, or seasoned pepper; salt; seasoned salt; paprika; garlic or onion salt or powder; or a little powdered mustard. Now add vinegar, using ¼ to ⅓ as much as oil, and toss gently. Use red- or white-wine vinegar if available, herb vinegar, cider vinegar, or dry sherry. Add more seasoning if necessary and serve at once.

#### TOSSED SALAD VARIATIONS

Vary a simple tossed salad of greens with the addition of green-pepper strips, sliced ripe or green olives, cut green onions, sliced radishes and/or cucumbers, sliced red or white onions, tomato wedges or small whole tomatoes, chopped nuts, slivered carrots, cooked peas or other vegetables, avocado slices, raisins, or tiny croutons. Or add fruits such as diced red apple, a few well-drained grapefruit or orange sections, diced melon, sliced fresh or canned pears, seedless or seeded grapes, drained fruit cocktail, or pineapple cubes.

#### APPLE, CARROT, AND RAISIN SALAD

Combine bite-size chunks of unpeeled red apple with shredded carrot and seeded raisins. Serve with mayonnaise.

#### CHINESE BAMBOO SHOOTS SALAD

2 cups canned bamboo shoots, drained and thinly sliced
2 tablespoons soy sauce
1 tablespoon sesame oil *
1 teaspoon sugar

Combine all ingredients and mix well. Allow to stand for 1 hour before serving, tossing occasionally. Serve with roast duck, chicken, or pork. Makes 4 servings.
* Substitute vegetable oil, preferably peanut, for sesame oil, if desired.

#### RANCHO SALAD

2 cups (one 1-pound can) kidney beans
About 2½ cups (one 1-pound, 3-ounce can) white beans or cannolini beans
About 2 cups (one 1-pound can) chick-peas
2 onions, coarsely chopped
2 green onions, coarsely chopped
3 pimientos, chopped
3 celery stalks, chopped
12 to 18 stuffed olives, sliced
⅓ cup chopped parsley
2 canned green chilies, chopped
Rancho Salad Dressing
Greens
Sliced tomatoes

Drain all beans and chick-peas. Combine with remaining ingredients except last 3; toss with the Dressing. Allow the salad to mellow for 1 or 2 hours in the refrig-

Tuna and Salmon Mold

Classic Chef's Salad

A variety of salad makings.‣

erator. Serve on a bed of greens with a garnish of sliced tomatoes. Makes 6 to 8 servings.

### Rancho Salad Dressing

2 garlic cloves
1 teaspoon salt
3 to 4 tablespoons vinegar
1 teaspoon pepper

Combine all ingredients.

### ROQUEFORT SALAD

6 to 8 cups bite-size pieces of salad greens
1 garlic clove
Salt to taste
¼ cup olive oil
1 tablespoon cider vinegar
1½ tablespoons fresh lemon juice
¼ teaspoon pepper
½ cup (about 2 ounces) crumbled Roquefort cheese

Place greens in a salad bowl that has been rubbed with garlic. Add salt, oil, vinegar, lemon juice, pepper, and Roquefort. Toss lightly. Serve at once. Makes 6 to 8 servings.

### CUCUMBER-ALMOND SALAD

2 cucumbers
Salt
1 cup dairy sour cream
¼ cup chopped almonds
2 tablespoons minced chives or green onion
1 teaspoon fresh lemon juice
Coarsely ground pepper to taste

Peel cucumbers and slice paper-thin. Sprinkle with salt and let stand while preparing remaining ingredients. Drain cucumbers and add remaining ingredients mixed with ½ teaspoon salt. Makes 4 to 6 servings.

### TOMATO, BACON, AND EGG SALAD

2 tomatoes
4 bacon strips, diced
3 hard-cooked eggs, quartered
4 cups broken salad greens
French Dressing (page 1622)
Salt and pepper

Peel and quarter tomatoes. Cook bacon until crisp, drain, and reserve 2 tablespoons fat. Mix tomatoes, bacon, eggs, greens, and fat. Moisten with French Dressing and season to taste. Makes 4 to 6 servings.

### DANISH SALAD

Combine ½ cup each of finely diced apples, cooked potatoes, beets, cooked veal, and pickled herring. Add a small diced dill pickle, a little minced onion, and vinegar to taste. Season to taste. Moisten with heavy cream. Mix lightly. Pack into 4 custard cups; chill well. Unmold; garnish with sliced hard-cooked eggs. Makes 4 servings.

### HOT-AND-COLD POTATO SALAD

6 cups diced cooked potatoes
1 medium green pepper, chopped
1 medium onion, chopped
1 cup diced celery
½ cup diced pimiento

1 cup chopped dill pickles
½ cup French Dressing (page 1622)
1½ cups mayonnaise
Salt and pepper
2 cups crushed potato chips
1 cup shredded sharp Cheddar cheese

Combine first 6 ingredients. Mix lightly with the French Dressing and let stand in refrigerator until thoroughly chilled. Stir in mayonnaise and salt and pepper to taste. Chill for several more hours. Just before serving, put in shallow 2-quart broilerproof baking dish. Mix potato chips and cheese and sprinkle on salad, covering completely. Put under broiler until cheese is bubbly, but salad remains chilled. Serve at once. Makes 6 to 8 servings.

### ALMOND COLESLAW

4 cups finely shredded cabbage
½ cup each of diced celery and cucumber
¼ cup diced green pepper
1 small onion, minced
½ cup toasted slivered almonds
½ cup mayonnaise
2 tablespoons each of light cream and vinegar
¼ teaspoon seasoned salt
Paprika

Mix vegetables, and chill. Just before serving, add remaining ingredients except paprika and mix well. Sprinkle with paprika. Makes 4 servings.

### ANISE GRAPE AND CABBAGE SLAW

1 cup diced unpeeled red apples
1 teaspoon fresh lemon juice
1 cup green seedless grapes, halved
2 cups medium-fine shredded green cabbage
¼ cup finely chopped celery
3 tablespoons dairy sour cream
1 tablespoon honey
¼ teaspoon crushed aniseed
½ teaspoon salt
⅛ teaspoon pepper
Romaine lettuce

Dice apples into lemon juice to prevent discoloration. Add grapes, cabbage, and celery. Combine next 5 ingredients. Add to salad. Toss lightly. Chill. Serve on romaine lettuce. Makes 6 servings.

### FRESH APPLE COLESLAW

2 cups finely shredded cabbage
2 cups diced unpeeled raw apples
½ cup dairy sour cream
¾ teaspoon dillseed
½ teaspoon salt
1 teaspoon fresh lemon juice
Pinch of pepper
½ teaspoon sugar
Head lettuce
Unpeeled diced apples for garnish

Combine first 8 ingredients. Toss lightly and serve on lettuce. Garnish with unpeeled diced apples. Makes 6 servings.

### SURPRISE SALAD

1 cup slivered red cabbage
1 cup slivered green cabbage
3 celery stalks, diced
½ cup slivered cooked ham
½ cup mayonnaise

Prepared mustard
Salt and pepper
⅓ cup pecan halves

Mix first 5 ingredients. Add mustard, and salt and pepper to taste. Garnish with nuts. Makes 4 servings.

### GERMAN SPINACH SALAD

1 pound small fresh spinach leaves
½ cup mayonnaise
½ cup dairy sour cream
6 anchovies, minced
1½ tablespoons each of chopped green-onion tops and minced parsley
1½ tablespoons each of vinegar and fresh lemon juice
½ garlic clove, minced
Cheddar-cheese cubes or garlic croutons

Wash and dry spinach. Mix remaining ingredients except cheese and add to spinach. Mix lightly and garnish with cheese. Makes 4 servings.

### MARINATED TOMATOES

Peel 6 tomatoes and cut up. Add ¼ cup French Dressing (page 1622), 1 garlic clove, and 2 tablespoons minced fresh herbs. Refrigerate; remove garlic. Makes 4 servings.

### TOMATO-AVOCADO SALAD

4 tomatoes
1 large ripe avocado
½ cup French Dressing (page 1622)
Salt and pepper
¼ cup crumbled Roquefort or blue cheese
Lettuce

Cut tomatoes into wedges but not all the way through so wedges can be separated like petals of a flower. Peel, seed, and cube avocado. Pile cubes on top of tomato. Spoon French Dressing evenly over avocado. Sprinkle with salt and pepper. Crumble cheese over top. Serve on nest of lettuce. (All sharp cheeses go well with avocado.) Makes 4 servings.

### VEGETABLE-AVOCADO SALAD WITH PAPRIKA DRESSING

4 medium onions, thinly sliced
Cider vinegar
Salt and pepper to taste
3 carrots, thinly sliced
2 or 3 bunches radishes, sliced
3 or 4 cucumbers, peeled and cut into 2-inch pieces
2 or 3 avocados
Lemon juice
Salad greens, shredded
Paprika Mayonnaise Dressing (page 1622)

Pour boiling water over onions and let stand for 5 minutes. Drain, cover with vinegar, and season with salt and pepper. Chill for several hours. Crisp carrots, radishes, and cucumbers in ice water. Peel and slice avocados; dip into lemon juice. At serving time, cover large platter with salad greens. Drain vegetables and avocado and arrange on greens. Serve with Paprika Mayonnaise Dressing. Makes 12 servings.

## GERMAN GOURMET MIXED SALAD

1 package (10 ounces) frozen artichoke hearts
¼ cup dry white wine
¼ cup water
 Mild French Dressing (page 1622) made with fresh lemon juice instead of vinegar
1½ cups thinly sliced raw mushrooms
3 to 4 truffles
½ cup Madeira
 Salt and pepper to taste
 Watercress or shredded romaine leaves
 Very thin tomato wedges
 Mayonnaise thinned with lemon juice

Cook artichoke hearts in white wine and water until tender. Drain, cut into ½-inch slices, and marinate in French Dressing. Marinate sliced mushrooms in French Dressing; marinate vegetables for 30 minutes. Peel truffles and simmer, covered, in Madeira for 5 minutes. Cool truffles in Madeira. Reserve 1 truffle and slice others fine. Drain vegetables and combine carefully with truffles. Discard marinade and Madeira. Add salt and pepper. Line a salad bowl with greens. Pile vegetables in middle to form a dome. Cut remaining truffle into rounds and use to decorate salad. Arrange tomato wedges around outside edge. Serve mayonnaise separately. Makes 4 servings.

**Note:** This rich mixed salad is ideal for a party, with cold ham, chicken, or roast beef, all handsomely dished up.

## VEGETABLE SALAD WITH DEVILED HAM

6 cooked potatoes, diced
6 cooked beets, diced, or 2 cups (one 1-pound can) diced beets, drained
4 carrots, diced
1 onion, chopped
 About ⅓ cup (one 2½-ounce can) deviled ham
1 teaspoon powdered mustard
1 cup mayonnaise
 Seasoned salt and pepper

Combine vegetables. Mix next 3 ingredients and fold in. Season to taste, and chill. Makes 6 servings.

## MIXED VEGETABLE SALAD

1 green pepper, cut into rings
1 cucumber, peeled and diced
2 large tomatoes, peeled and diced
1 red onion, cut into rings
1 package (10 ounces) frozen peas, cooked and cooled
1 tablespoon each of chopped chives and parsley
1 pimiento, chopped
1 carrot, shredded
½ pound (1 cup) cottage cheese
3 tablespoons fresh lemon juice
⅓ cup salad oil
 Seasoned salt and pepper

Mix vegetables and chill until ready to serve. Mix cottage cheese, lemon juice, and salad oil. Fold into vegetables. Season to taste. Makes 6 servings.

## SALADE RUSSE

¼ cup dry white wine
2 medium potatoes, peeled, cooked, and sliced, still hot
1 cup any cooked white fish
4 sour pickles, chopped
½ cup pitted ripe olives
½ medium cucumber, peeled and sliced
3 tomatoes, peeled and sliced
¼ cup fresh tarragon leaves, chopped (if available)
1 small head lettuce, broken
½ cup mayonnaise, thinned with a little milk
 Salt and pepper to taste

Pour wine over potatoes; chill. When ready to serve, mix remaining ingredients and add undrained potatoes. Makes 6 to 8 servings.

## ITALIAN SALAD

3 cups parsley (leaves only), chopped
1 cup diced boiled potatoes
3 hard-cooked eggs, chopped
½ cup French Dressing (page 1622)

Mix all ingredients, and chill. Makes 4 servings.

## VEGETABLE-RICE SALAD

½ cup uncooked rice
1 cup diced peeled tomatoes
1 cup sliced radishes
2 teaspoons salt
1 teaspoon paprika
1 teaspoon prepared mustard
½ teaspoon each of curry powder, pepper, and cayenne
3 tablespoons tarragon vinegar
7 tablespoons olive or salad oil
1 cup chopped watercress
1 cup finely diced raw carrots
½ cup pitted ripe olives
½ cup diced raw white turnip
 Mayonnaise

Cook, drain, and cool rice. Add tomatoes and radishes; chill. Mix seasonings, vinegar, and oil. Add to first mixture and mix well. Chill, and put into salad bowl. Moisten each one of next 4 ingredients with mayonnaise and shape each in a mound around edge of salad. Makes 4 servings.

## FRUIT SALADS

### SEAFOAM SALAD

 About 12 (one 1-pound, 14-ounce can) pear halves
1 cup pear syrup
1 box (3 ounces) lime-flavored gelatin
2 packages (3 ounces each) cream cheese
2 tablespoons milk
½ cup heavy cream, whipped
 Salad greens

Drain pears, reserving 1 cup of the syrup. Mash pears with fork or potato masher. Heat syrup, pour over gelatin, and stir until gelatin is dissolved. Beat cheese with milk until smooth and blended. Gradually beat in hot gelatin. Chill until slightly thickened. Fold in pears and cream. Chill in 1½-quart mold until firm. Unmold on greens. Makes 8 servings.

### OCTOBER SALAD

1 box (3 ounces) apple-flavored gelatin
2 cups hot water
⅛ teaspoon salt
⅓ cup each of coarsely chopped pitted dates and nuts
1 cup diced unpeeled red apples
1 cup diced unpeeled fresh pears
 Salad greens
 Ginger Mayonnaise Dressing (page 1622)

Dissolve gelatin in the hot water. Add salt and dates; chill until mixture is slightly thickened. Fold in nuts and fruit. Pour into 5-cup mold and chill until firm. Unmold on salad greens and serve with Ginger Mayonnaise Dressing. Makes 6 servings.

### CRANBERRY-CREAM SALAD

1 box (3 ounces) cherry-flavored gelatin
1 cup hot water
1 can (1 pound) whole-berry cranberry sauce
½ cup diced celery
¼ cup chopped walnuts
1 cup dairy sour cream
 Salad greens

Dissolve gelatin in hot water. Chill until thickened but not firm. Break up cranberry sauce with fork. Stir sauce, celery, and nuts into first mixture. Fold in sour cream. Pour into 1-quart mold and chill until firm. Unmold on greens. Makes 4 to 6 servings.

### APPLE-AND-ORANGE SALAD

Alternate slices of unpeeled red apple and orange on watercress. Serve with sweetened French Dressing (page 1622).

### APPLE GLACÉ WITH HONEY-CREAM CHEESE

Simmer 4 peeled cored apples in syrup made by boiling 2 cups pineapple juice, ½ cup sugar, and a little red coloring, until apples are tender and red, turning often. Drain; chill. Put on greens. Stuff with cream cheese softened with honey. Top with walnut halves. Makes 4 servings.

### JELLIED CINNAMON-APPLE SALAD

Dissolve ⅓ cup red cinnamon candies in 2 cups boiling water. Heat and pour over 1 box (3 ounces) red fruit-flavored gelatin dessert. Stir until dissolved. Chill until partially thickened. Fold in ¾ cup each of chopped celery and apple, dash of salt, and ⅓ cup chopped nuts. Pour into molds; chill until firm. Unmold on greens. Makes 4 to 6 servings.

### COTTAGE-CHEESE AND BLUEBERRY SALAD

¾ pound cottage cheese
 Dash of cayenne
 Salt to taste
1 pint fresh blueberries
 Watercress
 Sliced fresh, frozen, or canned peaches
 Mayonnaise

Mix first 4 ingredients lightly. Spoon in 6 mounds onto cress. Garnish each with peaches and serve with mayonnaise. Makes 6 servings.

### CHRISTMAS FRUIT SALAD

2 cups tangerine sections
1 cup grapefruit sections
1 cup diced pears
1 cup seedless grapes
2 tablespoons fresh lemon juice
Sugar
Cranberry or raspberry sherbet
½ cup chopped pistachio nuts

Combine first 4 fruits. Sprinkle with lemon juice and add sugar to taste. Chill. Put in 6 individual sherbet glasses. Top each serving with a small scoop of sherbet. Sprinkle with pistachio nuts. Makes 6 servings.

### JELLIED CHEESE RING

1 envelope unflavored gelatin
⅓ cup cold water
1 cup cottage cheese, mashed
½ cup crumbled Roquefort or blue cheese
½ teaspoon salt
⅔ cup heavy cream
Salad greens

Sprinkle gelatin over water and let stand for 5 minutes. Dissolve over hot water. Combine remaining ingredients except greens and blend with gelatin. Pour into oiled 1-quart ring mold and chill until firm. Unmold on greens and fill center with chicken, meat, or fish salad. Makes 4 servings.

**Note:** For dessert, surround ring with strawberries or other fruit.

### ORANGE AND DATE SALAD

3 medium oranges
1 cup diced celery
1 cup diced pitted fresh dates
2 tablespoons mayonnaise
Salad greens
6 slices of orange
6 whole fresh dates, pitted

Peel oranges, removing white membrane. Cut into sections. Mix with celery, dates, and mayonnaise. Put on greens on 6 individual plates. Garnish each with an orange slice and a whole date. Makes 6 servings.

### GRAPE, PEAR, AND CELERY SALAD

1½ cups seedless green grapes
2 pears, diced
2 celery hearts (white parts only), sliced
Cream Mayonnaise Dressing (page 1621)
1 or 2 large heads Boston lettuce
Additional grapes

Combine grapes, pears, and celery hearts. Toss with Cream Mayonnaise Dressing. Wash Boston lettuce and shake dry. Spread open. Cut out center with sharp knife to make cavity. Fill cavity with fruit salad. Serve surrounded with 2 rings of grapes. Makes 4 servings.

### WALDORF SALAD

Combine chunks of peeled tart apple, diced celery, and chopped walnuts with cooked salad dressing. Garnish with cranberry sauce.

### FRESNO FRUIT SALAD

2 medium cantaloupes
2 navel oranges
¾ cup seedless grapes
¾ cup sliced pitted fresh dates
½ cup dairy sour cream
½ teaspoon grated orange rind
1½ teaspoons sugar
Dash of salt

Cut cantaloupes into halves. Scoop out seeds and put halves on individual serving plates. Peel and section oranges. Mix with grapes and dates and fill cantaloupes with the mixture. Combine remaining ingredients; serve as dressing for salad. Makes 4 servings.

### ORANGE, BANANA, AND WALNUT SALAD

4 oranges
Salad greens
4 bananas
Chopped walnuts

Peel and slice oranges. Arrange on greens on 4 individual salad plates. Peel bananas, cut into quarters, and roll in nuts. Arrange on orange slices. Serve with any desired dressing. Makes 4 servings.

### PINEAPPLE WALDORF SALAD

Drain 2½ cups (one 1-pound, 4½-ounce can) pineapple chunks. Add chunks to 2 cups sliced celery and ¾ cup broken walnut meats. Chill. Just before serving, add enough mayonnaise to moisten, 1 tablespoon fresh lemon juice, and salt to taste; mix lightly. Makes 6 servings.

## SALAD DRESSINGS

**Note:** *For salad dressings based on Mayonnaise and Vinaigrette Sauce, including French Dressing, see the Sauce Cook Book, beginning on page 1619.*

### BUTTERMILK HORSERADISH DRESSING

*Serve with potato, cabbage, or tossed green salads, or on canned or fresh fruit.*

¾ cup buttermilk
2 tablespoons prepared horseradish
1 tablespoon vinegar
1 tablespoon sugar
¼ teaspoon salt
½ teaspoon prepared mustard

Combine all ingredients. Mix thoroughly. Chill in refrigerator. Makes 1 cup.

### SOUR-CREAM DRESSING

*Serve on green salads or vegetable combinations.*

1 teaspoon salt
1 tablespoon sugar
⅛ teaspoon cayenne
1 tablespoon fresh lemon juice
2 tablespoons vinegar
1 cup dairy sour cream

Combine all ingredients and stir until thoroughly mixed. Makes 1 cup.

### POTATO DRESSING

*Serve on lettuce, fish, or vegetable salads.*

1½ cups riced cooked potatoes
1 onion, grated

1 teaspoon powdered mustard
1 teaspoon salt
⅓ cup vinegar
1 cup undiluted evaporated milk
2 tablespoons chopped parsley
⅓ cup shredded raw carrot

Beat all ingredients until they are well blended. Makes 3 cups.

### COTTAGE-CHEESE DRESSING

*Serve with vegetable or fruit salads.*

½ cup cottage cheese
⅓ cup undiluted evaporated milk
¾ teaspoon salt
½ teaspoon sugar
1 teaspoon paprika
Dash of garlic or onion salt
2 tablespoons chopped parsley
1 tablespoon vinegar

Mix cottage cheese with milk. Add remaining ingredients. Makes 1 cup.

### AVOCADO DRESSING

*Especially recommended for fruit salads.*

¾ cup avocado pulp
3 tablespoons fresh lemon juice
2 tablespoons blue cheese
2 tablespoons heavy cream
½ teaspoon Worcestershire
¾ teaspoon salt
1 teaspoon prepared mustard

Sieve enough soft ripe avocado to make ¾ cup. Add lemon juice and mix well. Sieve blue cheese. Add to first mixture with heavy cream, Worcestershire, salt, and prepared mustard. Chill. Makes about 1 cup.

### COOKED SOUR-CREAM DRESSING

*For lettuce, cabbage, egg, or vegetable salads.*

3 tablespoons sugar
¾ teaspoon salt
1 teaspoon powdered mustard
2 teaspoons all-purpose flour
⅓ cup butter or margarine
1½ cups dairy sour cream
2 eggs, beaten
⅓ cup wine vinegar
⅓ teaspoon crumbled dried tarragon

Mix all ingredients. Cook, stirring constantly, until smooth and thickened. Cool; then chill. Makes 2¾ cups.

### COOKED BUTTERMILK DRESSING

*Serve on shredded cabbage, greens, fruit, or cooked-vegetable salads.*

2 tablespoons all-purpose flour
1 teaspoon powdered mustard
1½ teaspoons salt
⅛ teaspoon paprika
½ teaspoon celery seeds
2 tablespoons sugar
⅓ cup vinegar
1 cup buttermilk

Combine dry ingredients in top part of a double boiler. Add vinegar and buttermilk. Cook over boiling water, stirring constantly, until thick. Cover and cook for 10 minutes longer. Cool, and chill. Makes 1½ cups.

### SHERRY DRESSING
*Good on fruit salads.*

1 egg, beaten
¼ cup sugar
¼ cup sherry
　Dash of salt
2 teaspoons butter
　Juice of ½ orange
　Juice of ½ lemon
¼ cup heavy cream, whipped

Combine all ingredients except cream in top part of a double boiler. Cook over boiling water until slightly thickened, stirring. Chill. Just before serving, fold in cream. Makes 1 cup.

### FLUFFY FRUIT DRESSING
*Recommended for fruit salads.*

¼ cup sugar
1 tablespoon all-purpose flour
⅓ cup fresh orange juice
2 tablespoons fresh lemon juice
½ cup undiluted evaporated milk, whipped

Mix sugar and flour in small saucepan. Add orange and lemon juices. Cook, stirring, until thick. Chill. When you are ready to use dressing, fold in whipped evaporated milk. (Milk should be chilled before whipping.) Makes 1 cup.

## SALAMANDER

**SALAMANDER**—In culinary language, the word denotes a kitchen tool used to brown and glaze the top of cooked foods. The original salamander is a long iron rod with an enlarged and flattened end which is heated over a fire until it is white and then waved close over the food. Other salamanders may be metal discs or plates used in the same way and yet another is a small chimneyless portable stove used for the identical browning and glazing purpose.

Salamanders take their name from the lizardlike, heat-loving animal. The rod salamander is an old kitchen tool that goes back to the Middle Ages. Salamanders today are chefs' equipment when used at all; the coming of the modern broiler has made them obsolete.

**SALAMI**—One of a variety of sausages of Italian origin that can be eaten without being cooked first. There are Italian, German, Hungarian, French, and kosher salamis. The word is Italian and implies "salted," meaning that the meat is preserved. The singular of the word in Italian is *salame* and in colloquial usage this word is used for a person who is not very bright and is rather gullible.

Salamis differ from each other by their composition of meats, their spicing, their salting and curing, and their shape. Salami most often contains pork and some beef, although there are pure pork and pure beef salamis. The meat can be leaner or fatter and ground coarsely or finely. Salamis can be divided into two major groupings, hard and soft. The soft are the less chewy varieties of salami; kosher salami is an example. It is made and seasoned in the same way the hard salami is, but is softer because, after cooking, it is air-dried for only a short time or not at all. Most kosher salami comes in larger slices than the hard and is preferred by many for sandwiches because it is less chewy. Italian Genoa is a well known example of a hard salami; it is made of coarsely ground pork seasoned with garlic and sometimes wine. The salami is air-dried.

*Availability*—Salami in some form are available in most food stores. Kinds vary with the area.

*Storage*—Be sure slices of meat are flat before storage. Keep plastic-wrapped packages in wrapper. Wrap sliced meat in moisture-vapor-proof paper.

☐ Sliced, refrigerator shelf: 2 to 3 days
☐ Unsliced, dry and semidry varieties, kitchen shelf, casing uncut: indefinitely
☐ Unsliced, dry and semidry varieties, refrigerator shelf, casing cut: 2 weeks

*Nutritive Food Values*—Excellent source of protein, good source of iron, thiamine, riboflavin, and niacin.

☐ Hard, 3½ ounces = 450 calories
☐ Soft, 3½ ounces = 311 calories

### SAILBOATS
Cut 9 thin slices of salami (any kind) into quarters. Cut thin lengthwise slices from each of 36 small sweet pickles to make a smooth base. Use tip of knife to cut out wedge-shape strip on top side of each pickle. Fill hollow with cream cheese or cheese spread. Insert a quarter slice of salami into each to form a sail. Chill. Makes 3 dozen appetizers.

### SALAMI SWEET-AND-SOUR
¼ pound soft salami
2 cups diced potatoes
　Water
2 cups shredded red cabbage
1 green pepper, minced
2 tablespoons vinegar
2 tablespoons sugar
　Salt and pepper

Cut salami into slivers and brown lightly in skillet. Add potatoes and boiling water to cover. Bring to boil and simmer, covered, for 10 minutes. Add cabbage, green pepper, vinegar, and sugar. Cook for 7 minutes longer, or until potatoes are tender. Season with salt and pepper to taste. Makes 4 servings.

### SALAMI SKILLET
6 slices of bacon
¼ cup diced celery
2 tablespoons chopped green pepper
2 tablespoons all-purpose flour
1 can (14½ ounces) evaporated milk, undiluted
½ teaspoon salt
¼ teaspoon pepper
1 package (7 ounces) soft salami
2 hard-cooked eggs, sliced
1 cup wide noodles, cooked

Cook bacon until crisp. Remove from fat, drain and crumble. Pour off all but 2 tablespoons fat from skillet. In 2 tablespoons fat, cook celery and green pepper for 2 or 3 minutes. Blend in flour. Add milk, salt, and pepper and cook, stirring constantly, until thickened. Cut salami slices into quarters, reserving 4 whole slices for garnish. Add to first mixture with eggs and noodles; heat. Add bacon. Garnish with whole salami slices. Makes 4 servings.

### SALAMI OMELET
In a 10- or 12-inch skillet place 6 or 8 slices of salami (any kind), ¼ inch thick. Slowly brown on both sides (enough fat will be rendered for the omelet). Add 5 well-beaten eggs. With a fork distribute salami evenly. Cook until omelet takes form. Place under broiler until golden-brown. Cut as a pie to serve.

### SALAMI-CARROT SALAD
¼ pound hard salami
2 cups shredded carrots
¼ cup pickle relish
⅓ cup diced celery
½ cup mayonnaise

Cut salami into small cubes. Add other ingredients and mix well. Chill. Serve in lettuce cups, if desired. Makes 4 servings.

## SALLY LUNN

**SALLY LUNN**—A bread of English origin which has become a culinary specialty of our southern states. Traditionally, it is baked in a Turk's-head mold, however, in the south the batter is often baked in muffin pans. Although there have been so-called "quick Sally Lunns," the authentic one uses yeast as a leavening agent.

The origin of the name is obscure. It was once spelled *soleilune*, a French dialect version of "golden" or "sunshiny," which may indicate a French derivation. But the story most often told to account for the name is that the bread was invented and sold by a girl named Sally Lunn in the city of Bath, in England, around 1700. Sally Lunns are similar to Bath buns, but they do not have candied peel in them.

### SALLY LUNN RING
1 package active dry yeast
　or 1 cake compressed yeast
¼ cup water*
3 tablespoons sugar
2 medium-size eggs at room temperature
⅔ cup milk, scalded
3½ cups sifted all-purpose flour

½ cup melted shortening
1 teaspoon salt

Sprinkle or crumble yeast into water with 1 tablespoon of the sugar added. *Use very warm water (105°F. to 115°F.) for dry yeast; use lukewarm (80°F. to 90° F.) for compressed. Let stand for a few minutes, then stir until dissolved. Add remaining sugar and beat in eggs. Cool milk to lukewarm and add. Gradually stir in half of flour and beat until the batter falls in sheets from the spoon. Cool shortening to lukewarm and add. Mix well. Combine salt with remaining flour and add gradually. Mix well. Scrape down bowl. Grease top of dough to prevent crusting. Cover bowl and let dough rise in a warm place (80°F. to 85°F.) until doubled in bulk, about 1 hour. Punch down dough, cover, and let it rest for 10 minutes. Put dough in a greased 8½-cup gelatin mold or in a Sally Lunn or Turk's-head mold. Cover and let stand in a warm place to rise again until doubled in bulk, about 45 minutes. Bake in preheated moderate oven (350°F.) for 1 hour, or until browned. Serve hot with butter. Makes one 8½-inch Sally Lunn ring.

### RAISED SALLY LUNN MUFFINS

1 package active dry yeast
  or 1 cake compressed yeast
¼ cup water*
¾ cup milk
3 tablespoons sugar
1¼ teaspoons salt
3½ cups all-purpose flour
¼ cup soft butter or margarine
2 eggs

Sprinkle or crumble yeast into water. *Use very warm water (105°F. to 115° F.) for dry yeast; use lukewarm (80°F. to 90°F.) for compressed. Let stand for a few minutes, then stir until dissolved. Scald milk and pour over sugar and salt. Let stand until lukewarm. Stir in yeast and 2 cups of the flour. Beat well. Cover and let stand in a warm place until light, about 30 minutes. Beat in butter, eggs, and remaining flour. Break off pieces of the mixture, shape into balls, and put in greased 2½-inch muffin-pan sections. Let rise until doubled in bulk, about 45 minutes. Bake in preheated hot oven (400° F.) for about 15 minutes. Makes 2 dozen.

### QUICK SALLY LUNN

½ cup butter or margarine
  Sugar
2 eggs
1 cup milk
2 cups sifted all-purpose flour
3 teaspoons baking powder
¾ teaspoon salt
  Ground cinnamon

Cream butter; gradually add ⅓ cup sugar, creaming until light and fluffy. Beat eggs well; add milk. To the sugar mixture add sifted flour, baking powder, and salt alternately with liquid, beating until smooth. Turn into two greased pans (8 x 8 x 2 inches). Sprinkle with sugar and cinnamon. Bake in preheated hot oven (425°F.) for about 20 minutes. Cut each square into 9 pieces and serve warm. Makes 18.

**SALMAGUNDI**—A culinary term derived from the French word *salmigondis,* "hotchpotch." It is used to describe a stew made from leftover meats, seasoned with wine, vinegar, pickles, etc., or a salad plate of diced meats, pickled vegetables, and other salad ingredients, arranged, not tossed, and served with a dressing.

**SALMI or SALMIS**—A sauced dish usually made with partially cooked or leftover feathered game or domestic duck or goose and often finished by cooking in a chafing dish at the table. The word is French, short for *salmigondis.*

### SALMI OF DUCKLING

¼ cup butter or margarine
2 tablespoons each of chopped celery
  and carrot
1 tablespoon minced onion
¼ cup all-purpose flour
1⅓ cups canned consommé or bouillon
⅔ cup stewed fresh or canned tomatoes
4 servings leftover cooked duckling

Heat butter in saucepan and add next 3 ingredients. Cook for 2 or 3 minutes. Blend in flour. Add liquids and tomatoes and bring to boil. Simmer for 5 minutes. Add duckling and heat well. Makes 4 servings.

**SALMON** by *James A. Beard*—Called the greatest of sports fish, the king of fishes, salmon has been prized as food for centuries and is probably the best known of all fish.

The origins of salmon are interesting to speculate upon. During the ice ages, it is likely that salmon were migratory Arctic fish. As glaciers advanced and retreated, the earth's surface was reshaped and bodies of water re-formed or shifted. The fish that had originally been one family called the *Salmonidae* (salmon, trout, and char) were probably, during this epoch, dispersed over different parts of the world to the rivers and seas of Europe, Asia, and North America. Curiously enough, except for human transplanting of sal-mon, they inhabit only the waters of the Northern Hemisphere.

Pictures of salmon carved on bone have been found in France dating from about 12,000 B.C. Centuries after the cave man the Romans gave salmon its name. They were enthralled with the spectacle of hordes of leaping fish in the rivers of Gaul and so named them *salmo,* which comes from the verb "to leap." The *Salmo salar,* as the Atlantic salmon were scientifically named, eventually found its way into the literature and mythology of all Europe.

Only 300 years ago salmon flourished to such an extent in the rivers of Europe and North America that servants, being hired by new masters, accepted employment on the condition that they would be served salmon only a specified number of times a week. It had become the custom to bestow this commonplace food on the help almost daily. Salmon used to be found in the Loire, the Rhine, the Wye, the Hudson, the St. Lawrence, and the Connecticut—in nearly all the rivers of North America and Europe. Sadly enough, this is no longer true. Though salmon are hardy, they require two essentials, clean water and access to their spawning grounds. Polluted waters, dams, and other by-products of civilization have severely reduced the flow of salmon on both sides of the Atlantic. Fortunately, steps are now being taken, belatedly, to preserve the waters that have not become too polluted. With care, a fraction of the once abundant Atlantic salmon will remain.

The prospects are better for the Pacific salmon, which has become such a tremendous industry that preservation is vital to local and national economies. Pacific salmon are thus flourishing from Mexico to Alaska, and along the coasts of Siberia, Japan, and China.

Whereas there is only one variety of Atlantic salmon, there are five varieties of Pacific: sockeye (*Oncorhynchus nerka*), spring (*O. tschawytscha*), coho (*O. kitsutch*), pink (*O. gorbuscha*), and chum (*O. keta*). In addition there is the steelhead, which is more closely related to the Atlantic than to the other Pacific salmon, and the blueback, which is really a coho with darker markings.

There is one important difference in the life cycles of the Atlantic and Pacific salmon. Both, to reach their spawning grounds, ascend streams and rivers sometimes for a distance of hundreds of miles, jumping rapids and rocks with astonishing strength. When the place and time for spawning are reached, male and female pair off, and the female digs a nest with a fanning motion of her tail. The male guards her while she lays her eggs and then he fertilizes them. The process is repeated a number of times over a period of several days. The feats of climbing rivers and reproducing thoroughly exhaust the fish, understandably. Pacific salmon spawn only once and then die. Atlantic salmon may live to return to the sea and spawn several times.

When the young hatch in their nests, or redds, they live for a certain length of time from food retained in the shells and then break forth as tiny alevins. They spend from three to seven years in fresh waters before migrating to salt water as young salmon. During this time they change color from a rather varistriped to the silvery skin that one usually associates with salmon.

The history of salmon as food in the Western Hemisphere predates the discovery of America. The coastal Indians used salmon as a mainstay of their diet; for winter, it was salted, smoked, kippered, dried, or beaten into pemmican. If one goes to parts of Canada and up the Columbia River when the salmon are running, it is still possible to see the Indians fishing for salmon with spears, and smoking and curing it on the spot. In the West the Indians hot-smoked salmon over a campfire, suspending the fish in forked pieces of spirea wood and surrounding it with ferns. The early settlers in both the East and West of the United States salted and pickled salmon for winter use. Salmon bellies, salmon tips, fillets of salmon were all preserved in brine, and delicious this preparation can be, for one still finds it in certain regions of the country.

Fresh salmon is considered one of the world's great delicacies and is served in many of the finest restaurants as a *pièce de résistance*. Such three-star French restaurants as Oustau de Baumanière, La Tour d'Argent, and Pruniers; and in London, such restaurants as Pruniers (again), the Connaught Grill, and the Caprice serve fresh broiled salmon with Béarnaise Sauce, or poached salmon, hot or cold, with a *sauce verte*. Baumanière makes a specialty of a cold galantine of salmon, which is deftly and beautifully prepared with a stuffing, tied in a cloth, poached, and sliced in paper-thin slices for an hors-d'oeuvre.

Smoked salmon is one of the most expensive foods in the world. The European variety is more heavily smoked, usually, than the Nova Scotia and Columbia River varieties; on the other hand, the latter are saltier. Lox, or the favorite smoked salmon in Jewish delicatessens, varies in its salt content and thus in its price.

In England crimped, or cold, salmon is considered one of the prime delicacies of the social season and is featured as a buffet dish at gala balls and parties. Kippered salmon, which is a hot-smoke fish, meaning it is smoke-cooked, is also popular all through England and is served either hot or cold with various sauces and additives.

Salmon cheeks, which are just that, are one of the most prized portions of the fish. They are usually served sautéed Meunière and sometimes deep-fried, a superb treat either way.

Of course, it is canned salmon that is consumed in such astounding quantities throughout the world. Most of the canning is centered on the Pacific Coast, in Oregon, Washington, British Columbia, and Alaska. Millions of cans issue forth annually from spotless canneries, and close government inspection of the cans, the fish, and the processing make it one of the most sanitary products in the world. Canned salmon will stand any extremes of weather and temperature and remain fresh-tasting and flavorful.

The most valuable variety for canning is the sockeye. This is seldom seen fresh in the markets but is considered outstanding for canning because of its rich red flesh and firm tissue. The sockeye weighs up to fifteen pounds and is caught from southern Oregon to Alaska. Some sockeye has become landlocked and spends its life in fresh water. In this case, it bears such names as "kokanee," "kickaninny," and "redfish."

The spring or chinook, sometimes known as "the King," is another exceedingly valuable catch and is fished a great deal in the Columbia River, among other places. This species is one of the best of game fish, being known for rising to a lure and giving fishermen a fine fight. The spring grows very large, sometimes reaching seventy or eighty pounds in weight, but is nevertheless as delicate to the palate as smaller species. Coho, also known as "blueback" or "silver," or even "silverside," is popular with fishermen, too. It averages about three feet in length, and its silver skin is spotted with black. In addition to its value to the canning industry the coho is much appreciated in home kitchens for cooking and freezing. Not as fatty as the preceding species, but still a popular fish, is the chum, sometimes known as "dog salmon." It is not as highly regarded for fine eating as some of the other varieties, for it is apt to be dull in flavor.

**Availability and Purchasing Guide**—Fresh salmon is sold whole, in steaks, fillets, and large pieces. Frozen salmon steaks are available. Salmon is also available smoked and canned. Canned salmon roe is available.

In buying salmon, allow ½ to ⅜ pound per serving, and in the case of uncleaned fish, just as taken from the water, allow about 1 pound.

**Storage**

- [ ] Fresh; or smoked, refrigerator shelf: 1 to 2 days
- [ ] Fresh; or smoked, refrigerator frozen-food compartment, prepared for freezing: 2 to 3 weeks
- [ ] Fresh; or smoked, freezer, prepared for freezing: 3 to 4 months.
- [ ] Frozen, refrigerator frozen-food compartment: 2 months
- [ ] Frozen, freezer: 1 year
- [ ] Canned, unopened, kitchen shelf: 1 year
- [ ] Canned; or cooked, covered, refrigerator shelf: 3 to 4 days

**Nutritive Food Values**—Contains large amounts of phosphorus, potassium, some sodium, thiamine, riboflavin, and niacin, and some vitamin A. Canned salmon contains some calcium if the bones are eaten.

- [ ] Fresh, 3½ ounces, baked steak = 140 calories
- [ ] Canned, 3½ ounces = 164 calories

**Basic Preparation**—Fresh salmon can be baked, broiled, deep-fried, panfried, planked, sautéed, steamed, and stewed. Canned salmon should be drained and have the skin and bones removed before using. Smoked salmon is served cold in sandwiches, salads, hors-d'oeuvre, etc.

Salmon is rather an oily fish and is best when cooked simply. It is delicious either hot or cold. As is true with all fish, there is little connective tissue in salmon; therefore, it benefits by short cooking. Frozen fish, if it is not to be stuffed, is best cooked in its frozen state. There are several ways to tell when fish is cooked to its proper point. It will flake easily when tested with a fork or toothpick; it can be easily punctured with a fork; and it will lose its translucent appearance.

- [ ] **To Bake**—You may bake a whole fish, a piece of fish, or steaks. Season fish and place in a greased baking dish on foil and brush with butter or oil. Add seasonings and some wine, broth, or tomato sauce before baking. Place in preheated very hot oven (450°F. to 475°F.). Allow 10 minutes of baking per inch of thickness, measured at the thickest point. If the fish is frozen, double the time.
- [ ] **To Bake in Foil**—Place fish in an envelope made of aluminum foil and set on a baking sheet. Add any seasonings you choose. Pinch the edges of the foil to seal it tightly. Allow about 5 minutes at 450° F. for the heat to penetrate the foil. Then allow 10 minutes per inch of thickness for fresh fish, and double that amount of time for frozen. Serve with a tomato sauce or a mustard sauce.
- [ ] **To Bake Stuffed**—Ask your fish dealer to remove the scales, fins, and viscera. If the fish is to be served whole, leave head

and tail on. Clean and wash the fish well. Salt the interior, and then stuff with a highly seasoned bread stuffing, a shellfish stuffing, or thinly sliced vegetables, together with herbs and butter. If you have had the backbone removed, allow about 1 cup of stuffing per pound of fish; otherwise, about ¾ cup per pound. Close the opening of the fish with small skewers or with toothpicks, and lace with light string. Place on a buttered baking sheet or on a bed of finely cut leeks, carrots, onions, and celery. Oil the fish well, add a cup or two of white wine, if you wish, and bake at 450°F., allowing 10 minutes per inch of thickness. Baste with butter or oil and fresh lemon juice or white wine. Serve with a wine sauce made with the pan juices; with a tomato sauce, to which you might add the pan juices; with a mushroom sauce; or with lemon butter.

☐ **To Broil**—Steaks, fillets, split fish, or even whole fish, if they are fairly small ones, broil extremely well. You will find that if you broil on a generous piece of foil, you can use the margins of the foil as handles to turn the fish. Again, allow 10 minutes cooking time per inch of thickness, doubling the time for frozen (unthawed) fish. Baste with butter or with wine and butter. Broiled fish should be delicately browned on both sides. In the case of split fish, broil skin side to broiling unit first and then turn to flesh side. Serve broiled salmon with lemon butter, anchovy butter, Béarnaise sauce or sauce Maltaise. Crisp fried potatoes and a good wine are excellent accompaniments.

☐ **To Charcoal-Broil**—Steaks or fillets are best for charcoal broiling. If you place the fish in a hinged grill with a handle, it will be easier to turn over the charcoal. Oil the grill well, and brush the fish with oil or butter. Broil approximately 10 minutes per inch of thickness, depending on the strength of the charcoal heat. Serve with a Béarnaise sauce or with a barbecue sauce.

☐ **To Sauté**—Salmon steaks or fillets are ideal for sauté Meunière. For four 1-inch steaks place 3 tablespoons each of butter and oil in a heavy skillet, and heat. The oil will prevent the butter from burning. Cook the fish gently over medium heat, turning once very carefully with 2 spatulas. A 1-inch steak should take 10 to 12 minutes. Add a bit of white wine to the pan as you sauté. Remove fish to a hot platter and season to taste. Add chopped parsley to the pan, together with more butter, if necessary, and heat briefly before pouring over fish. Serve with plain boiled potatoes and wedges of lemon.

As a variation, add ½ cup *red* wine to the pan just before turning the fish, and let it cook down. It will lend a de-

**Broiled Salmon Steaks**

**Salmon with Cucumber Sauce**

licious flavor and a pleasant color.

☐ **To Deep-Fry**—Fillets, steaks, or strips of salmon may be deep-fried. The fish should be cut into even slices and rubbed with salt. Dip into batter or beaten egg and milk and then into flour, crumbs, or sesame seeds. Place carefully in a frying basket, very little at a time. Dip into fat heated to 375°F. on a frying thermometer and fry for 2 to 4 minutes, depending upon size of fish. Serve with lemon wedges and boiled parsley potatoes. Also try deep-fried parsley for a garnish that is unusual and delicious: Wash fresh parsley and dry well; dip for a minute into the hot fat.

☐ **To Poach**—This is probably the finest preparation for salmon whether it is to be served hot or cold. It is best done in a Court Bouillon, which may later be clarified and used for a sauce or for an aspic. Cooking and handling of salmon is made simple if the fish is first placed in cheesecloth, with ends of the cloth extending outside the fish boiler, to be used for turning or lifting the fish. Estimate 10 minutes per inch of fish measured at the thickest point, doubling the time for frozen fish.

### Court Bouillon

*Ingredients are based on 2 quarts liquid. If recipe is doubled, adjust seasoning accordingly.*

- 1 to 4 cups red or white wine and an equal amount of water, depending upon the size of the fish
- 1 tablespoon salt, or to taste
- 1 celery stalk
- 1 onion stuck with 2 cloves
- 1 carrot, sliced
- ¼ teaspoon thyme
- 1 teaspoon tarragon
- ½ teaspoon freshly ground black pepper
- 1 tablespoon chopped parsley
- 1 bay leaf

Combine all ingredients and boil for 10 minutes before adding fish.* If it is a very large fish, you will probably want to double this recipe. You may also adjust seasonings, using dill instead of other herbs.

* Salmon may also be poached in water, or in milk; or it may be steamed over hot water, if very tightly covered and sealed. The timing is the same as for "Poached Salmon."

After fish is cooked, remove carefully to a hot platter, if it is to be served warm. Serve with hollandaise sauce and tiny boiled potatoes. Some people prefer an egg sauce, made with a cream sauce to which chopped hard-boiled eggs and, sometimes, parsley have been added. This dish, incidentally, with boiled new potatoes and fresh peas, used to be the traditional New England Fourth of July feast.

If the fish is to be served cold, it should be allowed to cool slowly. The sauce or bouillon may be strained and clarified and used as the basis for an aspic to glaze the fish. However, the fish should first be skinned very carefully and decorated with cut vegetables, truffles, olives, or whatever else may be suitable. Serve cold salmon with either a good mayonnaise or a *sauce verte*. A vegetable salad is more or less standard as an accompaniment. Cold salmon makes a festive and delicious buffet dish.

☐ **To Freeze**—Cut fish into steaks after cleaning and eviscerating. Wash thoroughly. Dip fish into an ascorbic-acid solution to prevent yellowing and development of off-flavors. Mix 1 tablespoon ascorbic acid into 4 cups water and dip fish into solution for 20 seconds. Drain fish and wrap in moisture-vaporproof material, excluding as much air as possible. Seal.

# SALMON COOK BOOK

## FRESH SALMON

### DEEP-FRIED SALMON CUTLETS

- 2 cups flaked salmon steaks, about 1¼ pounds raw (directions for poaching, at left)
- 1 cup evaporated milk, undiluted
- 1 cup soft bread crumbs
- 1 teaspoon vinegar
- 1 teaspoon salt
- ⅛ teaspoon paprika
- 2 eggs
- ¾ cup fine dry bread crumbs
- Fat for frying

Mince salmon fine. Heat evaporated milk with soft bread crumbs, vinegar, salt, and paprika until scalded. Pour over 1 slightly beaten egg yolk, add salmon, and mix well. Fold in 1 stiffly beaten egg white. Chill for several hours. Shape into 8 cutlets. Roll in crumbs and dip into remaining egg mixed with 2 tablespoons cold water. Roll again in crumbs and chill for about 1 hour longer. Then fry in hot deep fat (370° to 375°F. on a frying thermometer) until golden-brown. Serve with creamy egg sauce, chili sauce, ketchup, or lemon sections. Makes 4 servings.

### SALTED SALMON

- 1 salmon (5 pounds)*
- 5 tablespoons sugar
- 2 tablespoons salt
- 6 sprigs of fresh dill
- 2 cups coarse salt

Clean fish and remove head, tail, backbone, and fins. Mix sugar and salt and rub over fish. Cut fish into 2-inch slices. Chop leaves from 4 sprigs of dill, saving remainder for later use. In the bottom of a large bowl place a layer of coarse salt and a sprinkling of dill leaves. Put a layer of fish pieces on top of this and continue layering, ending with a layer of salt. Place a weight on top of the fish and put in the refrigerator for 3 days. Serve cold with fresh dill to decorate. Makes 6 to 8 servings.

* The salmon *must* be fresh, not frozen. **Note:** This recipe, of Swedish origin, makes a wonderful smorgasbord dish; it can also be served as an entrée at luncheon.

## SMOKED SALMON

### SALMON HORSERADISH CONES

- ½ cup heavy cream
- 2 tablespoons grated horseradish
- ½ teaspoon salt
- 1 envelope unflavored gelatin
- 1 tablespoon vinegar
- 8 thin slices smoked salmon

Whip cream until quite stiff. Fold in horseradish (if possible, freshly grated, otherwise well-drained bottled or dried) and salt. Mix gelatin with vinegar and soften over hot water. Cool, and fold into first mixture. Shape salmon slices into cones and fill with mixture. Refrigerate for at least 2 hours before serving on plates with forks. Makes 8.

### SMOKED SALMON WITH CUCUMBER DIP

- 2 medium cucumbers
- ½ cup dairy sour cream
- 3 tablespoons cider vinegar
- 1 tablespoon minced chives
- ½ teaspoon crumbled fresh dill
- ¾ teaspoon salt
- ⅛ teaspoon pepper
- ¼ pound smoked salmon, very thinly sliced
- Pumpernickel bread
- Butter

Wash and peel cucumbers. Slice thin. Mix sour cream, vinegar, chives, dill, salt, and pepper. Pour over cucumbers and mix. Cover and chill for 2 to 3 hours. Put salmon on thin slices of pumpernickel, spread with butter. Serve as an appetizer, spreading cucumber mixture on top of salmon. Makes 6 servings.

### SCRAMBLED EGGS WITH SMOKED SALMON

- 4 thin slices of smoked salmon
- ¼ cup butter

9 eggs
½ cup light cream
Salt and pepper
Hot toast

Cut salmon into very thin strips. Sauté lightly in the butter in large skillet. Beat eggs with cream and add to skillet. Cook over low heat, stirring occasionally, until of desired doneness. Season with salt and pepper to taste and serve on or with buttered toast. Makes 4 servings.

# CANNED SALMON: APPETIZERS

### CURRIED-SALMON TRIANGLES

1 can (1 pound) salmon
⅔ cup mayonnaise or salad dressing
1 tablespoon chili sauce
1 tablespoon minced pimiento
1 tablespoon minced green pepper
1 teaspoon grated onion
¼ teaspoon curry powder
16 slices of toast, cut into triangles
Butter

Drain salmon and mash. Add remaining ingredients except toast and butter, and mix well. Butter toast triangles lightly and spread with salmon mixture. Garnish, if desired, with additional bits of pimiento and green pepper. Makes 64.

### SALMON BALLS

1 can (7½ ounces) salmon
1 package (3 ounces) cream cheese, softened
1 tablespoon chopped pickle
½ teaspoon Worcestershire
Mayonnaise to moisten
Chopped parsley

Drain salmon and mash. Mix with remaining ingredients except parsley. Shape into ¾-inch balls and roll in parsley. Makes about 3 dozen.

### SALMON DIP

1 can (1 pound) salmon
Juice of 1 lemon
2 teaspoons chopped chives
1 teaspoon minced onion
¼ teaspoon crumbled dried rosemary
6 peppercorns, crushed
Dash of ground cloves
½ teaspoon salt
1 cup dairy sour cream

Drain salmon and mash. Add remaining ingredients except sour cream and mix well. Fold in sour cream. Chill for at least 1 hour. Makes 2 cups.

# CANNED SALMON: SOUPS

### CREAM-OF-SALMON SOUP

2 tablespoons butter or margarine
1 tablespoon all-purpose flour
3 cups milk, scalded with 1 slice of onion
1 can (1 pound) salmon
Salt and pepper
Chopped parsley

Melt butter and blend in flour. Remove onion from milk. Gradually stir milk into butter-and-flour mixture. Cook, stirring constantly, until slightly thickened. Add salmon with its liquid, breaking up fish with fork. Season with salt and pepper to taste and serve with a sprinkling of parsley. Makes about 1 quart, or 4 servings.

### SALMON AND TOMATO BISQUE

1 can (1 pound) salmon
1 can (19 ounces) tomatoes
2 parsley sprigs, minced
1½ cups water
1 small onion, minced
2 tablespoons butter or margarine
2 tablespoons all-purpose flour
1 can (14½ ounces) evaporated milk
Salt and pepper
Cheese popcorn (optional)

Put salmon with its liquid into large saucepan. Add tomatoes, parsley, and water. Bring to boil and simmer for 20 minutes. In saucepan, cook onion in the butter for 2 or 3 minutes. Blend in flour. Remove from heat. Gradually add evaporated milk, put over heat and cook, stirring constantly, until thickened. Add salmon mixture. Season to taste with salt and pepper and heat well, but do not boil. Serve with a little popcorn floating on top, if desired. Makes about 1½ quarts, or 4 servings.

### SALMON AND TOMATO SOUP

1 medium onion, chopped
½ green pepper, chopped
2 tablespoons butter or margarine
3 cups diced potatoes
4 cups water
½ teaspoon crumbled dried thyme
1½ teaspoons salt
¼ teaspoon pepper
2 bouillon cubes
2 cups (one 1-pound can) tomatoes
2 cups (one 1-pound can) salmon
2 tablespoons sherry

Cook onion and pepper in the butter for 5 minutes. Add all ingredients except last 2 and simmer for about 15 minutes. Add salmon, broken into chunks, and the liquid from the can. Add sherry, and heat. Makes 6 servings.

# CANNED SALMON: MAIN DISHES

### SALMON WITH SOUFFLÉED CAPER SAUCE

Remove bones and skin from 2 cans (1 pound each) salmon. Break into large pieces in shallow baking dish. Heat in preheated moderate oven (350°F.) for about 15 minutes. Remove from oven. Cover with a mixture of ¾ cup mayonnaise mixed with 2 tablespoons chopped parsley, 3 tablespoons capers, and dash of cayenne; fold in 2 stiffly beaten egg whites. Broil for 5 minutes, or until sauce

is puffed and lightly browned. Makes 4 servings.

### CURRIED SALMON LOAF

1 box (3 ounces) lemon-flavored gelatin
1½ cups hot water
¼ cup fresh lemon juice
½ teaspoon salt
2 hard-cooked eggs, sliced
1 teaspoon finely minced chives
1 teaspoon capers
½ medium cucumber, peeled and sliced
1 can (1 pound) salmon, drained and flaked
½ cup mayonnaise
1 teaspoon curry powder
1 teaspoon instant minced onion
Salad greens

Dissolve gelatin in hot water, add lemon juice and salt, and chill until slightly thickened. Pour a little of mixture into loaf pan (9 x 5 x 3 inches). Arrange egg slices on gelatin and sprinkle with chives and capers. Chill until firm. Add a little more gelatin and cover with a layer of cucumbers. Mix remaining ingredients except greens and spread on cucumbers. Cover with remaining gelatin and chill until firm. Unmold on greens. Makes 6 servings.

### SALMON LOAF

1 can (1 pound) salmon
2 cups soft bread crumbs
2 eggs, slightly beaten
½ cup milk
2 tablespoons each of chopped onion and parsley
1 teaspoon salt
Dash of pepper

Mash salmon. Combine with remaining ingredients and put mixture in a greased loaf pan (9 x 5 x 9 inches). Bake in preheated moderate oven (350°F.) for 45 minutes or until firm. Makes 4 servings.

### SALMON DIVAN

4 packages (10 ounces each) frozen broccoli
¼ cup butter or margarine
¼ cup all-purpose flour
1 teaspoon salt
¼ teaspoon pepper
2½ cups hot milk
2 tablespoons sherry
4 cups (two 1-pound cans) salmon, in chunks
¼ cup grated Parmesan cheese
1 tablespoon fine dry bread crumbs

Cook broccoli according to package directions. Drain and put in shallow 2-quart baking dish. Melt butter and stir in flour, salt, and pepper. Add milk. Cook over moderate heat, stirring constantly, until mixture is smooth and thickened. Remove from heat and stir in sherry. Top broccoli with salmon chunks. Pour sauce over salmon. Combine Parmesan cheese and bread crumbs. Sprinkle over sauce. Bake in a preheated very hot oven (450°F.) for 15 to 20 minutes or until golden-brown and bubbly. Makes 8 to 10 servings.

## SALMON MOUNDS WITH CURRY-MUSHROOM SAUCE

1 small onion, minced
¼ cup melted butter or margarine
1 can (1 pound) salmon
  Milk
3 cups soft bread crumbs
2 eggs
¼ teaspoon poultry seasoning
¼ cup minced parsley
¼ teaspoon salt
  Dash of ground nutmeg
1 can (10½ ounces) cream-of-mushroom soup
½ teaspoon curry powder
½ teaspoon paprika
2 stuffed olives, sliced

Cook onion in the butter until golden. Drain salmon, reserving liquid. Add enough milk to liquid to make ½ cup. Mix onion, salmon, liquid, crumbs, eggs, poultry seasoning, parsley, salt, and nutmeg. Shape into 6 mounds in large shallow baking dish. Combine ½ cup milk, the soup, curry powder, and paprika. Pour around salmon. Top each salmon mound with a slice of olive. Bake, uncovered, in preheated moderate oven (350°F.) for about 45 minutes. Makes 6 servings.

## SALMON AND SHRIMP CASSEROLE

1 can (1 pound) salmon
1 can (4½ ounces) shrimps
1 can (3 or 4 ounces) sliced mushrooms, drained
2 tablespoons butter or margarine
2 tablespoons all-purpose flour
1 cup light cream
½ cup dry white wine
½ teaspoon salt
  Pepper
  Instant mashed potatoes, prepared
  Paprika

Drain salmon and flake with fork into large pieces; put in shallow baking dish. Add shrimps, drained and rinsed, and the mushrooms. Melt butter and blend in flour. Gradually add cream, stirring constantly. Stir in wine, salt, and pepper to taste. Cook, stirring, until thickened. Pour over fish and mushrooms. Spoon potatoes around edge of dish. Sprinkle with paprika. Bake in preheated hot oven (425°F.) for about 20 minutes. Makes 4 servings.

## SALMON-AND-POTATO BAKE

3 tablespoons butter or margarine
3 tablespoons all-purpose flour
1 teaspoon salt
⅛ teaspoon pepper
2 cups milk
1 can (1 pound) salmon, drained
4 cups sliced cooked potatoes
½ cup mayonnaise
½ cup shredded sharp Cheddar cheese
2 teaspoons Worcestershire
1 teaspoon prepared mustard
  Paprika

Melt butter and blend in flour, salt, and pepper. Gradually add milk and cook, stirring constantly, until thickened. Flake salmon and add to first mixture. Arrange in alternate layers with potatoes in shallow baking dish. Mix mayonnaise, cheese, Worcestershire, and mustard. Spread on top of mixture. Sprinkle with paprika. Bake in preheated moderate oven (350°F.) for about 30 minutes. Makes 4 servings.

## SALMON NEWBURG

3 tablespoons butter or margarine
3 tablespoons all-purpose flour
¼ teaspoon each of salt and powdered mustard
  Dash of pepper
1 cup milk
½ cup light cream
1 can (1 pound) salmon and liquid
2 egg yolks
2 tablespoons sherry
1 tablespoon grated Parmesan cheese
  Hot toast, biscuits, or waffles

Melt butter and blend in flour and seasonings. Gradually add milk and cream and cook, stirring constantly, until thickened. Add salmon liquid and stir a little of the hot mixture into egg yolks. Stir into mixture remaining in saucepan. Cook for about 2 minutes, stirring. Add sherry, Parmesan, and flaked salmon. Heat, and serve on toast. Makes 4 servings.

## SALMON-SPAGHETTI CASSEROLE

2 tablespoons butter or margarine
2 tablespoons chopped green pepper
1 small onion, chopped
1 can (1 pound) salmon, undrained
2 cans cream-of-mushroom soup
½ cup milk
2 pimientos, chopped
2 hard-cooked eggs, sliced
1 tablespoon chopped olives
1 package (8 ounces) spaghetti
¼ cup grated sharp Cheddar cheese

Heat butter in skillet. Add green pepper and onion and cook until tender. In 3-quart casserole combine salmon, soup, milk, pimientos, eggs, and olives. Add onion mixture and stir well. Cook spaghetti, drain, and put on top of salmon mixture. Sprinkle with cheese. Bake in preheated hot oven (400°F.) for about 30 minutes. Makes 6 servings.

## SALMON-STUFFED PEPPERS

4 green peppers, split and seeded
1 teaspoon instant minced onion
1 cup soft bread crumbs
1 egg
½ cup milk
  Salt and pepper to taste
1 teaspoon fresh lemon juice
1 can (7½ ounces) salmon, flaked
2 tablespoons butter or margarine

Parboil peppers in boiling salted water for 5 minutes; drain. Mix onion, ½ cup crumbs, and remaining ingredients except butter. Fill peppers with the mixture. Melt butter and mix with remaining crumbs. Sprinkle on top of peppers. Bake in preheated hot oven (400°F.) for about 15 minutes. Makes 4 servings.

## SALMON WIGGLE

1 can (1 pound) salmon
3 tablespoons butter or margarine
3 tablespoons all-purpose flour
½ teaspoon seasoned salt
½ teaspoon Worcestershire
⅛ teaspoon pepper
1½ cups milk
1 can (8½ ounces) peas, drained
  Hot toast, mashed potatoes, chow-mein noodles, or hot cooked rice

Flake salmon, but do not drain. Melt butter and blend in flour and seasonings. Gradually add milk and cook, stirring constantly, until thickened. Add salmon with its liquid and peas. Heat well and serve on toast. Makes 4 servings.

## SALMON PATTIES

1 can (1 pound) salmon
3 tablespoons water-ground cornmeal
1 tablespoon all-purpose flour
2 tablespoons vinegar
  Salt and pepper to taste
  Fat for frying

Flake salmon, but do not drain. Add remaining ingredients except fat. Shape into 8 flat patties. Fry on both sides in ½ inch hot fat in skillet. Drain on absorbent paper. Makes 4 servings.

## SALMON CROQUETTES

3 cups flaked cooked salmon
⅓ cup butter or margarine
⅓ cup all-purpose flour
¾ teaspoon salt
⅛ teaspoon pepper
1½ cups milk
1 tablespoon each of minced onion and parsley
1 teaspoon vinegar
1 cup fine dry bread crumbs
1 egg, slightly beaten
2 tablespoons cold water
  Fat for frying
  Creamy Egg Sauce (page 1620)

Mince fish fine. Melt butter in saucepan. Blend in flour, salt, and pepper. Gradually add milk and cook until very thick, stirring constantly. Add onion, parsley, vinegar, and fish and mix well. Chill for several hours. Shape into 12 croquettes. Roll in crumbs and dip into egg mixed with water. Roll again in crumbs. Chill for at least 1 hour. Then fry in hot deep fat (375°F. on a frying thermometer) until golden-brown. Drain on absorbent paper and serve with Creamy Egg Sauce. Makes 6 servings.

## SALMON SOUFFLÉ

1 can (7¾ ounces) salmon
  Milk
¼ cup butter or margarine
¼ cup all-purpose flour
½ teaspoon powdered mustard
¼ teaspoon salt
  Dash of cayenne
6 eggs, separated
1 tablespoon chopped parsley

Drain salmon, reserving liquid. Flake salmon. Add enough milk to the liquid to make 1 cup. Melt butter and blend in flour and seasonings. Gradually add milk mixture and cook, stirring constantly, until thickened. Beat egg whites until stiff and set aside. Beat egg yolks until thick. Stir a little of the hot sauce into yolks. Stir into sauce remaining in saucepan. Add parsley and salmon. Fold mixture into egg whites. Pour into well-greased 2-quart casserole. Bake in preheated moderate oven (350°F.) for 45 minutes, or until firm. Makes 6 servings.

## CANNED SALMON: SALADS

### SALMON-POTATO SALAD

1 can (1 pound) salmon
1 cup sliced celery
1½ cups cubed cooked potatoes
½ cup sweet pickle relish
½ teaspoon salt
¼ teaspoon pepper
1 tablespoon prepared horseradish
1 tablespoon minced onion
1 cup cooked salad dressing

Drain salmon, remove skin, and separate into large pieces in bowl. Add celery, potatoes, relish, salt, pepper, horseradish, and onion. Chill. Just before serving, add salad dressing; mix lightly. Makes 4 to 6 servings.

### SALMON WITH CUCUMBER SAUCE

1 can (1 pound) salmon
½ cup dairy sour cream
½ teaspoon salt
¼ teaspoon pepper
1 cucumber, peeled, chopped, and drained
Capers (optional)

Chill salmon; drain, remove skin, and break into chunks. Season sour cream with salt and pepper. Add cucumber, and mix. Serve on salmon. Garnish with capers if desired. Makes 4 to 6 servings.

### COLD SALMON MOUSSE

2 envelopes unflavored gelatin
½ cup water
2 cans (1 pound each) salmon
1 cup diced celery
½ cup minced green pepper
½ cup chopped pimiento
¼ cup fresh lemon juice
3 cups mayonnaise
1 tablespoon grated onion
¼ teaspoon pepper
Dill pickle, thinly sliced
Hard-cooked eggs, shredded
3 tablespoons chopped chives or green onion

Soften gelatin in the water. Dissolve over hot water; cool. Mash salmon, including liquid. Add celery, green pepper, pimiento, lemon juice, 1½ cups mayonnaise, onion, and pepper; mix well. Stir in gelatin. Pack into 2-quart mold or bowl. Chill overnight. Unmold on serving plate and garnish with pickle slices and hard-cooked eggs. Serve with remaining mayonnaise mixed with chives. Makes 12 servings.

**Note:** Recipe may be halved, if desired.

### SALMON LOUIS

1 can (1 pound) salmon
1 head lettuce
2 tomatoes, cut into sixths
½ cup mayonnaise or salad dressing
2 tablespoons each of heavy cream and chili sauce
2 tablespoons each of chopped green pepper and green onion
2 hard-cooked eggs
1 tablespoon chopped olives
½ teaspoon fresh lemon juice
Dash each of salt and pepper

Drain and flake salmon. Shred lettuce and put in a shallow salad bowl. Arrange salmon on lettuce. Put tomatoes around edge. Mix next 5 ingredients. Chop egg whites and add with olives, lemon juice, salt, and pepper to mayonnaise mixture. Chill, and serve on salmon salad. Garnish with sieved hard-cooked egg yolks. Makes 6 servings.

## CANNED SALMON: SANDWICHES

### CURRIED-SALMON SANDWICHES

1 cup flaked canned salmon
⅓ cup chopped celery
¼ cup mayonnaise
1 teaspoon curry powder
1 tablespoon pickle relish
12 slices of bread
2 eggs, beaten
½ cup milk
⅛ teaspoon salt
Dash of pepper
Butter or margarine

Mix salmon, celery, mayonnaise, curry powder, and relish. Spread on half of bread slices; top with remaining slices. Mix eggs, milk, salt, and pepper. Dip sandwiches into mixture and brown on both sides in hot butter in heavy skillet. Makes 6 sandwiches.

### SALMON-OLIVE SANDWICHES

1 can (7½ ounces) salmon
¼ cup chopped black olives
2 tablespoons chili sauce
1 tablespoon fresh lemon juice
8 slices whole-wheat bread

Mix all ingredients except bread. Spread between slices of bread. Makes 4 sandwiches.

**SALSIFY**—Another name for oyster plant, a biennial herb cultivated for its root which is used as a vegetable.

**SALT**—Sodium chloride (NaCl), a substance formed by the combination of one sodium atom with one atom of chlorine. It occurs abundantly in nature in the sea, in other natural brines such as the Great Salt Lake in Utah, and the Dead Sea, and in crystalline form, known as rock salt. In connection with food, salt is used as a flavoring and as a preservative.

Commercial salt, once almost solely produced by the evaporation of sea water, is nowadays largely manufactured from natural brines and rock salt. Salt is produced in different grades, the finest being table salt with the coarser grades being used for preserving and refrigeration.

Iodine is sometimes added to table salt to make iodized salt, of great importance in the prevention of goiter in regions such as the Midwest in the United States where natural iodine is scarce.

Salt, like water, is essential for man's good health. It has always played an important part in civilization. In Roman times salt was of such importance that part of every soldier's pay included an allowance for it. This *salarium* has come down to us as the word "salary." Cakes of salt were used as money and, like money, were taxed. Salt was considered to be the fitting medium for unalterable exchanges or covenants, according to the Bible, as a symbol of incorruption and purity. The Apostle, speaking of "the salt of the earth" (Matthew 5:13) can bestow no greater praise. The Devil is said to hate salt because of this purity, and in Scotland salt is thought to drive away witches.

Part of the reason that salt was considered to exemplify incorruption was its power of preserving food from spoiling. In the days when ice was available only in a natural state and had to be transported long distances, if indeed it was obtainable at all, foods had to be salted to preserve them. If there was no salt it was impossible to keep perishable foods, especially in hot weather. It is no wonder that spilling salt has long been considered unlucky.

Salt is also the world's best flavoring, bringing out the natural flavor of food. At tables today it is served in small salt shakers or dishes, often one to each person. But in the days when the substance was worth its weight in gold it was served in a huge salt cellar in the center of the table. This was often weighted at the bottom to prevent it from tipping over and spilling a grain of the precious stuff, not only because spilling salt was thought to be unlucky, but because it was so expensive. The vessel and its contents were so important that they were used to measure social rank and distinction. At the medieval table, those who sat between the host and the salt near the head of the table were "above the salt," or honored guests. Domestics and others with no social distinction were placed "below the salt." In the early days of the American Colonies, when salt was still expensive, this custom carried over to plantation homes in Virginia.

In this country salt was of the tremendous value it had been in earlier times. In the settling of the frontier in the Midwest, salt was the most expensive item required by the settlers. It was necessary, according to one merchant of prerevolutionary days to "cure their meat when they come into the buffalo country." In those days salt was as much as four times the price of beef. Not until the 19th century did the price drop as low as $2.50 a bushel.

*Availability and Purchasing Guide*—Salt is universally available. There are various types on the market:

*Cooking or Table Salt*—Fine-grained salt containing about 40 per cent sodium chloride plus such additives as sodium or magnesium carbonate to make the salt free-flowing. *Iodized* salts are table salts with potassium or sodium iodide added.

*Seasoned Salt*—Fine-grained cooking salt containing various combinations of sugar, monosodium glutamate, spices, starch, onion, garlic, and herbs. Among the special seasoned salts are *garlic salt, onion salt, celery salt,* and *hickory-smoked salt.*

*Flake Salt (also called Dairy, Cheese, or Kosher Salt)*—Coarse-grained sea salt with natural iodine and minerals. It has a far more pronounced taste than ordinary salt and is used in gourmet cooking and on breads, since it sparkles.

*Pickling Salt*—Fine-grained pure salt (without any additives). Since it leaves no cloudy residue, it is used especially when clear pickles are desired.

*Rock Salt*—Coarse-grained salt in small blocks or chunks used for baking oysters and clams and in ice-cream freezers.

*Salt Substitutes*—Fine-grained chloride compounds in which the sodium has been replaced by other chemicals such as calcium or potassium. They must not be used on a continuous basis without a doctor's advice.

**SALT PORK**—The side of a hog, cured; it is a fattier portion with less lean than bacon. The fat is cured by the dry-salt method and is not smoked. Salt pork is used for larding and barding since it does not have a smoked flavor that would change the flavor of the meat being larded. It is also used for flavoring and for adding fat to many dishes such as baked beans, clam chowder, stew, etc.

*Availability*—Year round, by weight and also prepackaged.

*Storage*—Refrigerate in original wrapper. Do not freeze.

☐ Refrigerator shelf: 2 to 3 weeks

*Nutritive Food Values*—Contains niacin,

thiamine, and riboflavin, some calcium and potassium, and a trace of iron.

☐ 3½ ounces, raw = 783 calories
☐ 3½ ounces, fried = 341 calories

*Basic Preparation*—To release its full flavor without saltiness or rawness, salt pork should be blanched. When used as a seasoning, it should be browned before being added to other ingredients or having other ingredients added to it. The browning is not necessary for larding or barding.

☐ **To Blanch**—Put salt pork, diced, in a large quantity of cold water. Bring slowly to a boil and simmer for 3 to 10 minutes, or longer depending on the amount of salt pork. Drain and plunge immediately into cold water to firm. Cut into desired shapes and brown slightly in skillet, preferably in the French manner with a little butter.

If the pork is not very salty, it may be soaked in cold water, but this is not as desirable as blanching it.

### SALT-PORK AND BEAN CHOWDER

1 cup dried pea beans
1 quart water
¼ pound salt pork, diced
1 onion, chopped
1½ teaspoons salt
¼ teaspoon pepper
1 cup diced potatoes
1 cup diced celery and leaves
1 can (19 ounces) tomatoes
2 tablespoons all-purpose flour
2 cups milk, heated

Put beans and water in large kettle. Bring to boil and boil for 2 minutes. Remove from heat and let stand for 1 hour. Cook pork and onion until lightly browned. Add with drippings to beans. Simmer, covered, for 1 hour. Add all ingredients except last 2 and simmer for 30 minutes. Thicken with the flour blended with a little cold water. Add milk. Makes about 2 quarts, or 4 to 6 servings.

### BEEF WITH RED WINE

3 pounds beef for pot roast
¼ pound salt pork, blanched and diced
Salt and pepper
½ cup water
1 cup dry red wine
1 onion, sliced
1 bay leaf, crumbled
½ garlic clove, minced
All-purpose flour

Brown meat on all sides with the salt pork in a heavy kettle. Sprinkle with salt and pepper. Place a rack in bottom of kettle under meat; add remaining ingredients. Cover and simmer for 3 to 3½ hours. Remove meat and thicken liquid with a flour-and-water paste. Add salt and pepper to taste. Make 4 servings.

**Note:** The salt pork is essential to the characteristic flavor of this dish.

### BROILED CORN WITH SALT PORK

¼ pound salt pork
1 medium onion, minced
3 cups cooked or canned whole-kernel corn
Salt and pepper
½ cup chili sauce

Cut pork into thin slices and partially sauté. Remove from skillet and drain off all but 2 tablespoons drippings. Add onion to drippings and cook for 2 or 3 minutes. Add corn and season with salt and pepper to taste. Divide into 4 individual broilerproof baking dishes. Top with the chili sauce and pork. Broil for 10 minutes. Makes 4 servings.

**SAMPHIRE** (Crithmum maritimum)—A succulent-stemmed perennial which grows along the rocky coasts of northwestern Europe and Great Britain. The plant grows to a height of one to two feet and has a small white or yellowish flower. It is also known as fennel, parsley pert, and St. Peter's herb. The crisp aromatic leaves and young stems are used for salads, pickles, and as a potherb.

**SAND DAB**—A lean, salt-water fish belonging to the flounder family, found in the waters off the California coast. A small fish, its flesh has a delicate subtle flavor. For this reason it is usually prepared simply.

*Availability*—Fresh, usually sold whole, in California only.

*Storage*—See Red Snapper, page 1540.

*Caloric Value*

☐ 3½ ounces, raw = 79 calories

*Basic Preparation*—See Red Snapper, page 1540.

### SAND DABS MEUNIÈRE

Skin the fish and sprinkle with salt and pepper. Roll in all-purpose flour and brown quickly in butter. Remove to a hot platter. Add a little more butter to skillet and heat until golden. Add the juice of 1 lemon and 1 tablespoon chopped parsley. Pour over the fish and serve at once.

**SANDWICH**—A dish made up of a filling such as sliced meat, cheese, a savory spread, etc., placed on one slice or between two or more slices of bread. In the United States and England the word is generally used to describe foods placed between slices of bread, whereas in Scandinavia and Germany, sandwiches are most often the single-slice-plus-topping variety, what we call here an "open-face" sandwich.

Sandwich sizes can vary from the long hero to the tiny bite-size tea sandwich;

they can be made with all sorts of breads and rolls; and the possibilities for filling are endless: moist creamy fillings, smooth spreadable fillings, sliced meats, fish, cheese, or poultry. In fact, almost anything that spreads or slices can be made into a sandwich, as nourishing or elegant as desired.

Sandwiches can be cold or hot. Among the hot sandwiches are those served with gravy and many covered with cheese and grilled under a broiler. A sandwich can be dipped into a mixture of milk and eggs and fried; or toasted in waffle irons; or cooked until crisp on a griddle. Still others can be wrapped in foil and grilled for a barbecue, speared on kabobs and toasted in special grills, or deep-fried.

The custom of placing food between slices of bread is an old one; workers in the field have long been fed that way. But the sandwich takes its name from John Montagu, fourth Earl of Sandwich (1718-1792), who, reluctant to leave the gaming tables long enough to dine, had cold beef sandwiches made for him so that he could eat as he played.

### BREADS

Use breads that are firm and easily spread with butter, cheese, etc. Crusts may or may not be trimmed according to the type of sandwich being made. Always use a sharp or serrated-edge knife when slicing to prevent the tearing of the bread. Bread can be plain or toasted. If sandwiches are trimmed, save crusts from bread in a tightly covered container and use them for stuffings, croutons, and casserole toppings, as well as for making bread crumbs.

Make good use of the variety of bread available. Apart from homemade breads and rolls, these store-bought breads make good sandwiches: white, rye, cracked-wheat, pumpernickel, and oatmeal breads; frankfurter and sandwich rolls; canned orange-nut, date-nut, chocolate, and brown breads; French and Italian bread; plain and seeded hard rolls; English muffins.

For hero sandwiches, small French or Italian loaves are good. Or, if the long loaves are used, they can be cut into individual hero sandwich sizes before filling. Plain and seeded hard rolls are also good for hero-type sandwiches.

For out-of-hand sandwiches, almost any bread can be used.

For hot open-face sandwiches served with meat and gravy, white, cracked-wheat, whole-wheat, or oatmeal bread, or even sandwich rolls can be used. For cold open-face sandwiches, these same breads plus rye and pumpernickel can be used.

For tea sandwiches, canned chocolate, nut, and brown breads; or crust-trimmed white, whole-wheat, cracked wheat, or oatmeal breads can be used.

### SPREADING

Spread butter or margarine to the edges of the bread to prevent the filling from soaking the bread. And use soft butter for easier spreading. One pound of softened butter or margarine spreads about 96 slices if you use 1 teaspoon per slice. Mayonnaise is preferable to butter when sandwiches have to be kept for some time, as when being carried to a picnic in warm weather. It will not melt as butter or margarine does. One pint of mayonnaise spreads about 50 average slices of bread.

### FILLINGS

To prevent tearing the bread when spreading a filling, use a blunt knife or spatula. If the crusts are to be trimmed, do this before spreading the filling. Spread the filling right to the edges of the slice of bread, or else the sandwich eater will feel cheated.

Many prepared sandwich fillings are available: deviled ham; luncheon-meat spread; liver pâté; chicken spread; sandwich spread; whipped cream cheese, cream cheese with pimientos, with olives and pimientos, with pineapple, with chives, with Roquefort, bars of date-and-nut cream cheese and clam-and-lobster cream cheese; chopped olive spread; blue-cheese spread; bacon-cheese spread; smoke-flavored cheese spread; and many others. Hot meat and poultry sandwiches can be varied by topping open-face sandwiches with sauce or gravy such as cheese sauce, meat-loaf sauce, tomato sauce, spaghetti sauce, curry sauce, brown or mushroom gravy, or à la king sauce.

### GARNISHES

Add assorted pickles and olives; cucumber, carrot, and celery sticks; salad greens; tomato slices or wedges; green onions; carrot curls; radishes; onion rings; green-pepper strips. With a sweet sandwich try dates, plumped prunes, maraschino cherries, or other fruits.

### SHAPES

■ **Pinwheel Sandwiches**—Cut bread into lengthwise slices and trim crusts. Flatten slices lightly with a rolling pin. Spread bread with a smooth filling and place sweet gherkins, olives, strips of pimiento or green pepper at one of the short sides. Starting at the side roll up tightly and wrap closely in wax paper. Chill. When ready to serve, cut into ½-inch slices.

■ **Rolled Sandwiches**—Use slices of soft bread with the crusts trimmed. Flatten with rolling pin. Spread with watercress or parsley butter or similar filling and roll up. Cover with a damp towel and refrigerate until ready to serve. For a

party look, push tiny sprigs of parsley or watercress into the sandwich ends.

■ **Ribbon Sandwiches**—Stack 2 slices of whole-wheat bread and 2 slices of white bread alternately with one or more fillings between slices. Press together and trim crusts. Wrap, and chill. Cut into ½-inch slices to serve.

■ **Checkerboard Sandwiches**—Prepare and cut ribbon sandwiches. Then stack 3 ribbon sandwiches so white and whole-wheat sections alternate. Spread filling between ribbons. Wrap; chill. To serve, cut into ½-inch slices.

■ **Open Sandwiches**—This kind of sandwich consists of one slice of bread only, spread with butter, mayonnaise, or another spread, and topped with any kind of fish, meat, or vegetable toppings, or a combination of all of these. Most open sandwiches are cold, but there are also hot ones where the topping of meat or fowl is covered with gravy.

Open sandwiches are eaten with a knife and fork. They are eaten for lunch, supper, and any-time snacks in Denmark, Sweden, Norway, Finland, and Germany, where they are standard fare. These countries excel at the art of making them as pretty as a picture by arranging the toppings not only for taste combinations, but with an eye for appearance. They use ingredients with contrasting colors such as hard-cooked egg and tomato, roast beef and chopped onion, or herring topped with dill sprigs, to name but a few of the endless combinations. Furthermore, the sandwiches are decorated with twists of lemon, cucumber, tomato, carrot curls, pickled red beets, and sprigs of parsley or dill.

To prepare handsome open sandwiches follow these rules:

Cut bread as thin as possible and use only firm breads that will not fall apart when spread with butter or mayonnaise. Crusts are generally trimmed from the bread. The filling is spread to the edges and the garnish piled on top.

### FREEZING SANDWICHES

To eliminate last-minute work, many sandwiches can be frozen prior to serving. All fresh breads freeze well. Spread bread generously with soft butter to keep fillings from soaking in. Package finished sandwiches individually wrapped and sealed in moisture-vapor-proof wrapping.

For fillings in sandwiches to be frozen use cooked egg yolk, peanut butter, cooked chicken, turkey, meat, fish, dried beef, or drained crushed pineapple. Do not use very moist fillings, cooked egg white, or raw vegetables. For binders use lemon, orange, pineapple, or other fruit juice, milk, dairy sour cream, or applesauce. Avoid mayonnaise or salad dressings; they separate when frozen.

# Sandwich Cook Book

**Chef's Club Sandwich**

## HEARTY HOT SANDWICHES

### HAMBURGER CORN-BREAD SANDWICHES

1 package corn-bread mix
1 pound beef chuck, ground
1 teaspoon salt
1/8 teaspoon pepper
1 onion, chopped
1 can (10½ ounces) cream-of-mushroom soup
1/4 cup milk
1 can (3 ounces) sliced mushrooms, drained
Chopped parsley
8 pimiento strips

Bake corn bread as directed on label, cut into 4 squares, and split. Put bottom halves on ovenproof platter. Mix next 4 ingredients and shape into 4 patties. Cook to desired doneness and put one on each bottom half of corn bread. Heat next 3 ingredients and put some on each hamburger. Add top halves of bread and more sauce. Heat in preheated moderate oven (350°F.) for about 10 minutes. Garnish with parsley and a cross of pimiento. Makes 4 sandwiches.

### CHILI BEEFBURGER SANDWICHES

1 pound beef chuck, ground
3/4 teaspoon salt
1 teaspoon powdered mustard
1½ teaspoons chili powder
1/2 teaspoon celery salt
1/4 teaspoon pepper
1/4 teaspoon garlic
2 tablespoons instant minced onion
1/4 cup tomato sauce or meatless spaghetti sauce
4 sandwich rolls, split and toasted

Mix all ingredients except rolls. Shape into 4 patties. Fry in greased skillet until of desired doneness. Serve between rolls. Makes 4 sandwiches.

### SWEET-AND-SOUR HAMBURGER SANDWICHES

1 pound ground beef
1/4 pound ground pork
1 teaspoon salt
1/4 teaspoon pepper
6 slices of canned pineapple
1 tablespoon soy sauce
1/3 cup firmly packed brown sugar
1 tablespoon Worcestershire
1/2 teaspoon ground cloves
1/3 cup wine vinegar
6 green-pepper rings
6 sandwich rolls or other rolls

Mix first 4 ingredients. Shape into 6 patties and brown on both sides in greased skillet. Pour off fat. Put a pineapple slice on each patty. Mix next 5 ingredients and pour over patties. Cover and simmer for 10 minutes. Put green-pepper rings on pineapple. Cover and simmer for 5 minutes longer. Serve hamburgers with some of the sauce between split rolls. Makes 6 sandwiches.

### HAMBURGER ROLLS

Cut deep slits in tops of 8 oblong hard rolls. Cook 1 pound ground beef chuck until browned, breaking up meat with fork. Add 2/3 cup tomato sauce, 3/4 teaspoon salt, 1/4 cup sliced stuffed olives, and 1 cup diced Muenster or Mozzarella cheese. Fill rolls and sprinkle with dried oregano. Wrap each filled roll in a piece of aluminum foil. Heat on rack over hot coals for 15 minutes, turning often. Makes 8 rolls.

### SLOPPY JOES

1½ pounds beef chuck, ground
1 onion, chopped
1½ teaspoons salt
1/8 teaspoon pepper
3 tablespoons all-purpose flour
1/2 teaspoon Worcestershire
1 cup ketchup
1¼ cups water
4 sandwich rolls, split and toasted

Cook beef, onion, salt, and pepper until meat loses its red color, stirring with fork. Blend in flour. Add Worcestershire, ketchup, and water. Simmer, stirring frequently, for 20 minutes, or until thick. Serve between rolls. Makes 4 sandwiches.

### ITALIAN SLOPPY JOES

3/4 pound Italian-style bulk sausage
3/4 pound ground round steak
3/4 teaspoon each of garlic powder and salt
1/4 teaspoon pepper
4 cans (8 ounces each) tomato sauce
3/4 teaspoon sweet basil
6 crusty French rolls
12 slices Mozzarella cheese (about 12 ounces)
Paprika

Mix sausage and beef and brown in saucepan. Stir in next 4 ingredients. Bring to boil and simmer for 1½ to 2 hours. Add basil and simmer for 30 minutes longer. Skim off excess fat. Slice rolls into halves lengthwise. Cover inside top half with 2 cheese slices and sprinkle with paprika. Broil until cheese melts. Spread meat mixture on bottom half of rolls. Close sandwiches and serve hot. Makes 6.

### STEAK ROLLS

2 tablespoons each of vinegar and water
Salt and pepper
1 cucumber, peeled and chopped
1 sweet onion, sliced
1½ pounds thinly sliced beef round steak
All-purpose flour
3 tablespoons shortening
8 sandwich rolls, split and toasted

Mix vinegar, water, 1 teaspoon salt, and 1/4 teaspoon pepper; bring to boil. Pour over cucumber and onion. Cover; refrigerate for several hours or overnight. When ready to serve, pound steak. Cut into 8 pieces. Roll in mixture of flour, salt, and pepper. Brown on both sides in hot shortening. Put a piece between halves of each roll. Serve with the sauce. Makes 8 sandwiches.

### FRENCH-TOAST SANDWICHES WITH CREAMED DRIED BEEF

Butter or margarine
1 jar (5 ounces) dried beef, shredded
3 tablespoons all-purpose flour
2¾ cups milk
1/2 teaspoon caraway seeds
1/4 teaspoon ground rosemary
Pepper
3 eggs
1/2 teaspoon salt
8 slices of white bread

Melt 3 tablespoons butter; add beef and cook for 2 or 3 minutes. Blend in flour; add 2 cups milk. Cook, stirring constantly, until thickened. Add seeds, rosemary, and pepper to taste. Keep hot. Beat eggs; add remaining milk and the salt. Dip bread into mixture and fry in hot butter until golden-brown on both sides. Serve beef between and over toast. Makes 4 sandwiches.

### BEEF TENDERLOIN SANDWICHES

8 slices of bread, toasted
Butter or margarine (about 2/3 cup)
1 garlic clove, minced
4 slices (4 ounces each) of beef tenderloin
Salt and pepper to taste
Sherry (about 1 cup)
1/2 pound fresh mushrooms, sliced, or 1 can (4 ounces) sliced mushrooms, drained
1/2 cup water

Spread toast with soft butter. For each sandwich cut 2 slices into triangles and put on serving plate. Melt 1/4 cup butter in skillet. Add garlic and cook for 2 or 3 minutes. Add tenderloin and season with salt and pepper. Brown on both sides. Reduce heat and add 3/4 cup sherry. Cover and simmer for 10 minutes, basting occasionally. Remove meat and reserve drippings. In another skillet melt 1/4 cup butter. Add mushrooms and cook until lightly browned. Add 1/3 cup sherry and the water. Pour into first skillet and simmer for 5 minutes. Arrange meat on toast and spoon hot sauce over. Makes 4 sandwiches.

### CORNED-BEEF AND CHEESE SANDWICHES, MUSTARD DRESSING

8 large slices of rye bread
Prepared mustard
Thinly sliced corned beef
Thin slices Cheddar cheese
Mustard Dressing
Pimiento strips (optional)

Spread bread with prepared mustard. Cover bread with corned beef and overlapping cheese slices. Spread with Mustard Dressing to within 1/2 inch of edges. Put under broiler until Dressing is bubbly and cheese is melted. Garnish with pimiento if desired. Makes 8 sandwiches.

#### Mustard Dressing

Mix thoroughly 1 cup mayonnaise, 3 tablespoons prepared mustard, 1 tablespoon prepared horseradish, 1 teaspoon

Worcestershire, ½ cup well-drained pickle relish, and a dash of hot pepper sauce.

### PORK AND CURRIED-COLESLAW SANDWICHES

8 thin boned pork chops
All-purpose flour
Salt and pepper to taste
1 tablespoon butter
1½ teaspoons curry powder
⅓ cup water
¼ cup mayonnaise
2 tablespoons vinegar
4 cups finely shredded or chopped cabbage
4 sandwich rolls, split and toasted

Roll chops in flour and fry in greased skillet until browned and done; season. Keep hot. Melt butter in skillet; blend in 2 teaspoons flour and the curry powder. Add next 3 ingredients and cook, stirring, until slightly thickened. Add cabbage and cook for a few minutes longer. Put 2 pork chops on each bottom half of rolls; top with slaw. Add roll tops. Makes 4 sandwiches.

### HAWAIIAN OMELET SANDWICHES

8 slices of toast
Butter
8 eggs, beaten
2 teaspoons soy sauce
½ teaspoon salt
½ teaspoon monosodium glutamate
2 green onions, chopped
½ green pepper, chopped
1 cup (one 8¾-ounce can) pineapple tidbits, drained
1 medium tomato, chopped
1 package (6 ounces) frozen king crabmeat, thawed and drained
4 slices of baked ham

Spread toast with butter. Cut 4 slices diagonally into halves. Arrange 1 whole slice on each plate with a toast triangle on either side. Mix eggs and seasonings. Heat ⅓ cup butter in large skillet; add onions and green pepper; cook for 5 minutes. Add eggs and cook until set around edge. Sprinkle with next 3 ingredients. When egg is completely firm, fold omelet and cook for 5 minutes longer. Put a slice of ham on each whole toast slice; cut omelet into 4 portions and put one on each ham slice. Makes 4 sandwiches.

### MONTE CRISTO SANDWICHES

For each sandwich use 3 slices of bread. Butter one slice first, then cover with a slice each of baked ham and cooked chicken. Butter both sides of second bread slice, put on top, and cover with a generous slice of Swiss cheese. Butter third slice, and put on top; press slightly, and secure with a toothpick. Trim off crusts, and cut into halves diagonally. Mix 3 slightly beaten eggs, ⅓ cup milk, and ⅛ teaspoon salt (makes enough for 4 servings or 12 triangles). Dip sandwich halves into egg mixture. Fry in butter or margarine in skillet until golden-

brown on all sides, adding more butter when necessary. Remove toothpicks. Three triangles make a generous serving.

### ITALIAN GRINDERS

Split small loaves of Italian bread, or cut 10-inch pieces from long loaves, and split. Brush inside generously with garlic-seasoned olive oil. Put together, sandwich fashion, wth layers of sliced salami, Mozzarella cheese, and flat anchovy fillets. Wrap in foil and heat in preheated moderate oven (350°F.).

### BAKED TUNA-CHEESE LOAF

1 can (7 ounces) tuna fish, drained
1 teaspoon instant minced onion
2 tablespoons chopped sweet pickle
1 cup grated sharp Cheddar cheese
1 loaf of French or Italian bread about 12 inches long
¼ cup butter or margarine
1 teaspoon prepared mustard or ¼ teaspoon powdered mustard

Mix first 4 ingredients. Cut bread into halves lengthwise and remove a small amount of the crumbs. Spread inside with butter and mustard, mixed. Spread tuna filling between 2 halves of bread. Wrap in foil and bake in preheated moderate oven (350°F.) for about 20 minutes. Cut into 4 crosswise pieces. Makes 4 servings.

### CURRIED-TUNA SANDWICHES

1 can (7 ounces) tuna fish
½ cup diced celery
¼ cup chopped almonds
½ cup flaked coconut
½ cup mayonnaise
¾ teaspoon curry powder
⅛ teaspoon pepper
1 tablespoon fresh lemon juice
8 slices of toast

Mix flaked tuna, celery, almonds, coconut, mayonnaise, curry powder, pepper, and lemon juice. Spread on toast and broil for 3 minutes, or until lightly browned. Makes 8 sandwiches.

### SEAFOOD CLUB SANDWICHES

8 slices of white bread, toasted
Soft butter or margarine
Lettuce leaves
1 can (7 ounces) tuna fish, drained and flaked
1 jar (3¼ ounces) smoked oysters
Whole cooked shrimps
Hard-cooked egg slices
Sliced tomatoes and cucumbers
Sauce Tartare (page 1622)

Spread toast with butter and top 4 slices with lettuce. Cover lettuce with tuna, then with more lettuce. Arrange oysters, reserving several for garnish, on second layer of lettuce. Cover with remaining toast, secure with picks, and cut sandwiches into thirds. Garnish with oysters and next 4 ingredients. Serve with Sauce Tartare. Makes 4 sandwiches.

### SHRIMPBURGERS

1 box (12 ounces) frozen shelled cleaned cooked shrimps
3 tablespoons butter or margarine

3 tablespoons all-purpose flour
¾ cup milk
1 cup cooked rice
½ cup grated sharp Cheddar cheese
1 tablespoon instant minced onion
1 teaspoon salt
⅛ teaspoon pepper
½ teaspoon curry powder
Fine dry bread crumbs
Shortening for frying
6 sandwich rolls, split, toasted, and buttered

Thaw shrimps and cut into small pieces. Make a sauce with butter, flour, and milk. Add shrimps, rice, cheese, and seasonings. Chill; shape into 6 patties. Roll in crumbs and fry in small amount of hot shortening in skillet until golden-brown on both sides. Serve between roll halves, with chutney if desired. Makes 6 sandwiches.

### Lobsterburgers

Substitute an equal amount of finely diced lobster for shrimps in the recipe above.

### CHICKEN-CHEESE SANDWICHES

6 slices of cooked chicken
6 slices of toast
6 slices of tomato
½ cup finely crumbled blue cheese
1 egg, beaten
½ cup minced canned mushrooms
3 bacon strips, halved

Put a slice of chicken on each toast slice. Top with a slice of tomato. Mix cheese, egg, and mushrooms. Spread on tomato and top each with a half strip of bacon. Broil until bacon is crisp. Makes 6 sandwiches.

### HOT TURKEY SANDWICHES WITH MUSHROOM SAUCE

8 slices of white bread, toasted
Sliced cooked turkey
2 cans (10½ ounces each) condensed cream-of-mushroom soup
½ cup water
½ cup shredded sharp Cheddar cheese
8 slices of bacon, partially cooked
Hot mashed potato (optional)

Cut 4 slices of toast into halves diagonally. For each sandwich put 1 whole slice of toast with a half on each side in baking dish or individual ovenware plate. Cover toast with turkey. Mix soup and water. Heat, stirring, until smooth. Spoon sauce over turkey and sprinkle with cheese. Top with bacon. Make a border of mashed potato around each sandwich. Put under broiler until cheese is melted and potato is lightly browned. Makes 4 sandwiches.

### CONTINENTAL CLUB SANDWICHES

⅓ cup soft blue cheese
⅓ cup mayonnaise
About 2 cups (one 1-pound can) sliced peaches, drained
1 cup (8 ounces) creamed cottage cheese
18 slices of white bread
6 slices of cooked turkey
12 lettuce leaves

Hero Sandwich

6 slices of baked or boiled ham
6 slices of Swiss or Gruyère-type cheese

Mix blue cheese and mayonnaise. Combine peaches and cottage cheese. Toast bread and spread 6 slices with blue-cheese mixture, using only half of mixture. Cover each with a slice of turkey and a lettuce leaf. Spread 6 more slices of toast with peach mixture and cover with a slice of ham, a slice of Swiss cheese, and a lettuce leaf. Put toast slices with peach mixture over toast with blue cheese, spread side up. Spread 6 remaining slices of toast with remaining blue-cheese mixture and close sandwiches. Cut each into 4 pieces, fastening each with a pick. Put on serving plates and, if desired, garnish with potato chips, radish roses, parsley sprigs, pickle chips, and green olives. Makes 6 sandwiches.

### SUNDAY-NIGHT WESTERN SANDWICHES
6 tablespoons butter or margarine
1 medium onion, chopped
1 medium green pepper, chopped
2 cups chopped cooked ham
12 eggs, slightly beaten
1 cup milk
1 teaspoon salt
½ teaspoon pepper
16 slices of toast

Heat 6 tablespoons butter in skillet; add onion, green pepper, and ham; cook for 5 minutes. Spread evenly in pan 1 x 10 x 15 inches. Mix remaining ingredients except toast and pour into pan. Bake in preheated moderate oven (350°F.), for 15 minutes, or until firm. Cut into 8 pieces and serve each between 2 slices of buttered toast. Makes 8 sandwiches.

### HAM RABBIT SANDWICHES
3 tablespoons butter or margarine
3 tablespoons all-purpose flour
½ teaspoon each of paprika and powdered mustard
2 cups milk
1½ cups diced cooked ham
1½ cups shredded sharp Cheddar cheese
Salt and pepper
6 English muffins, split and toasted

Melt butter in saucepan; blend in flour, paprika, and mustard. Add milk and cook, stirring constantly, until thickened. Add ham, cheese, and salt and pepper to taste. Heat, and serve between and over muffins. Makes 6 sandwiches.

### CHEESE--AND-EGG BARBECUE SANDWICHES
½ pound sharp Cheddar cheese
2 tablespoons minced green pepper
1 medium onion, chopped
1 tablespoon ketchup
1 egg, hard-cooked and chopped
2 stuffed olives, chopped
2 tablespoons butter or margarine, melted
6 sandwich rolls

Combine all ingredients except rolls and mix thoroughly. Spread on split rolls and put under broiler until cheese is melted. Makes 6 servings.

### FRENCH-TOASTED MOZZARELLA SANDWICHES
Cut ½ pound Mozzarella cheese into 6 slices. Put between ½-inch slices of Italian bread. Dip into milk, into flour, then into well-beaten egg. Fry in hot olive oil until sandwich is golden-brown on both sides and cheese is slightly melted. Makes 6 small sandwiches.

### DENVER CHEESE SANDWICHES
¼ cup butter or margarine
1 small onion, minced
½ green pepper, minced
6 eggs, beaten
⅓ cup milk
½ teaspoon salt
⅛ teaspoon pepper
6 slices of process Swiss cheese
12 slices of hot toast, buttered

Melt butter in large skillet. Add onion and green pepper; cook for 5 minutes. Add next 4 ingredients, mixed. Cover and cook over very low heat until firm. Top with cheese, cover, and cook for a few minutes longer. Cut into 6 servings and serve between slices of toast. Makes 6 sandwiches.

### PIZZA, WESTERN STYLE
1½ cups canned tomatoes, drained and chopped
½ teaspoon oregano
2 tablespoons olive oil
Salt and pepper
1 loaf Italian bread
Slices of Mozzarella, or Cheddar cheese (or cooked Italian-sausage slices, or anchovies)
Grated Parmesan cheese

Put tomatoes, oregano, and olive oil in saucepan. Season with salt and pepper to taste. Bring to boil and simmer for 10 minutes. Split bread lengthwise and spread with tomato mixture. Arrange cheese slices on top and sprinkle with grated cheese. Put under broiler until bubbly. Cut diagonally into 2-inch pieces. Makes 4 servings.

## HEARTY COLD SANDWICHES

### HERO SANDWICHES
Split hero loaves of bread lengthwise and brush inside and out with olive oil. On bottom half lay slices of Swiss cheese. Top with tomato slices, hard salami, pickled red pepper, ripe and pimiento-stuffed olives, flat anchovy fillets, and Italian parsley. Add top half of bread and cut sandwich into 3 crosswise pieces.

### HAM SALAD ROLLS
2 cups finely diced cooked ham
2 cups finely shredded cabbage
½ cup diced celery
½ green pepper, minced
1 hard-cooked egg, chopped
2 tablespoons prepared mustard
Dash of onion salt
2 frankfurter rolls
Salad dressing

Sweet-pickle slices

Mix first 7 ingredients. Open rolls; remove some crumbs from center and add to first mixture. Moisten salad with dressing and fill each roll. Garnish with pickle. Makes 8 sandwiches.

### DOWN-EAST SANDWICHES
Mash 2 cups (one 1-pound can) Boston-style baked beans. Spread on 4 slices of buttered toast. Add drained coleslaw, salt and pepper to taste, and a little ketchup. Top each with 2 browned sausage links and a second slice of buttered toast. Serve with pickles or olives. Makes 4 sandwiches.

### EGG-SALAD AND TONGUE SANDWICHES
Chop 6 hard-cooked eggs. Add 1 cup finely diced celery, 1 teaspoon instant minced onion, ½ teaspoon powdered mustard, ½ cup mayonnaise, and seasoned salt and pepper to taste. Toast and butter 12 slices of cheese bread. Other bread can be used, but cheese is especially good. Spread 6 slices with egg salad and put lettuce and sliced cold tongue on remaining toast. Put together, and serve with pickle relish. Makes 6 sandwiches.

### ROAST-BEEF AND BLUE-CHEESE SANDWICH
Spread white or whole-wheat bread with equal parts of blue cheese and soft butter, blended together. Top with slices of cold roast beef and sprinkle with chopped chives.

### CHEF'S CLUB SANDWICH
Toast and butter large oval slices of white bread. On bottom slice put baked or broiled ham and Swiss cheese. Add second slice of toast and top with lettuce, tomato slices, and crisp bacon. Add mayonnaise if desired. Add third slice of toast and top with sliced cooked chicken and lettuce. Add fourth slice of toast. Insert toothpick in center and top with a large green or stuffed olive.

### SARDINE SWISS-CHEESE SANDWICHES
2 cans (3¾ ounces each) sardines
12 slices of buttered rye bread
6 slices of Swiss or Muenster cheese
6 tomato slices

Arrange sardines on 6 slices of bread. Top with a cheese slice and a slice of tomato. Cover with remaining bread. Makes 6 sandwiches.

### TUNA-EGG THREE-DECKERS
18 slices of white toast
Butter or margarine
1 can (7 ounces) tuna, flaked
½ cup diced celery
Mayonnaise or salad dressing (about ⅔ cup)
¼ cup chili sauce
2 tablespoons pickle relish
6 hard-cooked eggs, sliced
⅓ cup sliced stuffed olives
12 tomato slices
Lettuce or other salad greens

Spread 6 slices of toast with butter. Mix tuna, celery, and 2 tablespoons mayonnaise. Spread on buttered toast. Top with 6 slices of toast. Spread with mixture of ½ cup mayonnaise, the chili sauce, and pickle relish. Cover with egg slices, olives, tomato, and lettuce. Top with remaining toast. Makes 6 sandwiches.

### EGGPLANT, MOZZARELLA, AND PIMIENTO LONG BOYS

Split four 6-inch lengths of French bread. Brush with olive oil and sprinkle with garlic salt. Slice 1 pound Mozzarella cheese and cover half of each length of bread. Add some pimiento slices. Peel and slice 1 medium eggplant ½ inch thick. Roll slices in flour and brown on both sides in hot fat. Season and put in overlapping slices on remaining halves of bread. Serve open. Makes 4 sandwiches.

### BLUE-CHEESE AND EGG SANDWICHES

Chop 3 hard-cooked eggs. Add 1 teaspoon instant minced onion, ¼ cup crumbled blue cheese, and ¼ cup mayonnaise or salad dressing. Mix well and season to taste with salt and pepper. Spread between slices of white or rye bread. Makes 4 sandwiches.

### POTATO, EGG, AND CHEESE SANDWICHES

2 medium potatoes, peeled
Salt
Boiling water
2 hard-cooked eggs
6 ounces sharp Cheddar cheese
1 medium sweet red or green pepper
½ small onion
Mayonnaise or salad dressing
Pepper
Prepared mustard and Worcestershire

Cook potatoes in boiling salted water until tender. Drain; using medium blade, put through food chopper with eggs, cheese, sweet pepper, and onion. Moisten mixture with mayonnaise. Season to taste with salt, pepper, mustard, and Worcestershire. Spread between slices of whole-wheat or pumpernickel bread. Makes 4 sandwiches.

### SKYSCRAPER SANDWICHES

Ingredients are listed starting with the bottom layer. To build these sandwiches assemble from the bottom.

■ **Barbecue Bonanza**—White toast, buttered; fried onion rings mixed with half-melted Cheddar cheese; rye toast, buttered; pork-roll slices, fried; hot-dog relish; white toast, buttered; shredded lettuce; hard-cooked egg, sliced; white toast, spread with mayonnaise; parsley.

■ **Broadway Special**—Rye or pumpernickel bread, buttered; chopped liver; Vienna bread, spread with mustard; Swiss-cheese slices; green-pepper strips; rye bread, buttered; salami or bologna; dill pickle, sliced; radish rose.

■ **Cold-Cuts Pyramid**—Pumpernickel bread, buttered; corned beef spread with mustard; white bread, buttered; shredded cabbage and green pepper with salad dressing; rye bread, buttered; Muenster cheese; wafer, buttered; smoked salmon; slice of red onion; fresh dill.

■ **Country-Club Luncheon**—Pumpernickel bread, buttered; cottage cheese and red caviar; Vienna bread, buttered; shrimp-and-celery salad; chicory; white bread, buttered; crisp bacon slices; tomato slices; wheat oval, buttered; watercress.

■ **Curry Surprise**—Whole-wheat bread, buttered; ham and chicken slices; whole-wheat bread spread with mayonnaise; hard-cooked egg and cucumber slices; white bread, buttered; shredded lettuce; tuna-fish salad; raisin bread; cream cheese, seasoned with curry powder; cashews, chopped; cut gingerroot.

■ **Roman Holiday**—Italian bread, buttered; hot eggplant, sliced and fried; Mozzarella cheese, sprinkled with oregano; Italian bread, spread with garlic-flavored olive oil; romaine and pimiento strips; Italian bread, buttered; anchovy fillets; olives and capers.

■ **Seafood Delight**—White bread, buttered; salmon- or tuna-and-celery salad; rye bread, spread with mayonnaise; cream cheese and olives; white bread with sandwich spread; crabmeat mixed with fresh lemon juice and green onion; rye bread; radish slices.

■ **Sunday-Night Supper**—White bread, spread with butter, seasoned with chopped mint; cold lamb, sliced; rye bread, buttered; salad of chopped cucumbers, onions, and radishes; white bread, buttered; watercress; deviled egg; gherkins.

■ **West-Coast Extravaganza**—Round of brown bread, buttered; cream-cheese pineapple spread; white bread, spread with mayonnaise; peanut butter and bacon strips; brown bread, buttered; shredded carrot with mayonnaise; white bread, buttered; stuffed olives.

## PICNIC AND LUNCH-BOX SANDWICHES

### TONGUE AND CHEESE SANDWICHES WITH CASHEWS

1 cup grated sharp Cheddar cheese
¼ cup mayonnaise
¼ cup finely chopped salted cashews
8 slices of whole-wheat bread
Thinly sliced smoked beef tongue
Lettuce or broken romaine leaves

Mix first 3 ingredients and spread on bread slices. Put tongue on 4 of the slices. Add lettuce and top with remaining bread slices. Cut into halves. Makes 4 sandwiches.

### CORNED-BEEF AND MUENSTER SANDWICHES

Spread 4 slices of whole-wheat bread with prepared mustard and 4 with mayonnaise. Put slices of corned beef on mustard-spread bread. Sprinkle with ¼ cup chopped green onion. Cover each with 1 slice of process Muenster cheese and top with mayonnaise-spread bread. Makes 4 sandwiches.

### PROVOLONE AND SALAMI SANDWICHES

Force 4 small sweet pickles and ½ pound each of Provolone cheese and cooked salami through food chopper, using medium blade. Add ¾ cup mayonnaise and mix well. Spread between 8 slices of bread to make 4 sandwiches.

### EGG, DEVILED-HAM, AND CHEESE SANDWICHES

Hard-cook 6 eggs, shell, and mash with 1 cup grated sharp Cheddar cheese. Add 2 teaspoons instant minced onion, 2 tablespoons ketchup, ½ teaspoon powdered mustard, ½ teaspoon Worcestershire, dash of hot pepper sauce, ¼ cup mayonnaise, and 2 small cans or 1 large can deviled ham. Mix thoroughly and spread between 8 slices of buttered white bread or toast. Makes 4 sandwiches.

### CREAM-CHEESE, CARROT, AND RAISIN SANDWICHES

2 packages (3 ounces each) cream cheese, softened
½ cup raisins
1 tablespoon grated lemon rind
1 tablespoon chili sauce
1 carrot, grated
⅓ cup chopped pimiento-stuffed olives
8 slices of white bread

Mix all ingredients except bread. Spread between bread slices. Makes 4 sandwiches.

### PICNIC BEAN SANDWICHES

2 cans (1 pound each) baked beans with tomato sauce
1 tablespoon Worcestershire
1 teaspoon onion salt
¼ cup ketchup
2 tablespoons sweet-pickle relish
1 teaspoon prepared mustard
8 split sandwich rolls, grilled

Combine all ingredients, except rolls, in saucepan or skillet. Heat thoroughly. Serve between roll halves. Makes 8 sandwiches.

### CURRIED-EGG SANDWICHES

6 hard-cooked eggs, chopped
½ cup mayonnaise
1 teaspoon curry powder or more to taste
½ cup chopped stuffed olives
½ teaspoon salt
¼ teaspoon pepper
8 slices of white bread, buttered

Mix all ingredients except bread. Spread between bread slices. Makes 4 sandwiches.

## SANDWICH FILLINGS

### Cheese

- Cheddar-cheese slices, fried ham, prepared mustard.
- Cottage cheese, chopped dill pickle, chopped stuffed olives, chopped nuts, salad dressing.
- Cottage cheese, chopped dill pickle, crumbled cooked bacon, a little mayonnaise, salt and pepper.
- Cottage cheese, minced green pepper and onion, on whole-wheat bread.
- Cream cheese, chopped almonds, and ripe olives or soy sauce.
- Cream cheese and pickled beets.
- Cream cheese, chopped dates, a few drops of fresh lemon juice.
- Cream cheese, chopped preserved gingerroot, a little milk.
- Cream cheese, prepared horseradish, onion, finely shredded dried beef, a little cream.
- Cream cheese-onion-bacon spread made with 1 package (8 ounces) cream cheese; 4 teaspoons instant minced onion; 2 tablespoons mayonnaise; ¼ teaspoon salt; ⅛ teaspoon pepper; ¼ teaspoon fresh lemon juice; 2 crisp bacon strips, crumbled.

Soften cream cheese. Add onion to mayonnaise and add to cream cheese with remaining ingredients. Makes 1 cup.
- Whipped cream cheese, orange marmalade, shredded lettuce.
- Cream cheese and raspberry jam.
- Pimiento-cheese spread and sliced pineapple on round slices of bread.
- Process American cheese, prepared mustard, sliced pineapple, bacon. Broil until bacon is crisp.
- Swiss cheese and mustard on rye bread with lettuce.

### Eggs

- Fried or scrambled eggs on whole-wheat bread with ketchup.
- Chopped hard-cooked egg, pickle relish, pimiento, salad dressing.
- Chopped hard-cooked egg, ripe olives, mayonnaise.
- Chopped hard-cooked egg, chopped ham, minced onion and green pepper, salad dressing.
- Chopped hard-cooked egg, green onion, raw spinach. Add mayonnaise and salt and pepper to taste.
- Chopped hard-cooked egg and watercress with mayonnaise and a few drops of fresh lemon juice.
- Chopped hard-cooked egg, sardines, mayonnaise, a little prepared mustard.
- Egg salad made with 3 hard-cooked eggs, chopped; 1 tablespoon pickle relish; 4 stuffed olives, chopped; ¼ cup finely diced celery; 1 teaspoon each of chili sauce and minced green pepper; ¼ cup mayonnaise.

Mix all ingredients thoroughly. Makes about 1 cup of filling.
- Sliced hard-cooked egg, sliced tomato, mayonnaise.

### Fish and Shellfish

- Anchovy fillets dipped into lemon juice on hot buttered toast.
- Heated frozen fried clams on hot buttered toast, tartare sauce.
- Heated fish sticks in toasted frankfurter rolls with tartare sauce, chili sauce, ketchup, or coleslaw.
- Salmon, minced celery, mayonnaise, curry powder.
- Sardine, sliced Swiss cheese, sliced tomato, and cucumber.
- Chopped cooked shrimps and canned chopped mushrooms, prepared mustard, softened cream cheese.
- Tuna, mayonnaise, very thin slices of peeled lemon.

### Meat and Poultry

- Crisp bacon, mashed or sliced banana with fresh lime juice, plain or curry mayonnaise.
- Chopped canned corned beef or tongue, sour-pickle relish, mayonnaise.
- Ground roast beef, chopped pickle and celery, prepared mustard, mayonnaise.
- Ground cooked steak and prepared mustard on toasted sandwich rolls.
- Mock-chicken made with 1 medium onion, minced; 1 tablespoon butter; ½ pound ground beef; ½ cup water; ½ teaspoon poultry seasoning; 2 tablespoons all-purpose flour; ½ cup undiluted evaporated milk; salt and pepper to taste; mayonnaise.

Cook onion in butter until golden-brown. Add beef, water, and poultry seasoning; simmer for a few minutes. Mix flour and milk; stir into meat mixture and cook until thickened. Add salt and pepper to taste. Cool, then chill. When ready to use, add enough mayonnaise to make mixture of spreading consistency. Makes about 1½ cups.
- Hamburger salad made with 1 cup crumbled leftover meat loaf or beef patties; ½ cup shredded raw carrot; 2 tablespoons diced celery; 1 tablespoon chopped green-onion tops; 2 parsley sprigs, chopped; ⅓ cup mayonnaise; salt and pepper to taste.

Combine all ingredients and mix well. Makes about 1½ cups.
- Ground beef cooked with chopped celery and onion, mixed with a little horseradish and salad dressing.
- Ground beef cooked with a little chopped onion, mixed with chili sauce and mayonnaise.
- Panbroiled thin steaks, butter mixed with chopped chives, in sandwich rolls.
- Ground bologna, carrot, and almonds; mayonnaise, cream, Worcestershire, salt.

- Ground cooked chicken or turkey with the skin, almonds, mayonnaise.
- Chopped cooked chicken or turkey, grated process American cheese, pickle relish, mayonnaise.
- Ground cooked ham or luncheon meat, cheese, sweet pickle, mayonnaise.
- Ground cooked lamb, chopped fresh mint, minced onion, mayonnaise, salt and pepper.
- Liverwurst, sliced tomato, lettuce, mayonnaise.
- Thinly sliced cooked meat, spread with mustard or chopped mustard pickle, pickle relish, ketchup, chili sauce, or tartare sauce.
- Sliced meat loaf, pickle relish, sliced hard-cooked egg, and salad dressing.
- Sliced meat loaf, tomato, and cheese, spread with prepared mustard.
- Cold slivered roast pork or other meat on toasted sandwich rolls with hot barbecue sauce.

### Peanut Butter plus:

- Apple butter, grated Cheddar cheese, fresh lemon juice.
- Mashed banana and French dressing.
- Mashed baked beans, chopped dill pickle, mayonnaise, salt, and pepper.
- Chopped celery and olives on whole-wheat bread.
- Chopped dates and fresh orange juice to moisten.
- Sliced hard-cooked eggs and mayonnaise with crisp lettuce. Sprinkle with salt and a little pepper.
- Chopped candied gingerroot and honey or mayonnaise.
- Slice of baked ham on raisin bread.
- Deviled ham, chopped sweet pickle, mayonnaise.
- Orange marmalade and a little chopped candied gingerroot with shredded lettuce.
- Thinly sliced salami and thinly sliced onion on rye bread. Add a dash of prepared mustard.
- Slices of ripe tomato on one slice of bread. On other slice, butter and chopped green onion.

### Miscellaneous

- Canned baked beans, crumbled crisp bacon, prepared mustard.
- Thinly sliced cucumber and green pepper on bread spread with dairy sour cream and prepared mustard.
- Chopped pecans or walnuts, minced celery, curry mayonnaise.
- Chopped pecans, mayonnaise, white pepper.
- Chopped raisins, dates, figs, and nuts, with mayonnaise.

Broadway Special

## OPEN SANDWICHES IN THE SCANDINAVIAN MANNER

Many of these sandwiches make excellent appetizers for special occasions. After spreading the desired slice of bread with butter, top it with any of the following fillings:

• Top slices of hard-cooked egg with slices of smoked eel and top these with thin slices of onion.

• Top potato salad with herring tidbits and chopped pickled beets. Garnish with olive slice.

• Top hot scrambled eggs with slices of smoked eel and sliced raw leeks.

• Top smoked herring fillets with a mound of chopped radishes. Make a hollow in the center of the mound and carefully drop in a raw egg yolk.

• Top shredded lettuce with smoked salmon paste piped through a pastry tube in a decorative pattern with a hollow in the center. Carefully drop a raw egg yolk into the hollow and top with a bit of prepared horseradish.

• Arrange lettuce cup on bread. Top with a piece of cold boiled fish and garnish with prepared horseradish and slices of tomato or pimiento.

• Top lettuce with cold scrambled egg and garnish with thin slices of smoked salmon.

• Spread bread with a thin layer of seasoned scraped raw beef. Top with lettuce and slices of hard-cooked egg and garnish with tiny cooked shrimps.

• Spread bread with mayonnaise and top with a lettuce leaf and cooked mussels. Garnish with a sprig of fresh dill.

• Spread bread with a relish spread and top with a cold fried fish fillet.

• Top a lettuce leaf with some elbow-macaroni salad and garnish with a roll of thinly sliced smoked salmon, cooked egg wedges, and a spoon of curry mayonnaise.

• Top bread with cooked shrimps and garnish with cheese and cucumber cubes. Top with a small spoon of mayonnaise.

• Top chopped fruit salad with a spoon of mayonnaise.

• Top bread with a lettuce leaf, topped in turn with slice of tomato, a sardine, and garnish with caviar, and a twist of lemon.

• Arrange cooked mussels on bread. Top with a salad of chopped celery and unpeeled apple mixed with mayonnaise.

• Top sliced cold meatballs with unpeeled cucumber slices and garnish with a cornucopia of sliced dried beef filled with whipped cream flavored with prepared horseradish and pimiento strips.

• Arrange cold thin slices of smoked ham on bread. Garnish with alternating slices of pickled beets and cucumbers, and spice with a little prepared horseradish.

• Spread bread with liver pâté and top with drained flat anchovy fillets. Garnish with prepared horseradish and a sprig of parsley.

- Arrange thin hard salami slices in overlapping rows. Top with scrambled eggs and thin slices of cooked leeks.
- Spread bread with pimiento cheese spread. Garnish with a crisscross of flat anchovy fillets, bits of chopped dill pickle, a carrot curl, and a sprig of watercress.
- Top thin slices of smoked ham with a spoon of tartare sauce and garnish with a tomato wedge and thin slices of unpeeled cucumber and a parsley sprig.
- Arrange thinly sliced smoked tongue on a lettuce leaf. Top with butter whipped with prepared horseradish and garnish

with sliced stuffed olives.
- Top thinly sliced prosciutto with potato salad and garnish with drained capers and julienne strips of pickled beets.
- Spread bread with liver pâté and garnish with tiny cubes of aspic made from beef bouillon. Top with bits of crisp bacon, a slice of tomato, and a bit of prepared horseradish.
- Top thinly sliced rare roast beef with relish mayonnaise and raw leeks sliced into small rings.
- Top thin slices of boiled ham with cold fried veal-kidney slices and a small

spoon of mayonnaise.
- Top a lettuce leaf with chopped hard-cooked egg salad sprinkled with curry powder. Garnish with a small strip of crisp bacon.
- Garnish cherry-tomato slices and slices of hard-cooked egg with a spoon of mayonnaise and chopped chives.
- Top thinly sliced Muenster cheese with mayonnaise piped through a star tip down the center of the sandwich. Add chopped radishes on one side and on the other side chopped chives.
- Spread dark bread with a sharp cheese

*Open Sandwiches in the Scandinavian Manner*

spread and top with a thin square of dark chocolate. Garnish with seedless grape halves.
- For small canapés, try the following: A lettuce leaf topped with a small wedge of Camembert garnished with a radish rose with some radish leaves.
- A slice of tomato topped with a teaspoon of smoked eel paste, tiny shrimps, and a parsley sprig.
- A thin slice of liver pâté on toast, garnished with a fried mussel, a small tomato wedge, and a parsley sprig.
- Spread bread with mashed smoked salmon. Top with a circle of chopped hard-cooked egg white. Mash hard-cooked egg yolk and beat in softened butter until creamy. Spoon mixture into the center of the egg whites.
- Mash smoked salmon and press through a star tip in a zigzag pattern down the center of bread. Sprinkle chopped hard-cooked egg on one side and chopped parsley on the other side.
- Mash liver pâté and mix with grated onion, chopped smoked ham, and chopped stuffed olives. Spread mixture on bread and garnish with a sweet pickle fan.
- Top bread with a thin slice of smoked salmon. Top with an unpeeled cucumber slice, a slice of hard-cooked egg, and a spoon of mayonnaise as well as a few drained capers to make a pyramid sandwich.
- Top bread with lettuce leaf, sliced hard-cooked egg topped with tiny cooked shrimps, and sprig of fresh dill.
- Top a cracker with a tiny lettuce leaf and a mixture of mayonnaise and grated sharp cheese. Top with a walnut half.
- A lettuce leaf is topped with fresh,

frozen, or canned crabmeat mixed with chopped celery and mayonnaise and then garnished with cooked chilled asparagus tips and a pimiento strip.

• Top with a ½-inch slice of unpeeled cucumber which has been hollowed out. Fill hollow with smoked-eel paste.

• With a star tip, pipe a ring of smoked-eel paste. Fill with center slices of stuffed olives.

• Top bread with slices of banana dipped into lemon juice. Garnish with a crisscross of flat anchovy fillets.

• Top bread or cracker with a mixture of softened cream cheese, chopped nuts, and chopped radishes. Garnish with a peeled and seeded grape.

• Top bread with a few rolls made of thinly sliced salami filled with whipped cream mixed with prepared horseradish.

• Spread bread with liver pâté and garnish with pickled mushrooms and a slice of tomato and a sprig of parsley.

• Spread bread with caviar. Make a small ring of finely chopped onions. Carefully drop in a raw egg yolk and garnish with a tiny lemon wedge.

• Beat prepared mustard into butter and spread on bread. Top with a thin slice of boiled ham, an unpeeled slice of cucumber, and a slice of peeled orange, and top with a maraschino cherry.

• For hot sandwiches try the following: Beat an egg white until stiff with a little salt. Pile the egg white on toasted bread, making a hollow in the center. Bake in preheated moderate oven (350°F.) until egg white is lightly browned. Remove from oven and while still hot carefully fill center with a raw egg yolk and a crisscross of flat anchovy fillets.

• Spread bread with caviar and top with sliced hard-cooked egg. Beat 1 egg white until stiff and mix with 2 tablespoons mayonnaise. Spoon mixture over hard-cooked egg and put under broiler until brown and puffy.

• Spread bread with chopped cooked well-drained spinach, top with cooked shrimps, and spread with egg-white and mayonnaise mixture as above. Broil as above.

• Top bread with cooked well-drained asparagus tips. Top with egg-white and mayonnaise mixture and broil as above.

• Top slices of smoked eel with thin slices of sharp cheese. Put under broiler until cheese is melted and bubbly.

• Prepare a thick white sauce and add chopped hard-cooked egg whites. Spoon while very hot over bread. Garnish with smoked salmon, chopped parsley, and sieved hard-cooked egg yolk.

• Fry mussels in a little butter with paprika and chopped parsley. Spoon on hot toast and serve immediately.

• Top bread with a mixture of grated sharp cheese, minced onion, and a little chopped pickle. Garnish with a crisscross of flat anchovy fillets and a small spoon of ketchup. Put under broiler until cheese is melted and bubbly.

• Roll a half slice of bacon around a mussel. Place filled roll on a small piece of bread. Put under broiler until bacon is crisp and bread is golden. Serve at once.

## SPECIAL-OCCASION SANDWICHES FOR APPETIZERS

### CHEESE-CRAB CANAPÉS

- 1 can (6½ ounces) crabmeat, flaked
- ⅓ cup mayonnaise
- 1 teaspoon prepared mustard
- ⅛ teaspoon salt
  Dash of cayenne
  Juice of ½ lemon
  Few parsley sprigs, chopped
- 6 slices of white bread
- ¼ cup grated Parmesan or Romano cheese
- 2 tablespoons fine dry bread crumbs

Mix all ingredients except last 3. Trim crusts from bread. Toast bread and spread with crab mixture. Mix cheese and crumbs; sprinkle on top of crab. Cut each into 4 triangles. Broil until lightly browned. Makes 2 dozen.

### COPENHAGEN COOLERS

- 1 envelope unflavored gelatin
- ½ cup cold water
- 1 cup boiling water
- 1 chicken bouillon cube
- 12 slices of toast
- 2 cans (4½ ounces each) deviled ham
- 3 or 4 hard-cooked eggs, sliced
- 3 or 4 tomatoes, sliced
- 1 cucumber, peeled and sliced
- 1 green pepper, cut into diamonds or other shapes

Soften gelatin in cold water. Add boiling water and bouillon cube and stir until cube is dissolved. Chill until slightly thickened. Spread toast with deviled ham and top with remaining ingredients in an attractive arrangement. Put on rack on cookie sheet and chill for 20 minutes. Spoon gelatin mixture over sandwiches to cover completely. Chill for about 30 minutes. Makes 12 open-face sandwiches. If preferred, sandwiches can be halved or quartered.

Note: The gelatin topping keeps these sandwiches fresh for hours. It can also be used on other sandwiches to keep ingredients fresh and crisp.

### ONION AND PARSLEY FINGER SANDWICHES

Coarsely chop 1 medium onion. Add 3 tablespoons chopped parsley and enough mayonnaise to make of good spreading consistency. Spread 4 slices of bread with the mixture. Top with 4 more slices. Cut off crusts and cut sandwiches into 3 or 4 finger-shape pieces. Makes 12 to 16 small sandwiches.

## SPECIAL-OCCASION SANDWICHES FOR LADIES' LUNCHEONS

### ALMOND SOUFFLÉ SANDWICHES

- 2 eggs, separated
- ½ teaspoon Worcestershire
- ½ cup chopped almonds
- ½ cup shredded Cheddar cheese
- 1 tablespoon mayonnaise
- 1 tablespoon chopped parsley
- ½ teaspoon salt
- 4 slices of toast

Beat egg yolks until thick. Add next 5 ingredients. Beat egg whites with salt until stiff and fold in yolk mixture. Pile lightly on toast. Heat under broiler until puffy and lightly browned. Makes 4 sandwiches.

### TURKEY OR CHICKEN SANDWICH LOAF

- 3 cups chopped cooked turkey or chicken
- 1 cup chopped celery
- ½ teaspoon grated onion
- 1 cup mayonnaise
  Salt and pepper
- 1 loaf (1 pound) sliced soft white bread
- ½ cup butter or margarine, softened
- ⅔ cup crumbled blue cheese (about 4 ounces)
- 1 package (4 ounces) cream cheese, softened
- 1 tablespoon milk
  Watercress

Mix first 4 ingredients to make filling. Season to taste with salt and pepper. Trim crusts from bread and place 3 slices in a row on sheet of foil or wax paper. Butter slices on one side and spread with filling. Continue adding slices, buttering and spreading them with filling, until each stack has 6 slices. Reserve any leftover slices for other uses. Press loaf together firmly. Beat cheeses and milk together until smooth. Spread on top and sides of loaf. Chill for several hours, or overnight. Cut into slices, put on serving plates, and garnish with watercress. Makes 6 to 8 servings.

### SAVORY CHEESE-AND-NUT SANDWICHES

- 1 package (8 ounces) cream cheese, softened
- 3 tablespoons each of chopped onion and green pepper
- 3 tablespoons chili sauce
- ⅔ cup chopped filberts or other nuts
- 3 hard-cooked eggs, finely chopped
- ½ teaspoon salt
  Dash of pepper
- 12 slices of white or whole-wheat bread
  Butter or margarine
  Ripe olives and tomato wedges

Mix first 8 ingredients. Spread on 6 slices of bread. Spread remaining 6 slices with butter. Put together and cut diagonally into 4 triangles. Garnish with ripe olives and tomato wedges. Makes 6 sandwiches.

### THREE-DECKER CHICKEN AND HAM SANDWICHES

Cut 24 slices of fresh bread into rounds, using a 3-inch cookie cutter. Butter. Spread 8 rounds with chicken-salad filling. To make, combine one 6-ounce can chicken, finely chopped, ¼ cup chopped blanched almonds, and ⅓ cup salad dressing. Season to taste with salt and pepper. Top with 8 rounds of bread. Spread with deviled ham (4½-ounce can). Top with 8 remaining rounds of bread.

Have 12 ounces cream cheese at room temperature. Cream well and add milk to make of good spreading consistency. Frost top and sides of sandwiches with cream-cheese spread. Put a border of chopped parsley around edge of each sandwich. Garnish with radish slices and small carrot curls. Chill. Makes 8 sandwiches.

### COCONUT-CHEESE SANDWICH LOAF

    4 packages (3 ounces each) cream
      cheese
 1¾ cups flaked coconut
    2 tablespoons mayonnaise
    1 unsliced sandwich loaf white bread
      (about 10-inch size)
    1 unsliced sandwich loaf whole-wheat
      bread (about 10-inch size)
    2 tablespoons soft butter or margarine
    1 bunch watercress, chopped
    2 tablespoons light cream (about)
      Red food coloring

Cream 2 packages of the cheese with a fork until soft and smooth. Add ¾ cup coconut and the mayonnaise and mix well. Trim crusts from top, bottom, and sides of bread. Slice each loaf lengthwise into 5 even slices. Spread a whole-wheat slice with half the cheese mixture and top with a white slice. Spread this white slice with 1 tablespoon of the butter and sprinkle with half the watercress. Repeat until there are 5 alternating layers of whole-wheat and white bread, ending with a whole-wheat slice. Mash remaining 2 packages of cream cheese with the cream. Spread on top and sides of loaf. Mix a few drops of food coloring with ¼ teaspoon water. Put remaining coconut on a sheet of wax paper, add coloring, and blend with fingers until coconut is tinted a delicate pink. Arrange in a border around edge of loaf. Wrap loosely in wax paper and chill for 3 hours, or longer. To serve, slice and serve with a garnish of watercress, if desired. Makes 8 to 10 servings.

## SPECIAL-OCCASION SANDWICHES FOR TEAS

### APRICOT-CHEESE SANDWICH FILLING

Soak ½ cup dried apricots in water overnight. Drain. Chop fine with knife or with wet scissors. Mix lightly with 1 cup creamed cottage cheese. Season with salt to taste. Especially good on Orange Tea Bread (page 1612). Makes 1½ cups.

### MINCED-CHICKEN SANDWICH FILLING

    1 cup finely minced chicken
    1 tablespoon mayonnaise
  ½ teaspoon prepared mustard
  ½ teaspoon horseradish

Mix all ingredients together. Makes about 1 cup filling.

### CURRY CASHEW SANDWICH SPREAD

Soften 1 package (3 ounces) cream cheese with a little milk and blend in 1 teaspoon curry powder and ¼ cup chopped cashew nuts. Especially good on brown or whole-wheat bread.

### WALNUT SWISS-CHEESE SANDWICH

Mix equal parts of grated or chopped Swiss cheese and chopped walnut meats. Season to taste with salt and cayenne. Moisten with enough mayonnaise or salad dressing to make of spreading consistency and spread on whole-wheat or rye bread.

### APRICOT-NUT SANDWICHES

Mix 1 cup dairy sour cream, 1 cup finely chopped walnuts, and 1 cup chopped dried apricots. Spread between 12 slices of buttered white bread. Makes 6 sandwiches.

### CREAM-CHEESE, CHERRY, AND PINEAPPLE SANDWICHES

    1 package (3 ounces) cream cheese,
      softened
  ⅔ cup finely chopped maraschino
      cherries
    1 can (8 ounces) date-nut or orange-nut
      roll, cut into 12 slices
    4 slices of pineapple (one 9-ounce can)

Mix cheese and cherries. Spread about 2 tablespoons cheese mixture on each of 4 bread slices. Cover with 4 more slices. Put a slice of well-drained pineapple over second bread slice. Top with remaining bread. Secure sandwiches with picks and cut each into 4 triangles. Makes 4 small sweet sandwiches.

## TEA BREADS FOR SPECIAL-OCCASION SANDWICHES

### CARROT-RAISIN BREAD

  ⅔ cup butter or margarine
    1 cup sugar
    2 eggs

 1½ cups sifted all-purpose flour
    2 teaspoons baking powder
    1 teaspoon ground cinnamon
  ¼ teaspoon salt
    1 cup finely grated carrots
    1 cup seedless raisins
  ½ cup chopped nuts

Cream butter and sugar until light. Beat in eggs. Sift dry ingredients together and gradually stir into first mixture. Add remaining ingredients and mix well. Pour into well-greased and lightly floured loaf pan (9 x 5 x 3 inches). Bake in preheated moderate oven (350°F.) for about 1 hour. Cool in pan for 10 minutes before turning out on rack to cool. Store overnight before slicing. This is especially good with cream cheese.

### ORANGE COCONUT BREAD

    3 cups sifted all-purpose flour
    3 teaspoons baking powder
    1 teaspoon salt
    1 cup granulated sugar
    1 cup packaged grated coconut, toasted
    1 tablespoon grated orange rind
    1 egg
 1½ cups milk
    1 teaspoon vanilla extract

Sift dry ingredients, including sugar. Stir in coconut and orange rind. Beat egg until light; mix with milk and vanilla and add to first mixture. Mix well, but do not beat. Pour into greased loaf pan (9 x 5 x 3 inches). Bake in preheated moderate oven (350°F.) for about 70 minutes. Cool on rack. Store overnight before cutting into thin slices. Good plain or toasted.

### CRANBERRY-NUT BREAD

      Water
      Juice and grated rind of 1 orange
    2 tablespoons butter or margarine
    1 cup sugar
    1 egg
    1 cup cranberries, chopped
  ½ cup chopped nuts
    2 cups all-purpose flour
  ½ teaspoon each of salt and baking soda

Add enough boiling water to orange juice to make ¾ cup liquid. Add grated rind and butter. Stir to melt butter. In another bowl, beat sugar and egg together and stir into orange mixture. Add cranberries and nuts. Sift together remaining ingredients and stir into first mixture. Pour into greased loaf pan (9 x 5 x 3 inches) and bake in preheated slow oven (325°F.) for about 1 hour. Cool on rack and store overnight before slicing.

### DATE-NUT LOAVES

    5 eggs
 1¼ cups sugar
    5 cups shelled pecans or walnuts,
      coarsely chopped
 1¼ pounds pitted dates, cut up
 1½ teaspoons vanilla extract
  ¾ teaspoon salt
 1¼ cups sifted all-purpose flour
 2½ teaspoons baking powder

Beat eggs until light. Gradually add sugar and continue beating until thick. Add nuts, dates, vanilla, and sifted dry ingredients. Divide into 2 loaf pans (9 x 5 x 3 inches), lined with wax paper. Bake in preheated slow oven (325°F.) for 70 minutes, or until done. Turn out on racks and peel off paper. Cool, and store overnight before slicing.

### ORANGE TEA BREAD

¼ cup soft shortening
¾ cup sugar
1 egg
3 cups sifted all-purpose flour
3 teaspoons baking powder
½ teaspoon baking soda
1 teaspoon salt
1 cup milk
½ cup fresh orange juice
¾ cup thinly sliced candied orange rind

Cream shortening and sugar until fluffy. Beat in egg. Add sifted dry ingredients alternately with milk and orange juice, beating until just blended. Stir in candied rind. Pour into well-greased loaf pan (9 x 5 x 3 inches) and bake in preheated moderate oven (350°F.) for 60 to 65 minutes. Cool in pan for 5 minutes. Remove to rack and cool thoroughly. Store overnight before slicing.

**SARDINE**—The name used to describe various small salt-water food fish with weak bones which can be preserved in oil. These include the pilchard, alewife, herring, and sprat. It is probably the French sardine, found in abundance around the island of Sardinia, from which the over-all name is derived. Fresh, sardines have an excellent flavor; canned, they are a mainstay of sandwich fixings.

Sardines are fatty fish. They differ according to kind, depending on locality. The North Atlantic coast around Maine and the Pacific coast in this country, as well as waters off the coasts of the United Kingdom, Norway, Denmark, Sweden, Finland, Portugal, Spain, South Africa, and Iceland provide various kinds of sardines.

In Europe sardines are important food fish. The silvery little fish are iridescent, silver below, and green or blue above. Sometimes they have small black spots. They travel quickly through the water, usually near or on the surface. They are usually fished with nets at night when they come to the surface to feed on the plankton. The moonlight shining on their silvery splashing has made them known as the "silver harvest."

*Availability* — Pilchards, weighing from 1½ to 2 ounces, are available fresh year round. Alewives and other types of sea herring used as sardines are available fresh, weighing 2 to 8 ounces, during the summer months. Sardines are also available salted and smoked. Larger sardines are sold as "smoked boneless herring." Canned sardines packed in oil as is or skinless and boneless are widely available. Sometimes tomato sauce forms the packing liquid. In Europe, Portuguese and French sardines are especially highly prized. Those from Portugal are usually packed in a high grade of pure olive oil; the French variety often have herb and spice mixtures added.

*Storage*

☐ Fresh, refrigerator shelf: 1 to 2 days
☐ Canned, kitchen shelf, unopened: 1 year
☐ Canned, refrigerator shelf, opened and covered: 4 to 5 days

*Nutritive Food Values*—Excellent source of protein and good source of calcium, iron, and niacin.

☐ Atlantic, canned in oil, 3½ ounces, solids and liquid = 311 calories
☐ Canned in oil, 3½ ounces, drained solids = 203 calories
☐ Canned in tomato sauce, 3½ ounces, solids and liquid = 197 calories

*Basic Preparation*—Fresh sardines are usually deep-fried, like any small fish.

☐ **To Deep-Fry Fresh Sardines**—Wash and clean the sardines. Dip in all-purpose flour, then in beaten egg. Roll in cornmeal or fine dry bread crumbs. Fry in hot deep fat (375°F. on a frying thermometer) until brown and crisp. Drain on absorbent paper and season with salt and pepper. Serve with Sauce Tartare (page 1622) or Italian Tomato Sauce (page 1627).

Drain canned sardines well on absorbent paper before using.

### DEVILED SARDINES

1 can (4 ounces) sardines in oil
2 garlic cloves, crushed
1 tablespoon each of minced onion and green pepper
1 tablespoon prepared mustard
1 teaspoon prepared horseradish
1 tablespoon water
2 tablespoons salad oil
½ teaspoon each of salt, celery salt, paprika, and pepper
⅛ teaspoon cayenne
Juice of ½ lemon
Lemon and tomato wedges, pickles (optional)

Drain sardines and arrange on serving plate. Mix garlic, onion, and green pepper. Add mustard, horseradish mixed with the water, and the salad oil. Mix thoroughly. Add seasonings and lemon juice. Mix well and pour over sardines. If desired, garnish with lemon and tomato wedges, and pickles. Serve as an appetizer or hors-d'oeuvre, with crackers, celery hearts, or potato chips, if desired. Makes 4 servings.

### SARDINE COCKTAIL

Drain one 15-ounce can large sardines. Cut into bite-size pieces and chill. When ready to serve place sardine pieces on lettuce. Cover with chilled cocktail sauce. Pass horseradish and hot pepper sauce. Makes 4 servings.

### SARDINES WITH SPINACH AND CHEESE

3 tablespoons butter or margarine
3 tablespoons all-purpose flour
1 teaspoon salt
¼ teaspoon white pepper
1½ cups diluted evaporated milk
1 teaspoon Worcestershire
¾ cup shredded sharp process cheese
1 can (15 ounces) sardines
1 package (10 ounces) frozen spinach
Paprika

Melt butter in top part of double boiler; blend in flour, salt, and pepper. Add milk and Worcestershire; cook over boiling water, stirring constantly, until thickened. Add ½ cup cheese and continue cooking until cheese melts. Heat sardines in skillet in their liquid. Cook spinach according to directions on package; drain well. Put hot spinach in greased shallow baking dish; top with drained sardines. Pour cheese sauce over sardines. Sprinkle with paprika and remaining cheese. Put in hot oven (400°F.) for 10 minutes, or until topping melts. Makes 4 servings.

### BROILED SARDINES ON TOAST

¼ cup butter or margarine
¼ cup soft bread crumbs
2 hard-cooked eggs, chopped
1 cup half-and-half (half milk, half light cream)
Salt and pepper
1 can (4 ounces) sardines in oil, drained
Buttered toast
Paprika

Melt butter in saucepan. Add crumbs, eggs, and half-and-half. Heat, and season to taste with salt and pepper. Broil sardines for about 5 minutes. Arrange on toast and cover with egg mixture. Sprinkle with paprika. Makes 2 servings.

### SARDINE SANDWICHES

1 can (4 ounces) sardines in oil, drained
1 hard-cooked egg, mashed
6 stuffed olives, mashed
Salt, paprika, and fresh lemon juice
Mayonnaise
8 slices of light rye bread

Mash sardines. Mix with egg and olives. Season to taste with salt, paprika, and lemon juice. Add mayonnaise to moisten. Spread between bread slices. Makes 4 sandwiches.

### SARDINE AND CHEESE SALAD

Lettuce or other salad greens
¼ pound Cheddar cheese, slivered
2 cans (4 ounces each) sardines in oil, drained
French Dressing (page 1622)

Line salad bowl with lettuce. Arrange cheese and sardines in bowl. Pour dressing over top. Makes 4 servings.

**SARSAPARILLA**—At one time sarsaparilla products were made with the flavoring extracted from the dried roots of several tropical smilax vines indigenous to Central and South America. The name is from the Spanish, a combination of *zarza*, "bramble or brier," and *parrilla*, "little vine."

The "wild sarsaparilla" early settlers of New England were so pleased to find was a different plant, a perennial herb of the genus *Arolia*, but its aromatic roots were treated as the tropical variety was.

Nowadays, all sarsaparilla products, the best known of which is a soft drink, are made from artificial flavoring.

**SASSAFRAS**—A handsome tree of the laurel family, one variety of which, *Sassafras albidum* or *variifolium,* is a native of North America. Its height ranges from thirty to sixty feet, although occasionally one may grow as high as ninety feet. The bark is rough and gray, and the bright green leaves are of three shapes, all on the same tree. These leaves, when dried and ground, are the prime ingredient of filé, a thickening and seasoning agent which forms the base of gumbo.

**SAUCE** *by James A. Beard*—A sauce is a liquid accompaniment to food, enhancing and complementing the dish with which it is served.

It must be confessed that during an earlier period of culinary history sauces were used not so much to enhance as to smother the unpleasant flavors of food resulting from lack of refrigeration. Ultimately, however, sauces grew to be esteemed as the highest refinements of cookery. Although some of the older cuisines of the world have produced distinctive sauces, such as the Chinese sweet and sour and the original chutneys and curries of India, it was French cuisine that brought saucing to its perfection.

Sauces fall into several categories, being derived largely from what are known as *les sauces mères,* or "the mother sauces." These include the two basic sauces made from stock, sauce espagnole, and sauce velouté; the basic white sauce, sauce béchamel; the two basic emulsified sauces, hollandaise and mayonnaise; and vinaigrette sauce, the oil and vinegar combination.

 **SAUCE ESPAGNOLE**

This is brown sauce made with meat broth, highly clarified, reduced, and thickened with a dark *roux*. Espagnole is well seasoned and has a satiny, *onctueaux* quality that imparts wonderful texture to the numerous sauces derived from it.

An offshoot of sauce espagnole that is also used as a base for other sauces is *demi-glace,* which is basic brown sauce cooked down after the addition of highly reduced veal broth. Sometimes tomato is added.

Both sauce espagnole and demi-glace may have *glace de viande* added, a rich beef or veal stock reduced to a glaze and then cooked a second time with bones and meat to bring out a gelatinous quality. The resulting product is a clear, hard jelly, used to finish sauces and meat dishes. It is as highly concentrated in flavor as beef extract.

Among the many sauces based on sauce espagnole are:

**Bordelaise**—Sauce espagnole, with addition of red wine, reduced, and shallots. Sometimes garnished with poached marrow. Classic with steaks and sometimes served with roast beef and lamb.

**Diable**—Sauce espagnole, with addition of white wine, vinegar, mustard, and cayenne pepper. Used for meats that require a bit of peppery flavor, such as grilled kidneys and pigs' feet, liver, veal chops.

**Italienne**—Sauce espagnole, with addition of tomato paste and *glace de viande.*

**Madère**—Sauce espagnole, with addition of Madeira wine, reduced. Served with ham, beef, duck, game (especially venison), sweetbreads, and kidneys.

**Périgueux**—Sauce espagnole, with addition of finely chopped or sliced truffles and Madeira. This elegant sauce is served with fine cuts of beef, with lamb, with chicken, and sometimes with duck.

**Piquante**—Sauce espagnole, with addition of vinegar, spices, and chopped gherkins. Used with meats receptive to sharply contrasting flavor, such as boiled lamb, roast veal, and sometimes boiled beef.

**Porto**—Sauce espagnole, with addition of port wine, reduced. Often served with sweetbreads, certain veal dishes, and chicken, and sometimes with mushrooms and mixed dishes.

 **SAUCE VELOUTÉ**

This is a white sauce made exactly like the espagnole, except that a white *roux* of flour and fat is used, and the meat flavor is veal broth, highly reduced. It is used for *chaud-froid* sauces, which have gelatin and cream added and are used for glazing chicken, fish, veal, ham, and other cold dishes, especially for buffet service. *Chaud-froid* sauces are sometimes highly seasoned, are always decorated, and often covered with aspic.

Among the sauces based on velouté are:

**Sauce Allemande or Parisienne**—Chicken velouté sauce enriched with cream and egg yolks.

**Sauce Normande**—Velouté sauce enriched with cream and egg yolks.

**Sauce Suprême**—Velouté sauce enriched with cream.

 **SAUCE BÉCHAMEL**

Béchamel is a sauce that might be fitted into any country's definition of a "white sauce" or "cream sauce," although to be a genuine cream sauce it must, of course, have cream added to it. In whatever form it is prepared, it should never be the badly seasoned library paste we so often find on vegetables, fish, and meats. It is a white sauce made with milk and a white *roux* of butter and flour, seasoned with salt and pepper, and sometimes with nutmeg or onion. In current usage the terms velouté and béchamel have become somewhat interchangeable. It used to be considered correct to make a velouté only with highly reduced *fonds*. Nowadays the housewife and the professional cook, alike, are apt to utilize the principle of béchamel for a basic sauce, making a *roux* of butter and flour and adding milk, chicken broth, veal broth, mushroom broth, vegetable broth, or fish or clam broth. Cream is often added to make a richer sauce.

A few of the variations on the basic white sauce are:

**Sauce Aurore**—Béchamel sauce, with addition of tomato. Served with some Italian dishes and with seafood and egg dishes.

**Caper Sauce**—Béchamel sauce, with addition of capers. Served with boiled lamb and occasionally with fish.

**Cheese Sauce**—Béchamel sauce, with addition of grated Gruyère, Cheddar, or other melting cheese. Served with vegetables, certain fish and seafood dishes, and occasionally with meat dishes.

**Curry Sauce, French style**—Béchamel sauce, with addition of small amount of curry, to flavor rather than heat. Much less pungent than traditional curry sauce. Served with chicken, veal, or lamb dishes.

**Sauce Mornay**—Béchamel sauce, with addition of Parmesan cheese, and sometimes cream. Served with fish, meat, poultry, and egg dishes, as well as with vegetables.

**Sauce Raifort**—Béchamel sauce, with addition of horseradish. Served with such dishes as boiled beef and beef tongue.

**Sauce Soubise**—Béchamel sauce, with addition of an onion purée and sometimes Parmesan cheese. Served with Saddle of Veal, Prince Orloff and saddle of lamb, also with certain breaded lamb, veal, and chicken dishes.

**Véronique**—Béchamel sauce, with addition of cream, seasonings, and white grapes. Served with fish and sometimes with chicken or as a *chaud-froid*.

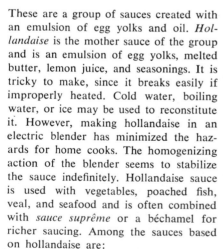

## THE EMULSIFIED SAUCES: HOLLANDAISE AND MAYONNAISE

These are a group of sauces created with an emulsion of egg yolks and oil. *Hollandaise* is the mother sauce of the group and is an emulsion of egg yolks, melted butter, lemon juice, and seasonings. It is tricky to make, since it breaks easily if improperly heated. Cold water, boiling water, or ice may be used to reconstitute it. However, making hollandaise in an electric blender has minimized the hazards for home cooks. The homogenizing action of the blender seems to stabilize the sauce indefinitely. Hollandaise sauce is used with vegetables, poached fish, veal, and seafood and is often combined with *sauce suprême* or a béchamel for richer saucing. Among the sauces based on hollandaise are:

**Béarnaise**—Basic hollandaise, with addition of reduced white wine vinegar or wine, shallots, and tarragon. Sometimes chopped fresh tarragon and parsley are added to the sauce just before serving. Served with fish, beefsteaks, liver, lamb, and other meats; occasionally with eggs; and infrequently with vegetables.

**Maltaise**—Hollandaise made with a seasoning of orange juice and orange zest, grated very fine. Served mostly with chicken and also with some vegetables.

**Mousseline**—Made with equal proportions of hollandaise and whipped cream, lightly salted. Used with asparagus, fish, and chicken dishes, and occasionally with egg dishes.

**Mustard Hollandaise**—Hollandaise with the addition of Dijon mustard. Served with grilled fish, lamb dishes, and some veal dishes. Sometimes a bit of anchovy is added for use with lamb.

*Mayonnaise* is an unheated emulsified sauce made with raw egg yolks or hard-cooked yolk, oil, vinegar or lemon juice, and seasonings. Another of the mother sauces, it is probably one of the most universally used of all sauces. There are many variations of mayonnaise, a few of which are given below:

**Sauce Aïoli**—A mayonnaise made by pounding garlic cloves in a mortar and then adding egg yolks and oil. Typical of Marseille and traditionally served with salt cod and accompaniments for Friday lunch. Also excellent with fish and seafood, if you are fond of garlic.

**Anchovy Mayonnaise**—Mayonnaise, with the addition of anchovies and sometimes garlic.

**Mayonnaise Rouge**—Mayonnaise, to which pounded lobster coral is added to give it flavor and color. Paprika is sometimes added also, but not in strong enough quantity to dominate the exquisite flavor of the mayonnaise.

**Mustard Mayonnaise**—Mayonnaise with Dijon mustard or powdered mustard added to taste.

**Mustard Cream Mayonnaise**—Mustard Mayonnaise with the addition of dairy sour cream.

**Sauce Tartare**—Mayonnaise, with the addition of mustard, chopped herbs, and, if desired, chopped pickle. The herbs might be dill, chervil, or tarragon. Sometimes garlic or onion is added, although these are not part of the original recipe.

**Sauce Verte**—Mayonnaise, to which finely chopped spinach and herbs are added. The spinach is used largely for color. The herbs may be any of several, but parsley should be one of them.

America has contributed these variations on mayonnaise:

**Louis Dressing**—Mayonnaise, with addition of garlic, chili sauce, and chopped egg. Sometimes parsley, chives, and other herbs are added also.

**Russian Dressing**—Mayonnaise, with addition of caviar, chili sauce, chopped onion and, often, chopped pickle. Seldom prepared twice in the same way.

**Thousand Island Dressing**—Mayonnaise, with addition of chili sauce and peppers, pimientos, and olives, all finely chopped. Horseradish is also sometimes added.

*Sauce Rémoulade* is a blend of mustard, a little *roux,* oil, vinegar, and salt and pepper. It is quite hot and not as heavily thickened as mayonnaise. It is oftentimes confused with *sauce verte.*

## THE VINAIGRETTE SAUCES

A vinaigrette sauce is basically composed of oil, vinegar, salt, and pepper. The proportions are three or four parts oil to one part vinegar. The best known version of vinaigrette sauce is French dressing and, indeed, the terms are often used interchangeably. Vinaigrette sauce is the primary dressing for salads in Europe. Nothing in the realm of food is easier to make, and when the vinegar and oil are of the best quality, this simple dressing is unsurpassed by any more elaborate preparation. There are countless variations on this dressing, some of which are listed here:

**Cervelle**—Add capers, onion, parsley, tarragon, and finely chopped cooked brains.

**Cressonière**—Add chopped hard-cooked eggs and watercress.

**Fines herbes**—Add finely chopped herbs.

**Garlic**—Add crushed garlic.

**Gribiche**—Add mustard, capers, chopped herbs, chopped pickle, chopped hard-cooked egg. Used with meats and fish.

**Roquefort**—Add crumbled Roquefort and chopped shallots or green onions.

## MISCELLANEOUS SAUCES

There are a few stray sauces that do not fall under any category whatsoever. Among them are:

**Barbecue Sauce**—This is an American invention, and there is no standard recipe. There are several approaches to barbecue sauce. One uses a tomato or ketchup base and includes garlic, herbs, and wine. Still another uses a sweet-sour base. And there are other quite popular ones that have a smoky flavor.

**Bread Sauce**—An English creation of bread crumbs, cream, and light seasoning. Used for game.

**Cumberland Sauce**—Another English creation, of currant jelly, mustard, port wine, and orange. Used for game and cold meats.

**Soup**—A strange entry, perhaps, but the fact is that canned, undiluted cream-of-mushroom, tomato, and other canned soups have worked their way into the American kitchen as sauces over the last few years.

**Spaghetti Sauces**—These are, for a great part, American variations on the classic tomato sauce and are used for pasta. The classic Italian tomato sauce is a blend of chopped, peeled, seeded fresh tomatoes, butter, sometimes a little ham and beef, a tiny bit of flour, herbs, usually basil and onion, with the possibility of the addition of sugar and tomato paste. It is long-cooked and put through a fine sieve. In the United States a far more successful tomato sauce may be made with canned Italian tomatoes or solid-packed tomatoes cooked down with butter or olive oil, basil, onion, and seasonings, and thickened with Italian tomato paste. It may be strained or not, as you wish. It is used for meats, fish, pastas, and as an additive to other sauces in Provençale and Italian cooking.

There is another group of preparations known as sauces which are generally condiments, rather than genuine sauces. Most of them are widely available commercially bottled. The important ones, which have become crutches in households and restaurants, are these: Beefsteak sauce, which comes under a number of trade names; chili sauce; cocktail sauces, basically derivatives of ketchup or chili sauce; gravy sauces; mushroom ketchup; soy sauce; teriyaki sauce; tomato ketchup; Worcestershire sauce, sometimes called *sauce Anglaise.*

 ## THE SAVORY BUTTERS

These savory butters, or *beurres composés,* are not strictly speaking sauces, but merely flavored butters. Since they are used as sauces, they are included here. Among them are:

**Amandine**—Melted butter to which sliced-toasted almonds have been added. Used for fish and vegetables.

**Anchovy**—Pounded anchovy fillets, and melted butter or softened butter, sometimes with garlic added. Used for steaks and fish.

**Bercy**—A reduction of white wine, shallots, and fresh lemon juice combined with melted butter and sometimes marrow. Used for beef and lamb.

**Blanc ("White Butter")**—Softened butter added bit by bit to a reduction of wine and shallots and whisked to an unctuous sauce without allowing the butter to melt completely. Used for fish.

**Chive**—Freshly chopped chives with melted butter or clarified butter. Used with fish, meat, vegetables, or eggs.

**Lemon**—Clarified butter with fresh lemon juice and sometimes lemon zest. Used for fish, veal, and egg dishes.

**Lobster Butter**—Pounded lobster meat, eggs, and tomalley blended with butter and sieved (shells are sometimes pounded and added to this as in crayfish butter).

Used in fish dishes and sauces.

**Maître d'Hôtel**—Chopped parsley, fresh lemon juice, salt, and pepper. Creamed with softened butter. Used extensively with meat, fish, and eggs.

**Mustard**—A blend of mustard and butter with the mustard proportioned to the dish and personal taste. Used with beef, kidneys, liver, and lamb. Also for sandwiches as a condiment.

**Noisette**—Brown butter to which toasted, chopped hazelnuts are added.

**Roquefort**—Softened butter blended with Roquefort cheese. Sometimes with mustard and brandy added. Used on grilled beef and as a spread on canapés.

**Shallot**—A blend of butter and chopped shallots, usually with parsley added and sometimes with a drop of vinegar. For meats.

**Shrimp**—Pounded shells and shrimp meat blended with butter. Sometimes seasoned with a touch of mace and used as an additive for sauces and as a garniture for fish.

**Tarragon**—Blended, chopped tarragon leaves pounded with a bit of parsley and combined with softened butter.

 ## DESSERT SAUCES

**Butterscotch Sauce**—Similar to caramel sauce in ingredients but buttery in flavor and almost always made with brown sugar.

**Caramel Sauce**—Made from caramelized sugar, cream, and flavorings.

**Chocolate Sauces**—There are a great variety of these, made to be served hot or cold, and ranging from chocolate-flavored custard sauces to those which are primarily a mixture of melted chocolate, cream, and flavorings.

**Custard Sauces**—A number of dessert sauces are based on a custard: either a *crème pâtissière,* which uses flour, eggs, sugar, and milk; or a *crème Anglaise,* which is made with egg yolks, sugar, milk or cream, and seasoned with vanilla or a liqueur.

**Fruit Sauces**—Made with fruit purées and sugar and seasoned with liqueurs; often used for hot desserts or fruit desserts.

**Hard Sauce**—A stiff mixture of butter, sugar, and flavorings. Used to a great extent with hot puddings, and traditional for plum pudding at the holiday season.

**Ice-Cream Sauce**—This is one of the most popular of convenience sauces for desserts. It is simply melted ice cream of good quality. Melted chocolate ice cream may be used for a coffee soufflé, for example, or coffee ice cream for a chocolate-flavored dessert.

**Maple Syrup**—Used in a number of guises

for a sauce.

**Sabayon Sauce**—A custard-like sauce resembling the Italian dessert zabaglione. It consists of beaten egg yolks and sugar, flavored with either wine or liqueur. Sometimes whipped cream is beaten in.

**Syrup Sauces**—A simple syrup base with various additives.

## GLOSSARY OF TERMS USED IN MAKING SAUCES

**Beurre Manié**—Butter and flour kneaded together. Used as a thickening agent.

**Bouquet Garni**—A blend of bay leaf, leek or onion, sometimes garlic, parsley, thyme, celery, usually tied together and used as a seasoning agent to be removed at will.

**Clarify**—Addition of egg white slightly beaten and shells to a stock before straining through linen or muslin.

**Déglacer**—To rinse a pan, usually with stock, wine, or spirits, to loosen particles or *fonds* which have gathered in a pan during cooking.

**Fond**—Juice of meat or fish created during cooking.

**Fond Blanc**—Chicken or veal stock.

**Fond Brun**—Beef, lamb, or game stock.

**Fumet**—Highly reduced essence or stock made of game, meat, or fish. Used as an additive in saucemaking.

**Glace-de-Viande**—Highly concentrated meat stock which is used as a glaze and an additive.

**Liaison**—Thickening agent of a sauce. This may be starch, flour, rice flour, potato flour, arrowroot, or cornstarch. In France, cream is used as a *liaison* but the thick, slightly matured unpasteurized *crème fraiche* has no counterpart in the United States. Cream in the United States requires the help of *roux,* arrowroot, or egg yolks. Other additives which may be used as *liaison,* and frequently are in French cooking, are blood, and bean or pea purées.

**Mirepoix**—Vegetables, usually leek, carrot, onion, celery, diced or cut into julienne, used in braising and sauce preparation.

**Reduce**—To boil vigorously to reduce water content.

**Roux**—A mixture of melted fat and flour. Used as a thickening agent.

**Zest**—The oily outside coating of lemon, lime, orange, or tangerine. Best removed by a zester or fine grater.

# How to Cook Superbly: The Basic Sauces, Brown and White

## by Helen Evans Brown

Some of the most useful bits of knowledge a cook can have are how to make good basic brown and white sauces. With the recipe I will give you for a basic brown sauce, what the French call *"Sauce espagnole,"* you can make all kinds of marvelous sauces for meat, poultry, game, and leftovers, merely by adding a little of this and that. I will also give you two basic white sauces: Béchamel and Velouté. Béchamel is simply milk thickened with a *roux* of flour and butter, while Velouté is made with white stock from veal or chicken broth. One or the other of these two sauces can be used to make hundreds of good-tasting dishes from Sauce Mornay (the classic cheese sauce) to cream soups, scalloped and gratin dishes, *crêpes farçis* (stuffed pancakes), all creamed dishes, and main-dish soufflés.

### BASIC BROWN SAUCE, SAUCE ESPAGNOLE

Some authorities claim that this sauce originated in Spain, hence its name. Others prefer the story that it is called "Spanish sauce" because Spaniards are dark-complexioned, just as the famous white sauce *Allemande* is named after the fair-skinned Germans. Either way, it's the Frenchiest of sauces.

**Equipment**—If you have the ordinary kitchen measures and a stock pot (a big pot or kettle that will hold at least 8 quarts) you're all set, although I do hope you have enough freezer room so that you can keep this sauce on hand. You'll use only a little each time, usually 1 cup, and if you freeze it in ½-pint containers you will have it when you need it.

½ cup each of diced carrot, onion, and celery
¼ cup diced ham
Butter (about ⅔ cup)

2 quarts Brown Stock
2 tablespoons minced parsley
½ teaspoon each of crumbled dried
  thyme and marjoram
¼ teaspoon whole allspice
1 small garlic clove
½ bay leaf
½ cup all-purpose flour
½ cup each of tomato purée
  and white wine
  Salt

First you make a *mirepoix*. All that means is that you cook the diced carrot, onion, celery, and ham in ¼ cup butter until the vegetables are very tender. Drain off the butter and save. Add the *mirepoix* to the 2 quarts of Brown Stock (or use 6 cans, 10½ ounces each, beef bouillon). Add the parsley, thyme, marjoram, allspice, garlic, and bay leaf, tied together in cheesecloth, and simmer for 2 hours, skimming when necessary. Remove bag of herbs and strain, pressing to extract juices from vegetables. To the butter you have saved, add enough butter to make ½ cup. Put it in a large saucepan and stir in flour. Cook, stirring, until it browns slightly (this is a brown *roux*); cool a minute, then stir in the strained liquid. Add the tomato purée and the white wine, and simmer for another 2 hours, skimming when necessary. This will give your sauce brilliance. It should be thick enough to lightly coat a metal spoon. Cook, pack in 1-cup jars, and freeze until needed. Add salt to taste at that time.

### Brown Stock

As you may have noticed in the instructions above, you can use canned beef bouillon in the place of this stock, but the superior product and the satisfaction you get from starting from scratch are worth the extra time it will take to make the real thing. If you are the thrifty type, you may have saved bones from beef as well as scraps of meat, and perhaps carcasses of chicken or turkey, or chicken gizzards and necks, and bits of veal. If so, you're ahead of the game as you can use these for your stock, making up the amount with some uncooked beef shanks. If you haven't, start saving now; you can collect bits that might otherwise be thrown away and freeze them until needed. You will want at least half meat and the rest bones. Beef is best and some should be raw. Some veal and poultry may be added, and even a small amount of pork—not ham, although you will need scraps of that for your sauce, and not lamb as the flavor is too definite.

5 pounds meat and bones
1 cup sliced carrots
1 cup sliced onions
1 cup sliced celery (outside stalk and
  leaves)
1 teaspoon salt
  Bouquet garni of 4 parsley branches,
  1 bay leaf, 1 thyme sprig or ¼
  teaspoon ground thyme, and

2 whole cloves
  Water

If you buy your meat and bones, have the butcher chop them into chunks. If they are leftovers and you have a cleaver, do it yourself. Brown the bones in a very hot oven (450°F.), then transfer to a large pot; add the vegetables, salt, and *bouquet garni*. (To make this, wrap the parsley around the bay leaf, cloves, and thyme, and tie with a white thread; or tie all the herbs and spices together in a piece of cheesecloth.) Cover with 2½ quarts cold water (if this doesn't cover the meat and bones completely, add more until it does), and put over high heat. As it comes to a boil, skim off the brown scum that rises to the top. Do this carefully until all the scum has been removed, then turn heat to very low, so that the liquid stops bubbling, and the surface seems barely to move, or "smile." Let it cook this way, really under a simmer, for anywhere from 5 hours to however long it takes for the meat to fall from the bones and have absolutely no taste; all the flavor has gone into the stock. Now strain, making sure that every drop is saved. Discard the well-drained meat and bones. You should have 2 quarts of stock. If there is more, continue cooking until it has reduced to that amount. If you have less than 2 quarts, make up the amount with water. Let the stock cool, uncovered, then refrigerate overnight. Next day, remove and discard the cake of fat that has formed on top. You now have 2 quarts of fine beef stock, rich enough so that it is lightly jellied.

### BASIC WHITE SAUCES, BÉCHAMEL AND VELOUTÉ

**Equipment**—You'll need no extra equipment for Sauce Béchamel, although I hope by now you have invested in a French whip, *fouet,* or similar wire whip, so useful for smoothing sauces and batters and for whipping. For Sauce Velouté, you'll need a stock pot or some large kettle or pot that will hold 8 quarts. Standard measuring cups and spoons are also in order.

### SAUCE BÉCHAMEL

3 tablespoons butter
3 tablespoons all-purpose flour
2½ cups milk
  Salt and pepper
⅓ cup light cream (optional)

For 2 cups sauce make a white or "blond" *roux* with 3 tablespoons each of butter and flour. Melt the butter, add the flour, and cook, stirring with a whip, for 2 minutes. Do not allow it to brown, even slightly. Now add 2½ cups milk, whipping as you add. Some authorities say that the sauce will lump unless the milk is heated, but I have never found this to be so. Bring just to the boil, then turn

heat very low, and simmer for at least 10 minutes, or until the sauce has been reduced to 2 cups. Add salt to taste, about ½ teaspoon, and a little pepper, preferably white for the sake of appearance. Béchamel sauce is very often finished with about ⅓ cup cream for extra richness. Carême, a famous French chef, also added 2 egg yolks and 1 tablespoon butter plus a little grated nutmeg.

This is as good a time as any to take up the problem of the addition of egg yolks to a hot sauce. Put the egg yolks in a small bowl and beat them slightly; then slowly beat in about ½ cup of the hot sauce. When mixed, pour this mixture into the remaining sauce, beating it as you add. Do not boil after the addition of the egg yolks.

### SAUCE VELOUTÉ

This sauce isn't quite as simple to make, as you need white stock as the base. However, a large batch can be made at one time and frozen in 1-cup jars.

¾ cup butter
¾ cup all-purpose flour
2 quarts White Stock*
1 small onion
2 whole cloves
½ bay leaf

Make a *roux* with the butter and flour, as in Sauce Béchamel. Add White Stock, the onion stuck with the cloves, and the bay leaf. Bring to a boil, turn heat low, and simmer for 1 hour, skimming if necessary. Cool, and use as directed; or freeze for future use. Makes 2 quarts.
*Sauce Velouté may be made with fish stock when it is to be used for seafood.

### White Stock

6 pounds veal bones and meat or
  6 pounds chicken backs, necks, and
  gizzards or 6 pounds (altogether)
  veal and chicken bones and meat
½ cup each of sliced carrot, onion,
  and celery
1 chopped leek (optional)
1 teaspoon salt
  Bouquet garni: 1 bay leaf, 4 parsley
  branches, 1 thyme sprig or ¼
  teaspoon ground thyme, and 1 whole
  clove, tied together

Have the meat and the bones chopped into pieces. Put them in a large pot with vegetables, salt, and herbs. Cover with 2½ quarts water. Be sure the water covers the meat and bones; add more if it doesn't. Bring to a boil and skim off all the scum that rises to the top. Turn heat very low so that the liquid barely moves and cook for about 5 hours, or until all the meat has fallen from the bones and the flavor has gone into the stock. Skim occasionally during the cooking. Strain, cool, then refrigerate. Next day, lift off and discard the fat that has hardened on top. You should have 2 quarts, partially jellied.

*Sauce Cook Book*

## BROWN SAUCES BASED ON SAUCE ESPAGNOLE

*(Recipe for Sauce Espagnole appears on page 1617)*

### DEMI-GLACE SAUCE

*For filet mignon or other fine cut of beef or for ham*

3 cups Sauce Espagnole
1 cup White Stock (page 1618)
1 tablespoon glace-de-viande or
  meat extract

Simmer all ingredients until reduced one-half. Makes about 2 cups.

### SAUCE BORDELAISE

*For all steaks and for beef tenderloin.
It is also very good on broiled mushrooms
or broiled mutton chops.*

You need marrow for this. Ask your butcher for 3 or 4 marrow bones and have him split them. Remove marrow and slice. Bring salted water to the boil, add marrow, and remove from heat. Let stand while preparing rest of sauce. Mince 1 small garlic clove and 1 shallot or green onion and sauté in 1 tablespoon butter until soft. Add ½ cup red wine (preferably, of course, a red Bordeaux, as this is how the sauce acquired its name, but a Cabernet or a Beaujolais will do), 1 cup Sauce Espagnole, and a dash of hot pepper sauce. Simmer until thickened, then add salt to taste, the drained marrow, 1 tablespoon fresh lemon juice, and 1 teaspoon minced parsley. Makes about 1¾ cups.

### CHASSEUR SAUCE

*For red meat, game, and poultry*

½ pound mushrooms, stems only, sliced
1 shallot, minced
2 tablespoons butter or margarine
¼ teaspoon salt
  Pepper to taste
¼ cup dry white wine
½ cup Sauce Espagnole
1 tablespoon tomato sauce
¼ teaspoon each of minced parsley
  and fresh tarragon

Reserve mushroom caps for other use. Sauté mushroom stems and shallot in butter. Add salt and pepper. Cook until

golden-brown. Add wine and cook until liquid is reduced to half of its original volume. Add remaining ingredients and simmer until slightly thickened. Makes about 1 cup.

### SAUCE DIABLE

*For deviled beef ribs, deviled turkey breast, or any meat that is grilled, where a hot sauce is desired*

Combine 1 cup Sauce Espagnole, 1 tablespoon prepared mustard, 1 tablespoon Worcestershire, a dash of hot pepper sauce, 1 tablespoon vinegar, and ¼ cup white wine. Simmer for 10 minutes and strain; then add salt to taste and 2 teaspoons minced parsley. Makes about 1¼ cups.

### DUXELLES SAUCE

*For eggs, fish, and chicken*

6 fresh mushrooms, chopped
2 tablespoons butter
¼ cup white wine
¼ cup Sauce Espagnole
1 tablespoon tomato purée
1 tablespoon minced parsley
  Salt and pepper

Sauté mushrooms in butter until moisture has evaporated. Add wine and simmer for a few minutes. Add remaining ingredients and stir until well blended. Reheat and season to taste with salt and pepper. Makes about ¾ cup.

### SAUCE ITALIENNE

*For kidneys, liver, pork chops, roast veal, chicken, and leftover cooked meats*

1 teaspoon chopped shallot
2 tomatoes, peeled, seeded, and
  chopped
¾ cup Marsala
½ cup Sauce Espagnole
1 tablespoon tomato paste
¼ cup chopped mushrooms
2 tablespoons finely diced cooked ham
½ teaspoon glace-de-viande or
  meat extract
  Few parsley sprigs, chopped

Put shallot, tomatoes, and wine in a saucepan and cook until tomatoes are soft and mixture has reduced to about one-half the original amount. Add Sauce Espagnole, tomato paste, mushrooms, and ham. Bring to a boil and cook for about 5 minutes. Add glace-de-viande and parsley. Makes about 1 cup.

### SAUCE MADÈRE

*For sweetbreads, ham, smoked tongue, veal, and beef tenderloin*

To 1 cup Sauce Espagnole add ½ cup canned tomatoes and ¼ cup Madeira or mellow sherry. Simmer until the volume is reduced by half. Strain, add a few grains of cayenne, salt to taste, and a good pinch of sugar. Makes about 1⅔ cups.

### SAUCE PÉRIGUEUX

*For beef, lamb, chicken, and sweetbreads*

3 or 4 truffles
½ cup Madeira

½ cup Sauce Espagnole
½ cup tomato sauce
2 tablespoons butter or margarine

Chop truffles and add to Madeira. Simmer for 5 minutes. Add Sauce Espagnole and tomato sauce. When sauce is hot, add butter and stir over low heat until butter is melted. Makes about 1¼ cups.

### SAUCE PIQUANTE

*For lamb, mutton, calf's liver, and game birds*

Cook together ½ cup chopped onions, 1 tablespoon butter, and ¼ cup wine vinegar until almost dry. Add 1 cup Sauce Espagnole and simmer for 5 minutes. Strain and add 2 teaspoons each of minced capers and gherkins. Season with salt and serve. Makes about 1½ cups.

### SAUCE AU PORTO

*For filet of beef, ham, veal, chicken livers, sweetbreads*

  Port wine
2 cups Sauce Espagnole
½ teaspoon glace-de-viande or
  meat extract
2 tablespoons soft butter

Put ½ cup port in saucepan, bring to boil, and boil until reduced to 3 tablespoons. Add Sauce Espagnole and simmer for 2 or 3 minutes. Add glace-de-viande and a little more wine, if desired. Simmer for 2 or 3 minutes to evaporate the alcohol. Remove from heat and beat in butter, a few small bits at a time. Makes about 2¼ cups.

### SAUCE ROBERT

*For pork roast, chops, or tenderloin*

Cook ½ cup minced onion in 1 tablespoon butter until the onion is soft. Add 1 cup Sauce Espagnole, 1 tablespoon vinegar, 2 tablespoons white wine, and ¼ teaspoon powdered mustard. Simmer for 15 minutes, add salt to taste, and strain before serving. Makes about 1¼ cups.

## WHITE SAUCES BASED ON SAUCE BÉCHAMEL AND SAUCE VELOUTÉ

*(Recipes for Sauce Béchamel and Sauce Velouté appear on page 1618)*

### SAUCE ALLEMANDE

*For poached fish, poultry, hot hors-d'oeuvre, and dishes which are to be topped with crumbs*

1½ cups Sauce Velouté
2 egg yolks
½ cup heavy cream
  Salt, white pepper, and fresh
  lemon juice

Heat Sauce Velouté until just simmering. Beat egg yolks and cream until blended. Gradually beat in, a few drops at a time, ½ cup of the hot sauce. Add remaining sauce in a thin stream, beating constantly.

Put mixture back in saucepan. Put over medium heat and bring to a boil. Cook, stirring, for 1 minute. Strain through a fine sieve. Add seasonings and lemon juice to taste. Reheat if necessary. Makes about 2 cups.

**Note:** When serving the sauce on fish, 1 to 2 tablespoons soft butter may be added, bit by bit, to finished sauce.

### SAUCE AURORE
*For poached eggs, chicken, sweetbreads, and seafood*

To 1 cup Sauce Béchamel add ¼ cup tomato purée and 1 teaspoon paprika. Makes about 1¼ cups.

### BERCY SAUCE
*For fish*

¼ cup butter or margarine
2 tablespoons minced shallots
½ cup white wine
½ cup fish broth
1 cup Sauce Velouté
1 tablespoon soft butter
2 teaspoons minced parsley
Salt and pepper

Melt butter and sauté shallots until translucent. Add wine and fish broth. Cook until reduced to half of its original volume. Beat in Sauce Velouté, soft butter, and parsley. Season to taste with salt and pepper. Reheat. Makes about 2 cups.

### Bercy Sauce for Meat

Substitute ½ cup beef or chicken bouillon for the fish broth.

### CAPER SAUCE
*For boiled lamb and fish*

Add 3 to 4 tablespoons well-drained capers to 1 recipe Sauce Béchamel.

### SAUCE CARDINAL
*For fish and shellfish*

2 tablespoons butter or margarine
2 tablespoons all-purpose flour
Salt and pepper to taste
½ cup hot fish stock or hot milk
1¼ cups heavy cream
½ teaspoon anchovy paste
½ teaspoon crumbled dried tarragon
½ cup cooked lobster meat, minced
½ cup cooked lobster meat, cut into ½-inch pieces

Melt butter. Remove from heat and blend in flour and salt and pepper. Cook over low heat, stirring constantly, until golden. Gradually add hot fish stock and cream, stirring constantly. Cook until thickened. Stir in anchovy paste and tarragon. Add lobster and heat thoroughly but do not boil. Keep hot in top part of a double boiler over hot water, stirring occasionally. Makes about 2½ cups.

### CHAUD-FROID SAUCE
*For glazing slices of chicken or game, or whole boiled chicken or salmon; it must be used before completely set.*

Heat 1 cup Sauce Velouté and add 1 envelope unflavored gelatin that has been softened in ¼ cup cold White Stock (page 1618), then dissolved over hot water. Add ¼ cup heavy cream. Makes about 1⅓ cups.

### CHEESE SAUCE
*For vegetables, fish, and some meat dishes*

Add ½ cup grated Gruyère or Cheddar cheese to 1 recipe Sauce Béchamel.

### CREAM SAUCE
*For "creaming" any vegetable or seafood*

To 1 cup Sauce Béchamel add from ¼ to 1 cup light cream. Heat; simmer until desired consistency. Makes 1¼ to 2 cups.

### CREAMY EGG SAUCE
*For fish*

To 1 cup Sauce Béchamel add 2 chopped hard-cooked eggs and ¼ cup light cream. Heat before serving. Makes about 2 cups.

### CURRY SAUCE, FRENCH STYLE
*For chicken, veal, or lamb dishes*

Add 1 to 3 teaspoons curry powder and 1 tablespoon fresh lemon juice to 1 cup hot Sauce Béchamel. Makes 1 cup.

### HERB SAUCE
*For any seafood or poultry*

To 1 cup Sauce Béchamel or Sauce Velouté add 1 teaspoon each of minced chives and parsley and ½ teaspoon minced fresh tarragon or marjoram. Heat, and serve. Makes 1 cup.

### SAUCE MORNAY
*Use whenever a cheese sauce is desired*

To 1 cup Sauce Béchamel add ⅓ cup heavy cream. Heat and add 2 tablespoons each of grated Gruyère and grated Parmesan cheese. (This is the classic recipe; ¼ to ½ cup grated Cheddar cheese may be used instead.) Makes about 1⅔ cups.

### SAUCE NORMANDE
*For fish, oysters, and mussels*

2 tablespoons butter
1 teaspoon all-purpose flour
1 cup liquid from cooking fish or shellfish, or bottled clam juice
2 egg yolks, slightly beaten
½ cup heavy cream
Salt and pepper

Melt butter and blend in flour; brown lightly. Gradually add liquid and simmer for about 10 minutes. Mix egg yolks and cream and stir into mixture. Bring to a boil and remove from heat. Season with salt and pepper to taste. Makes about 1½ cups.

### POULETTE SAUCE
*For chicken or frogs' legs*

1 cup Sauce Béchamel
2 egg yolks
1 tablespoon light cream
Juice of ½ lemon
1 teaspoon minced parsley

When white sauce is hot, beat some of the sauce into egg yolks beaten with cream. Add egg-yolk mixture to remaining sauce and cook over low heat, stirring constantly, until smooth and thick. Just before serving add lemon juice and parsley. Makes about 1 cup.

### SAUCE RAIFORT
*For boiled beef or beef tongue*

To 1½ cups Sauce Béchamel, add ½ cup grated horseradish; heat. Makes about 2 cups.

### RAVIGOTE SAUCE
*For hot or cold fish, meat, poultry, and vegetables*

2 tablespoons butter or margarine
1 tablespoon all-purpose flour
1 cup milk
¼ cup fresh lemon juice
1 tablespoon tarragon vinegar
1 tablespoon each of minced shallot, chervil, tarragon, and chives
Salt and pepper to taste

Melt 1 tablespoon butter and blend in flour. Gradually add milk and cook, stirring constantly, until slightly thickened. Add remaining ingredients and let stand for 5 minutes. Strain and serve hot or cold. Makes about 1¼ cups.

### SAUCE SOUBISE
*For lamb and veal*

1½ cups minced onions
2 tablespoons butter
2 tablespoons water
½ cup Sauce Béchamel
Salt and pepper to taste
Dash of ground nutmeg
2 tablespoons grated Parmesan cheese (optional)

Sauté onions in butter until they are translucent. Add water and stir well. Cook over low heat, covered, stirring occasionally, until onions are very tender but not brown. Onions must remain white or sauce will not be the right color. Press onions through a sieve or whirl in a blender. Beat in Sauce Béchamel, and heat. When hot add salt, pepper, nutmeg, and cheese, if desired. Makes about 1½ cups.

### SAUCE SUPRÊME
*For chicken, veal, or delicate vegetables*

5 tablespoons butter or margarine
2 tablespoons all-purpose flour
2 cups White Stock (page 1618)
1 small onion stuck with 1 whole clove
½ bay leaf
¼ cup heavy cream
1 tablespoon fresh lemon juice (optional)

Melt 4 tablespoons of the butter and stir in flour. Gradually stir in stock. Add onion with clove and the bay leaf and cook over low heat, stirring constantly, until smooth and thickened. Simmer for 10 minutes and then strain sauce. Stir in remaining butter and the cream. Beat in lemon juice if desired. Serve hot. Makes about 2¼ cups.

### SAUCE VÉRONIQUE
*For fish or chicken*

1 recipe Sauce Béchamel
1 cup small seedless white grapes
¼ cup heavy cream, whipped
Salt and pepper

Heat *Sauce Béchamel*. Simmer grapes in small amount of water for 2 or 3 minutes. Fold cream into hot sauce and season with salt and pepper to taste. Pour over hot fish or chicken and garnish with the grapes. Makes about 2½ cups sauce.

## SAUCES BASED ON HOLLANDAISE AND MAYONNAISE

### HOLLANDAISE

¾ to 1 cup butter
3 egg yolks
1 tablespoon cold water
1 tablespoon fresh lemon juice
Pinch of salt
2 tablespoons cold butter
Salt, white pepper, and fresh lemon juice

Melt butter and set aside. Beat egg yolks in top part of double boiler for about 1 minute. Beat in water, lemon juice, and salt. Place double boiler over simmering water, add 1 tablespoon butter, and continue to beat until mixture is smooth and creamy. Remove from heat and beat in remaining tablespoon of cold butter. Continue beating and gradually add melted butter by quarter-teaspoonfuls until mixture thickens. Season to taste with salt, white pepper, and lemon juice. Makes 1 to 1½ cups sauce.

**Note:** If Hollandaise Sauce separates, remove sauce from over the hot water at once and beat it vigorously with a rotary beater or electric mixer. If this doesn't work, make half of the recipe again; be sure there's only 1 inch of simmering water in double boiler, and stir sauce constantly. Then carefully stir in beaten mess you were tempted to pour down the drain. Don't overcook.

### BLENDER HOLLANDAISE SAUCE

3 egg yolks
2 tablespoons fresh lemon juice
¼ teaspoon salt
Pinch of white pepper
½ cup melted hot butter

Place egg yolks, lemon juice, and salt and pepper into the blender. Whirl for 2 seconds. Uncover and gradually drip in the melted butter. Sauce will thicken immediately. Makes ¾ cup.

### BÉARNAISE SAUCE
*For broiled or roasted red meats and fish*

1 teaspoon chopped shallots
½ teaspoon each of chopped fresh chervil and tarragon
12 peppercorns, crushed
2 tablespoons dry white wine
1 tablespoon vinegar
1½ cups butter or margarine
5 egg yolks
2 tablespoons light cream
Salt and cayenne

Mix shallots, chervil, tarragon, peppercorns, wine, and vinegar. Simmer until mixture is reduced to half. Melt butter, and pour off clear portion leaving whey behind; clear portion is clarified butter. Beat egg yolks with cream. Beat vinegar mixture into egg yolks and pour into top part of a double boiler. Cook over boiling water until creamy. While sauce is cooking beat constantly to avoid curdling. Gradually beat in clarified butter. Season to taste with salt and cayenne. Makes 1½ cups.

### BÉARNAISE TOMATE OR SAUCE CHORON
*For veal or lamb*

Add 2 to 3 tablespoons tomato paste to 1 recipe Béarnaise Sauce.

### SAUCE MALTAISE
*For chicken, broccoli, asparagus, or cauliflower*

Follow the recipe for Blender Hollandaise Sauce at left, substituting 1 tablespoon fresh lemon juice and 1 tablespoon fresh orange juice for the 2 tablespoons lemon juice. After sauce is blended, stir in 3 tablespoons fresh orange juice and 1 tablespoon grated orange rind. Makes about 1 cup.

### MOUSSELINE SAUCE
*For soufflés, fillets of veal, chicken, asparagus, or artichokes*

4 egg yolks
1 cup milk
2 tablespoons butter
Juice of ½ lemon
Pinch of ground nutmeg
Salt
¼ cup whipped heavy cream

Combine egg yolks and milk in top part of a double boiler. Cook over boiling water until hot. Add butter. Stir constantly until butter melts and sauce thickens. Add lemon juice, nutmeg, and salt to taste. Remove from water and fold in whipped cream. Makes about 1¼ cups.

### MUSTARD HOLLANDAISE
Follow recipe for Blender Hollandaise Sauce (at left), adding ½ teaspoon prepared Dijon mustard to finished sauce. If desired, 1 minced anchovy may also be added.

### MAYONNAISE

2 egg yolks or 1 whole egg
1 teaspoon sugar
1 teaspoon powdered mustard
1 teaspoon salt
2 tablespoons vinegar
2 cups olive oil

2 tablespoons fresh lemon juice

Put egg yolks and seasonings in small deep bowl. Beat with rotary beater or electric mixer until blended. Add vinegar very slowly, beating constantly. Add 1 cup oil, 1 tablespoon at a time, beating constantly. Add lemon juice and remaining 1 cup oil, 1 tablespoon at a time. Refrigerate. Makes 2 cups.

### SAUCE AÏOLI
*For fish, vegetables, and some meats*

12 garlic cloves, peeled
½ teaspoon salt
3 egg yolks
1½ cups olive oil
3 tablespoons fresh lemon juice, or more

In a mortar mash the garlic with the salt until garlic is puréed. In a deep bowl beat the egg yolks with a whisk until they are well mixed. Add the puréed garlic to the egg yolks and continue to beat with the whisk until mixture is well blended. Now add the oil, a drop at a time, whisking all the while. When several tablespoons have been added, add the rest of the oil very slowly in a thin stream, still whisking constantly. When the mixture is like a mayonnaise, whisk in the lemon juice. Add more salt if desired. If sauce is too thick, add additional lemon juice or water, ½ teaspoon at a time. Use more or less garlic and lemon juice, according to preference, but use only olive oil or the flavor will not be authentic.

To make this sauce in a blender, chop the garlic into small pieces with a knife and purée in the blender. Add the salt, egg yolks, lemon juice, and ½ cup of the oil and blend at high speed until thickened, a few seconds only. Slowly add the remaining oil in a thin stream and whirl until well blended. Adjust seasonings if necessary. Makes about 2 cups.

### ANCHOVY MAYONNAISE

To 1 cup mayonnaise, add 6 anchovy fillets, minced. If desired, add 1 garlic clove, minced.

### CREAM MAYONNAISE DRESSING
*For fruit salads*

Combine ½ cup heavy cream, whipped, 3 tablespoons mayonnaise, and 1 tablespoon grated fresh orange rind. Blend thoroughly. Makes about 1¼ cups.

### CUCUMBER-MAYONNAISE DRESSING
*For fish or vegetable salads*

½ cup mayonnaise
½ cup diced cucumber
Chopped green pepper to taste
Dash of tarragon vinegar
Salt and cayenne

Stir all together thoroughly. Makes 1 cup.

## CURRY MAYONNAISE
*For fruit or vegetable salad,*
*potato or macaroni salad,*
*seafood, poultry, or eggs*

Add 1 to 3 teaspoons curry powder to 1 cup mayonnaise. Makes 1 cup.

## GINGER MAYONNAISE DRESSING
*For fruit salads*

Mix ⅓ cup each of mayonnaise and dairy sour cream. Add 2 tablespoons chopped candied gingerroot. Makes about ⅔ cup.

## GREEN MOUSSELINE SAUCE
*For fish, asparagus, or other vegetables*

½ cup Sauce Béchamel (page 1618)
½ cup mayonnaise
2 tablespoons puréed cooked spinach
Pinch of dried tarragon
2 hard-cooked egg yolks, mashed
¼ teaspoon anchovy paste

Combine all ingredients and blend well. Chill until ready to serve. Makes about 1¼ cups.

## MUSTARD MAYONNAISE
*For cold fish*

Mix 2 teaspoons powdered mustard, 1 teaspoon sugar, 1 tablespoon malt vinegar, and 1 cup mayonnaise. Chill. Makes about 1 cup.

## MAYONNAISE ROUGE

To 1 cup mayonnaise, add the mashed coral from 1 cooked lobster.

## MUSTARD-CREAM MAYONNAISE

To 1 cup mayonnaise, add ½ teaspoon prepared mustard and ⅓ cup dairy sour cream.

## PAPRIKA MAYONNAISE DRESSING
*For potato or other vegetable salads*

Mix 1 cup each of mayonnaise and dairy sour cream and 1 tablespoon paprika. Chill. Makes 2 cups.

## SAUCE RÉMOULADE

3 hard-cooked egg yolks
½ teaspoon salt
⅛ teaspoon pepper
½ teaspoon powdered mustard
1 cup olive oil
2 tablespoons vinegar (or more to taste)
1 shallot, minced
Few parsley sprigs, chopped
1 tablespoon each of minced chervil, gherkins, and capers

Force egg yolks through a fine sieve. Blend with salt, pepper, and mustard. Gradually beat in oil, a few drops at a time, until all is added. Add remaining ingredients and beat well. Makes about 2 cups.

## CREAMY MAYONNAISE-ROQUEFORT DRESSING
*For greens or vegetable salads*

½ cup Roquefort cheese, crumbled
1 package (3 ounces) cream cheese
½ cup heavy cream
½ cup mayonnaise

1 tablespoon fresh lemon juice
1 tablespoon wine vinegar

Blend Roquefort and soft cream cheese. Beat in cream. When blended, stir in mayonnaise, lemon juice, and vinegar. Makes about 1¼ cups.

## SAUCE TARTARE
*For broiled fish, fried fish,*
*or soft-shell crabs*

1 cup mayonnaise
1 teaspoon each of prepared mustard, crumbled dried chervil, crumbled dried tarragon, and minced parsley
1 sweet pickle, chopped
1 teaspoon chopped chives or onions
Dash of garlic powder

Combine all ingredients and chill until ready to serve. Makes about 1¼ cups.

## SAUCE VERTE
*For cold salmon, striped bass,*
*other fish, or lobster*

15 leaves each of watercress and spinach
8 parsley sprigs
2 cups mayonnaise
Salt and pepper

Wash watercress, spinach, and parsley and cover with boiling water. Let stand for 5 or 6 minutes. Drain, put in cold water, and drain again, pressing out all the surplus moisture. Rub the wilted greens through a fine sieve. Mix thoroughly with mayonnaise. Add salt and pepper to taste. Makes about 2 cups.

## LOUIS DRESSING
*For crabmeat, especially,*
*but may be used on other seafood*

1 cup mayonnaise
½ cup chili sauce
¼ cup French Dressing, preferably made with tarragon vinegar (at right)
2 tablespoons chopped green olives
1 teaspoon Worcestershire
1 teaspoon grated horseradish
Salt and freshly ground pepper
¼ cup chopped scallions
2 tablespoons sweet pickle relish
Juice of ½ lime

Mix all ingredients together. Makes about 2 cups.

## RUSSIAN DRESSING
*For greens, meat, poultry, or eggs*

To ½ cup mayonnaise add ¼ cup chili sauce, 2 tablespoons pickle relish, and if desired, 2 tablespoons red caviar. Makes about ¾ cup.

## THOUSAND ISLAND DRESSING
*For seafood, greens, hard-cooked eggs,*
*or vegetables*

Mix 1 cup mayonnaise, ½ cup chili sauce, 2 tablespoons minced green pepper, 3 tablespoons chopped stuffed olives, 1 minced pimiento, 1 teaspoon grated onion or 2 teaspoons chopped chives. Makes about 2 cups.

## VINAIGRETTE SAUCES

### BASIC VINAIGRETTE SAUCE
½ cup olive oil
3 tablespoons vinegar
Salt and pepper

Combine oil and vinegar and beat until well blended. Season to taste with salt and pepper. Makes about ⅔ cup.

### FRENCH DRESSING
½ cup fresh lemon juice or vinegar
1½ cups olive or other salad oil
2 teaspoons salt
¼ teaspoon pepper
1 teaspoon powdered mustard
Dash of cayenne

Mix all ingredients in a 1-quart glass jar; cover tightly and shake until thoroughly blended. Store in the refrigerator. Makes 2 cups.

■ **Garlic French Dressing**—Follow recipe above adding 1 or 2 peeled garlic cloves to other ingredients.

■ **Sweetened French Dressing** — Follow recipe above adding 2 teaspoons sugar to other ingredients.

### CERVELLE SAUCE

To double the recipe for Basic Vinaigrette Sauce, add 1 tablespoon each of chopped capers, onion, parsley, and fresh tarragon. Add ½ cup chopped cooked calf's brains. Makes about 2 cups.

### CHIFFONADE DRESSING
*For mixed green or vegetable salads*

¾ cup French dressing
1 tablespoon minced parsley
2 tablespoons chopped pimiento
2 tablespoons green pepper
1 teaspoon minced onion
1 hard-cooked egg, finely chopped
1 teaspoon chopped cooked beet (optional)

Combine all ingredients and mix well. Makes 1¾ cups.

### COTTAGE-CHEESE FRENCH DRESSING
*For fruit, greens, and vegetables*

To ¾ cup French Dressing add 2 tablespoons cottage cheese, 1 tablespoon pickle relish, and 2 tablespoons chopped parsley. Makes about 1 cup.

### CRESSONIÈRE SAUCE

To 1 recipe Basic Vinaigrette Sauce, add 1 chopped hard-cooked egg and 2 tablespoons chopped watercress. Makes about 1 cup.

### DE LUXE FRENCH DRESSING

Use French Dressing recipe, adding several gashed garlic cloves, ⅓ cup chili sauce, 1 tablespoon prepared horseradish, and 1 teaspoon paprika. Makes about 2⅓ cups.

### GREEK GARLIC SAUCE
*For fish and vegetables*

6 medium potatoes
4 to 6 garlic cloves, minced
1 teaspoon salt
¾ to 1 cup olive oil
¼ cup fresh lemon juice

Boil potatoes in their skins. In a mortar pound garlic and salt to a smooth paste; or whirl in a blender. Peel potatoes; while hot, add them to the garlic mixture, blending everything to a smooth paste. Gradually add olive oil, a few drops at a time, alternating with lemon juice. The sauce should be very smooth and of the consistency of thick cream. Makes about 3 cups.
**Note:** The olive oil may have to be adjusted, since different kinds of potatoes absorb olive oil differently. Mealy potatoes are best for this sauce.

### GRIBICHE SAUCE
*For cold boiled beef, chicken,
fish, and shellfish*

3 hard-cooked eggs
½ teaspoon salt
1 teaspoon powdered mustard
Dash of pepper
1½ cups olive or salad oil
½ cup vinegar
½ cup chopped sour pickles
1 tablespoon capers
1 tablespoon mixed chopped parsley, chervil, tarragon, and chives

Separate the eggs and put the yolks in a bowl. Crush them until very smooth and add salt, mustard, and pepper. Beating vigorously, add oil a few drops at a time, until about 2 tablespoons have been added. Then add oil in a thin stream, beating vigorously. When mixture begins to thicken, add vinegar, a small amount at a time. Press out all the moisture from the pickles. Chop egg whites and add with pickles, capers, and herbs to the sauce. Makes about 3 cups.

### HERB DRESSING
*For greens, seafood, or meat*

To ¾ cup French Dressing add 2 teaspoons chopped fresh dill, marjoram, rosemary, summer savory, or other herbs. Makes ¾ cup.

### ROQUEFORT SAUCE

To 1 recipe Basic Vinaigrette Sauce, add 1 minced shallot or 2 tablespoons chopped scallions, and 2 tablespoons crumbled Roquefort cheese. Makes about 1 cup.

### HONEY DRESSING
*For fruit salads*

⅔ cup sugar
1 teaspoon powdered mustard
1 teaspoon paprika
¼ teaspoon salt
1 teaspoon celery seeds
⅓ cup strained honey
5 tablespoons vinegar

1 tablespoon fresh lemon juice
1 teaspoon grated onion
1 cup salad oil

Mix dry ingredients; add honey, vinegar, lemon juice, and onion. Pour oil into mixture very slowly, beating constantly with rotary beater. Makes 2 cups.

### MUSTARD DRESSING
*For rice, potatoes, or other vegetables*

Blend 2 tablespoons powdered mustard with enough water to make a thick paste. Dilute slightly with wine vinegar; add salad oil, beating until creamy. While beating, add sugar and salt to taste.

### TOMATO DRESSING
*For raw vegetable salads*

1 can (10½ ounces) condensed tomato soup
¼ cup water
¼ cup sugar
3 tablespoons grated onion
1 teaspoon powdered mustard
½ cup vinegar
½ cup salad oil
1 tablespoon Worcestershire
1 teaspoon paprika
Sprinkle of salt

Combine all ingredients thoroughly. Store in quart jar in refrigerator and use as needed. Shake well. Makes 3 cups.

## BARBECUE SAUCES

### BARBADOS BARBECUE SAUCE
*For beef, pork, lamb, chicken,
bologna roll, frankfurters, pears,
peaches, and bananas*

½ cup molasses
⅓ cup prepared mustard
½ cup vinegar
2 tablespoons Worcestershire
½ teaspoon hot pepper sauce
1 cup ketchup

Combine all ingredients and mix well. Makes 2⅓ cups.
**Note:** To use on frankfurters, brown franks, brushing with sauce several times until well glazed.

### DEEP-SOUTH HOT BARBECUE SAUCE
*For beef, pork, veal, chicken,
turkey, duck, liver, kidneys,
bologna roll, frankfurters, potatoes,
green and Lima beans*

1 onion, chopped
1 garlic clove, minced
2 tablespoons cooking oil
1 can (10½ ounces) tomato purée
1 cup chili sauce
1 cup vinegar
1 bottle (7 ounces) ginger ale
1 teaspoon cracked black peppercorns
2 teaspoons seasoned pepper
1 tablespoon salt
¼ cup sugar
1 tablespoon ground allspice
1 teaspoon ground mace
¼ teaspoon hot pepper sauce

Cook onion and garlic in oil for 10 minutes, stirring often. Add remaining

ingredients and simmer for about 15 minutes. Makes about 3 cups.
**Note:** To use on pork chops, brown chops. Cover with sauce and simmer until tender. Or cook on grill, brushing several times with sauce.

### CURRY BARBECUE SAUCE
*For beef, pork, lamb, veal, fish, chicken,
turkey, potatoes, onions, corn,
Lima and green beans, apples, pears,
peaches, and bananas*

2 tablespoons curry powder
1½ teaspoons garlic salt
1 tablespoon powdered mustard
2 tablespoons steak sauce
½ cup butter or margarine, melted
⅔ cup wine vinegar

Combine all ingredients and blend until smooth. Makes 1¼ cups.
**Note:** To use on fish, spread on fillets and cook on grill or in oven until done.

### HERB BARBECUE SAUCE
*For beef, pork, lamb, veal, chicken,
duck, rabbit, liver, kidneys,
bologna roll, frankfurters, meat loaf,
hash, potatoes, corn, carrots,
cabbage, peppers, Lima and green
beans, and onions*

1 cup ketchup
½ cup water
3 tablespoons tarragon vinegar
1 tablespoon steak sauce
¼ teaspoon each of ground marjoram, oregano, and thyme
Dash of garlic salt

Combine all ingredients. Makes 1⅔ cups.
**Note:** To use on steak or hamburgers, brown meat on both sides. Brush with sauce several times, or until cooked to desired doneness.

### HONEY BARBECUE SAUCE
*For ham, luncheon meat, or bologna*

Mix ¼ cup each of ketchup, honey, and fresh lemon juice and a few dashes of hot pepper sauce. Makes ¾ cup.

### PINEAPPLE-CHILI BARBECUE SAUCE
*For ham or bologna slices while broiling;
try on panbroiled meats, too.*

Mix ⅓ cup chili sauce, 2 tablespoons Worcestershire, 1 cup firmly packed brown sugar, ¾ cup pineapple juice, and 1 tablespoon fresh lemon juice. Makes 1⅔ cups.

### RED-HOT SAUCE
*For all kinds of barbecued meats*

10 pounds ripe tomatoes
8 medium onions
2 hot red peppers
1 cup sugar
1 cup white vinegar
1 teaspoon ground cinnamon
4 teaspoons salt

Quarter tomatoes. Peel and quarter onions. Seed and core peppers and cut into pieces. Put vegetables in kettle and cook until soft. Put through food mill.

Return to kettle and add remaining ingredients; cook until mixture begins to thicken. Reduce heat and simmer for about 45 minutes, stirring frequently. Makes about 2 quarts.

### SHERRY BARBECUE SAUCE
*For chicken*

Mix 1 cup sherry; ½ cup cooking oil; 2 tablespoons steak sauce; 1 tablespoon each of onion powder, powdered mustard, and brown sugar; 1 teaspoon garlic salt; and ½ teaspoon each of salt and pepper. Makes 1½ cups.

### SMOKY BARBECUE SAUCE
*For beef or other meat*

In saucepan mix 1 cup tomato juice, the juice and peel of 1 lemon, ¼ cup vinegar, ¼ cup liquid smoke, 2 tablespoons molasses, and 1 bay leaf; bring to boil. Makes about 1¾ cups.

## BUTTER SAUCES

### AMANDINE BUTTER
*For fish or chicken*

Melt ⅓ cup butter. Add 2 tablespoons shredded blanched almonds and sauté until nuts are lightly browned. Add 1½ teaspoons fresh lemon juice. Makes about ⅓ cup.

### ANCHOVY BUTTER
*For fish, eggs, or pasta*

To ⅓ cup butter, add 4 minced anchovy fillets and ½ teaspoon fresh lemon juice. Makes about ⅓ cup.

### BERCY BUTTER
*For beef and lamb*

2 teaspoons minced shallot
⅔ cup dry white wine
1 teaspoon fresh lemon juice
¼ cup butter, melted
2 teaspoons chopped parsley
Salt and pepper

Cook shallot, wine, and lemon juice until reduced to about one-fourth the original quantity. Cool; add melted butter, parsley, and salt and pepper to taste. Makes about ½ cup.

### BLACK BUTTER
*For eggs*

Heat ⅓ cup butter until quite brown. Add fresh lemon juice or wine vinegar to taste. Makes about ⅓ cup.

### BEURRE BLANC
(White Butter)
*For fish*

¼ cup dry white wine
¼ cup white-wine vinegar
1 tablespoon minced shallot
¼ teaspoon salt
⅛ teaspoon white pepper
1½ cups chilled butter, cut into 24 pieces

Fresh lemon juice

Put wine, vinegar, shallot, and seasonings in saucepan and boil until reduced to about 1½ tablespoons. Remove from heat and at once beat in 2 pieces of chilled butter. As butter softens and blends into the mixture, beat in another piece. Then put over very low heat and, beating constantly, continue adding successive pieces of butter until all are added. When all is blended in, remove from heat and add lemon juice to taste. Put in a slightly warm bowl and serve at once. Makes about 1½ cups.

### CHIVE BUTTER
*For fish, meat, or eggs*

To ½ cup melted butter, add 2 tablespoons finely chopped chives.

### COLBERT BUTTER SAUCE
*For fish*

1 recipe Maître d'Hôtel Butter (at right)
1 teaspoon glace-de-viande or beef extract
1 teaspoon chopped tarragon

Mix all ingredients together. Makes 1 cup.

### DRAWN BUTTER SAUCE
*For vegetables*

½ cup butter
2 tablespoons all-purpose flour
2 cups hot vegetable broth
2 tablespoons fresh lemon juice
Salt

Melt ¼ cup of the butter and stir in flour. Gradually stir in broth. Cook over low heat, stirring constantly, until smooth and thickened. Beat in remaining butter and the lemon juice. Add salt to taste. Makes about 2½ cups.

### LEMON BUTTER
*For fish, veal, and egg dishes*

Cut ½ cup butter into pieces and put in saucepan. When melted, skim off the foam and strain the clear yellow liquid into a bowl, leaving the milky residue in the bottom of the pan. Add 1 to 2 tablespoons of fresh lemon juice. Makes about ½ cup.

### LOBSTER BUTTER
*For fish dishes and sauces*

1 cup cooked lobster meat, legs, eggs, tomalley (coral), and shells
½ cup hot melted butter
Salt and pepper

Chop lobster meat, legs, etc., into small pieces or force through food chopper. Heat container or electric blender by filling with hot water. Drain and dry. Add lobster mixture. Pour in hot butter, cover, and blend at high speed. Pour into saucepan and heat until butter has warmed and melted. Blend again. Rub through a very fine sieve. As butter cools,

beat with a spoon and season to taste with salt and pepper. Makes about ⅔ cup.

### MAÎTRE D'HÔTEL BUTTER
*For meat and fish*

1 cup butter
1 tablespoon chopped parsley
Juice of 1 lemon
Salt and pepper

Cream butter and add parsley, lemon juice, and salt and pepper to taste. Makes 1 cup.

### MUSTARD BUTTER
*For beef, kidneys, liver, and lamb.
Also for use with sandwiches
as a condiment*

Melt ⅔ cup butter and, little by little, add 1 tablespoon prepared mustard. Makes ⅔ cup.

### NOISETTE BUTTER
*For fish*

Heat ½ cup butter until lightly browned. Add ¼ cup toasted chopped hazelnuts (filberts). To toast, put chopped nuts in preheated moderate oven (350°F.) for about 15 minutes. Makes ¾ cup.

### NORMAN WHITE BUTTER SAUCE
*For fish*

1 cup strained fish Court Bouillon (page 1594)
2 tablespoons white vinegar
1 cup butter, cut into pieces
Salt and pepper

Over very low heat simmer Court Bouillon and vinegar together for 10 minutes, or until liquid is reduced to ⅔ to ¾ cup. Add butter, 1 piece at a time, stirring constantly in the same direction. Add salt and pepper to taste. Pour into heated sauceboat as soon as butter is melted. Makes about 1¼ to 1½ cups.

### POLONAISE SAUCE
*For noodles, creamed meat or fish,
or vegetables*

1 cup fine white-bread crumbs
⅓ cup butter, melted
1½ teaspoons fresh lemon juice
1 tablespoon minced parsley

Brown crumbs in the butter. Add lemon juice and parsley. Makes about ⅔ cup.
**Note:** For green vegetables, add 1 chopped hard-cooked egg.

### ROQUEFORT BUTTER
*For grilled beef and a spread on canapés*

⅔ cup softened butter
¼ cup softened Roquefort cheese
1 teaspoon prepared mustard (optional)
1 tablespoon brandy (optional)

Cream butter and cheese together until well blended. If desired, add mustard and brandy, and blend. Makes about ¾ cup.

### SHALLOT BUTTER
*For meats*

½ cup butter
1 minced shallot

Bowknots with Anchovy Butter, peas, and sautéed mushrooms.

Cold spaghetti with French Dressing, tomatoes, and chopped mint.

Filled manicotti with Italian Tomato Sauce.

Few parsley sprigs, chopped
Few drops of vinegar (optional)

Mix well first 3 ingredients and add vinegar, if desired. Makes about ⅔ cup.

### SHRIMP BUTTER
*For an additive for sauces
and a garniture for fish*

Follow recipe for Lobster Butter (page 1624), substituting 1 cup shrimp meat and shells for the lobster meat, legs, etc. Add a little ground mace, if desired.

### TARRAGON BUTTER
*For fish*

2 tablespoons chopped tarragon leaves
Few parsley sprigs, chopped
½ cup softened butter

Pound tarragon and parsley together until thoroughly crushed. Add to butter and mix well. Makes ½ cup.

## CONDIMENT SAUCES

### COCKTAIL SAUCE

½ cup chili sauce
½ cup ketchup
2 tablespoons fresh lemon juice
2 tablespoons prepared horseradish
Worcestershire, salt, and hot pepper
sauce to taste

Combine all ingredients and blend well. Serve with shrimps, crabmeat, oysters, and clams. Makes about 1¼ cups.

### MAYONNAISE COCKTAIL SAUCE
*For shrimps or any seafood*

Blend together 1 cup mayonnaise, 1 cup chili sauce, 1 teaspoon Worcestershire, 2 teaspoons horseradish, 4 sweet pickles, minced, 2 celery stalks, minced, 1 small onion, minced (or 4 green onions, minced), 4 parsley sprigs, minced, and 1 tablespoon sugar. Refrigerate. Makes 2½ cups.

### HOT CONDIMENT SAUCE

2 quarts chopped ripe tomatoes (4 to 5 pounds)
2 carrots, chopped
3 onions, chopped
4 sweet red peppers
4 cups white vinegar
1 teaspoon pepper
¾ cup firmly packed brown sugar
2 tablespoons salt
½ teaspoon cayenne
2 teaspoons each of ground cloves, allspice, nutmeg, cinnamon, and ginger

Combine all ingredients in kettle. Bring to boil and simmer, stirring occasionally. Force mixture through a fine sieve. Again bring to boil and cook for about 30 minutes, stirring often. Fill hot sterilized jars; seal. Makes 2½ pints.

### HAWAIIAN TERIYAKI SAUCE
*For marinating chicken or pork*

Mix 1½ cups soy sauce, ¾ cup honey, 1½ teaspoons ground ginger, and ¼ teaspoon instant minced garlic.

### SOY-SAUCE DRESSING
*For coleslaw*

2 tablespoons soy sauce
1½ tablespoons water
½ cup salad oil
1 tablespoon ketchup
½ teaspoon instant minced garlic
¼ cup wine vinegar
1 tablespoon brown sugar
½ teaspoon paprika
¼ teaspoon pepper
2 dashes of hot pepper sauce

Mix all ingredients. Makes 1 cup.

## MISCELLANEOUS SAUCES

### AMÉRICAINE SAUCE
*For broiled lobster*

2 cups canned tomatoes
1 tablespoon olive oil
2 tablespoons butter or margarine
2 shallots, minced
1 garlic clove
1 tablespoon chopped parsley
1 tablespoon chopped chervil
3 tablespoons brandy

Cook tomatoes until they measure 1 cup. Strain. Heat olive oil with butter and sauté shallots until translucent. Add garlic, parsley, chervil, and tomato purée. Cook until shallots are tender. Add brandy and simmer for a few minutes longer. Remove garlic clove. Makes about 1½ cups.

### SWEET BASIL SAUCE
*For noodles*

3 garlic cloves
¼ cup minced sweet basil
1 tablespoon butter
¼ cup olive oil
2 tablespoons grated Parmesan cheese
½ cup hot water

With mortar and pestle, or knife on chopping board, mash and blend garlic and sweet basil into a creamy paste. Add butter, oil, and grated cheese. Mix thoroughly. Just before serving add boiling water. Stir well. Makes about ¾ cup.
**Note:** The sauce should be poured over cooked strained noodles, more grated cheese sprinkled on top of the dish, and it should be served immediately.

### ENGLISH BREAD SAUCE
*For roast chicken, other birds, and game*

½ cup soft bread crumbs
1 cup milk
1 small onion
1 whole clove
Pinch of ground mace
Salt and pepper
1 tablespoon butter
1 tablespoon light cream

Make sure bread is very finely crumbled. Pour milk into top part of a double boiler. Add onion stuck with clove and cook over boiling water until milk is scalded. Add mace. Sprinkle in crumbs and beat mixture with a whisk. Add salt and pepper to taste and half of butter. Cook, beating with the whisk, for 20 minutes. Beat in remaining butter and the cream. Remove onion and clove and serve at once. Makes about 1 cup.

### CHAMPAGNE SAUCE
*For ham, tongue, duck, and game*

1¼ cups champagne
¼ cup minced lean raw ham
¼ cup yellow raisins
2 teaspoons cornstarch
1 tablespoon water
1 tablespoon butter

Heat 1 cup of the champagne with ham and raisins. Simmer for 10 minutes. Mix cornstarch with water and add slowly to the hot sauce. Cook over low heat, stirring constantly, until smooth and thickened. Add the butter and stir until butter is melted. Stir in remaining champagne, reheat slightly, and serve immediately. Makes about 1½ cups.

### CHATEAUBRIAND SAUCE
*For broiled steak*

½ cup dry white wine
1 shallot, minced
2 tablespoons glace-de-viande or meat extract
1 tablespoon butter
1 teaspoon minced fresh tarragon
Dash of cayenne
¼ teaspoon fresh lemon juice

Cook wine with shallot until slightly reduced. Add remaining ingredients and reheat. Serve very hot. Makes about ½ cup.

### COLBERT SAUCE
*For broiled or roasted meat and fish*

¼ cup butter or margarine
1 tablespoon minced parsley
Pinch each of ground nutmeg and cayenne
3 tablespoons glace-de-viande or meat extract
1 tablespoon water or consommé
Juice of 1 lemon

Cream butter with parsley, nutmeg, and cayenne. Melt *glace-de-viande* with water. Gradually beat in butter mixture, a little at a time, alternating butter with lemon juice. Makes about ½ cup.

### CREOLE SAUCE
*For seafood, rice, spaghetti, tripe, or omelet*

2 tablespoons chopped onion
¼ cup chopped green pepper
1 garlic clove
¼ cup butter or margarine
2 tablespoons olive oil
2 tablespoons all-purpose flour
1 cup chopped peeled seeded tomatoes
½ cup beef stock
6 to 8 fresh mushrooms, sliced

1 tablespoon finely chopped parsley
Salt and pepper

Sauté onion, green pepper, and garlic in butter and olive oil. Sauté until onion is translucent. Remove garlic. Blend in flour. Gradually stir in tomatoes and beef stock. Simmer for 30 minutes over low heat, stirring occasionally. Add mushrooms and parsley and simmer for 5 minutes longer. Season to taste with salt and pepper. Makes about 1½ cups.

### CUMBERLAND SAUCE
*For duck, game, other hot or cold meat*

- 1 cup red currant jelly
- 1 cup port
  Juice of ½ lemon
  Juice of ½ orange
- 2 teaspoons each of grated lemon and orange rind
- 2 teaspoons prepared English mustard
  Salt and pepper to taste
- ¼ teaspoon each of cayenne and ground ginger

Melt currant jelly. Stir in port and fruit juices; cool. Blend in all other ingredients. Serve cold. Makes about 2¼ cups.
**Note:** This sauce improves if kept for a day or two before using.

### GREEK EGG AND LEMON SAUCE
*For meat, fish, and vegetable dishes*

- 3 egg yolks
- 1 whole egg
- 4 tablespoons fresh lemon juice
- 1 cup hot chicken bouillon

Beat egg yolks and whole egg until light. Add lemon juice gradually, beating constantly. Add hot bouillon, a little at a time, beating constantly. Makes 1½ cups.
**Note:** The trick is not to boil the sauce while adding the hot bouillon, or it will curdle.

### ENGLISH GOOSEBERRY SAUCE
*For boiled or fried fish and other fried foods, as well as with rich fowl such as duck or goose*

- 1 pint gooseberries*
- 1 cup water
  Handful of spinach or sorrel leaves (optional), chopped
- 3 tablespoons butter
- ⅛ teaspoon grated nutmeg
  Sugar to taste

Cook gooseberries and water together until berries are soft. Add spinach leaves and cook for 3 minutes longer. Drain and reserve juice. Rub berries and spinach through a food mill or a fine sieve. Return to saucepan and combine with juice. The purée should be of the consistency of a thin batter. If too liquid, boil over high heat until right consistency is achieved by evaporation. Add butter, nutmeg, and sugar to taste. Simmer for 2 or 3 minutes, stirring constantly. If no spinach is used, add a few drops of green food coloring for right color. Makes about 1 cup.

*One 15-ounce can gooseberries may be substituted for the fresh gooseberries and water. Use both berries and syrup.

### HORSERADISH SAUCE
*For cold cuts, braised, boiled, or roast beef, and fish*

- ½ cup heavy cream
  Salt
  Freshly grated horseradish
- 1 teaspoon vinegar or prepared mustard

Whip cream until stiff. Add salt and horseradish to taste. Stir in vinegar. Makes about 1 cup.

### MINT SAUCE
*For roast lamb or mutton*

- ½ cup cider vinegar
- 1 tablespoon sugar
- 2 tablespoons minced fresh mint leaves

Cook vinegar with sugar until syrup clears and just comes to a boil. Cool, and stir in mint. Makes about ½ cup.

### PIEDMONTESE BAGNA CAUDA
### (Hot Bath)
*For raw or plain boiled vegetables, boiled fish and meats*

- ½ cup butter
- ¼ cup olive oil
- 6 garlic cloves, sliced paper-thin
- 2 cans (2 ounces each) anchovy fillets without capers, minced

Over lowest possible heat (you may have to use an asbestos plate) cook together butter, olive oil, and garlic for 15 minutes. Do not let boil. Stir in anchovies and simmer until they dissolve. Keep the sauce hot over a candle or alcohol plate warmer. The sauce must never boil nor brown. Makes about 1¼ cups.

### CAUCASIAN PLUM SAUCE
### (Tkemali)
*For roast chicken or other fowl, and for shashlik*

- ½ pound prune-plums, pitted
- 2 or 3 garlic cloves, minced
  Salt and pepper
- 1 tablespoon minced parsley

Cook plums in water to cover. Drain, and reserve liquid. Rub plums through a sieve or purée in a blender. Stir sufficient plum liquid into the purée to achieve the consistency of cream. Add garlic, salt and pepper to taste, and parsley. Bring to a boil. Reduce heat and simmer for 5 minutes. Makes about 1¼ cups.

### SINGAPORE SATAY SAUCE
*For grilled meat*

- 1 garlic clove
- 1 small onion
- 1 cup roasted peanuts
- 2 fresh chilies
- 3 dried chilies
- 1 teaspoon sugar
- 1 small piece of tamarind
  Juice of ½ lemon
- 2 tablespoons water
- 2 tablespoons Coconut Milk
- 1 tablespoon soy sauce

In a mortar or electric blender, crush together garlic, onion, peanuts, chilies, sugar, and tamarind. Fry this paste in a dry frying pan for a few minutes. Add lemon juice, water, Coconut Milk, and soy sauce and bring to a boil. Reduce heat and simmer until sauce is thick. Makes about 1 cup.
**Note:** Satay Sauce keeps in refrigerator in a tightly closed jar for a few weeks.

### Coconut Milk
Soak ½ cup shredded coconut in 1 cup warm water. After 30 minutes, squeeze out coconut and strain liquid. Repeat this twice. Discard coconut pulp and use strained liquid.

### SWEET-AND-SOUR SAUCE
*For pork, vegetables, shrimps, or spareribs*

- 2 tablespoons butter or margarine
- ½ cup cider vinegar
- 1 cup water
- 3 tablespoons soy sauce
- ¼ cup sugar
- 2 tablespoons arrowroot or 1 tablespoon cornstarch
- 3 tablespoons Madeira
- 1 teaspoon chopped preserved gingerroot

Combine in a saucepan butter, vinegar, and water. Blend soy sauce with sugar and arrowroot. Gradually beat soy mixture into vinegar mixture. Cook over low heat, stirring constantly, until smooth and thickened. Stir in Madeira and gingerroot and cook until sauce becomes transparent. Makes about 2 cups.

### SWEET-SOUR MUSTARD SAUCE
*For fresh broiled or baked salmon*

- 1 tablespoon cornstarch
- 2 tablespoons sugar
- 2 tablespoons powdered mustard
- ½ teaspoon salt
- ⅛ teaspoon pepper
- 3 tablespoons cider vinegar
- 1 cup water
- 3 tablespoons butter or margarine

Mix cornstarch, sugar, mustard, salt, and pepper. Add vinegar, water, and butter. Bring to boil; cook until slightly thickened, stirring constantly. Makes about 1⅔ cups.

### ITALIAN TOMATO SAUCE
*For meats, fish, and pasta*

- ¼ cup olive oil
- 1 garlic clove, minced
- 1 medium onion, minced
- 1 can (32 ounces) Italian plum tomatoes, mashed
- 2 tablespoons tomato paste
- ½ teaspoon basil
  Salt and pepper
  Few parsley sprigs, chopped

Heat oil in saucepan. Add garlic and onion and cook for 2 or 3 minutes. Add tomatoes and tomato paste. Bring to boil and simmer for 15 minutes, or until of desired consistency. Add basil, and season with salt and pepper to taste. Add parsley. If desired, force sauce through a sieve before using. Makes about 3 cups.

## DESSERT SAUCES

### BUTTERSCOTCH SAUCE
*For puddings, cakes, and ice cream*

1½ cups firmly packed dark brown sugar
¼ cup all-purpose flour
1 cup boiling water
Dash of salt
¼ cup butter or margarine
3 tablespoons light cream or evaporated milk
1 teaspoon vanilla extract

Mix brown sugar with flour. Stir in boiling water and salt. Cook over low heat, stirring constantly, until smooth and thick, 6 to 8 minutes. Add more boiling water if sauce is too thick. Stir in remaining ingredients and blend well. Reheat and serve warm. Makes about 2 cups.

### CARAMEL SAUCE

1 cup sugar
1 cup boiling water
Dash of salt
½ teaspoon vanilla extract

In small heavy pan, heat sugar over low heat, stirring constantly, until sugar melts and is slightly browned. Very slowly add boiling water. Boil for 6 minutes. Add salt, and cool. Stir in vanilla. Makes about 1½ cups.

### CHANTILLY SAUCE

1 cup preserved chestnuts, drained
½ cup milk
½ cup heavy cream, whipped

Cook chestnuts with milk until chestnuts are very soft. Press mixture through a sieve, and cool. Fold in whipped cream. Chill until ready to serve. Serve on pudding, ice cream, or fruit. Makes about 1½ cups.

### CHOCOLATE SAUCE

2 ounces (2 squares) unsweetened chocolate
¾ cup milk
¼ teaspoon salt
1½ cups sugar
3 tablespoons light corn syrup
2 tablespoons butter
1 teaspoon vanilla extract

In saucepan over low heat melt chocolate in milk, stirring constantly. Beat until smooth. Add salt, sugar, and corn syrup. Cook, stirring occasionally, for 2 or 3 minutes. Add butter and vanilla. Makes 2 cups.

### BITTERSWEET-CHOCOLATE SAUCE

8 ounces (8 squares) unsweetened chocolate
2 cups sugar
1 can (14½ ounces) evaporated milk, undiluted
2 tablespoons strong black coffee
Dash of salt
1 teaspoon vanilla extract

Melt chocolate in top part of a double boiler over boiling water; add sugar; mix well. Cover; cook over boiling water for 30 minutes. Add evaporated milk, coffee, salt, and vanilla; beat until smooth and thick. Serve hot. Make ahead, if desired; cool, and refrigerate. Will keep for several weeks. Reheat over boiling water. Makes about 3 cups.

### CHOCOLATE CUSTARD SAUCE

4 egg yolks
¼ cup sugar
⅛ teaspoon salt
2 cups milk
2 ounces (2 squares) unsweetened chocolate
½ teaspoon vanilla extract

Beat egg yolks slightly. Add sugar and salt and mix well. Scald milk with the chocolate. Beat to blend. Stir into egg mixture. Cook, stirring constantly, over hot water until mixture is thickened and coats a metal spoon. Add vanilla. Cool, and chill. Makes about 2½ cups.

### CRÈME ANGLAISE
(Custard Sauce)

1½ cups milk
⅛ teaspoon salt
3 egg yolks
3 tablespoons sugar
Vanilla or almond extract

Scald milk in top part of a double boiler over simmering water. Mix salt, egg yolks, and sugar. Stir in small amount of hot milk, put back in top part of double boiler, and cook, stirring, until thickened. Cool. Flavor sauce with vanilla extract. Makes about 1¾ cups.

### CRÈME PÂTISSIÈRE

¾ cup sugar
6 egg yolks
⅓ cup all-purpose flour
⅛ teaspoon salt
2 cups milk
1-inch piece of vanilla bean

In heavy saucepan, combine sugar and egg yolks. Beat with wire whisk until thick and lemon-colored. Add the flour and salt and mix only enough to blend. Scald the milk with the vanilla bean. Gradually stir into egg-yolk mixture. Cook over low heat, stirring vigorously, until mixture boils. Then cook, stirring, for 2 minutes longer. Remove the vanilla bean. Strain and cool, stirring occasionally, to prevent a skin from forming on top. Makes about 2 cups.
**Note:** If vanilla bean is not available, substitute 1 teaspoon vanilla extract; add to finished mixture.

### WEINSCHAUM
(Wine Custard Sauce)
*For cakes, puddings, and fruits*

2 cups dry white wine
½ cup water
4 eggs
½ cup sugar

Beat all ingredients together in the top part of a double boiler over boiling water. Be sure boiling water is not touching bottom of top pan. Beat with a whisk or an electric beater until mixture thickens. Beat constantly and serve hot or cold. Makes 6 servings.

### FOAMY SAUCE
*For puddings or plain cakes*

1 cup confectioners' sugar
½ cup soft butter or margarine
2 egg yolks, beaten
2 egg whites, stiffly beaten
1 tablespoon brandy or rum

In top part of a double boiler cream confectioners' sugar and butter. Add egg yolks. Cook over simmering water, stirring constantly, until thickened. Fold in egg whites and brandy. Serve warm. Makes 4 to 6 servings.

### FRUIT SAUCE

2 cups (1 pound) peach jam
½ cup water
Grated rind and juice of 1 lemon
¼ pound dates, cut up
¼ cup chopped cherries
¼ cup slivered blanched almonds
1 teaspoon rum flavoring

Heat first 4 ingredients. Add last 4 ingredients. Refrigerate. Makes about 2½ cups.

### LEMON SAUCE

½ cup sugar
⅛ teaspoon salt
2 tablespoons cornstarch
1 cup boiling water
2 tablespoons butter
Juice of 1 lemon
1 teaspoon grated lemon rind

In saucepan mix sugar, salt, and cornstarch. Gradually stir in boiling water. Cook, stirring constantly, until thickened. Remove from heat; stir in butter, lemon juice, and grated rind. Serve warm. Makes 1¾ cups.

### ORANGE SAUCE

1 cup sugar
5 tablespoons all-purpose flour
⅛ teaspoon salt
Grated rind of 1 orange
½ cup fresh orange juice
Juice of ½ lemon
3 egg yolks
1 teaspoon melted butter
1 cup heavy cream, whipped

In heavy saucepan mix together sugar, flour, and salt. Add orange rind, fruit juices, and egg yolks. Cook over low heat, stirring, until thickened and smooth; add butter, and cool; fold in whipped cream. Makes about 2½ cups.

### HARD SAUCE

½ cup soft butter
1½ cups sifted confectioners' sugar
1 teaspoon vanilla extract or 2 tablespoons rum or brandy

Cream butter with confectioners' sugar until light and fluffy. Add vanilla. Chill. Makes 8 to 10 servings.

### CALIFORNIA-WALNUT SAUCE

*For ice cream, steamed pudding, or gingerbread, served hot or cold*

In heavy saucepan mix 1 cup light corn syrup, ⅛ teaspoon salt, ¼ cup water, and, if desired, ¼ teaspoon maple flavoring. Add 1¼ cups coarsely chopped walnuts. Bring to boil, cover; simmer for about 25 minutes. Cool, and cover tightly. Refrigerate. Makes about 2 cups.

### SABAYON

- 5 egg yolks
- 1 tablespoon cold water
- ¾ cup sugar
- ⅛ teaspoon salt
- ½ cup marsala, port, or sherry

In top part of a double boiler beat egg yolks with water until they are foamy and light. Whisk in sugar, salt, and wine. Beat over hot, not boiling, water until thickened and fluffy. This will take only a few minutes. Makes about 2 cups. To serve as dessert pile into sherbet glasses; serve hot. Makes 6 servings.

### ORANGE SYRUP

*For blueberry pancakes or dessert crêpes*

    Grated rind of 1 orange
- ½ cup fresh orange juice
- 1 cup sugar
    Salt
    Sections from 1 orange

Mix grated rind, orange juice, sugar, and salt and let boil in large saucepan until the consistency of maple syrup, 4 or 5 minutes. Add orange sections free of seeds and membrane. Serve hot or cold. Makes 1 cup.

### BROWN-SUGAR SYRUP

*For waffles or pancakes*

- 1 cup firmly packed brown sugar
    Dash of salt
- ½ cup water
- ¼ cup butter
- ¼ teaspoon vanilla extract

Cook all ingredients, except vanilla, in a large saucepan or skillet until thick, 3 or 4 minutes. Add vanilla. Makes 1¼ cups.

### VANILLA SAUCE

- ½ cup sugar
- 1 tablespoon cornstarch
- 1 cup boiling water
- 2 tablespoons butter
- 1 teaspoon vanilla extract
    Dash of salt

In small saucepan mix sugar and cornstarch. Stir in boiling water. Simmer for 5 minutes. Stir in butter and vanilla. Add salt. Serve warm. Makes 1¼ cups.

**SAUERBRATEN**—Beef prepared in a spicy, aromatic sweet-sour marinade to tenderize the meat and add flavor. The dish is of German origin and the word means "sour roast." Sauerbraten requires long cooking but, happily, no watching. The traditional accompaniments are dumplings, boiled potatoes, or noodles.

*Quick Sauerbraten with Potato Dumplings*

## SAUERBRATEN WITH VEGETABLES

```
 5 pounds pot roast of beef
   (round or rump)
 2 cups vinegar
 2 cups water
 1 onion, sliced
 ¼ cup honey
 2 teaspoons salt
10 peppercorns
 2 bay leaves
 6 whole cloves
 1 lemon, sliced
 2 tablespoons cooking oil
   Potatoes, carrots
   All-purpose flour
```

Put meat in large bowl. Combine next 8 ingredients; bring to boil. Cool, and pour over meat. Add lemon. Cover and refrigerate for 3 days. Turn meat each day. Remove meat from marinade, reserving marinade, and dry with paper towels. Brown on all sides in oil. Put on rack; strain marinade and add 1½ cups to the meat. Cover and simmer for 2½ to 3 hours, or until tender, adding more marinade if necessary. During last 45 minutes of cooking, add vegetables. Allow 1 potato and 2 carrots per serving. Remove meat and vegetables to platter. Thicken gravy with flour mixed with a little cold water; simmer for a few minutes and adjust seasoning. Makes 6 to 8 servings.

## SAUERBRATEN WITH SOUR-CREAM GRAVY

```
 4 to 5 pounds pot roast of beef (top or
   bottom round, or rump)
 1 tablespoon salt
 1 onion, sliced
10 peppercorns
 3 bay leaves
 3 whole cloves
 1 cup vinegar
   Water
 2 ounces salt pork
 2 tablespoons cooking oil
 2 tablespoons all-purpose flour
 2 tablespoons sugar
 6 gingersnaps, broken
   Salt and pepper to taste
 2 teaspoons monosodium glutamate
 ½ cup red wine
   Dairy sour cream
```

Rub meat with salt. Put in large bowl. Combine onion, peppercorns, bay leaves, cloves, vinegar, and 2 cups water and bring to boil. Cool. Pour over meat and add enough additional water to cover meat. Cover and refrigerate for 36 to 48 hours, turning meat each morning and night. Remove meat from marinade, reserving marinade. Pierce meat and insert strips of salt pork. Heat oil and brown meat on all sides. Put on rack in roasting pan.

Brown flour in oil remaining and add sugar, gingersnaps, salt and pepper, monosodium glutamate, and about 4 cups strained marinade. Cook until smooth and creamy. Pour over meat in roasting pan. Cover and simmer for 2½ to 3 hours, or until tender. Baste frequently while roasting. Add wine 30 minutes before meat is done. Remove meat. Add sour cream to gravy just before serving. Serve with Potato Dumplings (at right). Makes 6 to 8 servings.

## OVERNIGHT SAUERBRATEN

```
 2 pounds beef chuck steak about 1½
   inches thick
 1 teaspoon salt
 1 teaspoon ground ginger
 1 cup cider vinegar
 3 cups water
 1 medium onion, sliced
 2 tablespoons mixed pickling spice
 2 bay leaves
 ½ teaspoon peppercorns
 4 whole cloves
 2 tablespoons sugar
 2 tablespoons shortening
   All-purpose flour
```

Rub meat with salt and ginger; put in large flat dish. Combine remaining ingredients except shortening and flour; bring to boil. Cool; pour over meat. Cover and refrigerate overnight, turning once or twice. Remove meat from marinade, reserving marinade. Pat with paper towels and brown in shortening. Add 2 cups reserved marinade and half of onion and spices from marinade. Cover and simmer for 1½ hours, or until tender. Remove meat and thicken liquid with flour mixed with a little cold water. Simmer for a few minutes, then strain. Serve with Potato Dumplings (below) or with mashed potatoes. Makes 4 to 6 servings.

## QUICK SAUERBRATEN

```
 4 to 5 pounds pot roast of beef
   (rump or brisket)
   Water
 ¾ cup malt vinegar
 2 teaspoons salt
 3 tablespoons brown sugar
 ⅛ teaspoon each of ground cloves
   and allspice
 1 teaspoon each of monosodium
   glutamate and ground ginger
 1 bay leaf
 1½ teaspoons coarsely ground pepper
 ¾ cup chopped onions
   All-purpose flour
   Potato Dumplings
```

Brown meat in heavy kettle. Drain off fat. Put meat on rack, add ¾ cup water, and cover. Simmer for 1 hour. Remove meat and cut into ½-inch-thick slices; return to kettle. Bring to boil ¾ cup water plus remaining ingredients except flour and Dumplings. Pour over meat. Cover and simmer until fork-tender, about 1½ hours. Add water if necessary. Strain gravy and thicken with flour mixed with a little cold water; simmer a few minutes. Pour over meat; serve with Potato Dumplings. Makes 6 to 8 servings.

### Potato Dumplings

Brown 1 tablespoon minced onion in 2 tablespoons butter or margarine; add 1 slice of bread cut into small cubes, and brown. Prepare 2 envelopes (1 box) instant mashed potatoes as directed, but use only the amount of liquid indicated for 1 envelope. Beat in ¼ cup all-purpose flour and 2 beaten eggs. Season and add a few chopped parsley sprigs. Flatten a spoonful of mixture on your hand and put a few cubes of bread on dumpling. Roll into a ball. Repeat until the mixture is used. Drop into boiling water and cook until dumplings rise, 5 to 8 minutes. Sprinkle with buttered crumbs. Makes 8.

**SAUERKRAUT**—Pickled cabbage made from cabbage which has been cut fine and allowed to ferment in a brine made of its own juice, salt, and occasionally other spices.

*Availability and Purchasing Guide*—Year round sold fresh by bulk, canned, or packed in plastic film bags in the refrigerated-food sections of food stores. Sauerkraut juice is also available.

U. S. Grade A sauerkraut is white or cream-colored with long uniform shreds, crisp firm texture, and a good flavor.

### Storage

☐ Canned, kitchen shelf: 1 year
☐ Refrigerator shelf: 4 to 5 days

### Caloric Values

☐ Canned, 3½ ounces, solids and liquid = 18 calories
☐ Canned juice, 3½ ounces = 10 calories

### SAUERKRAUT

```
15 pounds firm white cabbage
 ⅔ cup salt
   Three 1- to 2-gallon crocks or
   one 4- to 6-gallon crock
```

Trim cabbage and quarter heads. Remove core and shred cabbage finely into 1/16-inch shreds. Mix cabbage with salt. Pack cabbage firmly into crock and cover with a clean cloth. Put a plate on the cloth and weight it with a piece of wood, so that the cloth is wet. As soon as fermentation begins, remove the scum and place a clean cloth and a board over the cabbage. Wash board daily. Keep cabbage at a temperature below 60°F. Let stand for at least a month. At this time heat the kraut to 180°F. and pack firmly into sterilized hot jars. Add sauerkraut juice to within ½ inch of the top of the jar. If there is not enough juice, make a brine of 2 tablespoons salt to each 1 quart water and pour over. Seal. Process in a boiling-water bath for 25 minutes for pints and 30 minutes for quarts. Makes 6 quarts.

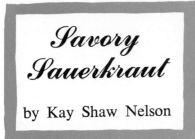

## Savory Sauerkraut

### by Kay Shaw Nelson

While traveling through the towns and countryside of delightful Alsace in northeastern France, I became enchanted with its rugged scenery, hospitable people, gingerbread architecture, and rolling fertile fields. But I was especially attracted by the many culinary specialties.

For Alsace, along with its neighboring province of Lorraine, is one of the great gastronomic regions of France. The local cookery can draw upon beautiful fruits and vegetables from luxuriant gardens and orchards; savory game from the Vosges Mountains; fresh fish from mountain streams and the Rhine River; and specially fed poultry. Jams of *mirabelle* plums; onions cooked to perfection in creamy tarts; delicious *pâtés* and terrines; tempting cheeses, such as Muenster; ham cooked in pastry; saddle of hare *à la crème;* spicy sausages and smoked meats; delicate pastries; and crayfish flan are only a few well-remembered gastronomic delights.

My most exciting and surprising discovery, however, was the sauerkraut, hitherto not a particular favorite of mine. So delicious was the *choucroute,* as the French call it, whether served by itself, garnished with a variety of smoked meats, cooked with pheasant, or baked in numerous ways, that I developed a new respect for the fermented cabbage. Since then I have encountered it on many occasions at home and abroad, but I have ever been grateful to the Alsatians for reintroducing sauerkraut to me.

The dish is not, of course, native to Alsace, or even to Germany just across the Rhine. Its origin dates back over 2,000 years to the Orient, when it was eaten by laborers building the Great Wall of China to combat deficiency diseases arising from a diet consisting primarily of rice. It is still popular in the East; in Korea pickled cabbage, mixed with an assortment of strongly flavored vegetables, is a staple food and considered essential to add vitamins to the sparse diet.

The invading Tartars, over 700 years ago, are credited with introducing the dish to eastern Europe where it has long been a popular and prized food. From there it was taken to Austria, where the name sauerkraut originated, thence to Germany and France.

Early German immigrants first prepared sauerkraut in America, where it was also readily received. Housewives, after the autumn harvest, chopped many heads of cabbage which, well sprinkled with salt, were placed in large earthenware or stone crocks. When nearly full, the sturdy containers were covered with a clean cloth, a board or metal plate, and a weight, most often a sizable stone. Almost daily, as a scum formed, it was removed and the cloth, board, and stone were washed. The "cooking" process, salt drawing out the sugary juice which bacteria fermented to produce a tangy flavor, took from twelve to fourteen days. At that time the sauerkraut was removed to a cool place and preserved with some of the brine in jars for later use. Although it is now readily available in cans, jars, packages, and sometimes in bulk for daily use, there are still some housewives who prefer to make their own.

In Europe controversies still rage over whether the German sauerkraut, cooked with numerous types of wursts and enjoyed with copious steins of robust beer, surpasses that of France. But the Alsatians, whether a burgher lingering over lunch or a farmer enjoying supper, will calmly point out that "There is *choucroute* and *choucroute.*" The inference is plain that only theirs, prepared with goose fat, bacon, juniper berries, and a glass of kirsch, has the real flavor.

Be that as it may, sauerkraut is a healthful dish rich in vitamins and phosphorus, calcium, and iron. It is also more versatile and adaptable than generally suspected. Made into soup or sandwiches, served as a salad or stuffing, combined with meats, poultry, or vegetables, raw or cooked, it is a savory dish. Its juice, mixed with an equal part of tomato juice and flavored with lemon juice, horseradish, or Worcestershire and salt and pepper, makes an agreeable cocktail. Not the least of its attractions is the fact that 1 cup of sauerkraut equals only 35 calories.

### ABOUT SAUERKRAUT

■ Bulk sauerkraut should definitely be drained and soaked in cold water for about 15 minutes before cooking. Squeeze out water by pressing between the hands. Canned sauerkraut may be washed in cold water to remove the briny taste.

■ The time of cooking is less for canned sauerkraut than for bulk.

■ A No. 2½ can (27 ounces) of sauerkraut, when drained, yields 1 pound.

■ For cooking sauerkraut, goose or pork fat is preferable; but butter may be used instead.

■ The preferred liquids for cooking sauerkraut are chicken or beef bouillon, tomato juice, or white wine.

■ Sauerkraut is an excellent accompaniment to sausages, frankfurters, ham or pork, spareribs, game birds, corned beef, and roast turkey.

Mashed or boiled potatoes, preferably in the skins, noodles, dumplings, or rice go well with sauerkraut.

### RUMANIAN SAUERKRAUT SOUP
½ cup diced carrot
½ cup snipped fresh parsley
½ cup chopped onion
½ cup chopped green pepper
About 3½ cups (one 1-pound, 11-ounce can) sauerkraut, drained
2 cans (10½ ounces each) condensed beef consommé
2 soup cans water
4 cups tomato juice
¼ teaspoon pepper
½ teaspoon salt
3 tablespoons uncooked rice

Combine all the ingredients in a large kettle. Mix well. Simmer, covered, for 1 hour. Serve with sour cream if desired. Makes about 2 quarts, or 6 servings.

### GERMAN FISH WITH SAUERKRAUT
1 pound fresh or frozen halibut or flounder fillets
1 cup cooked sliced mushrooms
About 3½ cups (one 1-pound, 11-ounce can) sauerkraut, drained
½ cup minced cooked carrot
1 can (10½ ounces) condensed cream-of-potato soup
¾ can milk
¼ teaspoon instant minced onion
⅛ teaspoon dillseed
1 cup chopped cooked ham
Salt and pepper to taste
Grated Parmesan cheese
1 tablespoon minced parsley

Cut fillets into 2-inch-wide strips. Combine mushrooms and sauerkraut and spread evenly in shallow 1½- to 2-quart baking dish. Sprinkle with carrot. Arrange fillet pieces on top. Combine potato soup, milk, onion, dillseed, ham, and salt and pepper in saucepan. Cook for 1 minute. Pour over fish. Sprinkle generously with Parmesan and with minced parsley. Bake, covered, in preheated moderate oven (350°F.) for about 35 minutes. Makes 6 servings.

### BAKED SAUERKRAUT AND CORNED-BEEF HASH
About 2 cups (one 1-pound can) sauerkraut, drained
4 whole cloves
1 medium onion
1¼ cups water
1 chicken bouillon cube
¼ teaspoon crumbled dried thyme
1 can (15½ ounces) corned-beef hash
1 can (8 ounces) tomato mushroom sauce

2 teaspoons prepared horseradish
1 apple, cored and very thinly sliced

Drain sauerkraut and wash in cold water. Put in saucepan. Stick cloves into onion. Add onion, water, bouillon cube, and thyme to sauerkraut. Simmer, covered, for 30 minutes. Discard onion. Spoon mixture into greased shallow baking dish. Combine remaining ingredients except apple slices. Spread evenly over sauerkraut. Top with apple slices. Bake in preheated very hot oven (450°F.) for 15 minutes. Makes 6 servings.

### SAVORY SAUERKRAUT CASSEROLE

½ pound dried yellow Lima beans
About 2 cups (one 1-pound can) sauerkraut, drained
½ teaspoon celery seeds
3 tablespoons brown sugar
1¼ cups tomato juice
Salt and pepper to taste
1 pound pork sausage meat
¾ cup chopped green peppers
Soft bread crumbs

Cook dried Lima beans according to package directions, but for a few minutes less than the stated time. Drain. Drain sauerkraut and wash in cold water. Mix with celery seeds, brown sugar, and tomato juice; season with salt and pepper. Fry sausage, draining off fat. Mince with fork. Add chopped peppers and cooked Lima beans. Arrange a layer of sauerkraut in greased shallow 1½-quart baking dish. Top with a layer of Lima beans and sausage. Repeat. Sprinkle with bread crumbs. Bake in preheated moderate oven (350°F.) for 25 to 30 minutes. Makes 6 servings.

### SAUERKRAUT BALLS

1 medium onion, minced
2 tablespoons butter or margarine
1 cup ground or finely minced cooked ham
1 cup finely minced corned beef
¼ teaspoon garlic salt
1 tablespoon prepared mustard
3 tablespoons minced parsley
⅛ teaspoon pepper
2 cups sauerkraut, drained and finely chopped
All-purpose flour (about ⅔ cup)
½ cup beef stock
2 eggs, well beaten
½ cup (about) fine dry bread crumbs

Sauté onion in butter until tender. Add ham and corned beef and cook, stirring often, for 5 minutes. Add garlic salt, mustard, parsley, pepper, sauerkraut, ½ cup flour, and beef stock. Mix well. Cook for 10 minutes, stirring often. Spread out on a platter to cool. Shape into 1-inch balls. Refrigerate for 1 hour. Roll sauerkraut balls in remaining flour, dip into beaten eggs, and roll in bread crumbs. Fry in deep hot fat (370°F. on a frying thermometer) until golden-brown. Drain on absorbent paper. Serve as appetizers with toothpicks. Makes about 5 dozen.

### TRANSYLVANIAN CASSEROLE

7 green onions
¼ cup pork fat or bacon
¼ cup chopped parsley
½ cup uncooked rice
Salt and pepper to taste
6 slices of bacon
½ cup minced green pepper
About 3½ cups (one 1-pound, 11-ounce can) sauerkraut, drained
1 can luncheon meat, sliced
1 package (1⅜ ounces) sour-cream sauce mix
1 cup milk
½ cup tomato juice
Chopped fresh dill or parsley

Mince onions with tops and sauté in fat until tender. Add parsley and rice; season with salt and pepper. Sauté for 10 minutes, stirring often. Set aside. Cook bacon until crisp. Drain off fat and crumble bacon. Add with green pepper to rice mixture. Combine well. Arrange half of sauerkraut in shallow 1½-quart baking dish. Cover with half of rice-bacon mixture. Arrange half of meat slices over previous layer. Repeat layers of sauerkraut and rice-bacon mixture. Combine sour-cream sauce mix, milk, and tomato juice. Mix well and pour over baking dish ingredients. Arrange remaining meat slices on top. Sprinkle with chopped dill. Bake, covered, in preheated slow oven (300°F.) for about 1 hour. Makes 6 servings.

### SAUERKRAUT SANDWICH

Arrange a layer of Swiss cheese, several slices of hot corned beef, and drained sauerkraut on a slice of dark rye bread spread with mustard. Cover with another slice of dark rye bread.

### CHOUCROUTE GARNIE

*I first tasted this Alsatian masterpiece on a crisp autumn day in a delightful Saverne restaurant while en route to the historic city of Strasbourg, situated along the Rhine River. It made a memorable luncheon. Since then it has been a favorite winter party dish as it can be made beforehand and is accompanied only by boiled potatoes and mustard. The well-seasoned sauerkraut can be served by itself with a roast, such as game, goose, duck, or pheasant, or with pork meats and sausages.*

2 pounds sauerkraut
3 medium onions, chopped
2 tablespoons bacon or pork fat
2 tart medium apples, peeled, cored, and chopped
6 peppercorns
10 juniper berries or ¼ cup gin
2½ cups white wine
12 link sausages
6 slices of cooked ham, ¼ inch thick
6 smoked pork chops or slices
6 frankfurters

Soak sauerkraut in cold water for 15 minutes. Squeeze dry between hands. Meanwhile sauté onions in fat until tender.

Add sauerkraut and toss with a fork. Cook for 5 minutes, stirring occasionally. Add apples, peppercorns, and juniper berries. Pour in white wine. Cook slowly, covered, for 1 hour. Meanwhile fry sausages. Drain off fat and put sausages on absorbent paper. Add with meats to sauerkraut. Cook, covered, for 30 minutes longer. Discard peppercorns and juniper berries. To serve, spoon out meats onto plate. Pile sauerkraut in center of large warm platter. Arrange meats and sausages over the top. This can be prepared beforehand and reheated. Serve with boiled potatoes and mustard. Makes 6 servings.

### HOT SAUERKRAUT AND BEAN SALAD

About 2 cups (one 1-pound can) sauerkraut, drained
⅛ teaspoon celery seeds
⅔ cup tomato juice
⅛ teaspoon pepper
¼ teaspoon instant minced onion
About 2 cups (one 15-ounce can) red kidney beans, drained
2 tablespoons chopped parsley

Combine sauerkraut, celery seeds, tomato juice, pepper, and minced onion in saucepan. Cook, covered, for 10 minutes. Add beans and cook, covered, for 5 minutes. Spoon into bowl to form a mound. Sprinkle with parsley. Makes 4 to 6 servings.

### VIENNESE SAUERKRAUT

1 medium onion, chopped
2 tablespoons bacon or pork fat
2 cups (one 1-pound can) sauerkraut
¼ teaspoon salt
½ teaspoon caraway seeds
¾ cup white wine
1 medium potato, peeled and grated

Sauté onion in fat until tender. Add remaining ingredients except potato. Simmer, covered, for 30 minutes. Add grated potato and simmer for 30 minutes longer, stirring occasionally. Makes 4 servings.

**SAUSAGE**—A preparation of minced or ground meat, usually seasoned with salt and spices and stuffed into a casing. Sausages may be made of all pork, all beef, or a combination of two or more meats. They may be fresh or smoked, dry or semidry; and they may be uncooked, partially cooked, or fully cooked.

Sausage has been an important meat staple for more than 5,000 years, and just about every country has produced its own special varieties. Not only has almost every country produced them, but individual cities became known for their specialties. Hence the number of city names given to sausages: Frankfurt, Genoa, Vienna, Bologna, Arles, Lyons. The idea behind their development was always the same: to utilize odd bits of meats and to preserve them by curing. The very name sausage is derived from

**Choucroute Garnie**

the Latin word for salt.

Since preservation was not so extreme a problem in the cooler climate of northern and central Europe, the sausages developed there were often fresh and cooked types: among the many from Germany are bockwurst, bratwurst, fresh thuringer, frankfurter, knockwurst, blood sausage, and liverwurst; from Austria, Vienna sausage; from Poland, kielbasa. In the warmer Mediterranean area where the summertime preservation of meat was a problem, the dried sausages predominated; the Italian cappicola, Genoa

salami, mortadella, and pepperoni; the southern French Lyons sausage; the Spanish chorizo. Interestingly enough, today when efficient refrigeration largely eliminates the need for preservation, many sausages are still cured or smoked because of the popularity of their distinctive flavor and color.

In the United States today more than 200 varieties of sausages and luncheon meats are sold. These include most of the favorite European types, either made here or imported, plus America's own contributions to the sausage world: the

fresh and smoked country-style pork sausage, in bulk and link form, and brown-and-serve links. In terms of preparation at home, all these products can be divided into two broad categories: one is those fresh and smoked sausages which must be cooked or heated before eating; the second is the ready-to-serve sausages and luncheon meats, usually sold sliced, which are served cold without further cooking or heating.

*Availability and Purchasing Guide*—A wide variety of sausages and luncheon meats are available in food stores throughout the United States. They may be sold in their casings as is, packaged, or sliced and packaged. Foreign specialty sausages are available in gourmet food stores and in stores catering to people of different national origins.

According to Federal law ingredients must be listed by their common or usual names and in the order of their predominance. State and municipal regulations governing products not involved in interstate commerce are often patterned after the Federal law.

**Cook-before-Eating**—Chief among these are the various fresh and smoked pork sausages sold country-style (spiral-shape), in links, bricks, and rolls. This group also includes bockwurst, a German sausage containing veal and some pork, milk, chives, eggs, and chopped parsley, with seasoning similar to frankfurters; kielbasa, a Polish pork-and-beef sausage often highly seasoned with garlic; mettwurst, a cured-beef and cured-pork mixture, seasoned with pepper and coriander.

**Cook-or-Heat-before-Eating**—These sausages include bratwurst, a German pork or pork-and-veal mixture seasoned with sage and lemon juice; knackwurst or knoblauch, similar to frankfurters, but seasoned with garlic.

**Heat-or-Eat-Cold**—Bologna and frankfurters are the best known of these sausages.

**Eat-Cold**—These are the dry sausages. Cervelat is the name of a classification of sausages which are generally smoked and made of finely ground beef chuck and pork, seasoned with salt, sugar, and pepper. However, goethaer cervelat is all pork. Salami is the name for another large classification of any sausages. The typical Italian salamis, which include Genoa salami, are made of cured pork and some lean beef, frequently moistened with red wine or grape juice and highly seasoned with garlic and spices. German salami, which also contain garlic, are less highly flavored and more heavily smoked than the Italian.

Other dry sausages include blood sausage, or blutwurst, made with fat pork, cooked meat, and gelatin-producing materials mixed with beef blood and spices; braunschweiger, a soft pink liverwurst; cappicola, a pork sausage seasoned with red hot or sweet peppers, salt and sugar, and mildly cured; chorizo, Spanish pork sausage, highly spiced; farmer cervelat, a pork-and-beef combination lightly seasoned and cured; frizzes, a cured pork sausage containing a small quantity of cured beef, and highly seasoned; Goteborg cervelat, a Swedish pork sausage,

salty and heavily smoked; headcheese, cured hog-head meat; liverwurst, a combination of ground pork and pork liver, either boiled or smoked, and seasoned with onions and spices; Lyons sausage, a French pork sausage, with garlic and spices, cured; mortadella, an Italian combination of cured pork and beef with added cubes of back fat, delicately spiced, and smoked; pepperoni, made of cured pork, and sometimes beef, seasoned with ground red pepper and other spices; souse, cured hog-head meat with vinegar pickle added for a sweet-sour flavor. Thuringer cervelat, a medium-dry pork-and-beef combination, mildly spiced; and Vienna sausage, a beef-and-pork mixture, small, cylindrical, pink, and mildly seasoned, sold canned.

**Storage**—Refrigerate all sausage with the exception of dry sausage which may be kept indefinitely in a cool place. Once casing on dry sausage is opened, refrigerate.

Sausage is not recommended for freezing because of its high fat content.

- ☐ Fresh, refrigerator shelf: 2 to 3 days
- ☐ Cooked or smoked, refrigerator shelf: 4 to 6 days
- ☐ Brown-and-serve, refrigerator shelf: 10 days
- ☐ Dry, kitchen shelf, casing uncut: indefinitely
- ☐ Dry, refrigerator shelf, casing cut: 2 weeks

**Nutritive Food Values**—High in fat with good amounts of protein, iron, and the B vitamins. Liverwurst is also high in vitamin A. The caloric values which follow are given for an edible portion of 3½ ounces:

- ☐ Blood sausage = 394 calories
- ☐ Bockwurst = 264 calories
- ☐ Bologna, all meat = 277 calories
- ☐ Bologna, with cereal filler = 262 calories
- ☐ Braunschweiger = 319 calories
- ☐ Brown-and-Serve sausage, browned = 422 calories
- ☐ Cappicola = 499 calories
- ☐ Cervelat, dry = 451 calories
- ☐ Frankfurter, all meat, raw = 296 calories
- ☐ Frankfurter, with cereal filler, raw = 248 calories
- ☐ Headcheese = 268 calories
- ☐ Kielbasa = 304 calories
- ☐ Knackwurst = 278 calories
- ☐ Liverwurst, fresh = 307 calories
- ☐ Liverwurst, smoked = 319 calories
- ☐ Mortadella = 315 calories
- ☐ Pork sausage, links or bulk, cooked = 476 calories
- ☐ Pork sausage, links, smoked (country-style) = 375 calories
- ☐ Salami, dry = 450 calories
- ☐ Salami, cooked = 311 calories
- ☐ Souse = 181 calories
- ☐ Thuringer, cervelat = 307 calories
- ☐ Vienna sausage, canned = 240 calories

**Basic Preparation**—All fresh and smoked pork sausages require cooking before eating, and smoked sausages labeled "cooked" or "fully cooked" usually are improved by heating. For example, frankfurters are fully cooked and may be eaten as purchased but heating is usually recommended for best flavor and palatability. Exceptions include their use in such foods as salads and sandwich fillings. Dry sausages need not be cooked.

☐ **To Panfry Pork Sausage Patties**—Shape meat into 3-inch patties about ½ inch thick, or if in a roll, cut off slices about ½ inch thick. Put in unheated skillet and cook over low heat until patties are well browned and thoroughly cooked. This takes about 15 minutes. Pour off excess fat as it accumulates.

☐ **To Panfry Pork Sausage Links**—Put sausage links in skillet and add about ¼ cup water. Cover and simmer for 5 minutes. (Don't boil and don't prick the links with a fork to let juice escape.) Drain off water and cook slowly uncovered until well browned and done. Turn links with tongs to brown evenly.

☐ **To Bake Pork Sausage Links**—(Good for cooking a pound at a time.) Spread sausage links in a shallow pan. Don't pile up. Bake in preheated hot oven (400°F.) for 20 to 30 minutes. Turn with tongs while baking to brown links evenly.

Broiling is not recommended for fresh pork sausage.

☐ **To Heat Frankfurters in Water**—Heat frankfurters in water just below the boiling point for 5 to 8 minutes. (Do not boil or pierce skins.) Remove from water with tongs. Or immerse frankfurters in boiling water, remove pot from heat; cover and let stand for 10 minutes.

☐ **To Broil Frankfurters**—Preheat broiler for 10 minutes, or as manufacturer directs. Brush frankfurters with cooking oil. Broil about 3 inches from heat, allowing 5 minutes on each side. Or split frankfurters lengthwise, not quite through, and broil, cut sides up, until lightly browned.

☐ **To Panbroil Frankfurters**—Cook whole frankfurters in small amount of hot fat in skillet, turning occasionally, until just browned. Or split lengthwise and brown the cut sides first, then the skin side.

Follow package directions for cooking where given.

# SAUSAGE COOK BOOK

## APPETIZERS

### MASKED LIVER MOLD

1½ pounds liver sausage
1 package (3 ounces) cream cheese
1 teaspoon Worcestershire
  Dash of onion salt
4 envelopes unflavored gelatin
¾ cup cold water
2 cans (12½ ounces each) consommé
  madrilene
  Red food coloring
  Fresh dill

Mix liver sausage, cream cheese, Worcestershire, and onion salt. Shape into a patty about 4½ inches wide and 3 inches thick. Chill. Soften gelatin in the water. Heat consommé and pour over gelatin. Stir until dissolved. Add small amount of coloring. Pour a ½-inch layer of the mixture into a 1½-quart mold. Chill until set. Cool remaining gelatin, but do not allow it to set. Spread a little of the liquid gelatin over congealed gelatin and top with liver mixture. Pour in more gelatin to surround liver mixture and cover top. Put remaining gelatin in shallow pan. Chill both until firm, preferably overnight. To serve, cut up gelatin in pan with sharp knife and put on serving dish. Unmold liver, cut into halves, and arrange on top of chopped gelatin. Garnish with fresh dill. Makes 12 servings.

### LIVER-SAUSAGE APPETIZER SALAD

1 cup diced liver sausage (firm type)
¾ cup pitted ripe olives, cut into halves
  or quarters
2 hard-cooked eggs, sliced
1 cup sliced celery
⅓ cup mayonnaise
1 teaspoon prepared mustard
2 teaspoons vinegar
½ teaspoon minced onion
  Salad greens

Mix liver sausage, olives, eggs, and celery. Combine remaining ingredients, except greens. Add to first mixture and toss lightly. Chill, and serve on greens. Makes 4 to 6 servings.

### PIGS IN BLANKETS

2¼ cups sifted all-purpose flour
1 teaspoon salt
¾ cup shortening
  Ice water
25 cocktail sausages

Sift flour and salt together. Cut in shortening. Add just enough ice water to hold ingredients together. Chill thoroughly. Roll out to ⅛-inch thickness. Cut squares large enough to cover little sausage with a "blanket" of pastry. Bake in preheated hot oven (400°F.) until pastry is golden-brown, about 15 to 20 minutes. Makes 25.

## MAIN DISHES

### OLD-FASHIONED PORK SAUSAGE

1½ pounds lean pork, ground coarsely
½ pound fat pork, ground coarsely
1½ teaspoons salt
1 teaspoon pepper
  Dash of cayenne or 3 dashes of
  hot pepper sauce
  About ⅛ teaspoon ground nutmeg
  Pinch of ground ginger
1 teaspoon crumbled dried thyme* or
  basil (or a combination of the two)

Combine lean pork with fat pork. Add rest of ingredients and mix well. Cover and let stand in refrigerator for about 2 days before using. For convenience in slicing, shape meat into rolls before refrigerating. Makes 2 pounds sausage meat.

* If desired, sage can be substituted for thyme.

### SAUSAGE RAGOUT

1 onion, chopped
1 garlic clove, crushed, or ¼ teaspoon
  garlic powder
1 tablespoon butter
½ pound mushrooms, sliced
½ pound sweet Italian sausage
½ pound fresh pork-sausage links
2 cups (one 1-pound can) tomatoes,
  drained
1 cup uncooked rice
1 small head lettuce, shredded
1 teaspoon salt
  Dash each of pepper and cayenne
2½ cups meat stock or bouillon
1 package (10½ ounces) frozen peas,
  cooked
2 pimientos, diced
¼ cup dried currants or white raisins,
  plumped in hot water (optional)

In casserole sauté onion and garlic in butter until limp. Add mushrooms and sausages cut into ½-inch chunks; cook for a few minutes. Add tomatoes and rice; stir together. Add lettuce, seasonings, and hot stock; you can use tomato liquid or liquid from peas as part of stock. Stir; bring to boil; cover. Bake in preheated hot oven (425°F.) for 30 minutes. Uncover; stir and cook for 10 minutes longer, or until rice is cooked. Stir in peas, pimientos, and currants. Makes 6 to 8 servings.

Note: For a different flavor, use 1½ cups fine noodles, uncooked, and add ½ cup more stock.

### SAUSAGE LOAF

1 pound pork sausage meat
1 medium onion, minced
2 cups soft bread crumbs
½ teaspoon poultry seasoning
  Dash of pepper
1 teaspoon prepared mustard
1 egg, beaten
½ cup evaporated milk
  Tomato slices
1 can mushroom gravy, heated
  Mashed potatoes and hot cooked peas
  Canned peach halves

Mix sausage thoroughly with onion, bread crumbs, poultry seasoning, pepper, mustard, egg, and evaporated milk. Pile lightly in loaf pan (9 x 5 x 3 inches). Bake in preheated moderate oven (375°F.) for 1 hour. Serve with slices of tomato and with mushroom gravy. Serve on platter with mashed potato nests, filled with cooked peas, and with peach halves. Makes 6 servings.

### SAUSAGE-BEAN CASSEROLE

1 box each of frozen cut green beans,
  wax beans, and Lima beans
2 tablespoons butter or margarine
2 tablespoons all-purpose flour
1 teaspoon salt
  Dash of pepper
  Dash of Worcestershire
1 cup milk
1 pound smokies

Cook beans separately according to package directions; drain. Mix lightly and put in baking dish. Melt butter; stir in flour, salt, pepper, and Worcestershire. Gradually add milk and cook until thickened, stirring constantly. Mix with beans. Score smokies and cook in skillet until done. Put on top of beans. Bake in preheated hot oven (400°F.) for 10 minutes, or until bubbly. Makes 6 servings.

### SAUSAGES IN ALE

1 pound link pork sausage
1 cup ale
2 bay leaves, crumbled
5 peppercorns
5 whole cloves
  Scrambled eggs
  Buttered toast
  Parsley

In heavy skillet, unheated, put sausage; cook slowly over low heat until nicely browned but not cooked. Pour off fat; add ale and spices tied in cloth to pan; simmer, covered, for 30 minutes. Check for dryness; add more ale if needed. Serve with scrambled eggs and toast tips garnished with parsley for brunch or supper treat. Makes 4 servings. Can be made in chafing dish. For the cocktail hour, use cocktail sausages and red wine, no ale and no spices except cloves.

**Note:** This dish may be made with dry white wine. Substitute wine for the ale.

### SAUSAGE, SWEET-POTATO, AND FRUIT BAKE

- 4 medium sweet potatoes, cooked, peeled, and sliced
- 2 cooking apples, cut into eighths
- 2 oranges, sectioned
- 1 package (1 pound) brown-and-serve sausages
- 2 tablespoons melted butter or margarine
  Brown sugar

Arrange sweet potatoes, apples, and oranges in casserole. Top with sausages. Pour butter over all and sprinkle with a little brown sugar. Bake, covered, in preheated hot oven (400°F.) for 15 minutes. Uncover and bake for 10 minutes longer, or until apples are tender. Makes 4 servings.

### SAUSAGE-POTATO POT

- 4 cups sliced potatoes
- 2 carrots, peeled and sliced
- 1 can (1 pound) whole onions, drained
- 2 tablespoons butter or margarine
- 2 tablespoons all-purpose flour
- 1 can beef bouillon
- ½ cup water
- ¼ teaspoon pepper
- 1 pound pork sausage meat
  Chopped parsley

Cook potatoes and carrots until almost tender. Put in casserole with onions. Melt butter and stir in flour. Gradually add bouillon and water, and cook until thickened, stirring constantly. Add pepper and pour over vegetables. Form sausage meat into patties and fry slowly until almost done. Put on top of vegetables. Cover and bake in preheated moderate oven (375°F.) for 20 minutes, or until all vegetables are tender. Sprinkle with chopped parsley. Makes 4 servings.

### SLAVIC SAUSAGE BAKE

- 1 pound fresh pork-sausage links
- 3½ cups (one 1-pound, 13-ounce can) sauerkraut
  Water
- 1 large onion, chopped
- 1 unpeeled apple, chopped
- 1 tablespoon brown sugar
- 1 tablespoon caraway seeds
- 2 bay leaves
- 6 whole cloves
- 4 peppercorns
  Salt
- 1 cup dairy sour cream
  Boiled potatoes

Cut sausage into 1-inch chunks. Drain sauerkraut and put in heavy pot. Barely cover with water; add onion, apple, sugar, and caraway seeds. Tie herbs in small square of cheesecloth and add to pot. Cook slowly for 1 hour, covered; add sausage and cook for another hour, or

until water is almost gone. Take out herb bag; add salt if necessary (sauerkraut may be salty enough), and stir in sour cream. Put in casserole and place in preheated hot oven (425°F.) for just long enough to get piping hot. Serve from casserole with boiled potatoes. Makes 6 to 8 servings.

### HOMEMADE KIELBASA SAUSAGE

- 3 pounds pork, coarsely ground
- 1 pound veal, coarsely ground
- 1 tablespoon crumbled dried marjoram
- 3 garlic cloves, finely minced
- 3 teaspoons salt
- 1 teaspoon pepper
- ¼ teaspoon ground allspice

Mix all ingredients together lightly but thoroughly. Stuff into sausage casings using a sausage-stuffing funnel. Cover the sausage with water and bake in preheated moderate oven (350°F.) until water has completely evaporated. To serve sausage, fry it with onion rings. Makes 4 pounds sausage.

### PASTA WITH SAUSAGE SAUCE

- 1 pound Italian sausage (sweet, hot, or half and half)
- 1 tablespoon olive oil
- 1 medium onion, chopped
- 2 garlic cloves, minced
- 1 can (6 ounces) tomato paste
  About 4⅓ cups (one 2-pound, 3-ounce can) Italian-style tomatoes
- ½ teaspoon sugar
- ½ cup chopped celery
- ½ teaspoon each of salt and crumbled dried basil
- 1 teaspoon chopped parsley
- 1 cup sliced fresh mushrooms or 1 can (4 ounces) sliced mushrooms, drained
- 1 tablespoon butter
- 1 tablespoon water
  Hot cooked linguine or spaghetti
  Grated Italian cheese

Cut sausage into ½-inch slices; brown lightly in oil with onion and garlic. Add tomato paste, tomatoes, sugar, celery, salt, and herbs. Simmer, covered, stirring occasionally, for 1½ hours. Sauce should be cooked down; add water only if necessary. Sauté mushrooms in butter and add with pan juices and water to sauce for last 30 minutes of cooking. Serve over cooked linguine, topped with grated cheese. Makes a meal with a tossed green salad and crusty sesame-seed Italian bread. Makes 6 to 8 servings.

### SCALLOPED SAUSAGE AND CORN

- 1 pound bulk fresh pork sausage
- 2 cups (one 1-pound can) cream-style corn
- 6 soda crackers, crumbled
- 1 cup milk
- 1 egg, beaten
- ½ teaspoon salt
  Dash each of pepper, cayenne, and ground nutmeg
- 1 large tomato, sliced

Make 6 small balls of sausage; crumble the rest. Brown balls and loose sausage; drain on paper towels. Mix loose sau-

sage with corn, crackers, milk, egg, and seasonings. Pour into greased casserole; top with tomato slices and sausage balls. Place casserole in pan with hot water 1 inch deep. Bake in preheated moderate oven (350°F.) for about 1 hour, or until set. Makes 4 to 6 servings.

### ITALIAN SAUSAGE AND RICE

- 1 pound Italian sausage (sweet, hot, or half and half)
- ½ cup chopped onion
- 1 garlic clove, minced
- ½ cup diced green pepper
- 1 cup sliced fresh mushrooms or 1 can (4 ounces) sliced mushrooms, drained
- 2 cups (one 1-pound can) tomatoes
- ½ cup ketchup
- ¼ teaspoon each of ground basil and oregano
- ½ teaspoon sugar
- ½ teaspoon salt
- 2 cups cooked rice (about ¾ cup uncooked)
  Few parsley sprigs, chopped
  Grated Romano or Parmesan cheese

Cut sausage into slices and brown lightly. Remove from skillet with most of the fat. In remaining fat cook onion, garlic, green pepper, and mushrooms. Add tomatoes, ketchup, herbs, sugar, and salt. Simmer, stirring frequently, for 5 minutes. Put rice in greased casserole, add sauce and sausage, and stir well. Bake, covered, in preheated moderate oven (375°F.) for 45 minutes; do not remove cover. Take out and let stand for 10 minutes before serving. Top with chopped parsley and serve with shaker of grated cheese. Makes 4 to 6 servings.

### SAUSAGE AND LIVER LOAF

- 1¼ pounds beef liver
- 2 stale hard rolls
- 1 small onion
- 1 garlic clove
- 1 pound bulk pork sausage
- 2 tablespoons minced parsley
- 2 tablespoons chili sauce
- 2 teaspoons salt
- 1 teaspoon Worcestershire
- ½ teaspoon pepper
- 1 egg
  Corn-flake crumbs

Blanch liver and put through fine blade of food chopper with hard rolls, onion, and garlic. Add sausage, parsley, chili sauce, salt, Worcestershire, and pepper and toss lightly; add egg to bind. Pack into a greased 1½-quart mold or loaf pan. If you like, sprinkle bottom and sides of pan with corn-flake crumbs. Bake in preheated moderate oven (350°F.) for 1¼ hours. Let stand for 5 minutes before turning out. Sprinkle top with corn-flake crumbs. Makes 6 servings.

### HOT SAUSAGE LOAF

- 1 pound bulk fresh pork sausage
- 1 medium onion, minced
- 1 can (4 ounces) mushrooms, chopped, and liquid
- 2 cups soft bread crumbs
- ½ teaspoon poultry seasoning

Sausage Loaf

Sausage-Bean Casserole

Sausage-Potato Pot

Sausage-Sweet-Potato
and Fruit Bake

½ teaspoon salt
Dash each of ground nutmeg and
pepper
1 teaspoon sharp prepared mustard
2 shakes of hot pepper sauce
1 egg, beaten
½ cup undiluted evaporated milk or
heavy cream
Paprika

With hands mix sausage, onion, drained mushrooms, crumbs, and dry seasonings. Stir in mustard, hot pepper sauce, egg, evaporated milk, and enough mushroom liquid to moisten if needed. Pile lightly in greased loaf pan (9 x 5 x 3 inches). Sprinkle with paprika. Bake in preheated moderate oven (375°F.) for 1 hour. Serve plain or with a sauce of thinned mushroom soup. Makes 6 to 8 servings.

### SAUSAGE AND CHICK-PEAS

1 pound Italian sausage (sweet, hot, or half and half)
1 to 2 tablespoons butter
1 large onion, chopped
1 can (8 ounces) tomato sauce
1 tablespoon chopped parsley
Pinch each of dried basil and oregano
2 cups (one 1-pound can) chick-peas or garbanzos, drained
Salt and pepper
Hot cooked rice or thin spaghetti

Cut sausage into ½-inch slices and brown lightly on all sides in butter. Add onion and more butter if needed. Cook, stirring constantly, until limp. Add sauce and herbs; simmer for 5 minutes. Add chick-peas. Simmer, covered, for 30 minutes. Season with salt and pepper to taste. Serve with rice. Makes 4 to 6 servings.

### QUICK SAUSAGE CASSEROLE

1 pound fresh pork sausage, bulk or link
2½ cups (one 1-pound, 4-ounce can) sliced apples
1 teaspoon all-purpose flour
2 tablespoons fresh lemon juice
Dash each of ground cinnamon, cloves, and nutmeg
¼ teaspoon salt
1 cup shredded sharp Cheddar cheese
Mashed potatoes

Brown sausage; put in greased casserole. Drain apple slices, reserving juice. Top sausage with layer of apple slices. Pour most of sausage fat from pan. Stir in flour, apple juice, lemon juice, and seasonings. Pour over apples. Add cheese. Bake in preheated moderate oven (350°F.) for 45 minutes. Serve with mashed potatoes. Makes 4 to 6 servings.

### SMOTHERED SAUSAGE-BEEF PATTIES

Mix ½ pound each of bulk fresh pork-sausage meat and ground beef chuck, 1½ cups soft bread crumbs, and ½ teaspoon poultry seasoning. Shape into 8 patties. Brown on both sides in skillet. Drain off fat. Blend ½ can (10½ oz. can) cream-of-mushroom soup, 1 cup water, and 2 tablespoons all-purpose flour. Pour around patties and cook until thickened. Makes 4 servings.

### SAUSAGE-STUFFED EGGPLANT

1 large or 2 medium eggplants
Boiling water
1 pound bulk fresh pork sausage
1 large onion, chopped
1 garlic clove, minced
½ cup diced celery
½ cup diced green pepper
2 cups (one 1-pound can) tomatoes
¼ teaspoon ground basil
1 teaspoon salt
Dash each of pepper and cayenne
½ teaspoon sugar
¼ cup each of dry bread crumbs and grated Parmesan cheese

Cut eggplant into halves lengthwise and parboil in salted water for 10 minutes. Remove carefully and let cool. With sharp-edge spoon scoop out pulp, leaving a shell of ½ inch. Brown sausage quickly; remove from heat, crumble, and drain on paper towels. Remove all but 2 tablespoons fat. Sauté onion, garlic, celery, and green pepper in sausage fat until limp. Chop eggplant pulp and add to pan with tomatoes, seasonings, and sugar; simmer for 5 minutes. Add sausage; cook for 5 minutes more. Pile mixture in eggplant shells in greased baking dish. Top with crumbs mixed with cheese. Bake in preheated moderate oven (375°F.) for 45 minutes. Makes 4 to 6 servings.

### SPANISH CASSEROLE

1 pound wide noodles
Salt
4 bacon strips, diced
2 mild onions, chopped
1 garlic clove, minced
½ pound fresh mushrooms, sliced
½ pound chorizos, sliced
½ cup julienne strips of cooked ham
1 can (8 ounces) tomato sauce
1 large tomato, peeled and diced
1 cup meat stock or bouillon
2 dashes of hot pepper sauce
1 cup grated sharp Cheddar cheese

Cook noodles in boiling salted water until tender; drain. In large skillet sauté bacon for 1 minute; add onions and garlic and cook until limp. Add mushrooms and cook for 5 minutes, stirring. Add chorizos and ham. Cook for a few minutes more, turning. Add tomato sauce, tomato, stock, 1 teaspoon salt, and the hot pepper sauce. Cook over low heat for 30 minutes. In greased 3-quart casserole put noodles, sauce, and cheese in layers, using ⅓ each time and ending with top layer of cheese. Bake, covered, in preheated hot oven (400°F.) for 45 minutes. Remove cover and cook for 15 minutes more. Makes 6 to 8 servings.

### CREAMED PEAS IN BOLOGNA CUPS

8 slices of large bologna, cut ⅛ inch thick
1 tablespoon butter or margarine
1 package (12 ounces) frozen peas
1 can cream-of-celery soup
1 teaspoon Worcestershire
¼ cup light cream or milk

Sauté bologna quickly on both sides in

the butter, letting edges curl to form cups. Cook and drain peas. Add soup, Worcestershire, and cream. Heat thoroughly and fill bologna cups with the mixture. If desired, garnish with parsley and a sprinkling of paprika. Makes 4 servings.

### SALAMI, EGG, AND NOODLE SKILLET

2 cups broken wide noodles
Salt
2 tablespoons butter or margarine
1 small onion, chopped
1 medium green pepper, chopped
¼ pound cooked salami, slivered*
1 pimiento, chopped
6 eggs, beaten
Pepper

Cook noodles in boiling salted water until tender; drain. Melt butter in skillet. Add onion and green pepper. Cook for 2 or 3 minutes. Add salami and cook until lightly browned. Add pimiento and cooked noodles; heat. Add eggs and stir until set. Season to taste. Makes 4 servings.
*Bologna may be substituted for the salami in the above recipe.

### LUNCHEON MEAT À LA KING

½ cup each of diced celery and green pepper
¾ cup water
1 can condensed cream-of-mushroom soup
2 pimientos, chopped
1 can (12 ounces) luncheon meat, diced
⅛ teaspoon pepper
Hot cooked rice, potatoes, or toast

In saucepan, cook celery and green pepper in the water for 5 minutes. Add soup and stir until blended. Add pimiento, meat, and pepper. Heat well and serve on rice. Makes 4 servings.

### FRIED BOLOGNA, POTATOES, AND ONIONS

¾ pound sliced bologna
4 tablespoons fat
1 cup sliced onion
4 cups thinly sliced raw potato
1 teaspoon salt
¼ teaspoon pepper

Sauté bologna in 1 tablespoon fat in skillet until lightly browned. Remove and set aside. Add remaining fat, onion, and potato to skillet. Cook slowly for about 25 minutes, or until potato is tender. As potato browns on bottom, carefully turn with a spatula. Add salt and pepper. Top with bologna and cook until heated. Makes 4 servings.

### SAUERKRAUT-SAUSAGE STUFFED PEPPERS

6 medium green peppers
About 2 cups (one 1-pound can) sauerkraut
½ cup minced green pepper
2 tablespoons brown sugar
¼ cup ketchup
1 tart medium apple, peeled, cored, and cubed
1 chicken bouillon cube
1½ cups water
Salt and pepper to taste

1 pound pork sausage meat
Seasoned fine dry bread crumbs
Grated Parmesan cheese
Paprika

Cut off tops of peppers. Cut off small strips from bottoms if necessary so peppers will stand upright. Remove seeds. Wash peppers and parboil in boiling water for 4 minutes. Drain. Drain sauerkraut and put in cold water for 15 minutes. Squeeze dry between hands. Put in saucepan with minced pepper, brown sugar, ketchup, cubed apple, bouillon cube, 1 cup water, and salt and pepper. Simmer, covered, for 30 minutes. Cook sausage. Drain off fat and mince sausage meat with a fork to separate. Combine with cooked sauerkraut mixture. Spoon into pepper shells. Sprinkle with bread crumbs, grated Parmesan, and paprika. Arrange in baking dish. Pour in ½ cup water. Bake in preheated moderate oven (350°F.) for about 30 minutes. Makes 6 servings.

## HOT HERO SANDWICHES

1 pound hot Italian sausage
3 tablespoons olive oil
4 large green peppers, cut into strips
½ teaspoon salt
2 loaves of Italian bread
Grated Parmesan cheese

Cut sausage into ½-inch chunks. Brown lightly in heavy skillet. Add oil, peppers, and salt. Simmer, stirring frequently, until peppers are limp but not brown. Heat bread in preheated hot oven (400°F.); take out, and cut each loaf into 3 pieces crosswise. Cut each piece into halves lengthwise. Put bread bottoms on cookie sheet. Divide cooked mixture evenly among bread pieces. Add oil from skillet to each, top with layer of cheese, and cover with bread tops. Slide back into oven for 5 minutes to crisp. Makes 6 sandwiches.

## APPLES AND SAUSAGES EN BROCHETTE

2½ cups (one 1-pound, 4-ounce can), apple slices, drained
1 pound small link sausages
4 small tomatoes, cut into wedges
Garlic salt
Sugar
8 frankfurter rolls

On skewers alternate apple slices, sausages, and tomato wedges. Sprinkle tomatoes with garlic salt and apple slices with sugar. Grill until sausages are done, 6 to 8 inches above coals heated to turn gray, turning frequently. Serve on heated rolls. Makes 8 servings.

**SAUSAGE SEASONING**—A blend of herbs and spices including white pepper, ground nutmeg, and ground coriander. It is used in homemade sausage, meat loaves, veal and poultry dishes, and in the batter for rolls to accompany ham and roast pork.

Sausage seasoning is available ground.

**SAUTÉ**—To cook a food in an uncovered shallow pan over brisk heat, using just enough fat to keep the food from sticking. This process is very different from what is sometimes called shallow-fat frying, where the foods are half submerged in the cooking fat. The name comes from the French verb *sauter,* "to jump," or "to make jump." Earlier the French cook turned the food in the pan by tossing it as we still toss flapjacks or pancakes, but today it is more usual to turn the food with a fork or spatula.

Sautéing is a very old cooking method designed to prepare foods quickly, using very little fuel in the process; and it is a cooking process used for the preparation of food all over the world. The primitive breads of the pioneer (flapjacks and hush puppies) and many elegant dishes of French cuisine are both examples of sautéing.

A sauté pan, a frying pan or skillet, should be of heavy metal with an even surface so that heat is evenly distributed and one entire surface of the piece or slice of food can be cooked at once before it is turned. Pans with warped or uneven surfaces do not serve well, nor do pans of thin metal; in the thin pan the surface of the food may be cooked too fast before the center of the slice is done; also the thinner pans tend to warp after relatively short use.

Butter, margarine, or butter mixed with a little cooking oil may be used for sautéing, but clarified butter is the best fat because it does not have any milky residue to burn or to cause food to stick to the pan. Other fats may be used as well, but they should be fresh, with a good odor when hot. Also, if the fat is meat drippings or melted poultry fat, it is essential that it be carefully strained or filtered to remove any solid particles. It is these solid particles which burn in the cooking and give an unpleasant smell to the kitchen and a burned taste to the food.

Foods that are to be sautéed must be reasonably tender; ancient fowl or sinewy game will be made tougher by this process. The food must be cut into small pieces or into slices thin enough to be cooked after having been sautéed for only a few minutes on each side. The number of minutes will vary according to the food; a rare hamburger should be turned over after about five minutes, while a pork chop will need to cook for fifteen minutes on each side. Meats, fish, poultry, vegetables, and fruits may all be sautéed, either plain, or after being dipped into flour or crumbs. The surface of the food should be dry so that it will become brown and crisp within the short

cooking period. Sometimes the pieces of food are pounded to make them even thinner so that they can cook in less time; veal escallops are prepared in this way. Only a small amount of food should be sautéed at one time, or the food may steam and this moisture will prevent the surface becoming crisp.

The term sauté is also used for the preparation of chicken dishes in which the whole joint of the chicken, as breasts, legs, wings, etc., are cooked, rather than a slice of chicken. For this the heat must be somewhat reduced and the cooking time increased. As some parts of a bird will cook more quickly than others, each joint should be removed from the pan as soon as it is tender, or it will become dried out.

Sometimes a sauce for a sautéed dish is made in the pan during the last minutes of cooking. Of course, in these dishes the pieces will no longer have a crisp surface. Or the pieces of cooked food may be removed from the pan when tender and kept hot while a sauce is made in the pan. If the fat has been measured carefully, there should be very little left, but unless the cook has used butter or a fat that can be incorporated in the sauce, it is better to drain off any remaining fat before proceeding with the sauce. The other pan juices should be used.

**SAUTERNE**—A delicate sweet golden wine high in alcohol, made in the Sauternes district of France and comprising not only the vineyards of the Commune of Sauternes but those of the adjoining Communes of Bommes, Barsac, Preignac, and Fargues. The Sauternes district adjoins that of Graves, but its soil is entirely different and the species of grapes cultivated in the vineyards of Sauternes are also entirely different. They are white grapes which are picked when overripe and from which is made the best of the naturally sweet wines. The wines are generally sold under the name of the estate producing it. The true sauternes are generally served as dessert wines. In California and New York State, a similar but somewhat drier wine is produced and is sold under the name sauterne. The drier type is usually served with fish or poultry. Both wines should be slightly chilled before serving. There are a few sweet sauterne wines made in the United States but the process of making them is much different from the true sauterne wine of France.

**SAVARIN**—A raised, nonsweet baba-like cake, rich in eggs and butter, baked in a ring mold and moistened with a rum syrup. Whipped cream is put in the center before serving.

### SAVARIN

1 package active dry yeast or 1 cake compressed yeast
¼ cup water*
¼ cup milk, scalded and cooled
2 cups sifted all-purpose flour
2 tablespoons sugar
½ teaspoon salt
4 eggs, slightly beaten
⅔ cup soft butter or margarine
1 teaspoon grated lemon rind
Rum Syrup
Whipped cream

Sprinkle dry yeast or crumble cake into water. *Use very warm water (105°F. to 115°F.) for dry yeast; use lukewarm (80°F. to 90°F.) for compressed. Let stand for a few minutes; then stir until dissolved. Put milk and flour in mixing bowl. Add yeast mixture, sugar, salt, and eggs. Beat with spoon or in electric mixer until a soft, sticky dough is formed. When thoroughly mixed, beat for 2 minutes with the hands, pulling up the dough and letting it slap back hard into the bowl. Then cover and let stand in a warm place for 45 minutes, or until the dough is doubled in bulk. Stir down and add butter in small pieces. Then beat with hands for about 4 minutes. Add lemon rind. Pour into a well-buttered 9-inch ring mold and let rise to the top of the pan, about 1 hour. Bake in preheated hot oven (400° F.) for 30 to 35 minutes. Turn out of mold and spoon hot Rum Syrup over cake until well saturated. Serve warm with the center filled with whipped cream. Makes 8 to 10 servings.

### Rum Syrup

In saucepan combine 1 cup sugar, 1½ cups water, and ½ cup rum. Bring to boil and simmer for 35 to 40 minutes.

**SAVORY**—An English culinary term that describes nonsweet foods served in small quantities at the end of a meal, after the dessert. The foods used for savories correspond to what we tend to serve as appetizers, hors-d'oeuvre, and canapés.

The reason for serving a savory was rooted in the English tradition of serving port and other fortified wines and spirits immediately after the dinner, when the ladies had withdrawn from the table leaving the gentlemen alone to enjoy manly talk without interference or inhibition. The taste of the wines clashed with the taste of the sweet dessert which had just been served, and the savory was introduced to clear the palate for the enjoyment of the wine. Many of the eighteenth-century savories were made of cheese,

one example being cheese fritters, made of a rich, eggy batter with grated Cheddar cheese and deep-fried. The recipe ends with the words: "These will eat very pretty." Another dish was called Ramekins. These were made of double Gloucester and Cheshire cheeses with butter and eggs added which were put into scooped-out rolls and baked, forming a soufflé-like mixture in the center.

**SAVORY, SUMMER (Satureia hortensis) and WINTER (S. Montana)**—Two closely related herbs which belong to the Mint family. The aromatic leaves of both plants are widely used for seasoning. Summer savory is a many-branched annual, growing up to eighteen inches on stems that are so weak that it falls down easily. The leaves are dark green. Winter savory is similar, although it is somewhat shorter and bushier. It tends to spread.

The aromatic resinous, although mild, flavor of the two herbs is similar, although summer savory is more delicate. Winter savory must be used with more discretion. Savory is known as the bean herb, because it goes so well with beans. It also adds piquancy to pâté, vegetable juice, consommé, chowder, and bean and lentil soups; chicken loaf, hamburger, lamb, veal, stews, and poultry stuffing; baked or broiled fish, cream cheese, scrambled eggs, herb bread, and stuffing; barbecue, fish, seafood, or poultry sauce; artichokes, beets, cabbage, peas, rice, sauerkraut, salad; stewed pears and quinces.

Savory has a long history as both a

culinary and medicinal herb. A native of southern Europe, it was known to the Greeks and Romans, who used it for all sorts of remedies. Many dishes fit for a king included savory. The master chefs of Richard II of England compiled a cook book in 1390 which included goose with "Sauce Madame": "Take sage, parsley, hyssop and savory, quinces and pears, garlic and grapes and fill the goose therewith and sew the hole that no grease come out and roast it well." Savory seems to have been more popular with sweet dishes than it is now: puddings, tarts, pastries, cakes, and conserves all could be flavored with savory. It was, in the words of one Englishman, "good for my Huswyfe's pot and pye."

But the herb was not limited to these two uses. The Elizabethan age was a great fancier of elaborate "knot" gardens, herb gardens planted and trimmed in elaborate shapes. Winter savory, which could be pruned into many forms, was found in many of these gardens. There was danger as well as delight in savory, however. An early 16th-century herbal warns: "It is forbidden to use it much in meats" because it "stirreth him that useth lechery." But, the herbal is quick to add, savory with wine will, "Make thee a good meek stomach." The French had found another good use for the herb. One Frenchman insisted that "the leaves and flowers applied unto the head in forms of a cappe or garland, doth awake the drowsily inclined." What person has not longed at some time for such a cap!

Savory is sold dried, either in whole leaves or ground.

### STEWED NAVY BEANS WITH SAVORY

2 cups (1 pound) dried navy beans
6 cups water
1 teaspoon salt
1 onion, peeled
½ teaspoon chopped fresh or dried savory

Wash beans and put in kettle. Add the water and bring to boil. Boil rapidly for 2 minutes. Remove from heat, cover and let stand for 1 hour. Add salt, onion, and savory and simmer for 1 hour, or until tender. Makes 6 servings.

**SCALD, TO**—In culinary usage to scald means to heat a liquid to just below the boiling point, as in scalding milk. Scalding also refers to pouring boiling water over a food, or plunging it into boiling water to harden it to facilitate peeling, or to kill surface organisms.

**SCALLION**—This name is given without much exactitude to several plants of the onion family: the green onion, the shallot, and the leek. To the truck gardener raising bulb onions for fall and winter use, the scallion or scullion is a bulb onion, of whatever variety, which does not develop a large bulb but grows into a slender plant with the same thickness from root to leaves. This is usually caused by inferior seed, poor soil, or bad weather. Also, the farmer who sows acres of onions has to thin his plants to give room for the development of the large bulbs. The small onions pulled during this thinning are bunched and appear in the market during most of the year, but particularly in the early spring. These are green onions and it is this vegetable which is most commonly called a scallion.

The green top of the shallot, harvested in early summer, and the young leek, harvested in the fall, are also marketed under the name scallion.

The word scallion, like shallot, means "onion of Ascalon," so it is probable that this vegetable was developed in ancient times near the Mediterranean coast of Palestine and Syria.

After trimming, the entire scallion is used, usually chopped or minced as a seasoning vegetable. It is generally added raw, but is sometimes cut into pieces and lightly sautéed in butter before being added to Lima beans, peas, etc. Scallions also form part of the serving of raw vegetable appetizers along with radishes, celery, raw cauliflowerets, and carrot strips.

**Availability and Purchasing Guide—** Available year round with the peak months May, June, July, and August.

Choose tender, crisp, young scallions with fresh green tops. Avoid bruised, yellowed, withered, damaged tops or nicks.

**Storage—**Wrap in moisture- vapor-proof paper and store in vegetable compartment of refrigerator. Tops may become slimy if stored too long.

☐ Refrigerator shelf or vegetable compartment: 2 to 3 days

**Caloric Value**

☐ 3½ ounces, raw = 46 calories

**SCALLOP—**A group of bivalve mollusks with ribbed rounded shells. Only the muscle which opens and closes the shell is used for eating. The shell itself is used as a natural dish in which foods such as Coquilles St. Jacques are cooked. There are two varieties, the tiny bay scallop and the large deep-sea scallop. Bay scallops have a shorter season and are less available than sea scallops, but they have a sweeter, more delicate flavor, and are more tender.

**Availability—**In the eastern part of the United States sea scallops are available fresh, frozen, and frozen breaded precooked. In other parts of the country, they are sold frozen, and frozen breaded fried. The peak of the season for fresh sea scallops is November to April. Bay scallops are available only in the East and only fresh, in the early fall.

**Purchasing Guide—**Fresh or thawed frozen scallops should have a sweetish odor and when packaged, there should be practically no liquid.

**Storage—**Scallops are highly perishable and should be kept not more than 1 to 2 days before cooking. They should be stored loosely covered in the coldest part of the food compartment of the refrigerator.

☐ Fresh, refrigerator shelf, raw: 1 to 2 days

☐ Fresh, refrigerator shelf, cooked: 3 to 4 days

☐ Fresh, prepared for freezing; or frozen, refrigerator frozen-food compartment: 2 to 3 weeks

☐ Fresh, prepared for freezing; or frozen, freezer: 1 year

**Nutritive Food Values—**A good source of protein. Low in fat, scallops have some calcium, a large amount of phosphorus, traces of riboflavin and niacin.

☐ Fresh, 3½ ounces, raw = 81 calories

☐ Fresh, 3½ ounces, steamed = 112 calories

☐ Frozen, 3½ ounces, breaded, fried, reheated = 194 calories

**Basic Preparation—**Wash thoroughly to remove bits of shell. Drain and pat dry. Scallops can be broiled, breaded and fried, sautéed, or baked. Cook them until just done. Do not overcook.

☐ **To Freeze—**Wash thoroughly. Open shell and remove meat. Drain and reserve liquid. Wash to remove shell fragments. Drain. Wash in brine solution of 4 cups water to 1 tablespoon salt. Remove after 3 or 4 minutes. Pack into freezer containers and cover with reserved liquid

and some of the brine. Allow ½-inch headspace. Seal.

### SCALLOPS MEUNIÈRE

2 pounds of sea scallops, washed and drained
½ cup milk
½ cup all-purpose flour
1 teaspoon salt
¼ teaspoon pepper
½ cup salad oil
¼ cup butter
2 tablespoons fresh lemon juice
2 tablespoons chopped parsley

Cut scallops into bite-size pieces if they are large. Pour milk over them and let stand for 2 minutes. Drain the scallops and coat with flour seasoned with salt and pepper. Sauté scallops in the oil until golden on all sides. Transfer to a heated platter. Wipe out the pan with paper towel. Heat butter until frothy, add juice and parsley, and pour over the scallops. Makes 6 servings.

### SCALLOP STEW

3 cups milk
1 cup heavy cream
2 tablespoons butter or margarine
2 teaspoons sugar
1 teaspoon Worcestershire
1½ teaspoons salt
¼ teaspoon pepper
1 pound sea scallops
Paprika
Chopped parsley

In top part of large double boiler, over boiling water, heat first 7 ingredients. Mince scallops and add to milk mixture. Cook for 5 minutes. Serve sprinkled with paprika and chopped parsley. Makes 4 servings.

### BROILED CURRIED SCALLOPS

Line broiler pan with foil. Arrange 2 pounds sea scallops in pan. Mix ¼ cup honey, 2 teaspoons curry powder, ¼ cup prepared mustard, and 1 teaspoon fresh lemon juice. Brush scallops generously with the mixture. Put broiler pan in lowest position under source of heat. Broil scallops for 10 minutes. Turn, brush with mixture, and broil for 10 minutes longer. Makes 6 servings.

### SCALLOPS SAUTÉ PROVENÇALE

1½ pounds bay scallops
All-purpose flour
6 tablespoons olive oil
2 garlic cloves, minced
Salt and pepper to taste
½ cup chopped parsley
Lemon wedges

Wash and dry scallops and roll in flour. Heat olive oil, add the scallops and cook for 2 or 3 minutes, stirring lightly. While cooking, add garlic and mix in well. Season with salt and pepper. Stir in parsley and serve at once with lemon wedges. Makes 4 to 6 servings.

### SCALLOPS NEWBURG

1 package (12 ounces) frozen sea scallops, thawed

3 tablespoons butter or margarine
1 teaspoon fresh lemon juice
1 teaspoon all-purpose flour
½ cup heavy cream
2 egg yolks, slightly beaten
2 tablespoons sherry
Salt and pepper
4 sandwich rolls
Paprika

Cut scallops into halves. Cook in 2 table-spoons butter for 3 minutes. Add lemon juice and cook for 1 minute. In another saucepan melt remaining butter and blend in flour. Add cream and cook until thickened, stirring constantly. Add egg yolks, sherry, and scallops; season to taste. Cut tops from sandwich rolls; scoop out centers and heat rolls in oven. Fill with scallops mixture. Garnish with paprika. Makes 4 servings.

### CREOLE SCALLOPS
2 cups (one 1-pound can) stewed tomatoes
1 package (12 ounces) frozen sea scallops, thawed
1 onion, chopped
½ green pepper, chopped
2 tablespoons all-purpose flour
¼ cup water
Salt and pepper
Hot cooked rice

In saucepan combine tomatoes, scallops, onion, and green pepper. Bring to boil and simmer for 5 minutes. Blend flour with water. Add to tomato mixture and cook until thickened, stirring constantly. Season to taste. Serve on rice. Makes 4 servings.

### SCALLOPS IN VERMOUTH
¼ cup butter or margarine
1½ pounds bay scallops
¼ cup dry vermouth

Melt butter. Wash and dry scallops and add to butter. Sauté for 2 or 3 minutes, or until just opaque. Add vermouth and heat gently. Makes 4 to 6 servings.

### MINCED SCALLOPS IN WINE-CHEESE SAUCE
1½ pounds sea scallops
½ cup dry white wine
½ teaspoon salt
Dash of cayenne
1 teaspoon instant minced onion
3 tablespoons butter
3 tablespoons all-purpose flour
½ cup heavy cream
1 cup grated sharp Cheddar cheese
½ cup buttered soft bread crumbs

Chop scallops fine. Put in saucepan with wine, salt, cayenne, and onion. Bring to boil and simmer, covered, for 10 minutes. Drain, reserving 1 cup broth. Melt butter and blend in flour. Add reserved broth, and cream. Cook, stirring constantly, until thickened. Stir in cheese and scallops. Put in 6 large shells or individual baking dishes. Top with crumbs and bake in preheated hot oven (400°F.) for 10 minutes. Makes 6 servings.

### SAUTÉED SCALLOPS WITH LEMON BUTTER
1½ pounds sea scallops
⅓ cup (about) fine dry bread crumbs
½ cup butter
¼ teaspoon salt
⅛ teaspoon pepper
Dash of paprika
1 tablespoon chopped parsley
3 tablespoons fresh lemon juice

Roll scallops in crumbs. Melt half of butter in skillet. Add salt, pepper, and paprika. Add scallops and sauté slowly for 8 minutes, or until golden-brown, turning gently to brown evenly. Remove scallops to a hot serving dish. Put remaining butter, parsley, and lemon juice in skillet. Heat, and pour over scallops. Makes 4 to 6 servings.

### SCALLOPS EN BROCHETTE
Skewer alternately whole sea scallops, fresh mushrooms, and squares of uncooked bacon. Grill over charcoal or in broiler for about 10 minutes, turning often and brushing with highly seasoned French dressing throughout the cooking.

### SCALLOPS BONIFACE
2 pounds sea scallops
Butter or margarine
2 small green peppers, seeded and chopped
½ cup chopped white leeks
⅓ cup sherry
¼ cup flour
2 cups milk
Salt, pepper, cayenne
Paprika

Wash scallops and drain. Melt ⅓ cup butter in a skillet. Sauté green peppers and leeks in it until leeks are golden. Add scallops and sherry and simmer for 10 minutes. Melt ¼ cup butter. Stir in flour. Gradually stir in milk and cook over low heat, stirring constantly, until smooth and thick. Add salt, pepper, and cayenne to taste. Add sauce to scallops and simmer for 5 minutes. Sprinkle with paprika and serve in patty shells or over rice. Makes 6 servings.

**SCALLOP, TO**—To bake in a casserole with milk or a sauce and often with crumbs, either as part of a mixture or arranged in alternate layers. The use of the word scallop to describe this type of baked food is thought to have been derived from the fact that the shells of scallops are often used as baking dishes.

**SCALOPPINE**—An Italian word, the English is escallop, for a prepared dish containing slices of meat or fish of any kind flattened slightly and fried. Nowadays the dish most often so called is veal, browned and cooked in a sauce of wine or tomatoes and seasonings.

**SCHNITZEL**—The German word for a veal cutlet which may be seasoned and garnished in a variety of ways.

### SARDELLENSCHNITZEL (Veal Cutlets with Anchovies)
3 pounds veal cutlet, ¼ inch thick
Salt and pepper to taste
All-purpose flour
Fat for frying
1¼ cups bouillon or water
3 anchovy fillets, chopped
1 cup dairy sour cream

Season meat with salt and pepper. Make incisions around edges so that meat will lie flat when cooking. Sprinkle one side of cutlets with flour. Fry in hot fat, floured side first, until golden-brown on both sides. Remove meat and stir 3 tablespoons flour into drippings in skillet. Gradually add bouillon and cook, stirring, until thickened. Put meat in sauce, cover, and simmer for 30 minutes. Add anchovies and sour cream, and heat. Add more salt and pepper to taste. Good with rice, mashed potatoes, or dumplings. Makes 6 servings.

**SCONE**—Plain or sweet biscuitlike tea cake, cooked on a griddle or baked in the oven. Scones are usually cut into triangular or diamond shapes. They originated in Scotland where they are often made of oatmeal.

# The Scones of Scotland

## by Alice Upham Smith

To walk into a baker's shop in Edinburgh or any other city in Scotland is to realize the almost infinite variety of delectable treats that can come from an oven. Tray after tray of scones, buns, baps, bannocks, and breads are there to choose from, as well as biscuits and cakes. I have heard it said that the Scots and the Viennese are the world's best bakers and I can vouch for Scottish baking after tasting the results during a year in Scotland.

It was lucky that bread came in small as well as large loaves because we each had our favorite kinds and would bring home four or five loaves when we went shopping. But it was the scones, hot out of the oven or off the griddle, that were the highlights of meals. Scones are the hot breads of Scotland. The word scone is

pronounced in the soft Scottish accent like scaun. As far as I can find, the name originally came from a parish in Perthshire which was the site of the historic abbey and palace where the kings of Scotland were crowned on the Stone of Destiny or Scone which is now under the Coronation Throne in Westminister Abbey. Tradition has it that this stone was Jacob's Pillow. The name is the only thing that is like a stone, however, for scones are as light as a feather and don't stay around long enough to gather any moss.

There are many varieties of scones, plain ones to eat with marmalade or honey for breakfast, richer sweeter scones to eat in front of a fire with tea, and oatmeal or griddle, also called girdle, scones, for lunch or supper.

All scones are quick and easy to make. One delightful old gentleman used to brag that his wife could have a batch of scones in the oven between the time guests rang the bell at the garden gate and walked up the short walk to the front door. The scones she served were made from a recipe that became one of my favorites to serve with chicken salad or cold sliced meat and a salad for Sunday supper. Guests always want the recipe. I confess I am not as deft and quick at making

them as my Scottish friend, however. Here is her recipe:

### TEA SCONES

2 cups unsifted all-purpose flour
½ cup sugar
2 teaspoons cream of tartar
1 teaspoon baking soda
¾ teaspoon salt
½ cup shortening
½ cup raisins or dried currants
2 eggs, slightly beaten
¼ cup milk

Sift dry ingredients together. Blend in shortening with pastry blender until mixture resembles fine bread crumbs. Add remaining ingredients. Mix with fork, divide into two parts, and turn each part out on floured board. Do not handle. Flatten with rolling pin into circles about ½ inch or more thick. Cut into triangles and put on greased and floured cookie sheet. Bake in preheated hot oven (400° F.) for 15 minutes, or until golden. Serve warm, slightly buttered. Makes about 16.

Oatmeal and Scotland go together, and in Scottish homes naturally there are oatmeal scones. They use a steel-cut oatmeal that is sometimes hard to find in this country. A variation using rolled oats just as they come from the package is quicker to make.

### OAT SCONES

1 cup unsifted all-purpose flour
1 cup old-fashioned rolled oats
½ teaspoon each of salt and baking soda
1 teaspoon cream of tartar
1 tablespoon sugar
¼ cup shortening
½ cup milk

Mix dry ingredients. Cut in shortening. Add milk, and with fork mix to a soft dough. Roll out on floured board to ½-inch thickness. Cut into triangles, put on greased cookie sheet, and bake in preheated hot oven (425° F.) for 15 minutes, or until browned. Serve warm. Makes 8 to 12.

Before stoves and ovens were common, scones were baked on a griddle, called a girdle, over an open fire, and griddle scones baked on top of the stove are still very popular. They look like plump pancakes but are eaten like biscuits with the usual trimmings. They were popular for evening snacks after a bridge game, and piles of them disappeared rapidly. Hungry youngsters can do away with them like magic. They were also served for lunch or supper. Sometimes there were two or three varieties of scone on the table as well as a loaf of bread and a cake. The scones made from the following recipe are the lightest I have ever eaten.

### GRIDDLE OR DROPPED SCONES
4 cups unsifted all-purpose flour
2 teaspoons each of baking soda and cream of tartar
1 tablespoon sugar
½ teaspoon salt
1 egg
2½ cups buttermilk

Mix all dry ingredients. Beat the egg well and add buttermilk to it; add to dry ingredients and mix to a fairly soft batter. Grease a griddle and drop mixture on by the tablespoonful. When brown on one side, turn and brown on the other. Wrap in a clean towel to keep warm. Makes about 4 dozen 2½-inch scones.

Griddle scones are a fine hot-weather bread because the oven does not have to be heated. All recipes for scones can be baked on a griddle if they are rolled about ¼ inch thick.

Potatoes are another economical food, so the thrifty Scots make potato scones. I like potatoes in any form, so I hunted high and low for the recipe to add to my collection, and here it is.

### KATY'S DROP POTATO SCONES
1 cup hot mashed potatoes
1 cup unsifted all-purpose flour
1 egg
¼ cup buttermilk
¼ teaspoon baking soda
½ teaspoon salt

Mix all ingredients together and drop by the tablespoonful onto a hot greased griddle. Smooth scones lightly with the back of the spoon. Cook for about 3 minutes on each side. Remove to a towel and cover to keep warm. Makes about 15.

Probably our buttermilk baking-powder biscuits developed from scones, but there are some differences in the recipes, and scones, being cut into triangles, seem a bit quicker to make.

### BUTTERMILK SCONES
2 cups unsifted all-purpose flour
1 tablespoon sugar
¼ teaspoon baking soda
2½ teaspoons baking powder
5 tablespoons shortening
¾ cup buttermilk

Sift dry ingredients together. Cut in shortening. Add buttermilk and mix with fork. Roll into 2 rounds about ½ inch thick and cut into triangles. Put on greased cookie sheet. Bake in preheated hot oven (400°F.) for 20 minutes, or until browned. Serve hot. Makes 12 to 16.

Try some scones next time you want a hot bread. As my Scottish friends would say, "They're bonny eating."

**SCORE, TO**—To slash with a knife, as when cutting the long fibers in a piece of less tender meat or the fatty surface of a piece of meat to allow fat to drain properly. Flank steak and round steak can be scored with a sharp knife to cut the long tough fibers. The fat of a ham or the fatty skin of a goose or duck can be scored decoratively to allow fat to escape and to give a decorative finish to the roast.

**SCRAMBLE, TO**—A method of preparing food by stirring it, usually applied to eggs which are beaten lightly with a fork, then sautéed in a small amount of butter. The eggs may be beaten with seasoning and a little milk, cream, or water before being poured in the pan; or they may be broken into the hot butter in the pan and mixed while they are being cooked. The first method gives a creamy golden-yellow scrambled egg while the second method results in scrambled eggs with a flecked white and yellow appearance.

To obtain soft creamy scrambled eggs they can be cooked in the top part of a double boiler over boiling water. For those who must be careful with calories it is possible now to scramble eggs in teflon-coated pans without any butter at all.

Chopped cooked meat, cheese, herbs, etc., can be added to scrambled eggs to give variety and interest.

**SCRAPPLE**—A very solid mush made from the by-products of hog butchering; the mush is sliced and fried for a breakfast or supper dish. Scrapple is the invention of the thrifty Pennsylvania Dutch farmers. Apart from the general ingredients, there is no set rule as to quantity and seasonings, so that scrapple is a highly individual product.

The basis for the making of scrapple is a broth produced by the cooking of the hog's head, liver, tongue, meaty bones, and other scraps. The meat that remains in the broth is ground, and other ground pork meat may be added. Meat and broth are then combined and seasoned, and the mixture is boiled. Originally, buckwheat flour was used to thicken the scrapple; this was the old German custom. But in the New World, the Pennsylvania Dutch preferred a mixture of buckwheat and cornmeal, and nowadays generally only cornmeal is used.

*Availability*—Scrapple, also known as Philadelphia scrapple, can be bought ready for frying, either packaged or canned.

#### Caloric Value
☐ 3½ ounces, unfried = 366 calories

*Basic Preparation*

☐ **To Panfry**—Cut scrapple into slices a little less than ½ inch thick. Roll in flour and panfry in bacon fat or other fat over medium heat, until crisp and well browned on both sides.

### HOMEMADE SCRAPPLE
1 pound pork liver
½ pound pork heart
1½ pounds boneless pork scraps
2½ quarts water
¼ teaspoon ground sage
⅛ teaspoon ground allspice (optional)
Salt and pepper to taste
3 cups buckwheat flour
3 cups cornmeal

Place pork liver, heart, and scraps in deep kettle. Cover with water. Boil until very tender. Drain meat; reserve. Chill broth and remove fat from surface. Trim meat and grind fine. Return broth and ground meat to kettle; add seasonings. Bring to a boil. Combine buckwheat flour and cornmeal. Trickle mixture slowly into boiling broth, stirring constantly to avoid lumping. Lower heat and cook, stirring very frequently, for about 1 hour, or until mixture is very thick and comes off the sides of the kettle. Rinse small bread pans or any molds with cold water. Pour hot scrapple into them. Cool. When cold, cut into slices or fingers and fry in shortening until crisp and brown on both sides. Makes 12 to 16 servings.

**SCROD**—A young cod or young haddock weighing from one and a half to two and a half pounds. A scrod is also a whole small cod split and boned for cooking. Young cod is sold in steaks, fillets, and whole, fresh and frozen. It is found all year round in the North Atlantic and North Pacific. Like all cod, it is one of the most useful food fishes. Since it is a lean fish it can be prepared in any number of ways—baked, broiled, sautéed, fried, panfried, steamed, etc.

**SCULPIN**—A fish of the family *Cottidae*. They are found in large numbers in temperate and cold regions of the Northern hemisphere, both in fresh and salt water. They are usually small and are characterized by a large head with a rough, spiny skull and a large mouth. Because of their excessive boniness they are not of any commercial importance as food. On the West Coast, however, the scorpion fish is sometimes called sculpin, although it is not a true sculpin at all. It is a kind of rockfish of the family *Scorpinaenidae*. They are most abundant off the coast of California where the most common scorpion fish is *Scorpaena guttata*. They have large heads and sharp spines, average about one foot in length, and are brown, red, or olive in color. They are sold whole and can be prepared in any of the ways that striped bass, another type of rockfish, is prepared. They are particularly good broiled or baked.

**SEAFOOD**—Properly speaking this word may be applied to any marine fish or shellfish used as food, but in popular usage it is apt to be confined to shellfish: the mollusks, such as clams and oysters, and the crustaceans, such as lobster.

### WHITE-FISH BOUILLABAISSE

- 1 carrot, diced
- 2 onions, chopped
- 2 leeks (white part only) or 4 green onions, sliced
- 1 garlic clove, crushed
- ½ cup olive oil
- 3 pounds any boned white fish, cut into 3-inch pieces
- 2 large tomatoes, diced, or 1 cup canned tomatoes
  Salt and pepper to taste
- 1 bay leaf, crumbled
- 2 cups fish stock, clam juice, or water
- 1 cup cooked shrimps, crab, or lobster
- 2 dozen scrubbed oysters, clams, or mussels in the shell
- 1 can (4 ounces) pimientos, diced
  Few saffron shreds
  Juice of 1 lemon
- 1 cup dry white wine
  French bread, sliced and toasted
  Chopped parsley

Cook first 4 ingredients in oil in large kettle until golden-brown. Add fish, tomatoes, salt and pepper, bay leaf, and stock. Bring to boil and simmer, covered, for 20 minutes. Add shellfish and simmer for 5 minutes, or until shells open. Add remaining ingredients except last 2. Heat well. Put toast in tureen and add soup. Sprinkle with parsley. Makes 6 to 8 servings.

### SEAFOOD SUPREME

- 2 cans (6½ ounces each) king crabmeat or 2 packages (6 ounces each) frozen crabmeat, thawed
- 2 lobster tails, cooked and cut up
- 1 pound cod fillets, poached
- 1 can (10 ounces) frozen shrimp soup, thawed
- 1 can (10½ ounces) cream-of-mushroom soup
- ½ cup heavy cream
- 2 tablespoons sherry
- ⅛ teaspoon pepper
- 2 tablespoons fine dry bread crumbs
- ¼ cup grated Parmesan cheese
  Paprika
- 2 tablespoons butter or margarine

Flake crabmeat, removing membranes. Add all but last four ingredients; mix well. Pour into shallow baking dish. Sprinkle with crumbs, cheese, and paprika. Dot with butter. Bake in preheated moderate oven (350°F.) for about 30 minutes. Makes 6 servings.

**SEAR, TO**—A culinary method of browning the surface of meat or poultry at a very high temperature to seal in the natural juices. Pot roasts and stew meat are seared on top of the range while roasts are seared in the oven. After the meat is seared, the temperature is lowered and the food is cooked slowly until the desired degree of doneness is reached.

**SEASONING**—An ingredient such as a condiment, flavoring, or spice added to food for the primary purpose of improving its taste.

**SEASON, TO**—To make food more palatable by the addition of salt, pepper, fresh and dried herbs, whole or ground spices, and various condiments, sauces, and flavorings.

**SEAWEED** by *Lucy Kavaler*—The most primitive large plants that still exist today are in the sea. Pick up a seaweed near the shore and it seems to be just a wetter, slimier version of the ones that grow on land. But the leaves, stems, and flowers are such in appearance only; the cells are not like those of higher plants. Seaweeds are members of a group known scientifically as *algae,* with a history that has been traced back to two-billion-year-old fossils. And this group has changed rather little over the ages; evolution has not carried it very far. Simple in structure although they are, seaweeds can be considered as food crops; they are consumed freely in Japan and are incorporated in a multitude of the processed foods we eat every day.

Wherever you go, you will find some form of seaweed: in the cold ocean off the rugged coasts of New England or Scandinavia, in the warm Pacific bounding California or Hawaii, in the Indian Ocean, in fresh-water ponds. There are giants nearly a mile wide and several miles long, tiny blobs, thin ribbons, leafy clusters, tangles of threads, delicate fern-like growths. In the shallow waters near shore one finds green, yellow-green, blue-green, and brown seaweeds; dimly seen in deep waters lie dark-red and purple ones waving their fragile beautifully wrought leaves.

Not all, to be sure, are edible, but there are so many wholesome varieties that almost every nation living on the sea has found ways of making seaweed palatable. A visitor to Edinburgh a hundred years or so ago would surely have heard street vendors crying "buy dulse and tangle," referring to a sweetened seaweed mixture with a taste similar to peanuts. British whalers gathered the leafy "laver" and it was virtually the only fresh vegetable they ate during their prolonged voyages. In parts of Wales it retains its popularity to this day. Among the Irish one can still find old men who cling to the timeworn custom of chewing dried dulse or crannogh in place of tobacco. As seaweed is particularly rich in iodine, it is a healthful chaw. On the opposite side of the Atlantic, therefore, goiter-prone South American Indians long ago learned to chew similar weeds as "goiter sticks."

Other health-giving attributes of seaweed gained recognition long before the dawn of modern medicine. During the Middle Ages monks consumed an algae jelly as a stomach remedy; it was probably effective, because one seaweed derivative is still used as a laxative.

The Japanese, masters of the art of seaweed cooking, insist that these algae belong in any well-balanced diet. For hundreds of years it was the custom for Japanese to celebrate their birthdays jointly as a national festival on December 31st. Instead of gorging themselves on delicacies, they ate healthful foods only: seaweed, vegetables, roe, and salmon. The tradition, although not the food, was abandoned after World War II. Two kinds of seaweed are basic to Japanese cooking: *kombu* or kelp, the large brown algae, and sheets of dried *nori* from the purple *Porphyra. Kombu* is a key ingredient in *dashi,* the soup stock that in turn is the basis of *miso,* the rich soup served for breakfast, lunch, and dinner, as well as tempura sauce, sukiyaki sauce, and a vast number of other dishes.

The great oriental contribution to hors-d'oeuvre is *sushi,* best described as a rice sandwich. The rice filling is boiled in *kombu* and wine and then is rolled either in a slice of raw fish or a piece of *nori.* This seaweed looks like a piece of slightly crumpled purple tissue paper, and the light shines through it unevenly as through a stained-glass window.

But so many useful food ingredients can be made out of seaweed that we find it in prosaic dishes as well as in exotic *sushi.* Lick an ice-cream cone, eat a portion of pudding, pour a glass of chocolate milk for the children, have a Bloody-Mary pick-me-up, down a mug of beer, even brush your teeth, and the chances are that a product derived from seaweed has entered your mouth. Ice cream is smoother, puddings gel, pie fillings are thicker, chocolate milk and syrups pour more easily and the flavor does not drop to the bottom, beer is clarified, meringues stiffened, and salad dressing homogenized. The source of all these wonders lies in such seaweed products as algin and sodium alginate, taken from the giant kelp, *Macrocystis*. Another weed, *Chondrus*, gives us Irish moss or carrageen and the *Gelidium* provides agar, familiar to high-school biology students as a culture medium and to cooks as a substitute for unflavored gelatin.

The properties given to foods by these seaweed derivatives are so incredible that they call to mind the old Scandinavian belief that the algae were magical. Sorcerers in those times stirred seaweeds into their potions. Modern science casts doubt as to the supernatural powers of those brews, but reveals that they must have been smooth, thick, evenly flavored, and easy to pour.

**SEED**—The fertilized ovule of a seed plant containing the embryo of the new plant and, usually, a food supply, enclosed in a seed coat. From prehistoric times seeds have been one of mankind's chief sources of food. Included among them are the cereals, such as wheat, barley, and rice; legumes such as Lima beans, peas, lentils, and peanuts; coffee; nuts; and the aromatic seeds used for flavoring: caraway, sesame, and poppy seeds, for example.

**SELTZER, SELTZER WATER**—A mineral water containing a great deal of carbon dioxide. It comes from Nieder Selters in the Wiesbaden district of Germany. The name is also now widely used to describe an artificially prepared bottled water of similar composition.

**SEMOLINA**—The purified middlings (medium-size particles of ground grain) of wheat. The word is derived from the diminutive of the Italian *semola*, "bran." The best semolina, the type used in the manufacture of macaroni, spaghetti, and other pastas, is obtained in the milling of durum wheat, a very hard wheat.

Semolina is used more widely in Europe than in the United States: the French bake a wheat bread with it, the Italians combine it with other grains in making polenta and gnocchi. It is also used for puddings. Semolina is available in this country in bulk and packaged. It can be prepared and used like farina.

**SESAME (Sesamum indicum)**—An annual tropical and subtropical herbaceous plant. It grows to a height of two to four feet, has a branching stem, leaves of various shapes, and pale rose or white flowers. Sesame has been grown since time immemorial for its tiny grayish-white or black seeds which have a sweet nutty flavor and which yield a bland oil when pressed. The cake left after the oil has been expressed from the seeds has also been used for food and fodder.

Sesame found its way into fiction via the *Arabian Nights*. Ali Baba the Sailor overheard the robbers directing the door of the cave where their treasure was hidden to "Open Sesame." Ali Baba copied them, much to his advantage. The term "open sesame" was used because in fact the sesame seeds pop out of their hulls very easily.

The seed was brought to the American South by the African slaves who called it "benne" or "bene" seed, an African name still used today in the South and elsewhere. Sesame seeds are popular in Southern cooking, especially in cakes and cookies. Bought whole and then toasted to bring out the flavor, the nutlike seeds can be used as a crunch garnish for appetizers, salads, and almost any dish calling for nuts. If they are not toasted first, they should be used in baked dishes, sprinkled over breads before baking, used instead of bread crumbs as a topping for meat and poultry casseroles, served instead of nuts in cakes and cookies. Sesame seeds toasted are good combined with cheese or used in sweet sauces. They are especially good with butter over noodles and vegetables.

In the Middle East today sesame seeds are crushed into a paste to spread on bread. The delicious Turkish halvah is a rich candy made primarily from sesame seeds.

*Availability*—Whole sesame seeds are widely available. Sesame oil is sold in health-food and specialty food stores.

*Caloric Values*

☐ Sesame seed, dry, 3½ ounces, whole = 563 calories

☐ Sesame seed, dry, 3½ ounces, decorticated = 582 calories

☐ Sesame oil, 3½ ounces = 884 calories

*Basic Preparation*

☐ **To Toast**—Spread seeds in pie pan and toast in preheated moderate oven (350° F.) for 10 to 15 minutes, until golden-brown.

### SOUTHERN SESAME SHRIMPS

Marinate peeled jumbo shrimps in equal parts of sesame oil, bourbon whiskey, and soy sauce for 2 hours. Grill or broil for 3 or 4 minutes on each side. Dip again into the marinade, roll in sesame seeds to cover, and return to the grill or broiler until the seeds are lightly colored on both sides.

### BURMESE GINGER BEEF

5 onions, chopped finely
4 garlic cloves, minced
2 teaspoons ground turmeric
2 fresh chili peppers or ½ teaspoon dried ground chili peppers
1-inch piece of fresh gingerroot, chopped, or 2 teaspoons ground ginger
2 teaspoons salt
3 pounds beef, cut into 1½-inch cubes
½ cup sesame or peanut oil
8 tomatoes, chopped
2 cups beef bouillon or 1 can (10½ ounces) consommé and ½ cup water

Combine onions, garlic, turmeric, chili peppers, gingerroot, and salt. Chop or pound together until very fine. Place beef in bowl and add spice mixture. Coat meat thoroughly on all sides. Refrigerate for several hours, turning frequently. Heat oil in deep saucepan until oil bubbles. Add beef and spice mixture and brown well. Add tomatoes. Cook, covered, over medium heat for about 10 minutes. Add bouillon. Simmer, covered, over low heat for about 1½ hours, or until meat is tender. Serve on rice. Makes 6 to 8 servings.

## SPICED SESAME CHICKEN

2 frying chickens (about 2½ pounds each), quartered
½ cup sesame seeds
⅓ cup cooking oil
¼ cup minced onion
2 teaspoons salt
½ teaspoon each of ground cardamom and ginger
1 garlic clove, minced
Dash each of ground cloves and chili powder
Pan Gravy

Wash and dry chicken pieces. Put, skin side down, in shallow broilerproof baking dish. Mix next 9 ingredients and brush some on chicken. Bake in preheated moderate oven (350°F.) for 30 minutes, basting frequently with remaining sesame mixture. Turn skin side up and bake for about 30 minutes longer. Put under broiler and brown lightly. Serve with Pan Gravy. Makes 4 servings.

### Pan Gravy

Remove chicken from baking pan. Blend 1 tablespoon cornstarch and 1 cup water. Stir into drippings. Cook, stirring, until thickened.

## SESAME HONEY BUTTER

¼ cup sesame seeds
2 tablespoons butter or margarine
1 cup strained honey

Toast seeds in butter for 10 minutes over low heat. They should be delicately browned. Add the honey, bring to a boil, reduce heat, and steep for 5 minutes. Serve hot over waffles, pancakes, or biscuits. This should also add food value and fine flavor to rice or to bread pudding. Makes 1¼ cups.

## SESAME WHOLE-WHEAT BREAD

2 packages active dry yeast or 2 cakes compressed yeast
3 cups water*
2 tablespoons sugar
2 teaspoons salt
2 eggs
¼ cup cooking oil
1 cup nonfat dry milk solids
¼ cup brewers' yeast
½ cup wheat germ
¼ cup sesame seed
3 cups whole-wheat flour
4½ cups sifted all-purpose flour

*Use very warm water (105°F. to 115° F.) for dry yeast; use lukewarm (80°F. to 90°F.) for compressed yeast. Sprinkle dry yeast or crumble cakes into water. Let stand for a few minutes; then stir until dissolved. Add sugar, salt, eggs, oil, milk, brewers' yeast, wheat germ, and sesame seed; beat hard for 2 minutes. Stir in flours. Turn out on floured pastry cloth or board and knead until smooth and satiny. Put in greased bowl; turn once, cover, and let rise until doubled, about 1 hour. Punch down and let rise for about 30 minutes. Shape into 3 loaves and put in greased loaf pans (9 x 5 x 3

inches). Let rise until doubled, about 1 hour. Bake in preheated moderate oven (350°F.) for about 45 minutes.

## SESAME-SEED ROLLS

Use roll mix or buy baked rolls (1 package of roll mix will make 12 rolls). Make according to package directions. Brush with beaten egg and sprinkle thickly with sesame seeds. Let rise, and bake according to directions.

## BENNE WAFERS

¾ cup melted butter
1½ cups firmly packed light brown sugar
1 teaspoon vanilla extract
1 egg
1 cup toasted sesame seeds
1¼ cups sifted all-purpose flour
¼ teaspoon baking powder
¼ teaspoon salt

Cream butter and sugar. Add vanilla and egg and beat until light. Stir in seeds, flour, baking powder, and salt. Drop by ½ teaspoonfuls onto greased cookie sheets; allow for spreading. Bake in preheated moderate oven (375°F.) for 10 minutes. Remove from pans at once. Makes 5 dozen.

## SESAME-ANISE COOKIES

1 tablespoon aniseed
2 tablespoons boiling water
¾ cup butter
⅔ cup sugar
⅛ teaspoon baking soda
2 eggs
2 cups sifted all-purpose flour
3 tablespoons sesame seeds, toasted

Combine aniseed and boiling water and steep while mixing dough. Cream butter with sugar and soda. Beat in 1 egg. Drain aniseed, and add. Stir in flour a little at a time. Mix well. Chill dough overnight. Roll out dough into ½-inch balls. Place on ungreased cookie sheets 1½ inches apart. Put a piece of wax paper over cookies and flatten to 1/16-inch thickness with bottom of a glass. Remove wax paper. Beat remaining egg and brush cookie tops. Sprinkle with sesame seeds. Bake in preheated hot oven (400°F.) for 7 to 8 minutes. Makes 12 dozen.

**SET, TO**—As a culinary term, the phrase means to become fixed, rigid, or more solid, and is applied to such foods as gelatin desserts or salads; or meats set with natural aspics. It is also applied to jam or jelly, where either natural or artificial pectin is used to set the mixture. Another culinary usage is to set a timer for a certain period in cooking or baking. An old-fashioned usage of the term was "to set bread," meaning to put the dough aside for rising.

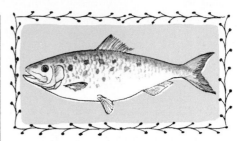

**SHAD**—An important food fish of the family *Clupeidae* which also includes herrings. Shad are found in coastal waters on both sides of the north Atlantic, in the Mediterranean, and off our Pacific coast. They differ from herrings chiefly in being larger and in the fact that they enter rivers to spawn. A few species of shad live permanently in fresh-water lakes: Killarney and some of the lakes of northern Italy, for example.

The common American shad, *Alosa sapidissima,* can reach a weight of fourteen pounds, but the average market weight ranges from one and a half to eight pounds, with four or five pounds most common. The fish has a compressed body with a rounded bluish back, silvery sides and undersurface. It is excessively bony, but the dark-pink flesh is delicious and its roe is a prized delicacy.

Shad is found in the Atlantic from the Gulf of St. Lawrence to Florida along the coast of the Gulf of Mexico. In the 1870's the Atlantic shad was successfully transplanted to the Pacific where it is now more plentiful than it is in eastern waters. Like the salmon, shad enters the warmer waters of rivers to spawn. It is at this point that it is caught. Shad is often named after a river, such as Delaware shad or Hudson shad, but this does not denote different species, simply the locality where the fish is caught.

Shad is a seasonal fish, and the spawning runs begin in Florida in December; they reach the Potomac in April, the Delaware and Hudson in April and May, and the Kennebec in May and June.

The bone structure of the shad is complicated and the large number of bones are a nuisance at the table. Boning a shad is a difficult job and should not be attempted except by skilled experts. However, fish markets will bone shad, or fillet it. The texture of the flesh is so delicate that the skin should be left on the fillets.

Broiled, baked, or planked, stuffed whole, or sautéed in butter, shad is superb eating.

*Availability*—Fresh shad is available whole, drawn, and in fillets from January through May. Canned shad is available year round.

Shad roe is available fresh and canned.

Fresh roe is usually from 5 to 6 inches long, 3 inches wide, and 1 inch thick. Canned roe is somewhat smaller.

**Purchasing Guide**—See Red Snapper, page 1540.

**Storage**—See Red Snapper, page 1540.

**Caloric Values**

☐ Fresh, 3½ ounces, raw = 170 calories

☐ Fresh, 3½ ounces, baked = 201 calories

☐ Canned, 3½ ounces, solids and liquid = 152 calories

☐ Roe, 3½ ounces, raw = 130 calories

☐ Roe, 3½ ounces, baked or broiled = 126 calories

### PLANKED SHAD

4- to 5-pound shad, split and boned
1 teaspoon salt
½ teaspoon pepper
1 teaspoon crumbled dried marjoram or ½ teaspoon ground coriander
1 cup melted butter

Oil wooden plank. Place plank in cold oven to heat. Bring heat up to hot (400° F.). When plank is thoroughly hot (time depends on size and thickness), reduce oven heat to moderate (375°F.). Place fish on hot plank. Sprinkle with seasonings and brush with some of the melted butter. Put into oven. Bake for 20 minutes, or until fish flakes when tested with a fork. Baste frequently with butter. Makes 4 to 6 servings.

### Baked Shad

Use a flat oiled baking pan or an oiled jelly-roll pan. Put fish on pan and season. There is no need to warm a glass or metal baking pan. Bake in preheated moderate oven (375°F.) as indicated above.

### BAKED SHAD WITH MUSHROOM STUFFING

5-pound shad
1 medium onion, minced
¼ cup butter
½ pound fresh mushrooms, chopped
¼ cup chopped parsley
½ cup seasoned bread crumbs
Salt and pepper
¼ pound bacon slices
About ½ cup hot water

Have fish split and boned, but leave head and tail on. Sauté onion in hot butter until soft. Add mushrooms and cook for 5 minutes. Add parsley and bread crumbs and cook for 3 minutes. Season to taste with salt and pepper. Stuff shad with mixture and sew edges together. Place fish on a rack in baking pan or in oiled baking dish. Cover with bacon and fasten strips with toothpicks. Add water. Bake in preheated hot oven (400°F.) for 10 minutes. Reduce heat to moderate (350°F.) and bake for 25 to 30 minutes longer, basting frequently. To test for doneness,

remove 1 bacon strip and see if the fish will flake when tested with a fork. Serve on hot platter with boiled parsleyed new potatoes and fresh green peas. Makes 6 servings.

### BAKED SHAD WITH HERB-BREAD STUFFING

2 onions, sliced
¼ cup butter
1 cup soft bread crumbs
¼ cup minced parsley
½ teaspoon thyme leaves
2 tablespoons minced celery leaves
1 teaspoon salt
1 egg, well beaten
1 split boned shad (about 4 pounds)

Sauté onions in the butter until golden. Add remaining ingredients except shad and mix well. Stuff fish with the mixture and sew or secure opening with toothpicks. Put in an oiled shallow baking dish and bake in preheated hot oven (400° F.) for 30 to 40 minutes. Good with parsley, potatoes and green peas. Makes 6 servings.

### GOLDEN BROILED SHAD

2 pounds boned shad fillets (with skin on)
1 tablespoon grated onion
2 tablespoons fresh lemon juice
½ cup butter
1 teaspoon salt
¼ teaspoon pepper
¼ teaspoon marjoram
Parsley sprigs

Put fish, skin side down, on greased broiler rack. Mix remaining ingredients except parsley. Spread half of the mixture on the fish. Broil 2 or 3 inches from unit for 6 to 10 minutes, or until fish flakes easily with a fork. Serve garnished with parsley. Makes 4 to 6 servings.

### SAUTÉED SHAD FILLETS

2 pounds boned shad fillets
Salt and pepper
Milk
Yellow cornmeal
Cooking oil
Sauce Tartare, page 1622

Cut fillets into serving pieces. Season with salt and pepper. Dip in milk, then in cornmeal. Sauté in hot oil until fish is browned on both sides and flakes easily with a fork. Serve with Sauce Tartare. Makes 4 to 6 servings.

### BROILED SHAD ROE WITH BACON

6 pair of shad roe (about 2 pounds)
Pepper to taste
Crumbled dried rosemary
12 slices of bacon
6 slices of buttered toast
Watercress

Prick the membrane of shad roe with a needle. Put in a saucepan. Cover with boiling water, add seasonings and simmer for 5 minutes. Drain roe and cut into 6 pieces. Put roe pieces on a rack in a broiler pan and cover with slices of bacon. Put 4 inches below source of heat and broil

until bacon is crisp. Serve on toast, garnished with watercress. Makes 6 servings.

### SMOTHERED SHAD ROE

½ cup butter
3 pair of shad roe (about 1 pound)
Salt and pepper to taste
Chopped parsley and chives
Watercress, lemon wedges, and paprika

Melt butter in skillet. Arrange roe in pan. Cover and cook for 5 minutes over medium heat. Turn roe, cover, and cook for 5 to 10 minutes longer, depending on size of roe. Season with salt and pepper and sprinkle with parsley and chives. Serve on hot plates. Garnish with watercress and wedges of lemon dipped into paprika. Makes 3 servings.

**Note:** Good with creamed potatoes.

**SHADDOCK or PUMMELO**—A citrus fruit, *Citris grandis,* native to the East Indies. It is similar to the grapefruit and may be its ancestor. It grows to the size of a watermelon, weighs up to twenty pounds, has a coarse thick rind and reddish, aromatic, but bitter flesh.

**SHALLOT**—A mild-flavored cousin of the onion, chive, garlic, and leek, which belongs to the *Liliaceae* or Lily family. The shallot derives its name from the ancient Palestinian city, Ascalon, where it probably was first grown. Shallots are greatly prized in fine cooking, especially French cooking, and they deserve the attention of any sensitive cook.

The shallot has a thick outer skin shading from reddish to gray, the bulb underneath greenish at the base and violet on the upper portion. It grows in clove form, with several cloves attached to a common disc. The Jersey, or "false" shallot, is of various shapes, often larger than the "true" shallot, with thin red skin, and bulb sometimes white but usually all violet.

The edible part of the shallot is the bulb which is used after summer maturity and dry storage just as the garlic or

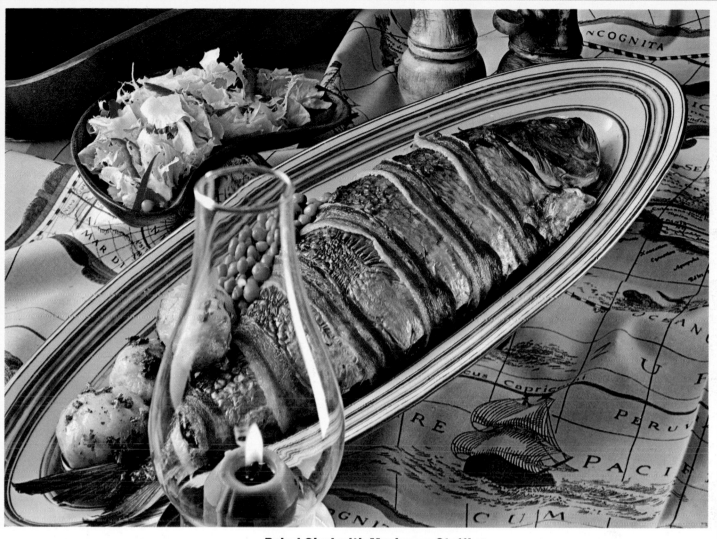

*Baked Shad with Mushroom Stuffing*

onion is used. The green tops are harvested in early summer and sometimes marketed as scallions.

The shallot grows in the southern United States and Europe. No wild shallots have ever been found, which suggests that they were developed by cultivation. The shallot is listed among the eighteen herbs grown in the kitchen garden of the monastery of Saint Gall near the shores of Lake Constance, during the 9th century. Charlemagne grew them in his great gardens at Aix-la-Chapelle, both for demonstration and for revenue.

Fresh shallots are used raw as a relish or may be used in salads or with vegetables as a seasoning ingredient. Dry ones are milder in flavor than regular onions but may be used in any of the ways that regular onions are used. They are frequently used in preference to onions in sauce recipes where a subtle flavor is particularly desirable.

*Availability*—Available in large food stores in large cities from October to May, with peak months March and April. They are sold green during the spring months, dried during the fall and winter.

*Purchasing Guide*—Fresh shallots should have fresh, crisp-looking bright-green leaves with no bruises, yellow or broken leaves. Bulbs should be ¼ to ¾ inch in width. Bunches should be well trimmed. Dried shallots should have firm, well-rounded cloves, not shrunken or shriveled in appearance.

*Storage*—Fresh shallots are perishable and should be wrapped in moisture- vapor-proof paper and stored in the coldest part of the refrigerator. Dried shallots can be stored in a cool dry place.

☐ Fresh, refrigerator shelf: 1 to 2 days
☐ Dry, kitchen shelf: 2 to 3 months

*Nutritive Food Values*—Fresh shallots are rich in vitamins A and C and in iron. Dried shallots contain less vitamin C.

☐ Fresh, 3½ ounces, tops only = 27 calories
☐ Dry bulb, 3½ ounces, raw = 72 calories

### SHALLOT-VEAL CHOPS

4 thick veal chops
¼ cup sweet butter or unsalted margarine
¼ cup diced boiled ham
6 shallots, diced
½ cup chicken or veal bouillon
½ cup dry white wine
2 egg yolks, beaten
1 teaspoon fresh lemon juice
Salt and pepper

Brown chops quickly on both sides in the butter. Add ham and shallots; cook for a few minutes longer. Add bouillon and wine; cover and simmer for 30 minutes, or until chops are tender. Remove chops to hot platter. Stir liquid into egg yolks, return to pan, and heat, stirring, until thickened. Add lemon juice and season with salt and pepper to taste. Pour over chops. Makes 4 servings.

## LAMB CHOPS AND SHALLOTS IN CASSEROLE

4 thick loin lamb chops
6 shallots, thinly sliced
¼ cup light cream
Salt and pepper to taste
2 tablespoons grated Parmesan cheese

Put chops in shallow casserole, cover with shallots, and add cream. Season, sprinkle with cheese, and bake, uncovered, in preheated moderate oven (350°F.) for 1 hour. Makes 4 servings.

## FRENCH SHALLOT-BEANS

2 packages (9 ounces each) frozen French-style green beans
4 shallots, thinly sliced
1 can (10½ ounces) condensed cream-of-chicken soup
¼ cup milk, evaporated milk, or thin cream
Salt and pepper to taste
1 tablespoon butter
Dash each of soy sauce and garlic salt
½ cup grated sharp Cheddar cheese

Cook beans, adding shallots for last 2 minutes of cooking. Drain and top with sauce made of remaining ingredients. Good served over rice or hominy. Makes 6 servings.

## SHALLOTS AND TOMATOES

3 tomatoes, large beefsteak type, peeled and sliced
2 shallots, diced fine
2 tablespoons chopped parsley
¼ cup olive oil
1 tablespoon basil vinegar or pinch of crushed basil and 1 tablespoon cider vinegar
Salt and pepper to taste

Put tomatoes in bowl and sprinkle with shallots. Add remaining ingredients, mixed well. Chill before serving. Makes 4 servings.

**SHEEP**—A ruminant mammal of the genus *Ovis,* native to the upland regions of the northern hemisphere and long domesticated for its flesh and wool. The flesh of a sheep under one year of age is generally considered to be lamb; the flesh of an older animal, mutton.

## SHEEPSHEAD or SHEEPHEAD—

A salt-water fish of the Gulf and Atlantic coasts of the United States, a cousin of porgies and scups. The sheepshead has large broad incisor teeth, much like a sheep. It is often caught far up in fresh water, as in the St. John's River, Florida. A brightly colored California fish with thick lips is also called a sheepshead but is properly a wrasse. There is also a fresh-water sheepshead, which belongs to the croaker family.

The flesh of all sheepshead is white, tender, and pleasant. They can be fried, sautéed, baked, etc., but they should be cooked in a manner to preserve their delicate flavor.

*Availability*—Sheepshead is available year round whole or filleted. Salt-water sheepshead is available mainly in the South and on the West Coast. Occasionally it is found in East Coast markets. The average market weight is 1½ pounds, although much larger ones are also available. Fresh-water sheepshead is available in the Midwest and the South. Sizes range from 2 to 8 pounds.

*Purchasing Guide*—See Red Snapper, page 1540.

*Storage*—See Red Snapper, page 1540.

### Caloric Values

☐ Salt-water, 3½ ounces, raw = 113 calories
☐ Fresh-water, 3½ ounces, raw = 121 calories

*Basic Preparation*—See Red Snapper, page 1540.

**SHELLFISH**—These belong to two very large classes, the mollusks and the crustaceans and are found in salt and fresh water. The mollusks have a soft structure and are partially or wholly enclosed in a one- or two-part shell. The former, called "univalve" mollusks, include the abalone, conch, and periwinkle. The latter, called "bivalve," include the clam, cockle, mussel, oyster, and scallop.

Crustaceans are covered with a crust-like shell and have segmented bodies. Among them are the crab, crayfish, lobster, prawn, and shrimp.

*Availability*—*Abalone,* fresh in California only, and canned; *conch,* in Florida and some large fish markets in northeastern cities only, frozen cooked and uncooked, and canned in some Italian food stores; *clams,* fresh alive-in-shell and shucked, frozen, canned, smoked and packed in jars, and in canned clam chowder; *crabs,* fresh, alive-in-shell, boiled-in-shell, and cooked meat, frozen cooked and deviled, and canned; *lobster,* fresh, alive-in-shell, boiled-in-shell, and as cooked meat, frozen, and canned; *mussels,* alive-in-shell, canned, and smoked and packed in jars; *oysters,* fresh, alive-in-shell or shucked, frozen, canned, smoked and packed in jars, and in frozen oyster stew; *scallops,* fresh shucked, frozen, canned, in a frozen dinner; *shrimps,* fresh, in shell, peeled, and peeled and cooked, frozen uncooked and unshelled, uncooked and cleaned, and precooked, canned in a variety of shrimp sizes and including tiny cocktail shrimps, in frozen shrimp soup, dinner, and chow mein; dried shrimps; and shrimp paste and shrimps in cocktail sauce in jars.

*Storage*—Wrap fresh shellfish in moisture-proof paper or place in tightly covered dish and store in coldest part of refrigerator. If it is not possible to refrigerate fresh shellfish thoroughly, cook and use promptly. Do not attempt to keep shellfish alive by placing in water. It will suffocate.

If shellfish is already cooked, refrigerate and use within a couple of days.

☐ Fresh, refrigerator shelf: 1 to 2 days
☐ Canned, kitchen shelf: 1 year
☐ Canned, refrigerator shelf, opened: 3 to 4 days
☐ Frozen, refrigerator frozen-food compartment: 1 month
☐ Frozen, freezer: 4 months

*Nutritive Food Values*—Shellfish are good sources of protein and iodine, and contain some amounts of the B vitamins. The crustaceans are higher in protein content than the mollusks.

## SHELLFISH-VEGETABLE CHOWDER

1 pound small shrimps
6 slices of bacon, diced
2 medium onions, chopped
1 can (6 ounces) minced clams
1 medium potato, diced
1 package (10 ounces) frozen succotash
2 cans (10¼ ounces each) frozen oyster-stew soup
3 cups milk
3 tablespoons butter or margarine
3 tablespoons flour
1 can (6 ounces) lobster, cut up
1½ cups heavy cream
½ cup dry sherry
Salt and freshly ground pepper to taste

Cover shrimps with boiling water and cook; drain, reserving the liquid. Peel and devein shrimps. In large kettle cook bacon until crisp. Remove bacon and pour off about half of fat. Cook onion in fat in kettle for 5 minutes. Combine shrimp liquid and liquid drained from clams; add enough water to make 4 cups. Add to onion with potato and succotash. Simmer for about 15 minutes. Add soup, milk, and blended butter and flour. Cook, stirring, until thickened. Add remaining ingredients including shrimps and drained clams, and heat. Makes 8 generous servings.

## CRAB AND SHRIMPS, DIXIE STYLE

1 small onion, minced
3 tablespoons butter or margarine
3 tablespoons all-purpose flour
1 teaspoon seasoned salt
¼ teaspoon seasoned pepper
½ teaspoon steak sauce
½ teaspoon grated lemon rind
1½ cups milk
½ cup light cream
1 can (4½ ounces) shrimps, drained and rinsed
1 can (6 ounces) crabmeat
Salt and pepper to taste
Split hot biscuits

Cook onion in butter until golden. Blend

in flour and seasonings. Add lemon rind, milk, and cream, and cook, stirring constantly, until thickened. Add shellfish, and heat. Season to taste and serve over biscuits. Makes 6 servings.

### HOT SHRIMP-CRAB SALAD

1 can (6 ounces) crabmeat
1 can (4½ ounces) shrimps, drained
1 cup diced celery
1 small onion, minced
½ medium green pepper, chopped
4 parsley sprigs, chopped
  Juice of ½ lemon
½ teaspoon salt
  Dash of cayenne
2 teaspoons Worcestershire
1 cup mayonnaise
¾ cup soft bread crumbs
2 tablespoons salad oil

Remove any pieces of shell from crabmeat. Rinse and clean shrimps. Mix lightly all ingredients except last 2. Pile in 4 oiled baking shells. Mix crumbs and oil; sprinkle on tops. Bake in preheated moderate oven (350°F.) for about 25 minutes. Makes 4 servings.

### SHELLFISH NEWBURG

1 can (6 ounces) crabmeat
1 can (5½ ounces) lobster
1 can (4½ ounces) shrimps
3 tablespoons butter
2 tablespoons all-purpose flour
½ teaspoon salt
⅛ teaspoon white pepper
  Dash each of cayenne and ground
    nutmeg or mace
2 cups milk
2 egg yolks, slightly beaten
2 tablespoons sherry
  Toast points

Pick over seafood; rinse shrimps. In top part of a double boiler or chafing dish over direct heat cook fish lightly in butter for 2 or 3 minutes. Blend in flour and seasonings. Gradually add milk and cook over boiling water, stirring constantly, until thickened. Stir small amount of mixture into egg yolks, put back in pan, and cook, stirring, for 2 or 3 minutes, but do not let sauce come to a boil. Stir in sherry and serve on toast. Makes 6 servings.

### SHELLFISH SOUFFLÉ

1 can (4 ounces) sliced mushrooms,
    drained
5 tablespoons butter
1 cup any cooked shellfish (alone or
    in combination)
  Mayonnaise
¼ cup all-purpose flour
½ teaspoon salt
  Dash of cayenne
1 cup milk
4 eggs, separated
1 cup grated sharp Cheddar cheese

Brown mushrooms lightly in 1 tablespoon butter. Add to seafood with enough mayonnaise to moisten. Put in 1½-quart soufflé dish or casserole. Melt ¼ cup butter and blend in flour, salt, and cayenne. Gradually add milk and cook, stirring constantly, until thickened. Beat egg

whites until stiff but not dry. Then beat yolks until thick. Stir yolks into hot mixture with cheese. Cool slightly and fold in egg whites. Pour over shellfish mixture. Set in pan of hot water; bake in preheated moderate oven (325°F.) for about 45 minutes. Makes 4 to 6 servings.

### SHELLFISH SALAD PLATE

On a bed of greens arrange whole cooked shrimps, lobster tails, and other seafood. Garnish with lemon and tomato wedges and serve with Green Sauce.

### Green Sauce

Use 1 part dairy sour cream to 2 parts mayonnaise and add minced parsley, green onion, watercress, and dill pickle to taste.

### CURRIED SHELLFISH

1 onion, minced
½ green pepper, minced
¼ cup butter or margarine
1 to 2 tablespoons curry powder
¼ cup all-purpose flour
2 cups chicken bouillon or consommé
1 tablespoon fresh lemon juice
1 can (4½ ounces) shrimps, drained
    and rinsed
1 can (5 ounces) lobster, drained
1 can (6½ ounces) crabmeat, drained

Cook onion and green pepper in butter for 2 or 3 minutes. Add curry powder and cook for 1 or 2 minutes. Blend in flour. Gradually stir in bouillon and cook, stirring constantly, until thickened. Add next 4 ingredients, and heat. Serve over rice if desired. Makes 6 servings.

**SHERBET**—A frozen dessert made of a fruit juice or purée, a sweetener, and water, to which milk, beaten egg white, gelatin, or marshmallow is added. It is the addition of the milk, etc., which differentiates a sherbet from a water ice.

Occasionally the word sherbet is also used to describe a cooling sweetened fruit drink or a fizzy drink made from tartaric acid, sodium bicarbonate, and sugar.

The classic French sherbet is made from fruit juices frozen with liqueurs or wines, each portion shaped by a special conical scoop and sprinkled with the same liqueur or wine.

### CITRUS MILK SHERBET

¾ cup light corn syrup
2 cups milk
  Grated rind of 2 oranges
  Grated rind of ½ lemon
¼ cup each of orange, lemon, and
    grapefruit juice
⅛ teaspoon salt
2 egg whites

Turn refrigerator control to coldest setting. Mix corn syrup, milk, rinds, and juices. Pour into refrigerator tray and partially freeze. Remove to cold bowl and beat until light and fluffy. Fold in beaten salted egg whites. Return to re-

frigerator tray and freeze until firm. Makes 4 servings.

### FIVE-FRUIT SHERBET

4 bananas
  Grated rind and juice of 1 orange
  Juice of 1 lemon
⅓ cup sugar
½ cup light corn syrup
¼ cup maraschino cherry juice
12 maraschino cherries
¾ cup canned crushed pineapple
1 egg white
  Dash of salt

Mash bananas with fork; add orange rind and juice and lemon juice. Stir in sugar, syrup, and cherry juice. Cut cherries into small pieces and add with pineapple to banana mixture. Beat salted egg white until stiff and beat into fruit mixture. Pour into refrigerator tray. Freeze until almost firm. Transfer sherbet to chilled bowl and beat with rotary beater until well mixed. Return to freezing tray and freeze until firm. Makes 8 servings.

### GUAVA SHERBET

1 envelope unflavored gelatin
¼ cup water
6 cups milk or light cream
2 cups honey
2 cups canned guavas, drained
    and mashed
1 teaspoon ground ginger

Soften gelatin in water. Scald milk; add gelatin and honey. Place in freezer trays. When liquid begins to freeze, empty into bowl and stir in mashed guavas and ginger. Return to freezer tray and freeze until solid. Makes 6 to 8 servings.

### LEMON OR LIME SHERBET

⅔ cup sugar
2½ cups water
½ cup fresh strained lemon or
    lime juice
⅛ teaspoon salt
2 egg whites

Simmer sugar and water for 10 minutes. Add to lemon or lime juice. Pour into a refrigerator tray. Put tray in lowest compartment of freezing unit. With temperature control at coldest point, freeze until partly frozen. Remove to ice-cold bowl; beat with chilled rotary beater or electric mixer until light. Fold in salted egg whites beaten until stiff but not dry. Return to refrigerator tray and freeze until firm. Makes 4 to 6 servings.

### ORANGE BUTTERMILK SHERBET

3 tablespoons sugar
1 teaspoon grated orange rind
½ cup fresh orange juice
⅓ cup light corn syrup
1½ cups buttermilk
1 tablespoon fresh lemon juice

Turn refrigerator control to coldest setting. Mix all ingredients and pour into refrigerator tray; partially freeze. Pour into chilled bowl and beat until fluffy. Return to tray and freeze until firm. Makes 4 servings.

Rainbow Sherbet Parfait

Five-Fruit Sherbet

Guava Sherbet

## PEACH SHERBET

1 cup sugar
1 cup water
2 cups fresh peach pulp
½ cup each of fresh orange and
  lemon juice
1 egg white
⅛ teaspoon salt

Boil sugar and water for 5 minutes. Cool. To make peach pulp, pit soft ripe peaches and press through sieve or food mill. Mix all ingredients. Put in crank-type freezer and freeze until firm. Makes about 1¼ quarts.

## RAINBOW SHERBET PARFAIT

Pour a little raspberry sauce into bottom of each parfait or other tall glass (fruit-juice glass can be used). Layer with various flavors of fruit sherbet such as orange, lime, lemon, and raspberry. Top each with a fresh or frozen raspberry. Serve at once or store in freezer.

## ROMAN PUNCH

*A famous 19th-century sherbet*

Soften slightly 1 quart commercial lemon sherbet. Beat together with 1 cup dark or light rum. Refreeze. Serve in sherbet glasses or scooped-out oranges or lemons. Cut a thin slice off the ends of oranges or lemons so that the fruit will stand upright on the plate. Makes 6 servings.

## STRAWBERRY SHERBET

1 teaspoon unflavored gelatin
¼ cup cold water
¾ cup sugar
2½ cups (one 1-pound, 4-ounce can)
  pineapple juice
1 pint fresh strawberries
⅛ teaspoon salt
1 egg white

Turn refrigerator control to coldest setting. Sprinkle gelatin on cold water and let stand for 5 minutes. Heat sugar and pineapple juice to boiling, stir into gelatin, and chill. Wash, drain, and mash berries; force through sieve. Add to pineapple mixture and pour into refrigerator tray. Partially freeze. Pour into chilled bowl and beat until fluffy. Fold in stiffly beaten salted egg white. Return to refrigerator tray and freeze until firm. Makes 6 servings.

## TANGERINE SHERBET

3 tablespoons sugar
1 cup tangerine juice
⅓ cup light corn syrup
1½ cups buttermilk
1 tablespoon fresh lemon juice

Set refrigerator control for fast freezing. Mix all ingredients and pour into refrigerator tray. Freeze sherbet until firm. Remove to cold bowl; beat with rotary beater until fluffy. Return to tray; freeze firm. Makes 4 servings.

## BRAZILIAN COCONUT SHERBET DRINK

Use 1 coconut for each helping. Prepare from 3 days to 1 week in advance.

With an icepick, a screwdriver, or any other sharp implement, make a hole in the soft end of a coconut. Insert a small funnel. Pour away all the coconut milk and use it for cooking. Fill coconut with light rum, brandy, or whiskey, but not Scotch. Plug hole with cotton. Stand upright in refrigerator. Serve ice cold in shell, with a straw.

## TURKISH STRAWBERRY SHERBET DRINK

Put 3½ cups hulled fresh strawberries in deep bowl and cover with 2 cups sugar. With a fork mash together berries and sugar. Let stand in refrigerator for 3 days, mashing once more each day. Strain mixture and bottle in sterilized bottles. Store upside down in a cool place. Serve diluted with water and chilled, or undiluted over ice. Makes about 2 pints.
**Note:** This sherbet may also be made with raspberries, apricots, lemons, grapes, oranges, or plums.

## TURKISH WATERMELON SHERBET DRINK

Peel a ripe watermelon and remove all seeds. Pound flesh or press through a food mill. Add sugar to taste and dilute with water. Strain, and serve chilled in glasses. Yield depends on size of melon.

**SHERRY**—A world famous Spanish apéritif or dessert wine, which comes originally from the Jerez district of southern Spain. The color varies from pale amber to dark brown and the taste from very dry to very sweet.

Sherry is made differently from other wines, and the making of it is a great art, practiced for centuries by skilled craftsmen. After the sweet juice from the pressed grapes has fermented in its own way, it is blended with many similar wines from different years. Brandy is added to the mixture and the beverage is allowed to age in special casks. Sherry improves with aging.

Various kinds of sherries have different names under which they are known and sold. The best pale dry sherries, used for apéritifs, are Amontillado, Fino, Vino de Pasto, and Manzanilla. The richest dark sweet sherries, drunk as dessert wines or like liqueurs, are called Oleroso, Amoroso, and Brown Sherry. Many vintners and shippers also sell sherries under their own brand names.

The best sherry comes from its original home in southern Spain. But excellent American sherries are made in California and upper New York State.

Sherry is used as an ingredient in such foods as soups, newburgs, sauces, and desserts. In cooking the alcohol evaporates and only the flavor remains. Cook-

ing sherry is the name given to a type of sherry sold in food stores which also contains salt. Its salt content should be kept in mind when adding it to any recipe specifying only sherry.

**SHIRR, TO**—In culinary usage the phrase describes a method of baking eggs. The eggs are broken into a buttered baking dish, seasoned with salt and pepper, and covered with a film of light cream. Then the tops are dotted with a little butter. The eggs are baked in a preheated moderate oven (350°F.) until the egg whites are just set, but the yolks are still soft.

**SHISH KEBAB**—A dish of meat, usually lamb, broiled on skewers. The name comes from the Turkish, *shish*, meaning skewer, and *kebap*, roast meat. Alternatively, it is spelled as shish kabob and it has come to mean as well a skewered combination of meat, fruits, and vegetables which may or may not have been marinated and seasoned with herbs and spices before broiling. The marinating is done to tenderize the meat so that it will cook quickly.

*Shish kebab* is a dish of Near Eastern origin. The nomad people roasted their meat in this convenient way over their campfires. Some, like the warriors of Georgia, a part of southern Russia, threaded the meat over their swords.

### SHISH KEBAB

Use lamb, mutton, or beef, cut into 1½-inch cubes. For vegetables, have any or all of the following: quartered tomatoes or whole small ones, slices of onion or whole parboiled small ones, cubes of eggplant or zucchini, and pieces of green pepper. Pieces of bacon can be used; bay leaves can be threaded next to the meat. A simple marinade is 1 part fresh lemon juice to 3 parts olive oil. When stringing meat and vegetables on skewers, push close together if you want meat rare and juicy; leave space between if you want it crispy and well done. It will take from 10 to 30 minutes to cook, depending on your taste.

**SHORT**—This word, applied to pastry, means very tender, flaky, and rich; usually desirable qualities, although a pastry can also be too tender or too short and fall apart. A short pastry is obtained by the use of a large amount of butter or other shortening.

**SHORTBREAD**—A thick cookie made with flour, sugar, sometimes eggs, and a proportionally large amount of butter or other shortening, which accounts for its name. It is of Scottish origin.

### SHORTBREAD

6 cups sifted all-purpose flour
1 cup sugar
2 cups (1 pound) soft butter
2 egg yolks

Mix first 3 ingredients very thoroughly with hands. Add egg yolks, one at a time, kneading dough well after each addition. Divide into 8 parts and roll each into a square or circle about ½ inch thick. Prick with fork. Bake in preheated moderate oven (350°F.) for 15 minutes. Reduce heat to slow (300°F.) and bake for about 30 minutes longer. Cut into eighths and return to oven until the edges are browned. Makes 64 triangles. Store airtight.

### NUT SHORTBREAD

1 cup soft butter or margarine
½ cup sugar
⅛ teaspoon salt
2½ cups sifted all-purpose flour
½ cup chopped nuts

Mix all ingredients thoroughly with hands; chill. Roll to ½-inch thickness. Cut with 1½-inch cookie cutters and bake in preheated slow oven (300°F.) for 20 to 25 minutes. Store airtight. Makes about 2 dozen.

### ORANGE SHORTBREAD

4 cups sifted all-purpose flour
¼ teaspoon salt
1 cup firmly packed light brown sugar
1 tablespoon grated orange rind
2 cups butter or margarine
1 egg white, slightly beaten
Candied cherries
Citron

Mix flour, salt, sugar, and orange rind. Cut in butter until crumbly. Work with hands until dough is smooth. Chill for 30 minutes. Roll ½ inch thick between 2 sheets of wax paper and cut with floured cutter. Brush with egg white. Cut candied cherries several times to form leaves of poinsettias on each cookie. Make stems with slivers of citron. Put on ungreased cookie sheets and bake in preheated moderate oven (350°F.) for 20 minutes. Makes about 3 dozen.

**SHORTCAKE**—Although shortcake can be a biscuit, cake, or cookie with a short flaky texture, it is more usually taken to mean a rich biscuit that forms the basis of a delicious dessert with the addition of fruit or berries and cream or whipped cream. The dessert is called "shortcake," too. Some shortcake desserts, in fact, are made from spongecake in Maryanne shapes or in layers. They may be served individually or can be made to resemble layer cakes.

Shortcake is a native American dessert.

It is best exemplified by the strawberry shortcake. The true strawberry shortcake or any other shortcake should be made with a biscuit dough.

### STRAWBERRY SHORTCAKE

3 cups all-purpose flour
4½ teaspoons baking powder
1 teaspoon salt
¼ cup sugar
Dash of ground nutmeg
¾ cup shortening
1 egg, beaten
½ cup milk (about)
2 tablespoons melted butter or margarine
1 to 1½ quarts sweetened strawberries
1 cup heavy cream, whipped

Sift together first 5 ingredients. Cut in shortening with pastry blender. Combine egg and milk; add to dry ingredients, stirring until all flour is moistened. Work dough a little with hand. Press half into greased 8-inch layer-cake pan. Spread with melted butter. Add remaining dough, pressing evenly into pan. Bake in preheated hot oven (450°F.) for about 30 minutes. Remove from pan. Lift top layer from bottom and put sweetened berries between the two layers and on top. Top with cream. Makes 8 to 10 servings.

**SHORTENING**—Any fat, liquid or solid, used in pastry, dough, or batter for the purpose of making the resulting product flakier, richer, and more tender. Those most generally used are the hydrogenated shortenings (lard, butter, margarine) and the edible oils. Occasionally used are rendered chicken fat and bacon fat. When the term "shortening" is used in a recipe without further specification, it is generally the hydrogenated shortening which is meant.

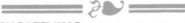

**SHOULDER**—A cut taken from the front section or forequarter of an animal. It is less tender than the hindquarter and requires tenderizing or longer cooking. Beef shoulder is usually referred to as chuck.

**SHRED, TO**—To tear or cut into small fragments or strips. This term is frequently used about the tearing up of such foods as dried beef or salt codfish.

**SHRIMP**—A ten-legged (decapod) crustacean, whose comparatively small size is responsible for its name; the Middle English *shrimpe* meant "puny person" and the name is akin to the Swedish *skrympa,* meaning "to shrink."

Shrimps vary considerably in size, ranging from the great Mexican and Gulf shrimps which swim in tropical waters, to the tiny half-inch creatures found in the cold waters off Scandinavia. The color of shrimps also varies but is some pale shade, usually brownish red or grayish green. The bright-pink color of the shell of cooked shrimps is due to a chemical change that takes place through exposure to heat.

Most shrimps available in markets are actually the abdomens and tails of shrimps. The heads, with their stalked eyes and feelers, are removed. The thorax, the front part of the body with the ten legs that give the shrimp its classification, has also been removed. What we see is the jointed rear section, consisting of a six-sectioned abdomen with five sets of elongated swimming paddles underneath, ending in a tail fin used to give a powerful impetus when the shrimp swims.

Shrimps are found along the Atlantic and Pacific coasts of the United States, as well as the Gulf coast. The Gulf shrimps are especially prized and provide the largest commercial supply. In southern states shrimps are often served for breakfast. The required accompaniment is hominy. One southern gentleman attested that during the shrimp season he had shrimps for breakfast every morning as well as a shrimp salad for Sunday-night supper and that he never tired of it.

The line of demarcation between shrimps, *scampi,* and prawns is not clearly defined. The difference between prawns and shrimps depends on where you live. In San Francisco and points north, prawns are large or jumbo shrimps; in Ireland they are Dublin Bay prawns, which M. André Simon, founder of The Wine & Food Society, claims are biologically the same as *scampi* and *langoustine,* from the waters of the Mediterranean, although he thinks that those of the south are larger and of a finer flavor. Then along comes famed Chef Conil, who says Dublin Bay prawns are *langoustines,* but not to be confused with *scampi.* To take the course of least resistance, let us allow that jumbo shrimps or prawns or *scampi* may all be cooked the same way, even if they have not been clearly established as relatives.

***Availability and Purchasing Guide***—Year round, fresh, frozen, and canned. Fresh shrimps are available in-the-shell; shelled; shelled, deveined, and cooked. They come in the following sizes:

Jumbo—under 20 per pound
Large—21 to 25 per pound
Medium—26 to 35 per pound
Small—35 and more per pound

Good quality fresh shrimps are firm to the touch and have a fresh, slightly sweet odor.

Frozen shrimps are available raw, in-the-shell; raw, in-the-shell but deveined; raw, shelled, and deveined; raw, shelled and deveined, individually glazed; cooked, shelled and deveined; breaded, uncooked; breaded, cooked; as well as in prepared dishes such as TV dinners, chow meins, creoles, curries, in cocktail sauces, stuffed and baked.

Canned shrimps come in jumbo, large, medium, and tiny cocktail size. They may also be sold in wet pack or dry pack. Shrimp paste is available canned.

Shrimps in cocktail sauce and shrimp paste are available in jars.

Dried shrimps are available in specialty food stores.

**Storage**—Wrap fresh shrimps in moisture-vapor-proof paper and store in the coldest part of refrigerator food compartment.
☐ Fresh, refrigerator shelf, raw: 1 to 2 days
☐ Fresh, cooked; and canned, opened, refrigerator shelf: 3 to 4 days
☐ Fresh, prepared for freezing; and frozen, refrigerator frozen-food compartment: 1 month
☐ Fresh, prepared for freezing; and frozen, freezer: 4 months
☐ Canned, kitchen shelf: 1 year

**Nutritive Food Values**—High in protein, low in fat.
☐ Fresh, 3½ ounces, raw = 91 calories
☐ Fresh, 3½ ounces, fried = 225 calories
☐ Frozen, 3½ ounces, breaded, raw = 139 calories
☐ Canned, 3½ ounces, wet pack, solids and liquid = 80 calories
☐ Canned, 3½ ounces, dry pack or drained solids of wet pack = 116 calories
☐ Shrimp paste, 3½ ounces = 180 calories

**Basic Preparation**

☐ **To Shell Fresh Shrimps**—For best results, shell before cooking. Hold tail end of shrimp in left hand, slip thumb of right hand under shell between feelers and lift off several segments of shell. Then, holding firmly to tail, pull out shrimp from rest of shell and tail.
☐ **To Devein**—With sharp knife, cut about ⅛-inch deep along outside curve of shrimp. Then lift out black vein, washing shrimp under water.
☐ **To Cook**—Shell and devein shrimps.

Drop into boiling salted water to cover; add 1 sliced small onion, 1 bay leaf, and a few celery leaves, if desired. Simmer, covered, for 2 to 5 minutes, or until pink. Drain and refrigerate.

Cook frozen shrimps in the same way, carefully breaking up block with fork. (Or follow package directions.)

☐ **To Broil or Fry**—Shell shrimps while raw and devein after slitting shrimps with a sharp knife. For butterfly shrimps, cut almost into halves and flatten. Dip into batter and fry in deep hot fat (375°F. on a frying thermometer) for 2 or 3 minutes, or until brown.

☐ **To Freeze**—Wash fresh shrimps thoroughly. Pack shrimps together closely. Freeze in small packages wrapped in moisture-vapor-proof wrapping material. Wrap tightly, excluding as much air as possible.

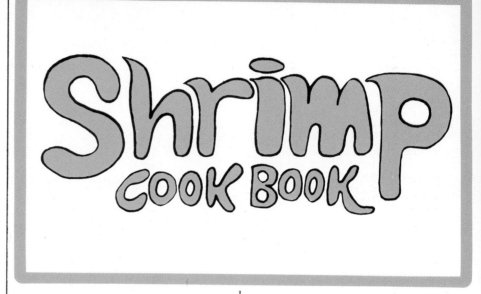

## APPETIZERS

### SHRIMP APPETIZER

1 cup mayonnaise
½ cup dairy sour cream
¼ cup ketchup.
1 tablespoon fresh lemon juice
Salt
1 pound cooked shelled shrimps

Combine mayonnaise, sour cream, ketchup, lemon juice, and salt to taste. This may be seasoned with chives, curry powder, dill, or garlic, according to taste. A variation is to add diced ripe avocado or minced celery or green pepper to the shrimps. For a party, serve shrimps on a large platter with sauce in the center. Serve individually in lettuce-lined dishes or in cocktail glasses, or heap on halved unpeeled ripe avocados. Makes 6 servings.

### SHRIMP COCKTAIL SUPREME

Arrange chilled cooked shrimps, preferably small ones, on lettuce leaves in cocktail glasses. For 6 cocktails make a sauce with 1 cup dairy sour cream, ¼ cup mayonnaise, 1 tablespoon fresh lemon juice, and 2 or 3 ounces caviar, black or red according to the state of the budget. Or snip 6 anchovy fillets into little pieces and use them instead. Pour sauce over the shrimps and serve garnished with a twisted lemon slice. Makes 6 servings.

### CHILI SHRIMP SQUARES

⅔ cup soft butter or margarine
1½ cups sifted all-purpose flour
½ teaspoon salt
1 teaspoon instant minced onion
1 teaspoon water
1 teaspoon steak sauce
1 cup finely chopped cooked shrimps
½ teaspoon chili powder
1 egg yolk
1 tablespoon milk

Cut butter into flour and salt. Soak onion for a few minutes in combined water and steak sauce. Add with shrimps and chili powder to first mixture, stirring with fork until blended. Roll out on floured board to ½-inch thickness and cut into 1½-inch squares. Put on greased cookie sheet and brush with egg yolk beaten slightly with milk. Bake in preheated moderate oven (375°F.) for about 30 minutes. Serve hot or cold. Makes about 2 dozen.

### MARINATED SHRIMPS

2 pounds jumbo shrimps, split
1 garlic clove, crushed
1 cup olive oil
¼ cup fresh lemon juice
⅛ teaspoon cayenne
1 teaspoon salt
2 green chili peppers, chopped
Thin slices of onion and orange

Cook shrimps and garlic clove in ¼ cup of the olive oil for 5 minutes. Discard garlic. Make a French dressing with the remaining olive oil, lemon juice, cayenne.

and salt. Add chili peppers and shrimps. Chill; serve garnished with onion and orange slices. Makes 6 to 8 servings.

### BROILED SHRIMPS AND PROSCIUTTO

Marinate peeled and cleaned shrimps in brandy. Wrap each one in a thin slice of prosciutto. String on skewers, alternating with small pieces of bay leaf, and broil over charcoal or in the oven for 3 minutes. Remove; roll skewers in melted butter, and then in crumbs; return to the broiler for 4 minutes. Serve with lemon wedges.

### TWICE-FRIED SHRIMPS FOR APPETIZERS

    2 pounds jumbo shrimps, shelled
      and deveined
      Seasoned all-purpose flour
    1 egg, slightly beaten
      Fat for deep frying
    ¼ cup butter
    ¼ cup olive oil
    2 large garlic cloves, mashed
    1 tablespoon minced parsley
    ½ teaspoon crumbled dried basil

Flatten each shrimp; roll well in flour (seasoned with 1 teaspoon salt and some pepper to each cup flour). Dip into egg, then fry in deep hot fat (370°F. on a frying thermometer) for 1 minute only. Drain. In a chafing dish or electric skillet melt butter and olive oil; add garlic, parsley, and basil. Heat for 1 or 2 minutes, add shrimps, and reheat. Serve on toothpicks. Makes 8 servings.

### SHRIMPS IN MARINADE

    2 pounds shrimps
    3 large red Italian onions, thinly sliced
    2 bay leaves, crumbled
      Salt and pepper to taste
      Hot pepper sauce
    1 lemon, thinly sliced
    ¼ cup capers
    ¼ cup chopped parsley
    2 teaspoons crumbled dried tarragon
      Olive oil
      Fresh lemon juice

Cook the shrimps in simmering salted water for 3 or 4 minutes. Drain and cool. Peel and clean. Arrange in a crock or dish in alternate layers with sliced onions, bay leaves, salt, pepper, and hot pepper sauce. Add lemon slices, capers, herbs, enough olive oil just to cover, and lemon juice to taste. Let the shrimps stand for 4 to 5 hours in the refrigerator to mellow. Delicious with thin rye-bread-and-butter sandwiches, radishes and cucumber salad. Makes 6 to 8 servings.

### SHRIMP PASTE

    2 pounds cooked shelled shrimps
    ½ cup butter
    ¼ teaspoon powdered mustard
      Pinch of ground mace
    1 tablespoon sherry
      Salt and pepper

Grind shrimps 3 times, or pound in a mortar. Cream with butter, mustard, mace, sherry, and salt and pepper to taste. Pack in a bowl or pot with a cover, and

**Shrimp Cocktail: Cooked Shrimps made with Cocktail Sauce**

chill. Serve with crackers for an appetizer, or for breakfast. Makes 6 to 8 servings.

### SHRIMP CANAPÉ OR SANDWICH SPREAD

- 1 package (8 ounces) cream cheese, softened
- 1 pound shrimps, cooked, cleaned, and ground
- ½ cup finely minced green onion
- ½ cup dairy sour cream or mayonnaise
  Salt and pepper to taste

Combine all ingredients. Add other seasonings if desired: garlic, dill, curry powder, chili powder, or such. Chopped almonds or olives may also be added. Spread on crisp crackers or toast triangles for an appetizer. Especially good on dark bread as a spread. Makes about 3 cups.

### SHRIMP AND ARTICHOKE APPETIZER

For a first course this is unexcelled. On individual plates arrange beds of very finely minced lettuce. On these lay large artichoke bottoms (canned or fresh cooked) and heap with shrimp salad. To each cup of diced shrimps add ¼ cup finely diced celery and ½ cup mayonnaise. Season with a few drops of fresh lemon juice and salt and pepper to taste. Press hard-boiled egg yolk through a sieve over the top of the shrimps. This is patterned after a specialty of one of San Francisco's well-known hotels, the Sheraton-Palace Hotel.

## SOUPS AND CHOWDERS

### SHRIMP BISQUE

- 1 pound shrimps
- 4 cups water
- 1 teaspoon salt
  Herb bouquet of parsley, crumbled dried thyme, and bay leaf
- 2 tablespoons uncooked rice
- 3 tablespoons butter or margarine
- 1 small onion, minced
- ½ cup minced carrot
- 2 tablespoons minced parsley
- 1 cup heavy cream
  Salt
- 1 teaspoon curry powder (optional)
  Croutons or finely minced parsley or chives

Combine shrimps, water, salt, and herb bouquet. Cook for 5 minutes. Strain broth and reserve. Shell and devein shrimps. Add rice to reserved broth and simmer until rice is soft. In the meantime heat butter. Cook onion, carrot, and parsley in it until soft. Add to broth along with the shrimps. Whirl in a blender until smooth, doing half at one time, or else grind shrimps before adding and force mixture through a sieve. Add heavy cream, and salt to taste and curry powder. Add milk or more cream to the desired consistency. Reheat or chill. If served hot, garnish with croutons; if cold, sprinkle with parsley. Makes 6 servings.

### Quick Shrimp Bisque

Combine 1 can frozen shrimp soup, thawed, ½ cup cleaned cooked shrimps, and 1 cup heavy cream; proceed as in Shrimp Bisque. Makes 6 servings.

### SHRIMP CHOWDER

- 2 pounds shrimps
- ¼ pound salt pork, diced
- ½ cup minced onion
- 2 cups diced potatoes
- 3 cups mixed milk and light cream

Cook shrimps as on page 1656. Drain, reserve broth, and shell and clean shrimps. Cook salt pork until brown and crisp. Reserve, and in the fat cook onion until soft. Combine onion, 2 cups of the shrimp broth, and diced potatoes. Simmer, covered, until potatoes are tender. Add shrimps, milk and cream, and diced pork. Heat through. Makes 6 to 8 servings.

### SHRIMP STEW

Cook 2 pounds of shrimps. Clean and cut into pieces if large. Add to 2 cups strained shrimp broth and 2 cups each of heavy cream and milk. Season. Heat; put in a tureen, add a little butter, and sprinkle with minced parsley. Makes 6 to 8 servings.

### SHRIMP SOUP ENGLISH STYLE

- 50 small raw shrimps
- ½ cup dry white wine
- 2 tablespoons butter or margarine
- 1 carrot, minced
- 1 onion, minced
- 1 small white turnip, peeled and minced
- 1 celery stalk, minced
- 4 cups fish stock
- 1½ teaspoons salt
  Juice of ½ lemon
- 1 teaspoon anchovy paste
  Croutons

Peel raw shrimps and devein. Wash and drain. Put shrimps into a saucepan. Add wine, cover, and simmer for 5 minutes. Press shrimps and liquid through a strainer or food mill or whirl in a blender. Melt butter and sauté vegetables in it until tender. Add fish stock and puréed shrimps. Add next three ingredients. Reheat slightly and serve sprinkled with croutons. Makes 6 to 8 servings.

### SHRIMP-OYSTER GUMBO

- 1 large onion, chopped
- 1 sweet red pepper, cut up
- ½ cup butter or margarine
- ⅓ cup all-purpose flour
- 6 cups water
- 1 can (19 ounces) tomatoes
- 2 teaspoons gumbo filé
- 1 box frozen okra, or 1 can (16 ounces) cut okra, drained
- 1 pound uncooked shrimps, peeled and cleaned
- 12 shucked oysters with liquid
  Salt and pepper
  Hot pepper sauce
  Hot cooked rice

Cook onion and pepper in the butter for

2 or 3 minutes. Add flour and brown lightly. Add water, tomatoes, and filé. Cover and simmer for 30 minutes. Add okra, shrimps, and oysters. Simmer for 10 to 15 minutes. Season with salt and pepper and hot pepper sauce to taste. Put a scoop of rice in center of each soup bowl and fill bowl with soup. Makes 6 servings.

### SHRIMP CAKES

- ¼ cup butter
- ¼ cup chopped onion
- 3 tablespoons all-purpose flour
- 1 teaspoon prepared mustard
- 1 cup light cream
  Salt and pepper
- 1 pound shelled cooked shrimps, chopped
  Cracker crumbs
  Butter
  Sauce

Melt butter and cook onion in it until soft. Stir in flour, mustard, cream, and salt and pepper to taste. When thick and smooth, add shrimps. Chill, form into cakes, roll in cracker crumbs, and sauté in plenty of butter. Serve with Sauce: Combine 1 cup mayonnaise, ½ cup chopped ripe olives, 1 tablespoon minced fresh dill, and 1 tablespoon fresh lemon juice. Makes 4 servings.

### SHRIMPS HAWAIIAN

- 2 pounds raw shrimps, peeled and deveined
- ¼ cup soy sauce
- ¼ cup pineapple juice
- ½ cup butter
- 6 slices of pineapple, sautéed
- ⅓ cup toasted slivered almonds

Marinate shrimps in soy sauce and pineapple juice. Sauté in butter. Serve on sautéed pineapple; sprinkle with toasted slivered almonds. Makes 6 servings.

### CREAMED SHRIMPS WITH AVOCADO

Make creamed shrimps by combining 2 cups cream or Béchamel sauce with each pound of cleaned shelled cooked shrimps, cut into pieces if large. Cover buttered toast with sliced avocado, ladle on creamed shrimps, and serve for breakfast or lunch. One pound shrimps makes 4 servings.

### SHRIMP CASSEROLE

- ½ pound mushrooms, sliced
- 2 tablespoons butter or margarine
- 1 medium onion, minced
- 2 large tomatoes, peeled, seeded, and chopped
- 2 tablespoons all-purpose flour
- ½ cup light cream
- ⅓ cup sherry
- 1 teaspoon Worcestershire
- ½ teaspoon hot pepper sauce
- 2 teaspoons salt
- ⅛ teaspoon pepper

**Shrimp-Oyster Gumbo**

3 pounds shrimps, cooked, peeled, and deveined
½ cup buttered soft bread crumbs

Sauté mushrooms in butter until tender. Add onion and tomatoes and cook for 10 minutes. Stir in flour and cream. Stir in sherry and seasonings. Add shrimps. Transfer to buttered casserole. Top with bread crumbs. Bake in preheated moderate oven (350°F.) for 20 minutes, or until top is browned. Makes 6 to 8 servings.

### SHRIMPS IN THE OVEN

Allow 6 jumbo shrimps for each serving. Split with scissors three-fourths of the way down the back, but do not remove shells. Arrange in individual dishes with the cut side spread open, and placed so that the wide part is in the center, the tails sticking up in the air. For each serving mix thoroughly:

3 tablespoons melted butter
2 tablespoons olive oil
¼ teaspoon salt
1 small garlic clove, minced
1 tablespoon white wine
2 teaspoons minced parsley

Pour this over the shrimps and bake in preheated hot oven (400°F.) for 8 minutes. Serve at once.

### SHRIMPS CREOLE

¼ cup bacon fat or other shortening
1 cup minced onions
½ cup minced green pepper
4 medium tomatoes, peeled and chopped
2 cups consommé or fish stock
½ teaspoon salt
Dash of cayenne
Herb bouquet of parsley, crumbled dried thyme, and bay leaf
2 pounds shelled raw shrimps

Melt bacon fat and cook onions and green pepper in it. Add tomatoes, consommé, salt, cayenne, and herb bouquet. Simmer, covered, for 40 minutes, stirring occasionally. Discard herbs and add shrimps. Simmer for 6 minutes. Correct seasoning and serve with rice. Makes 6 servings.

### SHRIMP EGG ROLLS

2 eggs
⅔ cup water
⅔ cup sifted all-purpose flour

½ teaspoon salt
Shrimp Filling

Beat eggs. Add water alternately with flour, sifted again with salt. Mix well. Lightly grease a 6-inch frying pan and pour in enough of the batter to make a very thin layer. Cook over moderate heat until just cooked through, about 1 minute. Pancake should not brown and it should be cooked on only one side. Cool. Put an equal portion of filling on each pancake, moisten the edges with slightly beaten egg, and roll, tucking in edges while rolling. Do not roll too tightly as the filling will swell a little. Pour an inch of cooking oil into a heavy frying pan and heat to 350°F. Cook egg rolls until golden-brown, about 5 minutes; turn and cook other side. Cool before freezing. To serve, heat while still frozen on a cookie sheet in preheated hot oven (400°F.) for 15 minutes, or thaw, and heat for 10 minutes. Makes 8 servings.

### Shrimp Filling

2 tablespoons finely diced carrot
2 tablespoons finely diced celery
2 tablespoons finely diced green onion
1 cup (one 5-ounce can) shrimps
1 tablespoon melted butter
½ teaspoon soy sauce
½ teaspoon monosodium glutamate
½ teaspoon sugar

Cook carrot and celery in salted water until tender. Drain. Add onion. Put shrimps through medium blade of food chopper. Add to vegetables with rest of ingredients. Mix well.

### CURRIED SHRIMPS IN PINEAPPLES

2 cups cooked cleaned shrimps
2 small fresh pineapples
2 tablespoons butter or margarine
½ pound fresh mushrooms, chopped
2 cups Thick White Sauce
2 teaspoons curry powder
Salt and pepper to taste
⅓ cup fine dry bread crumbs
⅓ cup grated Cheddar cheese

Cut shrimps into halves. Cut pineapples into halves and with a sharp knife scoop out meat. Cut pineapple meat into cubes. Mix pineapple cubes with shrimps. Melt butter and sauté mushrooms for 10 minutes. Add shrimps and pineapple cubes and cook for another 5 minutes. Add Thick White Sauce and curry powder. Season with salt and pepper. Spoon hot mixture into pineapple shells. Top with dry bread crumbs mixed with cheese. Place filled halves under broiler, covering pineapple leaves with foil to keep them from burning. Broil only until top is lightly browned. Serve with rice and chutney. Makes 4 servings.

### Thick White Sauce

Melt ½ cup butter or margarine. Stir in ½ cup flour. Gradually stir in 2 cups light cream or milk or evaporated milk. Cook over low heat, stirring constantly, until smooth and thick.

### SHRIMPS FLAMBÉS

Select jumbo shrimps and remove shells and veins. String on bamboo sticks. Dip into melted butter and grill or broil for 3 or 4 minutes on each side. Put on a platter, pour on 3 tablespoons hot brandy for each pound of shrimps, and flame. Serve on the bamboo sticks.

### SHRIMP KABOBS

Peel jumbo shrimps and remove veins. String on skewers, alternating with squares of bacon and pitted large ripe olives or cubes of pineapple. Dip into melted butter or cooking oil, and broil in a table broiler, over charcoal, or in the kitchen range, for 4 minutes on each side.

### QUICK SHRIMP SAUTÉ

1 cup butter
2 garlic cloves, crushed, or ½ cup minced onion
2 pounds raw shrimps, shelled and deveined
½ cup brandy
Salt and pepper
1 cup heavy cream (optional)

Heat butter and cook garlic in it until soft. Add shrimps and cook until shrimps turn pink. Add brandy, and flame. Season with salt and pepper to taste. Add cream if a sauce is desired. Serve at once on toast. Makes 4 to 6 servings.

**Note:** This is a fine dish to prepare at the table in the electric skillet or chafing dish.

### SWEET-AND-SOUR SHRIMPS

2 pounds cooked shelled shrimps
2 cups pineapple chunks
2 tablespoons grated green or crystallized gingerroot
1 green pepper, cut into long slivers
½ cup butter or cooking oil
1 cup pineapple juice
¼ cup sugar
½ cup vinegar
1 tablespoon soy sauce
2½ tablespoons cornstarch
½ cup water

Split shrimps. Combine shrimps, pineapple chunks, gingerroot, and green pepper. Heat butter and cook mixture in it for 2 minutes. Add pineapple juice, sugar, vinegar, and soy sauce. Mix cornstarch with water to make a paste. Stir into shrimp mixture and cook over medium heat, stirring constantly, until thick and clear. Serve with boiled rice. Makes 6 to 8 servings.

### SHRIMP CURRY

2 pounds shrimps
3 tablespoons butter or margarine
1 cup chopped onions
1 garlic clove, mashed
1 teaspoon salt
3 tablespoons all-purpose flour
2 tablespoons (or more) curry powder
1 cup canned whole tomatoes or peeled fresh tomatoes, chopped
Juice of ½ lemon

Salt and pepper to taste

Cook shrimps in water for 2 to 5 minutes according to directions on page 1656. Drain, and reserve 3 cups of the broth. Heat butter and cook onions in it until soft. Stir in garlic, salt, flour, and curry powder. Cook, stirring constantly, for 2 minutes. Add tomatoes, lemon juice, and reserved shrimp broth. Simmer, covered, for 10 minutes. Add shrimps and heat through thoroughly. Season with salt and pepper and add more curry powder if desired. Serve with rice and condiments, such as raisins plumped in sherry, French-fried onions, nuts, coconut or toasted coconut chips, crumbled crisp bacon, chutney, sliced or fried bananas, and chopped green onions. Makes 8 servings.

### SHRIMP SAMBAL

This is to serve with a curry, as one of the condiments. Shred 1 pound cooked shrimps and cook in 3 tablespoons butter for a few minutes. Add ½ cup grated coconut, 3 chopped green chilies, 2 pressed garlic cloves, and 1 tablespoon grated green gingerroot. Add salt to taste and chill before serving.

### SHRIMPS TERIYAKI

Split shrimps up the back with scissors and pull out the sand veins. Marinate in equal parts of pineapple juice, soy sauce, and bland cooking oil. Thread each shrimp onto a split bamboo or wooden stick that has been soaked in water. Broil or grill for 3 or 4 minutes on each side, and serve on the sticks.

### CHINESE FRIED SHRIMPS

Select large or jumbo shrimps and remove shells but not tails. Split down the back and pull out veins. Flatten with the bottom of a glass. Make a batter by beating 3 eggs and adding 1 cup milk, 1 cup all-purpose flour, 2 tablespoons cornstarch, 3 tablespoons cornmeal, and 1 teaspoon salt. Holding by the tail, dip each shrimp into the batter, then drop into deep hot fat (375°F. on a frying thermometer), and cook until brown. Drain on paper towels. The Chinese like to serve hot mustard and ketchup with these, putting one on each half of a small butter chip. The mustard is made by mixing powdered mustard with stale beer until the sauce is of the proper consistency.

■ **Variation**—Another quick way with fried shrimps is to dip them into mayonnaise (not salad dressing) and then roll them in crumbs before frying as above. This method allows for numerous variations. The mayonnaise may be flavored with any herb or spice, or the shrimps may be dipped into chopped nuts or grated cheese before the final breading. Or dip the shrimps first into mayonnaise, then into 2 parts crumbs to 1 part grated Parmesan cheese.

### GARLIC-GINGER SHRIMPS

Split shrimps up the back with scissors and pull out the sand veins. Make a marinade of equal parts of sherry or sake, soy sauce, and peanut oil or sesame oil, to which a pressed garlic clove and 1 tablespoon grated fresh or crystallized gingerroot have been added. Marinate for 3 to 4 hours, turning occasionally. Thread each shrimp on a split bamboo or wooden stick that has been soaked in water. Broil or grill for 3 or 4 minutes on each side, and serve on the sticks. Hot towels or finger bowls are needed. The shrimps can be peeled before cooking and served on picks, but they aren't quite as pretty, although they are delicious.

### SHRIMP JAMBALAYA

    2 tablespoons ham fat or lard
    2 tablespoons all-purpose flour
    1 cup chopped ham
    ½ cup chopped onion
    1 garlic clove, minced
    2 pounds raw shrimps, shelled and
      deveined
    2 cups canned whole tomatoes or fresh
      tomatoes, peeled and chopped
      Pinch of cayenne
    1½ cups raw rice
    ½ teaspoon crumbled dried thyme
    2 teaspoons chili powder
    1 teaspoon salt
      Boiling water

In deep heavy saucepan heat ham fat and brown flour in it. Add ham, onion, garlic clove, and shrimps. If shrimps are very large, cut into pieces. When onion begins to turn golden, add tomatoes, cayenne, rice, thyme, chili powder, salt, and enough boiling water to moisten mixture. Simmer, covered, until rice is tender, stirring occasionally with a fork. Check frequently to see if additional boiling water is needed as rice absorbs moisture. The jambalaya should be moist, but not mushy or soupy. Serve with a tossed green salad and a dessert. Makes 8 servings.

### DEVILED SHRIMPS

    5 tablespoons butter
    ¼ cup all-purpose flour
    ½ teaspoon paprika
    ⅛ teaspoon pepper
    ½ teaspoon powdered mustard
    1 teaspoon grated onion
    1½ cups milk
    1½ cups cooked cleaned shrimps
    1 pimiento, minced
    ½ cup sliced stuffed olives
    2 tablespoons dry white wine
      Salt to taste
    1 to 2 tablespoons fine dry crumbs

Melt ¼ cup butter; blend in next 5 ingredients. Gradually add milk and cook, stirring constantly until thickened. Add remaining ingredients, except crumbs. Pour into shallow 1-quart baking dish and top with crumbs. Dot with 1 tablespoon butter. Bake in preheated hot oven (400° F.) for 15 minutes, or until crumbs are browned. Makes 4 servings.

### SHRIMPS COOKED IN BEER

Shell and devein shrimps before cooking. Drop shrimps into boiling beer and water, using 3 parts stale beer to 1 part water. Use 1 tablespoon salt for each quart water, a few peppercorns, 1 or 2 bay leaves, and a sprinkling of celery seeds. Simmer, covered, for 2 to 5 minutes, or until pink. Drain, cool, and serve as is. **Note:** No sauce is needed when shrimps are cooked this way. When cooking shrimps in water, try adding some of the herb-combination products sold especially for shrimps.

### GRILLED JUMBO SHRIMPS, VENETIAN STYLE

    2 pounds raw jumbo shrimps
    1 garlic clove, crushed
      Pepper to taste
      Juice of 1 lime
    ¼ cup olive oil
      Garlic Butter

With scissors or sharp knife, split each shrimp shell on underside down to tail; try not to cut meat. Put shrimps in bowl with next 4 ingredients. Stir well to coat shrimps. Cover and refrigerate for at least 2 hours. Push onto skewers and grill 6 inches from heat over low charcoal fire, turning frequently. This takes about 15 minutes. If grilling in broiler, remove shells first. Serve with Garlic Butter. Makes 4 servings.

### Garlic Butter

Mix ½ cup melted butter, 1 teaspoon Worcestershire, 1 tablespoon fresh lemon juice, ¼ teaspoon hot pepper sauce, 1 mashed garlic clove, and salt to taste. Serve in saucers as a dip for shrimps.

### SHRIMPS CACCIATORE

    1 pound raw shrimps, shelled and
      cleaned
    1 medium onion, minced
    ½ medium green pepper, minced
    2 garlic cloves, minced
    ¼ cup olive oil
    2⅓ cups (one 1-pound, 3-ounce can)
      tomatoes
    1 can (10¾ ounces) spaghetti sauce
      with mushrooms
    ½ cup dry red wine
    2 teaspoons salt
    ¼ teaspoon pepper
    ¼ teaspoon ground allspice
    1 bay leaf, crumbled
    ¼ teaspoon ground thyme
      Dash of cayenne
      Hot cooked spaghetti

Put shrimps in salted cold water; bring to boil. Drain. Cook onion, green pepper, and garlic in oil for 5 minutes. Add remaining ingredients except shrimps and spaghetti. Simmer, uncovered, for about 20 minutes. Add shrimps, and heat. Serve on spaghetti. Makes 6 servings.

### SHRIMP POTPIE

    1 can (4 ounces) chopped mushrooms,
      drained
    1 small onion, minced
    5 tablespoons butter or margarine

1 pound shrimps, cooked
3 tablespoons all-purpose flour
1 teaspoon salt
⅛ teaspoon pepper
2 cups milk
1 tablespoon chopped parsley
1 cup cooked diced potatoes
½ cup cooked green peas
Standard pastry (recipe using 1 cup flour)

Cook mushrooms and onion in 2 tablespoons of the butter for 5 minutes; add shrimps. Prepare white sauce with remaining butter, the flour, salt, pepper, and milk. Pour over shrimp mixture and add remaining ingredients except pastry. Turn into 1-quart casserole; top with pastry. Bake in preheated hot oven (425° F.) for about 20 minutes. Makes 4 servings.

### INDIAN SHRIMP BALLS

3 cups (3 cans, 4½ ounces each) cooked deveined shrimps
1 tablespoon instant minced onion
1 tablespoon water
2 eggs
1 teaspoon ground coriander
½ teaspoon each of ground cuminseed, powdered mustard, and ground turmeric
1 teaspoon salt
⅛ teaspoon garlic powder
3 tablespoons all-purpose flour
⅓ cup water
Cooking oil or melted shortening
Curry Sauce
¼ cup evaporated milk or coconut milk
1 teaspoon fresh lemon juice

Put shrimps through food chopper twice, using finest blade. Soften instant minced onion in 1 tablespoon water, and add. Blend in eggs, spices, and flour. Mix until of almost pastelike consistency. Add water and cook for 5 minutes, or until mixture almost sticks to the pan. Shape into balls 1½ inches in diameter. Brown in hot oil. Drain. Add to Curry Sauce. Cook gently for 5 minutes. Add milk and heat for 1 to 2 minutes. Do not stir, to prevent breaking shrimp balls. Add lemon juice and serve on hot cooked rice. Makes 6 servings.

**Note:** For cocktail size, make ¾-inch balls and serve on toothpicks.

#### Curry Sauce

¼ cup instant onion flakes
3 tablespoons water
2 tablespoons cooking oil or shortening
1¼ teaspoons curry powder
⅛ teaspoon garlic powder
¾ teaspoon salt
1¼ cups water

Soften onion flakes in 3 tablespoons water. Fry in oil until onion begins to brown. Add curry powder and garlic powder. Stir and cook for 1 to 2 minutes. Add salt and water. Cook, uncovered, for 10 minutes to form a medium-thick sauce. Makes about 1½ cups.

### SHRIMPS WITH DILL AND MUSHROOMS

1 pound shrimps
½ cup butter
1 pound mushrooms, sliced
½ cup all-purpose flour
¼ cup dry white wine
2½ cups milk
½ cup heavy cream
1 tablespoon chopped fresh dill or dillweed
Salt and pepper
1 tablespoon brandy (optional)

Cook shrimps as directed on page 1656. Shell, devein, and if large, cut into pieces. Melt 1 tablespoon of the butter. Sauté mushrooms in it until soft. Melt remaining butter. Stir in flour and cook until golden. Gradually stir in wine, milk, and cream. Cook, stirring constantly, until thick and smooth. Stir in dill and salt and pepper to taste. Combine shrimps, mushrooms, and sauce. Add brandy, if desired. Heat in top part of a double boiler over hot water; serve on rice, toast, or toasted English muffins. Makes 6 servings.

## SALADS

### SHRIMP AND CELERY SALAD

2 cups cooked shrimps, chilled
1 cup sliced celery
1 tablespoon minced onion
1 tablespoon fresh lemon juice
½ cup mayonnaise
Salt and pepper to taste
Salad greens

Cut shrimps into halves lengthwise and mix with remaining ingredients except greens. Serve on greens. Makes 4 servings.

### EXOTIC SHRIMP SALAD

2 pounds shrimps, cooked and shelled
1 cup sliced water chestnuts
¼ cup minced green onions
¼ cup minced celery (white part only)
1 cup mayonnaise
2 teaspoons curry powder
2 tablespoons soy sauce
Lettuce, litchi nuts, toasted slivered almonds

Combine shrimps, water chestnuts, green onions, celery, mayonnaise, curry powder, and soy sauce; toss well. Pile in nests of lettuce and garnish with canned litchi nuts. Sprinkle with toasted slivered almonds. Makes 6 servings.

### SHRIMP MACARONI SALAD

1½ cups uncooked elbow or other macaroni
¾ cup diced celery
¼ cup sliced green onions
3 radishes, sliced
½ cup mayonnaise
1 tablespoon vinegar
1 teaspoon prepared mustard
½ teaspoon celery seeds
2 cans (4½ ounces each) shrimps, drained and rinsed
Seasoned salt and pepper to taste
Salad greens

Cook, drain, and cool macaroni. Mix with remaining ingredients except greens. Chill until ready to serve. Serve on greens. Makes 4 to 6 servings.

**Note:** Make this in advance to blend flavors.

### SHRIMP-GRAPEFRUIT SALAD

1 pound shrimps, cooked, shelled, and deveined
½ cup minced celery
1½ cups grapefruit sections, coarsely chopped and drained
½ cup mayonnaise, or more to taste
4 grapefruit shells
Additional grapefruit sections
Shredded salad greens

Combine shrimps, celery, grapefruit sections, and mayonnaise, and blend thoroughly. Pile into grapefruit shells. Decorate with additional grapefruit sections. Serve shells on a bed of shredded salad greens. Makes 4 servings.

**SHRUB**—A beverage made from liquor, fruit juice, fruit rind, and sugar. The combination is mixed together and aged in crockery, glass, or wood containers and then strained. It is often served iced, diluted with plain or carbonated water. A nonalcoholic version may be made from acidulated fruit juice and iced water.

The eager guesser who follows up the romantic connotations of the name "shrub" may decide that the beverage was first drunk at garden parties or that the original fruit for shrub was grown on a bush. Actually, the history of the word is a great deal more prosaic. It comes from the Arabic *sharab,* meaning "drink" which is also the root of the word sherbet.

Any kind of fruit may be used to make shrub. In earlier days in America it was usually combined with brandy or rum. One 1836 recipe for Currant Shrub by a Charlottesville cook declares: "The Shrub is indifferent unless the Rum is good."

One of the advantages of shrub as a punch in Colonial days was that it kept well throughout the year because of the alcohol it contained. An 1831 Virginia cook book promises that their Cherry Shrub "will keep all Summer, in a dry cool Place, and is delicious mixed with water."

Another old recipe, for a nonalcoholic Shrub, is "frosted," that is, served in small glasses with an Orange Sherbet topping. The recipe calls for juice from lemons, oranges, pineapple, and "pickled Fruit" which are mixed with a sugar-spice syrup. The name "shrub" is really just a reminder of older days and recipes. Most old-time fruit drinks—shrubs, bounces, flips—are scarcely distinguishable from each other in ingredients.

### SHRUB

Thin peel of 2 lemons
1½ cups fresh orange juice

½ cup fresh lemon juice
2 quarts rum
4½ cups sugar
5 cups water

Put lemon peel, orange juice, lemon juice, and rum in a large covered jar or crock. Let stand for 2 days. Dissolve sugar in the water and add to first mixture. Remove lemon peel. Let mixture stand for 12 days before bottling. Makes about 4½ quarts.

**SHUCK**—An outer covering such as a husk, pod, or shell. Corn is shucked by having the husk stripped from it. Oysters are shucked by being removed from their shells.

**SIDE**—In culinary terms, a side is one-half of the body of an animal, as a side of beef. Salt pork or bacon is often referred to as "side meat."

**SIFT, TO**—To put dry ingredients such as flour, sugar, baking powder, baking soda, confectioners' sugar, or spices through a very fine sieve or sifter to aerate them.

Sifting should be done before measuring since these ingredients pack down and do not measure accurately if not sifted. After sifting they are measured by spooning them lightly into a measuring cup. The top of the cup is leveled with a knife. Then the dry ingredients are sifted again to blend them properly.

Confectioners' sugar is sifted to prevent lumps. In making angel food or spongecake the dry ingredients are sifted three times to incorporate as much air as possible since these cakes are dependent for their success on a large amount of air in the batter.

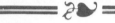

**SIMMER, TO**—To cook a food in water or other liquid at just below the boiling point. Usually this is done slowly and gently for a long period of time. It is a preferred method for many foods that would be toughened by higher heat, such as shrimps or eggs, and for delicate foods that would separate into pieces through the violent motion of rapidly boiling water, such as fish. Soups are simmered to develop the richest flavor, sauces are simmered until of the desired consistency, tough meats are simmered until tender, dried fruits until plump, etc.

**SINGE, TO**—To remove the remaining down, feathers, or pin feathers from a plucked fowl or the bristles from a pig, by exposing them to a flame, or to a hot iron, often one especially made for the purpose.

**SKATE**—A salt-water fish with huge wing-like pectoral fins, a broad flattened body, and a slender elongated tail. It belongs to the ray family of which there are a number of varieties in Atlantic and Pacific waters. Skates can grow very large; the common gray skate of Europe, a popular food fish, can reach a weight of 100 pounds. The body is bony and it is the fins which are used for cooking. The flesh is gelatinous, and it has a delicate and distinctive flavor.

Skate is generally poached and served with brown butter sauce or with tomato sauce. It is eaten somewhat differently from other fish. The flesh is scraped off the wings with knife and fork in long strips rather than cut through.

*Availability*—Available fresh during the fall and winter months in fish markets on the east and west coasts.

*Storage*—See Red Snapper, page 1540.

*Caloric Value*

☐ 3½ ounces, raw = 98 calories
**Basic Preparation**—See Red Snapper, page 1540.

#### SKATE WITH BROWN-BUTTER-AND-CAPER SAUCE

Cut large-size wings into serving pieces and use small wings whole. Poach skate in Simple Court Bouillon for a few minutes. Drain and dry thoroughly. Put fish in serving dish. Pour Brown-Butter-and-Caper Sauce over it. Serve immediately.

##### Simple Court Bouillon

Combine 1 quart water, 3 tablespoons fresh lemon juice or 1 tablespoon vinegar, and 1½ teaspoons salt. Bring to a boil and cook for 3 minutes before using for poaching fish.

##### Brown-Butter-and-Caper Sauce

Heat butter until well browned. Season with fresh lemon juice to taste. Add capers, about 1 tablespoon for each 1 cup melted butter.

**SKEWER**—A thin pin or rod of wood or metal. It is used for fastening meat or poultry during roasting in order to keep its shape. Small pieces of meat, vegetables, and fruit are also strung on skewers for broiling such dishes as *shish kebab*.

**SKIM, TO**—In culinary usage the phrase means to remove the top layer from a food or beverage. This layer may be referred to as "crust," "foam," "froth," or "scum." The most common examples are the froth which rises to the top of jam or jelly during cooking, the cream which rises to the top of unhomogenized milk, the fat and/or froth on soups and stews, the fat on gravies and sauces, and the crust or surface which solidifies on puddings.

**SKIN, TO**—To strip or peel the skin from a food, either with a knife or with the hands.

**SLICE, TO**—To cut thin flat pieces from a food with a knife.

**SLIVER**—A long slender piece of meat, cheese, pie, etc. "To sliver" means to slice foods into small thin strips. Blanched almonds are slivered; meats, firm fruits, and vegetables are slivered for salads, soups, creamed dishes, etc.; garlic can be slivered and forced into meats.

Foods can be slivered with a sharp knife and also on the coarse blade of a grater.

**SLOE**—The fruit of the blackthorn, *Prunus spinosa,* which grows wild in woods and hedges in most parts of the British Isles. The sloe, in French it is called *prunelle,* is edible but not usually picked to be eaten. Its chief use is to flavor sloe gin.

In the United States the name sloe is also given to the fruit of the native plum tree (*Prunus americana*) which is occasionally used for jams, jellies, and conserves. The fruit of the American tree is small and bitter and generally yellow or reddish-yellow in color.

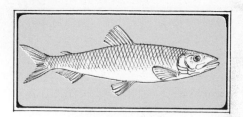

**SMELT**—Any of several small fish belonging to the family *Osmeridae*. Their backs are greenish and translucent, sides and belly are silvery; a school of smelts gives the impression of streaking silver. Smelts live in both Pacific and Atlantic coastal waters. They are a migrating fish and they ascend rivers and lakes to spawn. The name is also used for various silversides of the family *Atherinidae,* which resemble the true smelt, notably the jack smelt and top smelt found along the Pacific coast.

Their flesh is delicate, rich, and oily, so much so that the Indians of the Pacific coast used to dry the fish and burn them for light, and called them "candlelight fish."

*Availability*—Fresh smelts are available from September to May. Frozen and canned smelts are available year round.

*Purchasing Guide*—See Red Snapper, page 1540.

*Storage*—Wrap in moisture- vapor-proof paper and store in coldest part of refrigerator.

☐ Fresh, refrigerator shelf: 1 to 2 days
☐ Fresh, prepared for freezing; and frozen, refrigerator frozen-food compartment: 1 month
☐ Fresh, prepared for freezing; and frozen, freezer: 4 months

*Nutritive Food Values*—Contain some calcium, large amount of phosphorus, some thiamine, riboflavin, vitamin A, and a small amount of niacin.

☐ Fresh, 3½ ounces, raw = 91 calories
☐ Canned, 3½ ounces, solids and liquid = 200 calories

*Basic Preparation*—Smelts can be boned or not boned before broiling or frying. If boned uncooked, split the fish in the usual manner at the back, remove the bone, and cut off the head. To bone them cooked, remove the head and backbone at one time.

☐ **To Broil**—Split and clean smelts. Brush with melted butter or margarine. Dip into milk or cream and roll in bread or cracker crumbs until well coated on all sides. Broil in the usual manner, basting with additional butter.

☐ **To Sauté**—Dip the cleaned and split fish into seasoned flour and sauté them quickly in hot butter or shortening. Serve with Sauce Tartare (page 1622) or fresh lemon juice.

☐ **To Fry**—The fish may or may not be boned. Dip smelts into crumbs, beaten egg, and crumbs again. Fry in deep hot fat (375°F. on a frying thermometer) for 3 to 5 minutes. Drain and season to taste.

☐ **To Freeze**—Clean fish and eviscerate. Wash thoroughly. Dip into solution of 1 tablespoon ascorbic acid and 4 cups cold water for 20 seconds. Drain, and wrap in moisture- vapor-proof wrapping, excluding as much air as possible. Seal.

#### SMELTS WITH CAPER SAUCE

2 pounds smelts
⅓ cup undiluted evaporated milk
⅓ cup all-purpose flour
⅓ cup yellow cornmeal
2 teaspoons salt
⅛ teaspoon pepper
 Fat for frying
¼ cup butter
 Juice of ½ lemon
1 tablespoon each of capers and minced parsley

Dip fish into evaporated milk, then roll in combined flour, cornmeal, and seasonings. Heat enough fat to cover the bottom of frying pan. Fry fish for 5 minutes on each side, or until well browned and done. Meanwhile, melt butter and add lemon juice, capers, and parsley. Pour over hot fish. Makes 4 servings.

**SMETANA, SMITANE**—This culinary term refers to dishes cooked with sour cream. *Smetana* is a Russian word meaning "sour cream," an ingredient much used in all Slav cooking. *Smitane* is the French version of the word.

**SMOKE, TO**—To preserve, or cure, by exposure to smoke. Foods smoked are meat, fish, poultry, shellfish, cheese, salt, and nuts. Nowadays some of these are not actually smoked but have a smoked flavor brought about by the addition of liquid or powdered "smoke." Meats, however, are still smoked with wood, actually a hardwood sawdust heated with an electric coil. There is no actual fire and a tremendous amount of smoking is done with a comparatively small amount of sawdust. The artificial liquids and powders used for "smoking" contain salt, charcoal, dextrose, spices, herbs, onion, and other powdered vegetables, monosodium glutamate, and papain.

**SMORGASBORD**—A word we have adopted from the Swedish *smörgåsbord* and a food custom we have adapted to our own style of informal service. The Swedish word derives from three words, *smör,* butter, *gås,* goose, and *bord,* table. The first two combined in *smörgås* mean bread and butter, or open sandwich, so bread and butter table it was, and it did contain that, but also a few other matters which were served, buffet style, as a first course, much as the Russian *zakuski* were served. In the United States the name, without its Swedish accents, is now used to denote an entire meal served buffet style, with all the dishes arranged to be selected from by the individual diner. It is a favorite party meal because of the ease of service and is well liked by hearty eaters, as the rule is that one may return as many times as he wishes to sample everything on the table.

#### SWEDISH SMÖRGÅSBORD

The *smörgåsbord* is perfectly suited to modern American living. In Sweden it is usually served as the first course, but in this country we like to make it the whole meal, and include hot dishes, dessert, and coffee.

A *smörgåsbord* can be as simple or as elaborate as you wish, but the table should always look colorful, bountiful, and inviting. To display dishes at different heights, try placing a box in the center of the table under the cloth, if the cloth is large enough, or on top and covered with napkins. Attention should be given to garnishes made with parsley, cress, fresh dill, olives and pickles, hard-cooked eggs, pimiento, tomatoes, oranges, lemons, cucumbers, radishes, carrots, turnips, beets, and such.

The food in a *smörgåsbord* should be eaten in a special order, as courses. One starts with bread and butter, sardines, anchovies, and herring, served, if desired, with small, hot boiled potatoes, flavored with dill. Next come the other cold fish dishes, such as lobster salad, fish in aspic, and smoked salmon. These are followed by helpings of cold sliced meats and vegetable salads. The hot foods are eaten next; then comes an assortment of cheeses. Swedish Applecake or fruit with Dream Cookies make good desserts. No need to overcrowd a plate, it's perfectly proper to take several trips to the table.

These recipes may be doubled, tripled, and so on, to serve larger groups.

#### JANSSON'S TEMPTATION

2 quarts thinly sliced potatoes
1 can (3½ ounces) Swedish boned anchovies, cut up
1 small onion, chopped
 Pepper
2 cups milk

In 2½-quart baking dish put alternate layers of potatoes and anchovies, ending with potatoes. Sprinkle each layer with onion and pepper. Pour milk over top. Cover, and bake in preheated hot oven (400°F.) for 30 minutes; uncover and bake for 30 minutes longer, or until potatoes are tender. Makes 12 servings.

### HERRING AU GRATIN

- 2 salt herring
- 8 medium potatoes, cooked and sliced
- 1 onion, chopped
  Pepper to taste
- 2 tablespoons fine dry bread crumbs
- ¼ cup butter

Clean herring and soak in water for at least 12 hours. Skin, and remove bones. Cut into ½-inch pieces. Arrange herring, potatoes, and onion in alternate layers in baking dish. Sprinkle each layer with pepper. Sprinkle bread crumbs over top and dot with butter. Bake in preheated hot oven (425°F.) for 30 minutes. Makes 12 servings.

### SALT HERRING SALAD

- 1 salt herring
- 2 cups diced cooked potatoes
- 1½ cups diced pickled beets
- ¼ cup diced sweet pickles
- 1 large apple, peeled and diced
- 1 small onion, minced
- 1 cup diced cooked veal
- ¼ cup vinegar
- 2 tablespoons water
- 1 tablespoon sugar
- ¼ teaspoon pepper
  Cream cheese
  Shredded hard-cooked egg yolk
  Apple wedges

Clean herring and soak in water for at least 12 hours. Skin, and remove bones. Cut into cubes. Mix herring, potatoes, beets, pickles, diced apple, onion, and veal. Toss lightly. Combine vinegar, water, sugar, and pepper; pour over salad ingredients. Toss lightly until all is well seasoned. Chill for several hours. Garnish with softened cream cheese put through a pastry tube, egg, and apple. Makes 12 servings.

### FISH SALAD IN CLAMSHELLS

*For 12:* Mix 2 cups chopped cooked fish (crabmeat, tuna, or lobster) with mayonnaise to moisten. Season to taste with salt and pepper. Put a spoonful into each shell half. Top with mayonnaise; garnish.

### SHRIMPS BOILED WITH DILL

Allow 2 or 3 large shrimps per serving. Wash and drop into boiling salted water to which a few sprigs of fresh dill have been added. Simmer for 3 to 5 minutes, or until pink and tender. Drain, and chill. Serve with Sharp Sauce, below.

#### Sharp Sauce

- 4 egg yolks
- 1 teaspoon salt
- ½ teaspoon pepper
- 1 tablespoon prepared mustard
- 2 teaspoons powdered mustard
- ½ teaspoon Worcestershire

Dash of hot pepper sauce
- 2 teaspoons sugar
- 3 tablespoons vinegar
- 1 cup salad oil
  Chopped chives

Beat egg yolks slightly. Add remaining ingredients except oil and chives. Beat until smooth. While beating, slowly add oil. Chill until serving time. Sprinkle with chopped chives. Makes 1½ cups.

### SALMON TROUT IN ASPIC

- 3 salmon trout (about 1½ pounds each) or other mild fish
- 4 cups water
- 1½ teaspoons salt
- 8 peppercorns
- 1 bay leaf
- 1 small onion
- 3 tablespoons vinegar
- 1 envelope unflavored gelatin
- ¼ cup cold water

Clean fish, but leave heads on. Combine remaining ingredients, except last two; bring to boil; add fish; cover, and simmer for about 10 minutes, or until fish flakes with fork. Lift fish to serving plate. Chill. Soak gelatin in the cold water, dissolve in 1 cup strained hot fish stock. When cold, pour over fish. Chill until serving time. Garnish. Makes 12 servings.

### OYSTERS IN ASPIC

- 18 to 24 oysters
- 1 envelope unflavored gelatin
- ¼ cup cold water
- 1 cup hot water
  Juice of ½ lemon
- ¼ teaspoon salt
  Garnishes

Simmer oysters in own liquid until edges curl. Chill; drain. Put in shallow dish. Soften gelatin in the cold water. Add the hot water; stir until dissolved. Add lemon juice and salt. When cold, pour over oysters. Chill. Unmold. Garnish as desired. Makes 12 servings.

### SEAFOOD SALAD

- 3 cups flaked cooked fish (cod, flounder, sole)
- 2 packages (1 pound each) frozen shrimps, cooked and chopped
  Juice of 1 lemon
- 1 cup chopped celery
- 2 tablespoons chopped chives
  Mayonnaise
  Salt and pepper
  Garnishes

Combine first 5 ingredients. Add enough mayonnaise to moisten, and salt and pepper to taste. Chill until serving time. Mound on chilled serving plate and garnish as desired. Makes 12 servings.

### JELLIED VEAL LOAF

- 1 veal shank
- 3 pounds boneless veal
- 6 cups water
- 1½ tablespoons salt
- 12 peppercorns
- 1 bay leaf
- 1 medium onion
- 3 tablespoons vinegar
- 3 whole cloves

Have butcher cut veal shank into 3 or 4 pieces. Put with remaining ingredients in large kettle. Bring to boil; cover, and simmer for 2½ hours, or until meat is very tender. Remove meat from stock, and when cold, force through coarse blade of food chopper. Cook bones in stock for about 30 minutes longer. Strain stock through cheesecloth. There should be 1 quart; if more, boil to reduce amount; if less, add water. Add ground meat, and cook for about 5 minutes. Pour into loaf pan (9 x 5 x 3 inches). Store in refrigerator for several hours, or overnight. Unmold; slice. Makes 12 servings.

### GLAZE FOR BAKED HAM

One half hour before ham is done, score and spread with a mixture of 1 beaten egg white, 1 tablespoon powdered mustard, and 2 teaspoons sugar. Sprinkle with 3 tablespoons fine dry bread crumbs. Bake in preheated moderate oven (350°F.) until well browned.

### COOKED VEGETABLE SALAD

- 8 cups cooked (four 10-ounce packages frozen) vegetables: carrots, peas, snap beans, Lima beans, etc.
- ¾ cup mayonnaise
- ¼ cup dairy sour cream
  Onion salt
  Salt and pepper

Combine cold vegetables with mayonnaise and sour cream. Season with onion salt and salt and pepper to taste. Makes 12 servings.

### MARINATED CUCUMBERS

- 3 or 4 cucumbers
- ½ cup vinegar
- ¼ cup water
- 2 tablespoons chopped parsley or dill
- 3 tablespoons sugar
- ½ teaspoon salt
- ⅛ teaspoon pepper

Peel and slice cucumbers very thin. Add remaining ingredients. Refrigerate for at least 2 hours before serving. Makes 4 cups.

### SWEDISH MEATBALLS

- 1 egg
- 1 cup milk
- ½ cup fine dry bread crumbs
- 3 tablespoons chopped onion
  Butter
- 2 tablespoons water
- 2 teaspoons salt
- ½ teaspoon pepper
- 1½ pounds ground beef
- ½ pound ground pork

Beat egg; add milk and bread crumbs; let stand for a few minutes. Brown onion in 2 tablespoons butter. Combine crumb mixture and other ingredients. When smooth, shape into 1-inch balls. Brown in butter, add the water; cover, and simmer for 20 minutes.

To make with gravy: Pour off all but 1 tablespoon fat; sprinkle 2 tablespoons flour over meatballs. Add 1½ cups milk and ½ cup cream; bring to boil. Cover; simmer for 20 minutes. Makes about 60.

### SWEDISH BROWN BEANS
3 cups dried brown beans
3 quarts water
2 teaspoons salt
⅓ cup molasses
⅓ cup vinegar

Wash beans and soak overnight in the water. Cook in same water for 2½ hours, or until tender, adding more water when necessary. There should be about 1 cup water when beans are done. Add salt, molasses, and vinegar; cook for about 20 minutes longer, stirring often. Makes 12 servings.

**Note:** If the brown beans are unavailable, kidney or pea beans can be used.

### SWEDISH APPLECAKE
2½ cups fine dry bread crumbs
1¼ cups firmly packed light brown sugar
1 teaspoon ground cinnamon
2 cans (1 pound, 4 ounces each) pie-sliced apples
2 cans (1 pound each) applesauce
Juice of 1½ lemons
½ cup butter
Custard Sauce

Combine bread crumbs, brown sugar, and cinnamon. Mix apples, applesauce, and lemon juice. In well-buttered baking pan (13 x 9 x 2 inches) put alternate layers of crumbs and apple mixture, with a good layer of crumbs on bottom and top. Dot each layer of crumbs with butter. Bake in preheated hot oven (400°F.) for 45 minutes. Serve warm or cold with Custard Sauce. Makes 12 servings.

**Note:** Thick homemade applesauce may be used in place of canned apples and applesauce, and whipped cream or ice cream served instead of Custard Sauce.

#### Custard Sauce
Scald 2 cups milk in top part of a double boiler. Beat 5 egg yolks; add ¼ cup sugar and ⅛ teaspoon salt. Pour milk gradually over egg yolks. Return to double boiler, and cook over simmering water, stirring constantly, until mixture coats spoon. Cool.

#### DREAM COOKIES
1 cup butter
1 cup sugar
1 teaspoon vanilla extract
2 cups sifted all-purpose flour
Pinch of salt
1 teaspoon baking powder
Blanched almonds, split

Cream butter. Add sugar and beat until fluffy. Add vanilla. Stir in flour sifted with salt and baking powder; mix until smooth. Form into small balls. Put on ungreased cookie sheet; press half almond on top of each. Bake in preheated slow oven (300°F.) for 20 minutes, or until lightly browned. Makes about 6 dozen.

## GARNISHES FOR SMÖRGÅSBORD

### LEMON, ORANGE, TOMATO, CUCUMBER, OR HARD-COOKED EGG
1. With sharp knife make diagonal cuts outside to center.
2. Twist to separate halves. Decorate cut sides with pimiento, capers, parsley, or sprinkle with paprika. Use singly, or spear an assortment on a skewer and stick into turkey, ham, etc.

### PICKLE FANS
Thinly slice medium-size sweet pickle lengthwise to within ¾ inch from end. Spread to form fan.

### SERRATED SLICES OR TWISTS
Use oranges, lemons, limes, cucumbers.
1. Cut away small lengthwise strips of peel.
2. Slice, use as is, cut into halves, or cut slices three-fourths way through center, then twist.

### SLICED VEGETABLE GARNISH
Thinly slice 1-inch pieces of carrot, cucumber, or whole radishes to within ⅛ inch of opposite side. Put in ice water for several hours to open.

### RADISH FLOWERS
Cut away sections of peel of radish to within ½ inch of bottom, or make crisscross cuts through radishes several times. Let stand in ice water for several hours to open.

### ROSES FROM BEETS OR WHITE TURNIPS
For beets: Parboil large beets for 10 minutes, or until skins slip off.
1. With sharp knife cut petal-shape scallops around lower end of beet; turn point of knife down and in.
2. Cut around beet, removing ¼ inch from sides above petals.
3. Start from a point ¼ inch above and midway between 2 petals of first row, cut down and in until knife touches tops of first row of petals. Continue around to form second row of petals.
4. Cut around beet, removing ¼ inch from sides above second row of petals, as in step 2.
5. Continue steps 3 and 4 until rose is complete, making 4 or 5 rows of petals depending on size of beet.
For turnips: Pour boiling water over white turnips and let stand for 5 minutes. Peel, and follow procedure for beets. To make pink roses, dip cut turnips into beet liquid or red food coloring. Wrap roses and refrigerate until serving time.

### DAISIES
With a sharp knife tip, cut out V-shape sections from edge of a slice of carrot, white turnip, or cucumber. Put a small

round of contrasting color in center; use carrot on white, ripe olive or black grape on color.

# AMERICAN SMORGASBORD

### MENU

SLICED COLD ROAST BEEF
AND TURKEY,
HORSERADISH COCKTAIL SAUCE
HAM BALLS WITH
SOUR-CREAM SAUCE*
PARSLEY RICE
BAKED BEANS
MARINATED VEGETABLE SALAD*
SLICED CUCUMBERS, RADISHES,
WATERMELON PICKLE
SLICED CHEESE: EDAM, MUENSTER,
CARAWAY, OR CHEDDAR
SEEDED BREAD STICKS, RYE BREAD
ASSORTED CRACKERS
BUTTER
CHERRY-PORT MOLD*
POUNDCAKE
COFFEE

Recipes for 12 servings are given for starred dishes. Use standard recipes for other dishes, or buy foods ready-prepared.

### HAM BALLS WITH SOUR-CREAM SAUCE
2 pounds ground cooked ham
½ cup minced onion
½ teaspoon pepper
2 eggs, slightly beaten
Sour-Cream Sauce

Mix all ingredients except Sauce and shape into balls, allowing about ¼ cup of mixture for each ball. Put in baking pan (13 x 9 x 2 inches). Bake in preheated hot oven (400°F.) for 35 to 40 minutes. Serve with Sour-Cream Sauce. Makes 12 servings.

#### Sour-Cream Sauce
⅓ cup butter or margarine
⅓ cup all-purpose flour
1⅓ cups water
2⅔ cups dairy sour cream
¾ teaspoon each of marjoram and dillseed
Salt and pepper

Melt butter and blend in flour. Add water, sour cream, marjoram, and dillseed. Cook, stirring constantly, until thickened. Cook for 10 minutes longer. Add salt and pepper to taste. Sauce can be kept warm over hot water. Makes 4 cups.

### MARINATED VEGETABLE SALAD

1 package (1 pound) frozen Lima beans
1 package (9 ounces) frozen green beans
1 package (1 pound) frozen green peas
1¼ teaspoons salt
⅛ teaspoon pepper
2 pimientos, chopped
1 tablespoon grated onion
3 tablespoons vinegar
1 cup mayonnaise
   Salad greens, tomato wedges

Cook Lima beans, green beans, and peas separately as directed on the package labels. Drain. Combine vegetables and add salt and pepper. Cool. Add remaining ingredients except greens and tomatoes and toss lightly. Chill thoroughly. Serve in bowl with a garnish of greens and tomato wedges. Makes 12 servings.

### CHERRY-PORT MOLD

1½ cups port
4 cups (two cans, 15 ounces each) pitted drained Bing cherries
2½ cups cherry syrup, drained from cherries
2 cups cold water
3 packages (3 ounces each) cherry-flavored gelatin dessert
   Sweetened whipped cream

Pour port over cherries and let stand overnight. Drain port from cherries and set aside. Combine cherry syrup and ½ cup of the water. Heat, add gelatin, and stir until dissolved. Add wine and remaining water. Chill until slightly thickened. Then fold in cherries and pour into a 2-quart mold or individual molds. Chill until firm. Unmold and serve with sweetened whipped cream. Makes 12 servings.

**SNAIL**—A land gastropod mollusk, greatly admired by the French and Italians as a table delicacy. Even the ancient Romans prized them and perfected the art of fattening them for the table.

France is the great snail-consuming country. Vineyard snails are the most popular, but since there are not enough of them to supply the demand, other varieties, including the *petit-gris* of southern France, are also used.

The Anglo-Saxon palate has never really taken to snail eating, but gourmets say that they love them. As a matter of fact, snails have very little taste of their own; they serve as a vehicle for a highly flavored butter sauce.

Snails are served in their shells. The final cooking is best done in specially grooved snail dishes which prevent them from rattling around as they would in an ordinary pan. Purists serve them with special snail forks and pincers that hold the shell as the meat is removed.

*Availability*—Fresh snails, live-in-the-shell, are available year round in fish markets in the larger eastern cities. The fresh snails available in retail stores rarely measure more than 1 or 1½ inches in diameter.

Canned snails and snail shells are available in specialty food stores.

*Storage*—Fresh live snails must be cooked immediately. They cannot be kept.

☐ Canned, kitchen shelf, unopened: 1 year

☐ Fresh, cooked; and canned, opened, refrigerator shelf: 1 day

*Caloric Value*

☐ 3½ ounces, raw = 90 calories

*Basic Preparation*

☐ **To Prepare Fresh Snails**—Soak in warm water just long enough to break the membrane that covers the shell. Any snails that do not have heads out of shells should be discarded. Bring remaining snails to a boil in salted water or Simple Court Bouillon, page 1663. Drain, and remove snails, using a small oyster fork or nutpick. Cut off tip of head and small black part at end of snail. Rinse with cold water or white wine. Wash shells if to be used in recipe. For stuffing snails see To Serve with Snail Butter, below.

☐ **To Prepare Canned Snails**—Put snails in deep bowl. Cover with lukewarm water; soak for 2 minutes. Drain. For 50 snails combine 1 cup water, 1 cup dry white wine, 1 teaspoon instant garlic, and 1 bay leaf. Cook until liquid is reduced to 1 cup; strain. Reheat and simmer snails in liquid for 3 to 5 minutes. Drain snails. Wash and dry snail shells. For stuffing snails, proceed as directed below.

☐ **To Serve with Snail Butter**—Put into each shell a piece of prepared Snail Butter (below) the size of a hazelnut and 1 snail. Press firmly. Spread more Snail Butter on the snail, so that only the Snail Butter shows on the opening.

The snails may now be chilled for later cooking or finished immediately. Place shells in snail pan or pack them closely into shallow baking pan. Place in preheated hot oven (425°F.) for a few minutes, or until heated through thoroughly. Serve piping hot.

### SNAIL BUTTER

½ cup butter
2 tablespoons minced green-onion tops
1 to 3 garlic cloves, mashed, or garlic to taste
3 tablespoons minced parsley
   Salt and pepper

Cream butter until soft. Beat in green onions, garlic, and parsley. Season with salt and pepper to taste. Mix until thoroughly blended. Makes about ½ cup.

**Note:** This garlicky well-seasoned butter is also good for broiled fish, seafood, and red meats.

### SNAILS FORESTIÈRE

24 mushroom caps
½ can (24) snails, drained
½ cup sweet butter
1 garlic clove, crushed and chopped fine
¼ cup finely chopped parsley
   Salt and pepper to taste

Broil or sauté mushroom caps. Fill each cap with one snail. Whip butter until soft. Add garlic, parsley, and salt and pepper. Place a dab of butter mixture on top of each snail and broil until butter has melted and mushrooms are hot. Makes 4 servings.

**Note:** No snail shells are required.

**SNAP BEAN**—A variety of the common garden bean, which includes both round and flat green and yellow or wax beans and the so-called Italian green beans. Snap beans are also called green beans or string beans. They are native to the New World, and both the North and South American Indians used them long before the white man came. From the Americas, these beans were transplanted to Europe and are now one of the world's most popular vegetables. Americans like snap beans that are large, but in Europe smaller beans are preferred. France and Italy grow inch-long green varieties that are incredibly tender and delicious.

*Availability*—Fresh snap beans are available year round from Florida, New York, New Jersey, and many other truck garden areas.

Canned green beans are sold whole, whole vertical pack, French style, and cut. Yellow beans are sold cut. Some green beans are packed in vinegar as dilly beans.

Frozen green beans are sold whole, cut, or Frenched. Yellow beans are sold cut. Frozen Italian green beans are also available.

*Purchasing Guide*—Buy fresh, crisp, firm beans that snap when broken. Young tender vegetables are characterized by pale-green or golden-yellow color with very small beans on the inside. Beans should be uniform in size and free from blemishes. Most beans grown today are stringless.

**Storage**

☐ Fresh, refrigerator shelf: 1 to 2 days
☐ Fresh, prepared for freezing; and frozen, refrigerator frozen-food compartment: 2 to 3 months
☐ Fresh, prepared for freezing; and frozen, freezer: 1 year
☐ Canned, kitchen shelf: 1 year
☐ Canned, refrigerator shelf, opened: 2 to 3 days

**Nutritive Food Values**—Small amounts of vitamin A, iron, and thiamine. Green beans have more vitamin A than yellow beans.

Caloric values which follow are given for an edible portion of 3½ ounces.

☐ Fresh green, raw = 32 calories
☐ Fresh green, boiled and drained = 25 calories
☐ Canned green, regular pack, solids and liquid = 18 calories
☐ Canned green, regular pack, drained solids = 24 calories
☐ Frozen green, cut style, boiled and drained = 25 calories
☐ Frozen green, French style, boiled and drained = 26 calories
☐ Fresh yellow or wax, raw = 27 calories
☐ Fresh yellow or wax, boiled and drained = 22 calories
☐ Canned yellow or wax, regular pack, solids and liquid = 19 calories
☐ Canned yellow or wax, regular pack, drained solids = 24 calories
☐ Frozen yellow or wax, boiled and drained = 27 calories

**Basic Preparation**—Trim beans, cutting off the tough ends, and cut beans into style desired. Cook, covered, in a small amount of water to which salt is added. Allow 15 to 30 minutes for whole fresh beans; 10 to 15 minutes for cut beans, fresh or frozen; and 8 to 12 minutes for Frenched beans, fresh or frozen.

☐ **To Freeze**—Use only young, tender, firm beans with no blemishes. Trim beans and cut into style desired. Blanch in boiling water for 2 minutes for Frenched, 2½ minutes for cut, and 3 minutes for whole beans. Chill in cold water for 3 to 5 minutes. Drain. Pack into containers, leaving ½-inch headspace. Seal. They can also be frozen on trays in a single layer and then poured into freezer containers for a loose pack.

### GREEN BEANS IN SOUR-CREAM SAUCE
1½ pounds green beans
    Salt
1 tablespoon minced onion
3 tablespoons butter
3 tablespoons all-purpose flour
1 tablespoon minced parsley
3 tablespoons fresh lemon juice
¾ cup dairy sour cream
    Pepper

Wash beans and cut as desired. Cook in small amount of boiling salted water until tender. Drain, reserving 1 cup of the liquid. Keep beans warm. Sauté onion in the butter for 2 or 3 minutes. Blend in flour. Add parsley and reserved liquid. Cook, stirring constantly, until thickened. Add lemon juice and sour cream; heat but do not boil. Season to taste with salt and pepper and pour over beans. Makes 6 servings.

### GREEN BEANS AND WHOLE ONIONS
2½ cups (one 1-pound, 4-ounce can) cut green beans
2½ cups (one 1-pound, 4-ounce can) whole onions
    Salt and pepper to taste
    Chopped pimiento (optional)

Drain liquid from vegetables and cook until reduced by one half. Add vegetables and salt and pepper. Add pimiento, if desired. Heat quickly, and serve. Makes 8 servings.

### HOT GERMAN BEANS
1 pound fresh wax beans or 2 cups (one 1-pound, 3-ounce can) wax beans
4 slices of bacon
1 onion
1 tablespoon sugar
¼ cup cider vinegar
⅛ teaspoon ground thyme
½ teaspoon monosodium glutamate
    Salt and pepper

Cook fresh beans in a small amount of salted water until tender. Drain; reserve liquid. Or drain canned beans, reserving liquid. Cut up bacon and sauté onion and bacon until onion is golden. Add liquid drained from beans. Cook until liquid is reduced to ¼ cup. Add next 4 ingredients and beans. Reheat, and season to taste with salt and pepper. Makes 4 servings.

### WAX BEANS WITH PIMIENTO AND PICKLE RELISH
2½ cups (one 1-pound, 4-ounce can) wax beans
½ pimiento, cut up
2 tablespoons pickle relish
    Salt and pepper to taste

Drain liquid from beans. Cook liquid until reduced by one half. Add beans and heat quickly. Add remaining ingredients and serve at once. Makes 4 servings.

### ITALIAN-GREEN-BEAN SALAD
1 package (9 ounces) Italian green beans, cooked
2 tomatoes, quartered
2 peeled medium potatoes, cooked, chilled, and quartered
    Salad greens
½ cup Basic Vinaigrette Sauce (page 1622)
1 tablespoon capers
2 tablespoons minced pimiento-stuffed olives

Arrange beans, tomatoes, and potatoes on greens in salad bowl. Pour Sauce over top. Mix capers and olives and sprinkle

on vegetables. Makes 4 servings.

### GREEN BEANS ORIENTAL
2 packages (9 ounces each) frozen French-style green beans
    Salt
1 can (19 ounces) bean sprouts
1 can (8 ounces) water chestnuts, drained and sliced
½ cup grated Parmesan cheese
6 tablespoons butter
2 tablespoons all-purpose flour
¼ teaspoon pepper
    Dash of cayenne
¼ teaspoon Worcestershire
2 cups heavy cream
1 cup finely chopped unblanched almonds

Cook beans in boiling salted water for 5 minutes; drain. Put in shallow 2-quart baking dish in alternate layers with bean sprouts, water chestnuts, and cheese. Melt 4 tablespoons butter and blend in flour, 1¼ teaspoons salt, the pepper, cayenne, and Worcestershire. Add cream, and cook until thickened, stirring constantly. Pour over vegetables, lifting mixture with a fork so sauce will coat all vegetables. Melt remaining butter, and add almonds. Sprinkle on top of mixture in baking dish. Bake in preheated hot oven (425° F.) for 15 to 20 minutes, or until heated and nuts are browned. Makes 8 servings.

**SNOWBALL**—In cookery, a snowball is a round cookie, cake, or ball of ice cream. The cookie or cake may be rolled in confectioners' sugar or frosted with white frosting and rolled in coconut to give a snowball appearance. Ice-cream balls are rolled in coconut and served with a chocolate or other sauce.

### COCONUT COOKIE SNOWBALLS
1 cup soft butter or margarine
2 cups granulated sugar
2 eggs
1 teaspoon vanilla extract
5 cups sifted all-purpose flour
1 teaspoon baking soda
2 teaspoons baking powder
½ teaspoon salt
¾ cup dairy sour cream
1 cup flaked coconut
    Colored sugar

Cream butter and granulated sugar until light. Add eggs and vanilla and beat well. Add sifted dry ingredients, sour cream, and coconut; mix well. Chill several hours. Shape into 1-inch balls and sprinkle with colored sugar. Put on ungreased cookie sheets and bake in preheated moderate oven (375° F.) for about 10 minutes. Makes about 6 dozen.

### VANILLA ICE-CREAM SNOWBALLS
Shape vanilla ice cream with a spoon or scoop into serving-size balls. Roll in flaked coconut and freeze until firm. To serve, pile in a chilled bowl or serve individually with chocolate or other sauce. (See Dessert Sauces, page 1628.)

**SODA**—Chemically, soda is a sodium compound of any one of many varieties. In reference to food it is most often sodium bicarbonate or sodium acid bicarbonate, a crystalline salt used in the manufacture of baking powder, carbonated beverages, and effervescent salts.

But in popular language, a soda is a drink made from carbonated water and flavored syrups and/or fruit, most often with the addition of ice cream. Ice cream sodas may have some milk added and may be topped with whipped cream, cherries and/or nuts.

**SODA CRACKER**—A plain white cracker, usually square and characteristically salted on top, made chiefly of flour, water, shortening, and a leavening agent. Although these crackers cannot be baked with home equipment, commercially made soda crackers are widely available. They are good served with seafood cocktails, salads, and soups, and crumbled for use as toppings on casserole dishes.

**SODA POP**—A bottled soft drink made with carbonated water and added flavoring, usually a sweet syrup.

**SODA WATER** (Carbonated Water)— A beverage charged with carbon dioxide under pressure, a process which produces a liquid which bubbles, fizzes, or sparkles when opened. The term does not include beverages in which the gas is produced within the beverage by the natural process of fermentation. The carbon dioxide in soda water is produced from sodium bicarbonate by the action of sulphuric or other acid. As a beverage, soda water is always cooler than plain water held at the same temperature because the escaping gas carries off part of the heat stored in the water.

Plain soda water is widely available bottled. It is used in combination with various flavorings to produce soft drinks, and combined with liquor for high balls and other alcoholic drinks.

*Fillets of Sole en Casserole*

**SOFT ROE or MILT**—See Roe, page 1558.

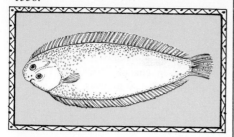

**SOLE**—A salt-water flat fish. The most important species, and the one most highly prized as a food fish, is *Solea vulgaris,* the true common sole, which is found only in European waters. It is an elongated oval in shape, is almost completely surrounded by fins, and varies in color from dark brown through pale gray, but is generally an olive-brown with blackish markings. The average size at maturity is one foot, but specimens twice that long are not uncommon. Its taste and texture are incomparable.

The best European sole is the Channel (Dover or English) sole. The lemon sole is another European species and does not provide as fine eating as the true sole.

French cooking has scores of recipes for preparing true sole in both plain and extremely fancy ways, with dozens of sauces. Yet for freshness and utter deliciousness, nothing beats a fresh Dover sole, grilled or broiled, served with a little butter and a squeeze of lemon.

Various related flat fishes belonging to other genera are fished in American waters and marketed as "sole."

***Availability***—Channel or Dover sole, generally frozen and high in price, is imported from England, Belgium, the Netherlands, and Denmark, and is available in large cities in the eastern part of the United States, and in some of the big cities in other parts of the country.

American "sole" or "lemon sole" is available year round, sold whole or in fillets, fresh or frozen.

***Purchasing Guide***—See Red Snapper, page 1540.

***Storage***

☐ Fresh, refrigerator shelf, raw: 1 to 2 days

☐ Refrigerator shelf, cooked: 3 to 4 days

☐ Frozen, refrigerator frozen-food compartment: 2 to 3 weeks

☐ Frozen, freezer: 1 year

***Nutritive Food Values***—Good source of protein, low in fat.

☐ 3½ ounces, raw = 79 calories

***Basic Preparation***—Wash fish and pat dry. Prepare as directed in recipes, cooking fish as little as possible to keep it firm.

### SOLE MEUNIÈRE

Coat fish or fillets with all-purpose flour. Cook over medium heat in hot butter until fish is browned. Turn once during cooking. Season with salt and pepper. Transfer to hot serving dish. Brown butter remaining in the pan and pour over fish. Sprinkle with a little lemon juice and minced parsley.

**Note:** This is the classic French way of cooking sole; it brings out the fish's delicate flavor.

### SOLE IN VERMOUTH

1 cup dry vermouth
1½ pounds sole fillets
4 egg yolks
⅔ cup butter or margarine
1 tablespoon heavy cream
Salt and pepper to taste

Heat vermouth in a skillet. Wrap fish loosely in cheesecloth and poach in the vermouth for about 10 minutes. Put fish on a broilerproof platter. Reduce vermouth to about ⅔ cup. In top of a double boiler combine egg yolks, butter, cream, and vermouth. Cook over hot, not boiling, water, stirring constantly, until thickened. Season. Pour over fish and brown quickly under broiler. Sauce may curdle slightly, but flavor is delicious. Makes 4 servings.

### FILLETS OF SOLE EN CASSEROLE

Few parsley sprigs, chopped
2 green onions, chopped
1 teaspoon salt
⅛ teaspoon white pepper
1 cup white wine
½ cup water
2 pounds sole fillets
3 tablespoons butter or margarine
2 tablespoons all-purpose flour
1 cup heavy cream
1 egg yolk

Put first 6 ingredients in skillet and bring to boil. Add fish and poach for about 10 minutes. Remove fish to a shallow broilerproof casserole; reduce liquid to 1 cup. In top part of a double boiler melt 2 tablespoons butter and blend in flour. Add fish liquid and half of cream. Cook, stirring, until thickened. Mix remaining cream and the egg yolk. Pour small amount of sauce over mixture, stirring. Pour back into double boiler and cook for a few minutes longer, stirring constantly. Add remaining butter, and pour sauce over fish. Brown under broiler. Makes 6 servings.

### HORSERADISH SOLE

Poach fish as in recipe for Fillets of Sole en Casserole. Serve hot with following sauce: Mix 1 cup dairy sour cream, 2 tablespoons grated lemon rind, 3 tablespoons prepared horseradish, and ¾ teaspoon salt.

### SOLE BONNE FEMME

6 fillets of sole
½ cup white wine
½ cup strong fish stock
Juice of 1 lemon
5 tablespoons butter
Salt and pepper
1 tablespoon all-purpose flour
2 egg yolks
½ cup sliced fresh mushrooms

Put sole fillets into a well-greased shallow casserole. Pour white wine, fish stock, and half of lemon juice over fish. Dot top with 3 tablespoons of the butter and sprinkle with salt and pepper. Bake in preheated moderate oven (350°F.) for 10 to 15 minutes, or until fish flakes. Drain juices from pan into a saucepan and thicken with a mixture of 1 tablespoon butter and the flour. Beat hot sauce into egg yolks. Sauté mushrooms in remaining butter with remaining lemon juice. When tender, add to the sauce. Reheat. Pour sauce over fish and put under broiler until sauce is golden-brown. Makes 6 servings.

**SORGHUM**—A genus of grasses with a large number of species, cultivated throughout the world for food, forage, and syrup. They are tall annuals, resembling maize, and they grow from three to fifteen feet tall. The grains are smaller and rounder than those of the true cereals such as wheat. The sorghums, although less nutritious than maize, require very little water and can be grown in regions where maize will not flourish.

Sorghums were among the first of the wild plants to be domesticated by man. They originated in Africa and Asia: Egyptian cultivation can be dated before 2200 B.C. and they were grown in China and India at an early date.

There are four main types of sorghums: grass, grain, broomcorn, and sugar.

Grass sorghums are used entirely for hay and pasturage. The grain sorghums, grown in the United States since 1874, include Durra, Milo, Shallu, Kaoliang

(Chinese sorghums), Feterita, and Hegari. The grain or seed is used for livestock food and the plants for foliage. Commercial uses include alcohol, beer, oil, and starch. In Asia, India, and Africa grain sorghums are a staple human food.

Broomcorns, grown in the United States since 1797, have a panicle with long branches, known as the "brush." These branches are used for carpet and whisk brooms.

The sugar sorghums did not flourish in the United States until 1853. They are tall and leafy and their canelike stalk contains a sweet juice which can be boiled down into a syrup. This syrup has been used as a molasses substitute. It is, indeed, often called molasses, although the true molasses is a by-product of the syrup of the sugar cane. In sorghum, the syrup is not crystallized into sugar, but rather used in a pure concentrated form. During the Civil War sugar was very scarce in the North, and sorghum syrup was used instead of molasses. Nowadays sorghum syrup is generally available only in the southeastern section of the United States.

### Caloric Value

☐ 3½ ounces = 257 calories

**SORREL or DOCK**—A hardy perennial herb which dates back to 3000 B.C. and still grows wild in Asia, Europe, and North America. Several of its varieties, which differ in shape of leaves and strength of flavor, are cultivated. All varieties are acid to some degree.

The mildest variety is dock (*Rumex Patientia),* also called spinach dock and herb patience dock. A tall plant, growing over five feet tall, its foot-long mild leaves are used in the spring as a salad green or potherb. French sorrel (*Rumex scutatus*) has shield-shape leaves and branches which tend to fall over. It has an acid sour flavor, but not so sour that it cannot

be used in salads. The most acid of the three plants is garden or belleville sorrel, also known as sour dock (*Rumex Acetosa).* Both its Latin and its popular name, sour grass, reflect its acidity. It has oblong green leaves, as long as four inches; their flavor is almost nonexistent in the early spring, but from this mild beginning they develop great acidity. Garden sorrel is used, as is French sorrel, for cream soups, for purées to accompany liver, cutlets, ham, lamb, and shad; for omelets, Swedish bread, salads; and with vegetables such as cabbage, lettuce, beet tops, or spinach. It is often used in Jewish cookery to make a sorrel soup, *schav.* The classic preparation uses a creamy sauce as the base for soup or a purée.

*Availability*—Sorrel is available in eastern markets in small supply all year round, as it is raised locally during the summer months and comes from Florida during the winter months.

*Purchasing Guide*—Buy sorrel with crisp clean leaves which are bright green in color. Avoid seedy or woody stems, yellowed or wilted leaves.

*Storage*—Wash and trim. Shake off as much of the water as possible and store in plastic bag in refrigerator or in vegetable compartment. If preferred, wash just before using.

☐ Refrigerator shelf or vegetable compartment: 2 to 3 days

*Nutritive Food Values*—Very high in vitamin A, with small amounts of calcium and phosphorus, and some vitamin C.

☐ 3½ ounces, raw = 28 calories
☐ 3½ ounces, cooked and drained = 19 calories

*Basic Preparation*

☐ **To Cook**—Remove stems and wash leaves thoroughly in warm water. Put leaves in kettle and cook, covered, for 6 to 8 minutes, or until tender, stirring once after 1 to 2 minutes of cooking. Add a little boiling water if necessary. The water that clings to the leaves may be enough. Drain if necessary and chop coarsely, if desired. Season with salt, pepper, and butter to taste. Serve as greens.

### SORREL SOUP

1½ cups sorrel leaves
2 tablespoons butter or margarine
6 cups water or bouillon
1 egg yolk
  Salt
6 slices of bread, toasted

Chop sorrel and wash thoroughly. Cook in a heavy saucepan, covered, until leaves are wilted. Add butter; when it is melted, add water. Simmer for 10 minutes. Beat egg yolk slightly and beat in some of the

hot soup. Add this mixture to remaining hot soup and reheat but do not boil. Season to taste with salt. Put a slice of toasted bread in each soup bowl and spoon soup over toast. Makes 6 servings.

### Sorrel Soup with Rice

Add ¼ cup uncooked rice to the soup and simmer for 30 minutes. Then thicken with egg as above.

### Sorrel Soup with Vermicelli

Add ¼ cup broken vermicelli to the soup and simmer for 15 minutes. Then thicken with egg as above.

### CREAM-OF-SORREL SOUP

¼ pound sorrel
10 spinach leaves
6 to 8 lettuce leaves
2 leeks (white part only), chopped
1 medium onion, chopped
3 tablespoons butter
1 cup hot water
1 cup milk
½ cup heavy cream
1 egg yolk
  Salt and pepper

Remove stems from greens. Wash, dry, and chop the leaves. Cook leeks and onion in the butter for 3 or 4 minutes. Add leaves and the hot water. Simmer for 3 or 4 minutes, or until leaves are tender. Add some of the milk and whirl in electric blender or force through a coarse sieve. Add remaining milk, and heat. Beat cream and egg yolk and add to hot mixture. Heat, and add salt and pepper to taste. Makes about 3 cups, or 4 servings.

### SORREL PURÉE

3 pounds sorrel
2 tablespoons butter or margarine
1 tablespoon all-purpose flour
2 tablespoons heavy cream
  Salt and pepper

Cook sorrel as directed in Basic Preparation. Drain thoroughly and force through a coarse sieve. Melt butter and blend in flour. Add purée and cream and cook, stirring, until thickened. Add salt and pepper to taste. Makes 4 to 6 servings.

### GARDEN SORREL

1 pound sorrel
2 tablespoons butter or margarine
1 egg yolk
¼ cup cold milk
  Salt and pepper

Wash sorrel and remove hard stems. Put sorrel in a heavy saucepan. Cook, covered, over low heat until wilted, for about 10 minutes. Add butter and simmer for another 5 minutes. Beat egg yolk with milk and stir some of the hot sorrel broth into egg mixture. Add this mixture to remaining sorrel. Cook over low heat, stirring constantly, until thickened. Season to taste with salt and pepper. Serve with hard-cooked eggs, sausage, or ham. Makes 4 servings.

# Menus

100 Menus
to help you plan
more varied meals
for your family with
the recipes in this volume

*Recipes for all starred dishes found in this volume.*

## BREAKFASTS

Apples and Sausage
en Brochette*
Scrambled Eggs
Corn Bread    Rose-Hip Jam*
Coffee or Tea

———◆———

Grapefruit and Orange Sections
Homemade Scrapple*
Poached Eggs
Quick Corn Relish*
Coffee or Tea

---

Mixed Fruit Juices
Homemade Kielbasa Sausage*
Rice Pancakes*
Sesame Honey Butter*
Coffee

———◆———

Melon with Berries
Ham Balls with Sour-
Cream Sauce*
Sally Lunn Ring*    Butter
Coffee or Tea

---

Vegetable Juice
Salmon Patties*
Toasted English Muffins
Orange Marmalade
Coffee or Tea

———◆———

Raspberries and Blueberries
Quick Sausage Casserole*
Buttered Rye Toast
Spiced Tomato Relish*
Coffee

---

Sliced Peaches or Nectarines
Scrambled Eggs with
Smoked Salmon*
Oat Scones*    Butter
Tea

———◆———

Whole Pears
Crisp Bacon
Broiled Tomatoes
Baked Rice and Cheese*
Coffeecake
Coffee

## LUNCH or SUPPER

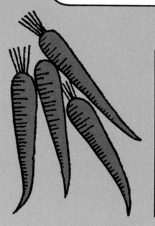

Banana and Mandarin
Orange Cups
Fried Ham Slices
Hashed Potatoes with
Rosemary*
Melba Toast
Whipped Butter
Coffee

———◆———

Baked Rosy Rhubarb*
Broiled Chicken Livers
New Orleans Rice Fritters*
Coffee with Chicory

---

Persimmons or Papaya
Shrimp Cakes* (omit Sauce)
Broiled Pineapple Rings
Sesame Whole-Wheat
Bread,* Toasted
Tea

———◆———

Strawberries and Cream
Golden Broiled Shad* or
Broiled Fresh Albacore*
Scalloped Corn
Coffee

---

Tomato Soup
Broiled Sardines on Toast*
Coleslaw
Five-Fruit Sherbet*

———◆———

Rumanian Sauerkraut Soup*
Sour Cream
Dark Rye Bread and
Salami Sandwiches
Rice Pudding*

---

Shellfish-Vegetable Chowder*
Pilot Crackers    Butter
Baked Rhubarb Meringue*

———◆———

Vegetable Juice
Fresh Grapefruit Shrimp
Salad*
Shredded Salad Greens
Rice à l'Impératrice*

---

Greek Rice Soup*
Copenhagen Coolers*
Buttered Crisp Rye Wafers
Fruit Cup

———◆———

Purée of Rice* with Sorrel
Salad Niçoise*    Crackers
Turkish Watermelon Sherbet
Drink*

---

Chicken Bouillon
Shrimps in Marinade*
Grilled Cheese Sandwiches
Sweet Cucumber Relish*
Frosted Date-Nut Bars*

———◆———

Quiche Lorraine with
Cream Cheese*
Marinated Vegetable Salad*
Jellied Rhubarb*

---

Meat and Vegetable Salad*
Onion and Parsley Finger
Sandwiches*
Custard Rice Pudding*

———◆———

Salami Skillet*
Marinated Cucumbers*
Hard Rolls    Butter
Peach Sherbet*

Corn and Shrimp Casserole
Grape, Pear, and Celery
Salad*
Buttered Whole-Wheat Toast
Hot Tea

_____

Masked Liver Mold*
Mixed Vegetable Salad*
Assorted Crisp Breads
Popcorn Balls*

---

Cream-of-Sorrel Soup*
Egg-Salad-Stuffed Tomatoes*
Melba Toast
Fresh Rhubarb Betty*

_____

Broiled Shrimps and Prosciutto*
Macaroni, Cheese, and
Sour Cream Salad*
Toasted Corn Muffins
Apple Relish*

---

Tomato Soup
Hamburgers on Toasted Rolls
Beet and Cabbage Relish*
Coffee Ice Cream
Chocolate Sauce*

_____

Cold Cuts
Hot Cheese-Potato Salad*
Garlic Italian Bread
Baked Quinces*

---

Iabochnii Sup (Apple Soup)*
Bread Sticks
Frankfurters and Hot-Potato
Salad*
Sliced Tomatoes
Gingerbread
Butterscotch Sauce*

_____

Ham Jambalaya*
Fresh Apple Coleslaw*
Cucumber Pickle Relish*
Rye Crisp
Frozen Cheese and
Raspberry Dessert*

---

Fish Salad in Clamshells*
Baked Smoked Ham
Glaze for Baked Ham*
Cooked Vegetable Salad*
Hot Rolls    Butter
Rhubarb-Apple Pie*

_____

Sage-Cheese Appetizer*
Ham-Cheese Rice Bake*
Almond Coleslaw*
Tangerine Sherbet*

---

Zakuski (Appetizers)*
Soldatskie Shchi
(Soldiers' Sauerkraut Soup)*
Pumpernickel   Sweet Butter
Iablochnii Krem (Cream of
Apples)*

_____

Shashlik*
Griby v Smetane
(Mushrooms in Sour Cream)*
Salat iz Morkovi i Kisloi
Kapusty (Carrot and
Sauerkraut Salad)*
Kissel*

---

Overnight Sauerbraten*
Potato Dumplings*
Broccoli or Brussels
Sprouts
Celery and Carrot Sticks
Rumanian Raisin Compote*

_____

Veal Rosemary*
Viennese Rice*
Orange and Date Salad*
Crisp Seeded Rolls
Butter
Sabayon*

---

Sorrel Soup*
Spiced Sesame Chicken*
Pilaf    Green Beans
Tomato-Avocado Salad*
Strawberry Sherbet*

_____

Grapefruit Cup
Baked Red Snapper,
Florida Style*
Wax Beans with Pimiento and
Pickle Relish*
Dill Pickle Salad*
Coconut Cookie Snowballs*

---

Hot Sausage Loaf*
Brown Rice
Buttered Green Cabbage
Corn sticks
Apple Glacé with Honey-
Cream Cheese*

_____

Sweet-and-Pungent Pork*
Baked Potatoes   Spinach
Shredded Chinese Cabbage
and Carrot Salad
Cooked Buttermilk Dressing*
Angel Food Cake
Bittersweet-Chocolate
Sauce*

---

Oysters in Aspic*
Rockfish en Papillote*
Vegetable-Avocado Salad with
Paprika Dressing*
Bread Sticks    Butter
Orange Buttermilk Sherbet*

_____

Chicken Consommé
Sweet-and-Sour Shrimps*
Fried Rice*
Sliced Radish and
Watercress Salad
Almond Cookies
Preserved Kumquats

---

Baked Turkey and Rice*
Salat iz Tsvetnoi Kapusti
s Vinogradom (Cauliflower
and Grape Salad)*
Hard Rolls    Butter
Turkish Dreams*

_____

Beef with Red Wine*
Whipped Potatoes
Green Beans and Whole
Onions*
Assorted Raw Relishes
Russian Cream*

---

Burmese Ginger Beef*
Yellow Rice*
Mixed Green Salad
East Indian Rose Pudding*

_____

Lamb Chops and Shallots
in Casserole*
Saffron Rice*
Waldorf Salad*
Rhubarb Flummery*

---

Shrimp and Artichoke
Appetizer*
Salmi of Duckling*
Rutabaga au Gratin*
Raisin Pie*

_____

Glazed Roasted Stuffed
Rock Cornish Hens*
Pecan Stuffing*
Green Peas and Corn
Rhubarb-Onion Relish*
Celery and Romaine
Hearts
Pears Condé*

---

Russian Sturgeon Champagne
Soup*
Salat iz Teliatini s
Ogurtsami (Veal and
Cucumber Salad)*
Crisp Rye Wafers
Sweet Butter
Russkii Iablochnii Pirog
(Apple Pie)*

_____

Sesame-Baked Rosefish*
Sveziye Podzharenyye
Ogurtzy (Braised
Cucumbers)*
Romaine and Tomato Salad
Fresh Raspberry Pastries*

Menus

Pork-and-Pepper Casserole
with Fruited Black
Bean Sauce*
Pimiento Rice
Rancho Salad*
Corn Bread   Butter
Guava Sherbet*

---

Rosemary Chicken with
Tangerine Rice*
(with Peas, Avocados,
and Apricots)
Bibb or Boston Lettuce
French Dressing*
Ice Cream
Chocolate Drops*

Chicken Quenelles*
Curried Rice*
Broiled Tomato Slices
Spinach and Chicory Salad
Raspberry Pudding*
Refrigerator Oatmeal
Cookies*

---

Shrimp Paste*   Crackers
Choucroute Garnie*
Boiled Potatoes   Mustard
Italian Rum Cake*

Florentine Pork Roast
Arista*
Baked Yams
Cold Green Beans and
Broccoli
De Luxe French Dressing*
Rhubarb and Strawberry Pie*

---

Ikra iz Baklazhanov
(Eggplant Caviar)*
Melba Toast
Jugged Rabbit*
Green Lima Beans
Corn on the Cob
Christmas Fruit Salad*
Sesame-Anise Cookies*

Roast Leg of Veal or Lamb
Sauce Soubise*
Stewed Navy Beans with
Savory*
German Gourmet Mixed
Salad*
Cherry-Port Mold*
Cookies

---

Salt-Pork and Bean Chowder*
Grilled Jumbo Shrimps,
Venetian Style*
French Rice Salad*
Whole-Wheat Italian Bread
Lime Sherbet* with
Raspberry Sauce*

Lamb Ragout in Carrot-
Potato Ring*
Jellied Cabbage Salad*
Cottage-Cheese Dressing*
Sesame-Seed Rolls*
Margarine
Raspberry Peach Glacées*

---

Sausage and Liver Loaf*
Sauerkraut*
Rye Bread   Whipped Butter
October Salad*
Ginger Mayonnaise Dressing*
Butterscotch Rice Pudding*

Bif Strogonov
(Beef Stroganoff)*
Buttered Noodles with
Poppy Seed
Salat iz Krasnoi i
Beloi Rediski
(Red and White
Radish Salad)*
Pumpernickel Bread
Indian Ravo*

---

Celery   Ripe and Green Olives
White-Fish Bouillabaisse*
Toasted Sliced French Bread
Strawberry Shortcake*

Ham Nuggets in Raisin
Sauce*
Noodles
Harvest Relish* on
Leaf Lettuce
Savarin*

---

Tomato Juice
Cucumber Sticks
Hot  Shrimp-Crab  Salad*
Anise, Grape, and Cabbage
Slaw*
Hot Buttered Rolls
Orange Gelatin with
Weinschaum (Wine Custard
Sauce)*

Pasta with Sausage Sauce*
Parmesan Cheese
Pimiento, Capers, and
Artichoke Heart Salad
French Dressing*
Melon with Berries

---

Sausage-Stuffed Eggplant*
Italian Green Beans
Salat iz Repy i Ogurtsov
(Turnip and Cucumber
Salad)*
Sour-Cream Dressing*
Fruit Cup   Dream Cookies*

Planked Shad*
French-Fried Potatoes
Shallots and Tomatoes*
Endive with Avocado Dressing*
Lemon Sherbet*
Old-Fashioned Rosewater
Sugar Cookies*

---

Shrimp Egg Rolls*
Broiled Chicken
Caucasian Plum Sauce*
Chinese Bamboo Shoots Salad*
Kompot iz Apelsin i
Chernosliv (Prune Orange
Compote)*

Shellfish Soufflé*
(made with Crabmeat)
Sauce Cardinal*
Peas and Mushrooms
Orange, Onion, and
Watercress Salad
Herb Dressing*
Corn Sticks
Tangy Rhubarb Ice*
Shortbread*

---

Clam Pilaf Casserole*
German Spinach Salad*
Popovers   Butter
Sour-Cream Devonshire Pears*

Scallops in Vermouth*
Surprise Rice Croquettes*
Cooked Green Bean and
Carrot Stick Salad
Chiffonade Dressing*
Buttered Whole-Wheat Toast
Rhubarb Tangy Fresh
Applesauce*
Orange Shortbread *

---

Celery and Crabmeat Salad*
Cheese Omelet   Peach Relish*
Raised Sally Lunn Muffins*
Butter
Iranian Raisin Cake*
Caramel Sauce*

Borsch Poproshche
(Very Quick Borsch)*
Salmon-Stuffed Peppers*
Asparagus and Tomato
Salad
Creamy Mayonnaise-
Roquefort Dressing*
Banana and Orange Cup

---

Boiled Smoked Tongue
Champagne Sauce*
Buttered Spinach or
Swiss Chard
Hashed Brown Potatoes
Poires à l'Impératrice*

Twice-Fried Shrimps*
Broiled Chicken Livers
Sherry Barbecue Sauce*
Green Beans Oriental*
Hot Buttered Rolls
Sugared Fresh
Pineapple Slices

---

Pea Soup    Rye Croutons
Sauerbraten with Vegetables*
(Potatoes and Carrots)
Fresno Fruit Salad*
Benne Wafers*

---

Consommé    Cheese Crackers
Baked Sauerkraut and Corned-
Beef Hash*
Cucumber-Almond Salad*
Old-Time Rice Pudding*
with Brown-Sugar Syrup*

---

Shrimp Bisque*
Onion Melba Toast
French Beef Salad*
Basic Vinaigrette Sauce*
Vienna Bread
Sweet Butter
Fresh Fruit
Assorted Cheeses

---

Shrimp Appetizer*
Ravioli (with Hamburger
Filling)*
Parmesan Cheese
Mixed Green Salad with
Ripe Olives
Melon Ball and Grape Cup
Espresso

---

Spanish Chicken with Rice*
Orange, Grapefruit, and
Avocado Salad with
Fluffy Fruit Dressing*
Buttered Toasted Hard Rolls
Chocolate Cake

---

Cheese-Crab Canapés*
Saffron Veal*
Buttered Wild or Brown Rice
Endive and Pickled Beet Salad
Vanilla Ice-Cream Snowballs*
Chocolate Sauce*

---

Smothered Sausage-Beef
Patties*
Mashed Winter Squash
Collard Greens
Sliced Red Apple and
Chicory Salad
Ginger Mayonnaise Dressing*
Rich Rice Pudding*

---

Sauerkraut Balls*
Lamb Chops with Artichokes*
Italian Rice and Peas*
Romaine or Dandelion Salad
Sherry Wine Gelatin
Sabayon Sauce*

---

Cream-of-Salmon Soup*
Salmagundi Salad with
Salami and Liverwurst*
Buttermilk Scones*
Butter
Sliced Peaches
Raisin-Filled Cookies*

---

Slavic Sausage Bake*
Wilted Cucumbers
Finnish Bread*    Butter
Rainbow Sherbet Parfait*

---

Layered Spinach Curry
Casserole^
(with Lamb)    Rice
Condiments: Banana Slices,
Chopped Green Pepper
and Tomatoes, Toasted
Coconut, Lemon Wedges,
Toasted Sliced Almonds
Onion Buttered French Bread
Pineapple and Strawberries
with Honey

---

Rosemary Chicken in Cream*
Buttered Green Peas with
Cut Asparagus Tips
Radish Salad*
Toasted Cranberry-Nut Bread*
Date Rice Pudding*

---

Cold Roast Beef
Swedish Brown Beans*
Tomato-Cumin Chutney*
Roquefort Salad*
Kompot iz Narezanykh Popolam
Grush i Vishen (Pear
Halves and Cherry Compote)*

## QUANTITY COOKING MENUS

Roast Loin of Pork
Olad'i s Lukom (Baked
Onion Dumplings)*
Cranberry-Filbert Relish*
Romaine
Herbed Sour-Cream Dressing*
Spongecake

---

Salmon Trout in Aspic^
Swedish Meatballs*
Jansson's Temptation*
Pickled Beets
Dilled Cucumbers
Crisp Rye Bread
Butter
Swedish Applecake*

---

Boneless Baked Ham*
Scalloped Potatoes*
Baked Beans*
Marinated Cucumbers*
Gingerbread*
Whipped Topping

---

Ham Loaf in Raisin Sauce*
Scalloped Corn*
Jellied Cranberry and
Orange Salad*
Parker House Rolls*    Butter
Chocolate Brownies*

---

Brunswick Stew*
Celery Sticks    Radishes
Hot Corn Bread*    Butter
Lemon Fluff Dessert*

---

Mixed Fruit Juices
Tuna à la King*
Hot Biscuits*
Jellied Tomato-Juice Squares*
Vanilla Ice Cream
Fudge Sauce^ or
Butterscotch Sauce^
Cookies

---

Italian Spaghetti and Meatballs*
Grated Italian Cheese
Mixed Green Salad
Toasted Buttered
Italian Bread Slices
Bisquit Tortoni

---

Oven-Barbecued Steaks^
Creamed Potatoes and Peas
Assorted Relishes
Pan Rolls*    Whipped Butter
Deep-Dish Cherry Pies*

---

Glazed Baked Ham
Swedish Meatballs*
Cold Potato Salad*
Macaroni Salad*    Baked Beans*
Tomatoes    Lettuce
Apple Crisp*

---

Chicken Hawaiian*
Chow-Mein Noodles
Pineapple Salad with Cream
Cheese
Assorted Breads    Butter
Vanilla Ice Cream
Almond Cookies

---

Melon Wedges
Chili con Carne*
Fluffy Rice
Large Corn Chips
Cabbage and Green-
Pepper Slaw*
Sherbet
Frosted Date-Nut Bars*

---

Cranberry Juice Cocktail
Turkey Pie with
Pastry Crust*
Fruit Salad
Parker House Rolls*
Angel Delight*

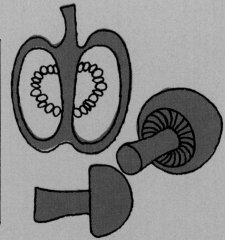

*Recipes for all starred dishes found in this volume.

# GENERAL INFORMATION

### The Ingredients and Measurements Used in Recipes

All recipes in this book have been tested in the Woman's Day Kitchens with standard American measuring cups (8 ounces = 16 tablespoons), measuring spoons (1 tablespoon = 3 teaspoons), and other standard kitchen equipment. All measurements are level. Liquids are measured in standard 8-ounce glass measuring cups, at eye level.

All sugar is granulated white sugar unless otherwise specified.

All flours, cake and all-purpose, are sifted before measuring unless otherwise specified. No self-rising flour is used.

All baking powder is double-acting baking powder.

All brown sugar is firmly packed when measured.

All confectioners' sugar is sifted before measuring.

All pepper is ground black pepper unless otherwise specified.

Fats and shortening are measured at room temperature, packed firmly into measuring cup and leveled with a straight knife. They are scraped out with a rubber spatula.

Salted butter or margarine, packed in ¼-pound sticks, is used unless otherwise specified. 1 stick = ½ cup = 8 tablespoons = ¼ pound.

1 tall can evaporated milk (14½ ounces) contains 1⅔ cups undiluted evaporated milk. Sweetened condensed milk is an entirely different product, and cannot be used interchangeably with evaporated milk.

⅓ to ½ teaspoon dried herbs can be substituted for each tablespoon fresh herbs. Crumble herbs before using to release flavor.

Before starting to cook or to bake, read the recipes carefully. Assemble all ingredients and equipment. Follow recipe exactly. Do not increase or decrease recipe unless you are a skilled enough cook to recognize what adjustments must be made as to ingredients, pan sizes, and/or cooking time.

### Cooking Temperatures and Times

Cooking temperatures and times are approximate for meat. They depend not only on the weight and kind of meat, but also on its shape, temperature, and its bone and fat contents. A meat thermometer was used in testing.

Cooking times for meats are as recommended by the National Live Stock and Meat Board, 36 Wabash Avenue, Chicago, Illinois 60603.

### Oven Temperatures

| TEMPERATURES (Degree F.) | TERM |
|---|---|
| 250 to 275 | VERY SLOW |
| 300 to 325 | SLOW |
| 350 to 375 | MODERATE |
| 400 to 425 | HOT |
| 450 to 475 | VERY HOT |
| 500 to 525 | EXTREMELY HOT |

**Important**—Preheat oven for 10 to 15 minutes before placing food in it. Many a cake has been spoiled by being placed in a barely heated oven. Baking times are based on the assumption that the oven is already at the stated temperature.

Check the oven temperature control frequently, especially if baking times vary from those given in recipes. (This can be done with a portable oven thermometer.) If a control is consistently off, call your public utility. They should be able to reset the oven temperature control.

### Caloric Values

The caloric values, where mentioned, for each food are based on 100 grams, about 3½ ounces edible portion, as mentioned in Composition of Foods, Agriculture Handbook No. 8, Agricultural Service of the United States Department of Agriculture, Washington, D. C., revised December 1963.

## COMPLETE RECIPE INDEX—Volume 10—825 Recipes

*All starred recipes are for **Quantity Cooking.**

*All starred recipes are for Quantity Cooking.

**\*All starred recipes are for Quantity Cooking.**